VLADIMIR LENIN
HOW TO BECOME A LEADER

VLADLEN LOGINOV

VLADIMIR LENIN
HOW TO BECOME A LEADER

TRANSLATED FROM THE RUSSIAN BY LEWIS WHITE

GLAGOSLAV PUBLICATIONS

VLADIMIR LENIN – HOW TO BECOME A LEADER

by Vladlen Loginov

Translated from the Russian by Lewis White

Edited by Geoffrey Swain

Publishers Maxim Hodak & Max Mendor

Cover and interior layout by Max Mendor

© 2019, Vladlen Loginov

Introduction © 2019, Geoffrey Swain

© 2019, Glagoslav Publications

www.glagoslav.com

ISBN: 978-1-78267-061-2

A catalogue record for this book is available from the British Library.

This book is in copyright. No part of this publication may be reproduced, stored in a retrieval system or transmitted in any form or by any means without the prior permission in writing of the publisher, nor be otherwise circulated in any form of binding or cover other than that in which it is published without a similar condition, including this condition, being imposed on the subsequent purchaser.

CONTENTS

INTRODUCTION 7

WHAT COLOUR WERE LENIN'S EYES? 19

PART ONE – ORIGINS

AMONG THE ROOTS OF THE FAMILY TREE 25
THE SIXTIERS 34
SIMBIRSK 43
SCHOOL 54
1ST MARCH 1881 64
THE MAN OF THE HOUSE 72
GRADUATION 79

PART TWO – BROTHER OF A HANGED MAN

KAZAN 86
KOKUSHKINO 92
A MUDDLED PAPER 98
SAMARA 103
FAMINE 112
SELF-DETERMINATION 117
WARD NO. 6 126

PART THREE – THE LEAGUE OF STRUGGLE

IN THE CAPITAL 135
INITIAL RECOGNITION 143

THE MARXIST SALON	150
AWAKENING	154
NIKOLAI PETROVICH	158
LEADER OF THE PETERSBURG SDS	166
IN DISTANT LANDS	172
THE BIRTH OF A PARTY	180

PART FOUR – PRISON & EXILE

SOLITARY CONFINEMENT	185
THE HYDRA OF REVOLUTION	193
BY IMPERIAL DECREE	202
'CIVILISED' EXILE	211
THE WEDDING	221
FAMILY	231
WORK	238
A SPLIT IN THE SOCIAL DEMOCRATS	243
A NEW ERA	248
THE ANTI-CREDO	254

PART FIVE – THE TURN OF THE 20TH CENTURY

THE TRIPLE ALLIANCE	265
TWO PASSPORTS	275
A MORAL DOUSING	285
PERSONAL RELATIONS	296
THE WIND OF CHANGE	300
LENIN	305
INDEX OF NAMES	314

INTRODUCTION

Vladlen Loginov is no newcomer to the study of Lenin's life. He published an article on the theme of Lenin and the Bol'shevik newspaper *Pravda* in 1962 at the height of the Khrushchev thaw and has retained an interest in Lenin's career ever since. Loginov knows his Lenin back to front, so it is perhaps surprising that in this detailed account of the young Lenin, he sets himself a rather modest task. The image of Lenin, Loginov believes, has been over-politicised in the twentieth century and as a result the more literature that appears, "the more confused the issues surrounding the analysis of Lenin's life and activities become". An antidote is necessary, in Loginov's view, and "this book's intention", as he makes clear in the preface, "is not to offer an explanation, but to present some material for consideration, a few details of his biography hitherto unknown to the reader, to apply some additional touches to Lenin's portrait". Emulating the German nineteenth century historian Leopold von Ranke, who argued that the facts should speak for themselves, Loginov wants Lenin's life to speak for itself.

Not all the details given here are "hitherto unknown" to western scholarship, but very many are. Simply adding a few new details to the Lenin story, however, is not the main achievement of this book, for all the modest intentions of the author. The great strength of Loginov's work is to put Lenin in the context of his time, to show that he was a product of his time. As Loginov puts it, "the circumstances and events of each era did influence actions, did determine the destiny of lives, and did define modes of living just as profoundly as familial heritage." Does the reader need to know about Lenin's paternal and maternal grandparents? Well, yes, because this information shows how upwardly mobile Lenin's family was. At the apex of Russian society in the nineteenth century little changed, the Tsar still ruled as an absolute monarch. Below the surface, however, Russian society was being transformed in the middle years of the nineteenth century and Lenin's family was part of that process.

Lenin's father was only a generation away from serfdom, someone who advanced a successful career through education, first at the Astrakhan Gymnasium and then Kazan University. Unsurprisingly, he believed all his life that others could benefit through education in the same way, devoting his life to the cause of education for all. He was a man of the "Sixties", the decade when Tsar Alexander II, the liberator of the serfs, seemed to be encouraging further reform. Until the Tsar closed them down in 1862, an early sign that his reputation as a reformer was exaggerated, Lenin's father was active in establishing Sunday Schools to educate the poor. Later, his move from being a successful classroom teacher to becoming an education bureaucrat, a schools' inspector, reflected his commitment to a universal programme of education - and this included the Muslim Chuvash people of the Volga region, at the request of his father Lenin gave a local Chuvash teacher Greek lessons so that he could enter university.

On his mother's side, Lenin's Jewish ancestry has always been the subject of speculation, grist to the mill of those on the political right who think of all Marxists as Jews and rant about a Judeo-Bol'shevik conspiracy to subvert society. The main point about his maternal grandparents, however, has nothing to do with ethnicity but upward mobility, they too were members of a family moving smartly up the social ladder. The family adopted Christianity to escape the poverty of village life in the Jewish Pale of Settlement, idealised in the twentieth century by the 1970s musical *Fiddler on the Roof*. They moved to St. Petersburg, where Lenin's grandfather, no longer hampered by the limitations on Jewish access to higher education, became a successful doctor, respectable enough to marry into the minor aristocracy; and he retired to run the small estate of Kokushkino not far from the river Volga. It was the purchase of this estate in 1859 which gave the family and its heirs, Lenin included, the status of hereditary nobles.

By the time Lenin was born in 1870, his was a family of some means. His parents had their own house, a couple of servants and the estate at Kokushkino to retreat to in the summer. A decade later, things were beginning to unravel. Russian society was changing and the era of reform was over. Alexander II was assassinated in 1881 and the new Tsar Alexander III epitomised reaction rather than reform – Autocracy, Orthodoxy and the National Spirit became the watchwords of the day. One of Alexander III's early targets was education. For him, the primary education of peasant children should be the concern of the Orthodox Church rather than the state, and the education of Muslim peoples like the Chuvash was simply unnecessary. Lenin's father, who was not a religious man, found the growing presence of the church in educational affairs difficult to handle. As a schools' inspector, he was employed on a five-year contract, but when this was renewed in January 1886 it was only for a one-year term; the man of the "Sixties" was out of tune with the spirit of the reactionary "Eighties". Tragically, Lenin's father died a few days after the news about his contract was received. What he had achieved through a life-long commitment to education was being dismantled.

Did the apparent fall from grace of his father give Lenin's elder brother a personal motive to hate everything that Alexander III stood for? Something turned the scholarly young scientist into a terrorist. Although only just completing his undergraduate studies, he was already being courted for a future academic career at St. Petersburg University. Yet he threw in his lot with the bomb-makers who hoped to kill the Tsar on 1 March 1887. His arrest and subsequent execution in May had a devastating impact on the Ulyanov family. From being successful and respected members of the local community, they became pariahs overnight, shunned even by old friends. The need to start a new life meant that the Kokushkino estate had to be sold, and to make matters worse, no sooner had Lenin been accepted for study at Kazan University, than he was expelled for taking part in a student demonstration. Throughout all this, Lenin's mother proved a power of strength. It was his mother who repeatedly pleaded with the authorities for Lenin's re-admission to university, even travelling to St. Petersburg in person to confront the Minister of Education. In the circumstances, it is not surprising that, once he qualified as a lawyer with a first class degree from St. Petersburg University awarded on 15 November 1891, Lenin felt obliged to return to his family and support his mother.

What was the impact on Lenin of his brother's execution? All biographers agree that after his brother's execution, over the summer of 1887, Lenin read and re-read Nikolai Chernyshevsky's novel *What is to be done?*, his brother's favourite book. Chernyshevsky's novel, written in 1863, called on intellectuals to devote their lives to the service of the people, and it became a bible for the Populist movement. Populists were socialists who looked to Russia's traditional forms of society for a model of the society of the future. For them the traditional peasant village commune [*obshchina*], which administered taxes and allocated land for ploughing on a shared communal basis, was a primitive form of democracy and collective ownership which could be used to revolutionise Russian society. It had been the main Populist political party, the People's Will or *Narodnaya Volya*, which successfully assassinated Alexander II and which Lenin's brother had joined for his failed attempt on the life of Alexander III. What did Chernyshevsky teach Lenin over the summer of 1887? Were his future actions motivated be the desire to seek revenge for his brother? All biographers agree that the events of summer 1887 changed Lenin's life. The question is, how much?

The only other detailed study of the young Lenin available in English argues that the summer of 1887 was what made Lenin Lenin. The desire for revenge and the ideas of Chernyshevsky were what turned an obedient school-boy into the future dictator. Nikolai Vladislavovich Volsky, better known by his pseudonym Nikolai Valentinov, published *The Early Years of Lenin* in 1969, drawing on his one-time friendship with Lenin and his later writings as a Parisian émigré. Valentinov picks up on some of the same themes as Loginov - he refers to Lenin's father as "a passionate enlightener" and draws a splendid picture of Lenin's happy childhood, especially skating in the winter and the summer trips to Kokushkino. He is clear that, at school, Lenin had shown little interest in politics and so he suggests that, if it had not been for the events of May 1887 "Vladimir Ulyanov would never have become Lenin"; the execution of his brother was "the key to understanding how Lenin became a revolutionary".[1]

According to Valentinov, the central element of that process was Lenin's reading of Chernyshevsky, not only over the summer of 1887 but while forced to live in Kokushkino after his expulsion from Kazan University in December 1887. He remained isolated in Kokushkino until autumn 1888 and, according to Valentinov, read everything Chernyshevsky had ever published in the bound volumes of the journal *The Contemporary* or *Sovremennik*, which his father had lovingly collected and archived. Valentinov sees Lenin going "into his own kind of mystic communication with the goal, the ideas and feelings of his brother", as he explored Chernyshevsky's writings; "it was in this fashion that he embarked upon his career as a revolutionary", Valentinov suggests, and he devotes the last three chapters of his study to Chernyshevsky's influence on Lenin: "a comparison of Chernyshevsky's teaching about how to make a revolution and the views displayed by Lenin in the years

---

1   N. Valentionov. The Early Years of Lenin. Ann Arbor: University of Michigan Press, 1969. p. 79.

1905-05 and 1917-19 reveal their stunning analogy and correspondence," he concludes, adding that Lenin's revolutionary inheritance had "little in common with Marx".[2]

Loginov's interpretation is very different. He picks up his theme that Lenin was a product of his times and argues that Lenin's intellectual development continued long after September 1888 when he was allowed to leave Kokushkino and live once again in Kazan, although not study at the university. Here there were other influences on his life, besides Chernyshevsky. He continued to mix with student groups and, contradicting Valentinov, Loginov shows the influence of Marx. It was in Kazan that he first attended a talk about Marx's ideas and settled down to read *Das Kapital* for himself. In spring 1889 he narrowly avoided a police crack-down on the student discussion groups he frequented by moving to the family's new small-holding at Alakevka, where he again read avidly. By the time he moved to Samara after graduating, to practice as a lawyer, he had begun to call himself a Marxist. In Loginov's view, this was part of a process of intellectual evolution at least as important as his brother's execution, a process in which two things stand out.

First, there was the famine of 1891, which showed clearly that the bureaucratic apparatus of the Russian autocracy simply could not cope with a social crisis of this magnitude. But while opponents of the regime were united in believing that the famine showed up the incompetence and inhumanity of the Tsarist system, the experience of the famine heightened disagreements between Populists and Marxists. Populists believed that the new society it hoped for, based around the peasant commune, could prevent capitalism from coming to Russia. Marxists believed that capitalism was already coming to Russia, and that one of the causes of the famine was nothing other than the increased marketisation of Russian grain production. Populists and Marxists had long disagreed about the vitality of the peasant commune – whether it was thriving and therefore capable of reviving Russia along communal lines, or disintegrating as capitalist relations penetrated the country more and more. The famine made these discussions all the more acute, with Populists suggesting that the Marxist obsession with unraveling the objective causes of the famine reflected a lack of sympathy for the peasantry – they seemed glad that capitalism had hit the village, even if it did bring famine in its wake.

---

2   Ibid. pp. 134, 205, 280.

Aside from the famine, but indirectly related to it, the second major impact on Lenin's thought at this time came from the book written by V. E. Plotnikov *The South Russian Peasant Economy* in 1891. Lenin wanted to get to the bottom of the issue of the vitality of the peasant commune. To this end, he started to read the reports issued by local councils [*zemstvos*] and then came across Plotnikov's detailed study of the peasant economy. This showed clearly that, in southern Russia at least, capitalist differentiation was taking place amongst the peasantry and the village commune was disintegrating as an economic institution for regulating and equalizing the use of plough land. Plotnikov provided the empirical detail needed to confirm Lenin in his belief that the Marxists were correct. Capitalism was coming to Russia and it was undermining the traditional form of peasant society on which Popluists placed so much hope. The evidence showed that the Marxists were right and the Populists were wrong.

Loginov is surely right to look to the whole of Lenin's intellectual world in the period 1887-91 to explain how he became a revolutionary, rather than just focusing on the execution of his brother and the influence of Chernyshevsky, as Valentiov does. It was not just Chernyshevsky, but the famine and Plotnikov. Discussing the evolution of Lenin's ideas, Loginov asserts: "It would seem that at least two conclusions must be drawn in this regard: firstly, that his system of beliefs was formed over a reasonably extended period, and secondly, that this process was not defined by the books he read alone." The logic of Loginov's position is this: if in later life Lenin was accused of rarely changing his mind and forcing his viewpoint on others, the process of establishing those views took years of reading and debating with friends. There was no thunderbolt, it was an evolutionary process, but his conversion to Marxism was completed by 1891 and by 1892 his revolutionary career had begun.

If Lenin became a revolutionary in 1892, when did Lenin become Lenin? Loginov counters Valentinov's view that it was summer 1887, but his answer to this question is very straightforward and a little unsatisfying. Loginov argues that it was just after the first issue of his long-planned underground newspaper *Iskra* appeared, when, in early 1901 he first signed himself "Lenin". Loginov is very convincing that Lenin was a product of his time and that there was far more to his intellectual formation than Valentinov's obsession with Chernyshevsky, but surely Lenin became Lenin when he began to express the ideas that would later become known as Leninism. What defined Lenin as a political leader, rather than being just one of many Marxist revolutionaries, were the ideas he expressed in his political pamphlet of 1902 *What is to be done?*, consciously borrowing the title from Chernyshevsky. This pamphlet held within it the explanation for his splitting of the Russian Social Democratic Labour Party at its Second Congress in 1903 to form the Bol'sheviks as a separate and distinct political faction. Although those ideas would not be fully formed until 1902, it is possible to suggest that the first signs of Leninism can be seen almost as soon as Lenin arrived in St. Petersburg in August 1893.

In April 1894 Lenin wrote the pamphlet which first made his name in the capital's Marxist circles, "Who are the friends of people, and how do they fight the Social Democrats?" Although the thrust of the pamphlet, as the title suggests, was the well-established and ongoing struggle between Populists and Marxists, it also contained, as Loginov correctly notes, a more Leninist notion. A theme that emerges is the need to move working class protest on from "smoldering discontent" to "awakening consciousness". The occasional riot or an isolated strike had to be replaced with something more organised and better planned, and the only way for there to be effective organization and planning, was for the workers to become conscious of their place in society and the tasks assigned them by the class struggle. How to bring class-consciousness to the workers of Russia would become Lenin's concern until the success of the October Revolution in 1917. The logic of what Loginov tells us, despite his assertion that Lenin became Lenin in 1901, is that Lenin was on his way to becoming Lenin as soon as he reached the capital. Those issues which would become his specific concern were already troubling him.

In discussions about working class consciousness, Lenin did not have a lot to go on. His experience of the working class was relatively limited. He made his first contacts with workers early in 1894 and soon became a popular lecturer addressing workers' circles, known affectionately as "baldy". Along with the future Menshevik leader Yulii Martov, Lenin was keen to move beyond workers' circles and the concept of change through education towards agitation and change through strike action. Strikes did take place in December 1894 and in January-February 1895, and Lenin's group produced leaflets and even helped win some concessions from the employers. Inevitably the question arose, how best to lead this movement? The initial step was easy to state, but difficult to achieve in the conditions of the Tsarist autocracy. The émigré community of Social Democrats, with its access to funds, needed to be brought together with all the militant labour groups growing up in St. Petersburg and elsewhere. Lenin was allocated the key role here, visiting Switzerland, France and Germany, before bringing together the workers' groups of the capital with the aim of producing a newspaper, the *Workers' Cause*. All went well at first. By autumn 1895 more pamphlets had appeared, more strikes had been successful, and the first issue of the *Workers' Cause* had been published under Lenin's editorship. Then, in December 1895, Lenin was arrested.

Unable to give any further direct guidance to the working class movement, Lenin was alarmed by what happened next. Despite the arrest of Lenin and other leaders, leaflets continued to appear and strikes continued to take place. Although these strikes were not covered in the Russian press, the foreign press gave detailed accounts, and K. M Takhtarev, one of the leading labour activists of the day, was clear that the leaflets produced by surviving members of Lenin's group, combined with the fact that the employers had begun to make concessions, had an enormous impact on the workers. The pressure of labour unrest was such that by January 1897 the government had decided to shorten the working day. At one level, then Lenin should have been delighted. As Loginov notes, Lenin was clear that "nothing had such a powerful organisational and educational influence on the working masses as active struggle itself". However, more fundamentally Lenin was alarmed, because without the firm leadership he had offered, the workers were slipping towards what he would call in *What is to be done?* "trade union consciousness".

Loginov gives a rather neutral account of the events of 14-17 January 1897, events which are arguably of great significance in understanding why Lenin was so convinced that the working class needed clear and firm leadership. True to his Rankean view that he will give no explanation and let the facts speak for themselves, Loginov simply describes how Lenin, having been held in prison since December 1895, was sentenced to exile and given three days, 14-17 January 1897, to arrange his affairs before heading east to Siberia. His group of comrades, the League of Struggle for the Emancipation of the Working Class, met on consecutive evenings, well into the night to discuss developments since the arrests of December 1895. Loginov tells us, quoting a participant, that "the bias towards a peculiar 'democratism' and 'workerphilia' . . . elicited a degree of hot temper." He then explains, how, as 1896 had developed, Takhtarev had increasingly argued that the centre of gravity of the League of Struggle should be pushed down to factory based mutual aid funds, funds permitted by the authorities to operate legally, and the existing Central Group, the guiding leadership structure composed of intellectuals should be abandoned.

As the strike movement had developed in 1896, so ever more mutual aid funds had begun to operate and some workers, supported by Takhtarev, developed the idea of the funds becoming a legal core of the labour movement, rejecting the idea that the leading Central Group of the League of Struggle had the right to lead the labour movement. During his last days in St. Petersburg, the last days of his contact with the labour movement of the capital, Lenin learned that the workers seemed to have abandoned all the lessons he had taught them. Lenin was opposed to the idea that the mutual aid funds should lead the workers' struggle, a concept referred to in the jargon of the day as "workerphilia". He argued on 14-17 January 1897, just as he would in *What is to be done?*, that workers would revert to trade unionism pure and simple if they were not led by conscious Social Democrats. Takhtarev, on the other hand, felt that the League of Struggle should serve the labour movement, responding to its needs, and not always insist on leadership. Here in essence was the dispute which in 1903 would lead to the split within the Russian Social Democratic Labour Party and the emergence Bol'sheviks. As Lenin left Petersburg in January 1897 for years of exile and emigration, his last direct contact with the St. Petersburg labour movement was disturbing to say the least, and his fears about the inherent trade union instincts of workers would follow him to Siberia and beyond. His own experience of the labour movement had been that, without clear leadership, workers left to their own devises could develop only trade union consciousness.

While Lenin was in Siberia, there was plenty of evidence that the 'workerphilia' tendency was not only still strong but moving towards what Lenin feared most, an accommodation with the liberal opposition to the autocracy. In 1897 two May Day appeals were produced: one was traditionally Social Democrat in tone, calling for political freedom and the eight-hour day; the other, however, was reformist in tone, Economist, to use the contemporary jargon, calling simply for the right to strike and the right to form trade unions, demands that liberals had no qualms about supporting. A proclamation of 1899 was limited to health and welfare issues, again issues which liberals could support. By autumn 1900 a workers' committee brought together the mutual aid funds of the capital; it had contact with what was left of Lenin's Union of Struggle, but refused to follow its directives.

Between 1898-1902, sixteen issues of the underground newspaper *Workers' Thought* appeared. It provided workers with a sounding board for their opinions, with no clear editorial line. It registered the diverse views of workers and recounted the reality of factory struggle through its network of worker correspondents. It called for militant strike action in the struggle with capitalism for improved economic conditions, but was critical of demands put on the movement by "repentant intellectuals". In spring 1899, with the support of Takhtarev who had become its editor, *Workers' Thought* produced a 'Supplement' supporting the ideas of the revisionist German Social Democrat Edward Bernstein and reproducing one of his articles on the possibility of reform within the capitalist system.³ All these developments were of great concern to Lenin, workers were not only reverting to trade unionism, but slipping under liberal influence.

Lenin spent part of his exile destroying the ghosts of the past, writing *The Development of Capitalism in Russia* and *The Heritage We Renounce* aimed at destroying Populism once and for all. However, he also looked to the future, preparing for his return from exile and in this context his concern was the distinction between trade union and political consciousness; his translation of Sidney and Beatrice Webb's study of the *Theory and Practice of British Trade Unionism* enabled him to explore the very worst of trade union reformism. Mostly while in Siberia he avoided the squabbles of exile, but when the left-leaning liberal Yekaterina Kuskova wrote a so-called *Credo*, aimed at placing the labour struggle for economic improvements within a purely liberal framework of opposition to the Tsar, he contacted other Social Democrat exiles to draft a joint response. As Lenin would later put it in *What is to be done?* "following the tail" of the labour movement, rather than leading it, could lead to the workers drifting towards support for liberal reforms.

Once released from exile, Lenin found the situation was not quite as bad as he feared. The year 1899-1900 had been the heyday of Economism, after which it seemed to be on the decline. Leaflets circulating in Petersburg even in 1900 regularly took a revolutionary tone, demanding "Away with Autocracy" and "Long Live Political Freedom".⁴ The following year saw

---

3   *A. K. Wildman*. Making of a Workers' Revolution: Russian Social Democracy, 1891-1903. Chicago: University of Chicago Press, 1967. pp. 113, 120-124.
4   Ibid. p. 84.

the Obukhov Defence of May 1901, when workers in St. Petersburg's Obukhov factory demanded the eight-hour day and fought with police when attempts were made to restore order. Lenin believed, as Loginov makes clear, that the influence of "workerphilia" and Economism was not a reflection of the strength of their ideas, but of the weak organisation of the revolutionary tendency and that was what he was determined to put right. Lenin's purpose in founding his underground newspaper *Iskra* was to unite these revolutionary tendencies and see off all talk of Economism.

Certainly, then, Lenin became Lenin with *Iskra* in 1901 and the project of seeing off Economism once and for all. But just as Loginov argues that Lenin becoming a revolutionary was a process rather than a single event, it could be argued that Lenin becoming Lenin was a process, not an event like the first use of the pseudonym "Lenin". That process could have begun as early as 1894, and was surely a central part of Lenin's intellectual development during his time in prison and Siberian exile. Indeed, uniting the revolutionary tendency of Social Democracy against liberal Economism was not Leninism, it was a task Lenin carried out in association with his future Menshevik opponents Martov and Alexander Potresov. Leninism as such would appear only once the Economists had been defeated and the issue became one of establishing the correct relationship between the Social Democratic Party and the labour movement, a relationship which ensured that the workers were led by class conscious representatives.

When the Second Congress of the Russian Social Democratic Labour Party was held in London in 1903, the easy bit was defeating the Economists. What split the party into Bol'sheviks and Mensheviks was Lenin's insistence that class-consciousness could only come from political struggle beyond the labour movement, and for that to happen, the workers needed to be led. And not only did they have to be led, but, for that leadership to be successful, a specific form of discipline and hierarchical structure in the party organization was essential. The full ramifications of the disputes of 1903 were far from being in place in January 1897 as Lenin prepared for exile, but he first glimpsed elements of that future struggle when he learned of Takhtarev's proposals to move the centre of gravity of the labour movement towards legally permitted mutual aid funds and away from the underground social democratic League for the Emancipation of Labour.

A note on Russian names

Russians have three names, a given name, the name of their father or patronymic, and a family name. Lenin was Vladimir Ilych (son of Ilya) Ulyanov. In practice, the family name is used only rarely and on very formal occasions, the respectful form of address is name and patronymic. Loginov refers on occasion to Lenin's father as Ilya Nikolayevich, and at times he calls Plekhanov, the founder of Russian Marxism, Georgi Valentinovich. One of the many forms of endearment in the Russian language is to refer to someone by their patronymic alone; in her memoirs, Lenin's wife Nadezhda Krupskaya refers to Lenin as Ilych. These usages have not been explained in the text, since they are clear from the context in which they appear.

Geoffrey Swain
Professor Emeritus
University of Glasgow

VLADIMIR LENIN – HOW TO BECOME A LEADER

WHAT COLOUR WERE LENIN'S EYES?

Physiognomy lost any semblance of credibility long ago. It is no coincidence that card sharks are said to have the most likeable faces. Yet it is to the face one always looks for first impressions. These may prove accurate, or turn out to be wholly deceptive. One can miss the genius secreted behind an exterior of rank ordinariness, or the mediocrity which guises as brilliance.

When Maxim Gorky met Lenin for the first time, he remarked: "I had expected Lenin to be different. There seemed something lacking in him. His hands tucked into his waistcoat in a cocky stance, the guttural way he rasped the letter R. On the whole – too simple, nothing of a '*leader*' about him at all."[5]

There can be no doubt that Lenin's appearance left such a first impression. Gleb Krzhizhanovsky wrote, "His short stature, in a regular worker's cap, would easily have been lost in the crowd in any factory quarter. An agreeable, swarthy face with a touch of the Asiatic to it – that is about the sum of what there is to say about his outward aspect. With equal ease, Vladimir Ilyich, dressed as he was in a simple rural coat, could have merged with any throng of Volga peasants – there was something in his appearance that seemed to have stemmed directly from these lower classes, as if one of them from birth."[6]

Interesting, then, that many years later, Boris Pasternak, on a wholly separate thread, expressed a similar idea to Krzhizhanovsky's: "The genius is nothing other than the rarest and greatest representative of the ordinary rank and file of the age, its immortal expression. The genius is closer to the average person, more akin to him, than to the many varieties of exceptional people. The genius is the *quantitative extreme of a mankind which is qualitatively homogeneous*."[7]

---

5   Vospominaniya o Vladimire Ilyiche Lenine: Five volumes. Moscow, 1969. Vol. 2. p. 238.
6   Ibid, p. 10.
7   Literaturnoye obozreniye. 1978. No 4. p. 105.

Perhaps this is the perspective from which to approach an analysis of such a complex historical figure. However, one need only recall that the old Bol'shevik academic Krzhizhanovsky was not only an ardent supporter of Lenin, but also a close friend, to recognise the precariousness of this starting position: those who did not embrace the revolution, and hence Lenin, will view his appearance completely differently.

One such person was Alexander Ivanovich Kuprin. On 26th December 1918, he, along with the journalist O. L. Leonidov, had met with Lenin; in February 1921, by now living as an émigré in Paris, he published his study *Instant Photography*.

Lenin, he wrote, "is short in stature, square-shouldered and lean. There is nothing unpleasant, pugnacious or deep-thinking about his appearance. He has high cheekbones and his eyes are slanted... The dome of his skull is broad and elongated, but not at all as exaggerated as it appears in photographs... The remaining wisps of hair on his temples, as well as his beard and whiskers, bear witness to the red-headed firebrand he was in youth. His hands are large and very unsightly...

I was continually drawn to his eyes... naturally narrow, Lenin additionally tends to screw up his eyes, likely an attempt to conceal his short-sightedness, and this coupled with the rapid glances he makes occasionally suggest a squint, and perhaps an air of cunning. But it was rather their colour that struck me most...

Last summer in the Paris zoological gardens, observing the golden-red eyes of the lemurs, I exclaimed to myself: finally, I've found the colour of Lenin's eyes! The sole difference is that lemurs' pupils are large and restless, while Lenin's are piercing dots from which blue sparks fly."[8]

Of course, it is not that Lenin was not a "red-headed firebrand" in youth, but that he became to Kuprin a symbolic figure, the personification of that hated "red distemper" and as such, to the writer, even Lenin's eyes took on an apparently "golden-red" hue.

Krzhizhanovsky, on the other hand, wrote, "As soon as one looks into Vladimir Ilyich's eyes, into those extraordinary, piercing, deep brown eyes, full of force and vigour, one already senses that the person before you is far from ordinary. Most portraits of Vladimir Ilyich fail to

---

8   Quoted in: *D. Volkogonov*. Lenin. Politichesky Portret: Two books. Moscow, 1994. Book 1. pp. 29-30.

convey the impression of distinctive giftedness that quickly supplants the first impression garnered from his outward appearance…"[9]

A. V. Lunacharsky left his own sketch: "His face was especially splendid when serious, somewhat roused, perhaps a little angry. It was then that his eyes, under that heavy brow, would sparkle with a remarkable intellect and intensity of thought. What could be more splendid than eyes which communicate intensity of thought! And with that, his whole face took on an air of extraordinary strength."[10]

The Samara barrister Grigory Klements offers this portrait in 1924: "He was a young man, short in stature, but sturdily built, with a fresh, ruddy face upon which the moustache and beard – reddish in colour – barely showed through, and gently wavy red hair on his head. He looked no older than 23. One was struck by the large head with heavy white brow. His small eyes seemed permanently screwed up, his look serious, thoughtful and cautious. A rather ironic, restrained smile would play across his thin lips…"[11]

Judging by the photographs of Vladimir Ulyanov that survive from 1891, Klements' portrait is an accurate one. It is also interesting to recall the accounts given by those for whom Lenin was an unknown.

On one occasion in 1904, Lunacharsky, who had only recently become acquainted with Lenin, visited the studio of the renowned sculptor Naum Aronson.

Lunacharsky recounts, "Lenin removed his coat and in his usual lively manner went round the studio and curiously, but without comment, examined the plaster casts, marbles and bronzes… Aronson took me to one side:

'Who is that?', he whispered in my ear…

'A friend of mine…'

Aronson nodded his bushy head:

'He has a remarkable appearance.'

'He has?' I asked with surprise, as I had been disappointed that Lenin, who I had long considered a great man, seemed to me too much like your average … canny *muzhik*.

---

9   Vospominaniya o Vladimire Ilyiche Lenine: Vol. 2. pp 10-11.

10   Lenin vsegda s nami. Vospominaniya sovetskikh i zarubezhnykh pisatelei. Moscow, 1969, p. 19.

11   Kommuna. Samara. 1924. 24th April.

'He has a remarkable head,' Aronson told me, looking at me excitedly.

'Couldn't you persuade him to pose for me? I'd only do a small medallion. He'd make a very fine Socrates, for instance.'

'I don't think he'll agree to it,' I said.

Nonetheless, I relayed all this to Lenin, including his apparent resemblance to Socrates. Lenin literally roared with laughter, burying his face in his hands."[12] Aronson's wonderful marble bust of Lenin decorated the Central Lenin Museum in Moscow for many years.

During one meeting with the young Bol'shevik Ivan Popov, later a writer and playwright, Lenin used the expression "physical strength of intellect" when speaking about Georgi Plekhanov. Popov asked: "What is that, Vladimir Ilyich, the physical strength of intellect? I don't understand." Lenin replied, "Well, one can immediately recognise and distinguish the physical strength of an individual. An individual enters the room, you look at them, and you see that they are strong physically... Such is Plekhanov's intellect. You only need look at him to recognise he has the most powerful mind, one which prevails against everything, capable of weighing up everything at once, cutting to the heart of the matter – there is nothing one can conceal from him. And one has the sense that it exists objectively, like a physical force."[13] Lenin produced just such an impression on those around him.

To this we may add another quite authoritative and 'impartial' testimony: the German professor Otfrid Foerster, who could count many eminent figures among his patients through the years, met Vladimir Ilyich in the 1920s. He recounted, "Everyone who hadn't yet become engaged in Lenin's great undertaking fell under the magical spell of his formidable personality upon meeting him... I had occasion myself to experience the strength of his spirit.

I now see him before me as if in life, with his stocky frame, his elastic movements, his magnificent skull, like the dome of a mighty building; from his eyes, which in one moment roved calmly in open glances, the next narrowing, as if to better take the world in his sights, the constant flow of his intellect sparkled forth.

---

12   *A. V. Lunacharsky. Vospominaniya i vpechatleniya.* Moscow, 1968. pp. 84-85.

13   Lenin vsegda s nami. pp. 94-95.

His facial expressions were marked by their fabulous liveliness, each feature betraying the constant intensity of his mental processes and his profound internal tension."[14]

Today we know an incomparable amount more about Lenin than did his contemporaries. 55 volumes of his collected works have been published, as well as 40 volumes of the Lenin Collection, 14 volumes of *Decrees of the Soviet Government,* 12 volumes of the *Biographical Chronicle* and hundreds of memoirs. In all this published material, around 30,000 documents associated with Lenin have emerged. Nonetheless, until recently, approximately 6,500 such documents have remained in the archives. Of these, 3,000 are official documents merely signed by Lenin. Around 2,000 are so called "marginalia" - notes scribbled on books, newspapers, other letters and so on. However, there are around 1,000 letters, memoranda and resolutions of real substance. An entire volume of the most fascinating documents relating to Lenin – over 400 previously considered 'top secret' – has recently been made available.

However, the remarkable thing is this: the more literature appears, the more confused the issues surrounding the analysis of Lenin's life and activities become. New myths appear to replace the old. The difficulty is not so much in the 'mystery' of Lenin as a figure, as much as it is in the previously mentioned over-politicisation of his image.

After the revolution of 1917, portraits of Lenin replaced icons of the Virgin Mary with child and images of the tsar and his heir in the "red corners" of peasant huts. His image, independent of the real-life man, became a kind of symbol of the "new faith", of the battle of 'poor' against 'rich', the struggle for justice. For millions, it became an object of near religious veneration.

As a result, any serious act of state in the Soviet Union, or any political leader, was regarded as legitimate only with Lenin's 'blessing'. And in this table of ranks, each leader is either a "devoted disciple" or a "glorious successor" of his cause. This is, in fact, why searching for the roots of modern problems in Lenin's past deeds is at the very least unfair, since it has now become a wholly separate narrative: it is akin to blaming Christ for the Crusades and the bonfires of the Inquisition since in both cases the name and word of God is evoked.

---

14   Pravda. 1925. 21st January.

As Krzhizhanovsky reflected, "When over the course of human history individuals appear who, like pillars of fire, illuminate the road of life for others, and when we call such individuals geniuses, we often to fail in our attempts to explain the genius of these people."[15]

This book's intention is not to offer an explanation, but to present some material for consideration, a few details of his biography hitherto unknown to the reader, to apply some additional touches to Lenin's portrait.

So what colour *were* Lenin's eyes? Were they really a "fiery-red"?

Objective testimony does exist: in 1895, gendarmerie officials composed a verbose portrait of the leader of the "League of Struggle for the Emancipation of the Working Class", Vladimir Ulyanov: "Height – 2 *arshins*, 5½ *vershoks* [166.7 cm – *author*], medium build, of amiable appearance, blond, straight hair on his head and eyebrows, reddish moustache and beard, *brown eyes*, average-sized, round head, average-sized, high forehead, average nose, round face, regular features, ordinary mouth, round chin, average-sized ears."[16]

---

15   Vospominaniya o Vladimire Ilyiche Lenine. Vol. 2. pp. 9-10.
16   Krasny Arkhiv. 1934. No. 1 (62). p 139.

PART ONE – ORIGINS

AMONG THE ROOTS OF THE FAMILY TREE

The Biographical Chronicle of V. I. Lenin begins with the following entry:

"10th (22nd) April

Vladimir Ilyich Lenin (Ulyanov) is born.

Vladimir Ilyich's father – Ilya Nikolayevich Ulyanov, a school inspector at the time of Vladimir's birth, later Director of Public Schools of Simbirsk Province. He came from a lower middle class family in Astrakhan. His own father had previously been a serf.

Lenin's mother – Maria Alexandrovna, the daughter of A. D. Blank, a doctor."

It is curious that Lenin himself knew so few details of his family tree. In his family, as in the families of other such non-gentrified ranks, it was not done to go digging into one's genealogical heritage; it was only after Lenin's death that interest in such issues began to grow, namely among his sisters, who carried out the research. In completing the thorough questionnaire issued for the 1922 party census[17], to the question of his paternal grandfather's occupation, Lenin answered honestly: "I don't know."[18]

Three generations of Lenin's ancestors were certainly serfs. His great-grandfather, Nikita Grigoryevich Ulyanin, born in 1711, and his eldest son, Vasily Nikitich Ulyanin, born in 1733, lived in the village of Androsovo in Nizhny Novgorod Province.

---

17 The party census, conducted in spring 1922, aimed to purge the party of so-called "unreliable" elements. Social background, participation in the Revolution and ideological literacy were ascertained.

18 *V. I. Lenin.* Polnoye sobraniye sochineny. Vol. 44. p. 150.

According to the 1795 census review, Lenin's grandfather, Nikolai Vasilyevich, was a 25-year-old bachelor recorded as living in the same village. However, from 1791, he was recorded as absent (according to documents in the Astrakhan archive) – whether he escaped or was released to pay cash levies [*obrok*] and bought his way out of serfdom is unclear, but in Astrakhan, Nikolai Vasilyevich was transferred to the category of state peasant in 1799, before moving into the ranks of the lower middle classes as a tailor in 1808.

His vital statistics are recorded as: "Height – two *arshins*, six *vershoks* [168.9 cm – *author*]. Hair, moustache and beard light brown. Light, clear complexion. Brown eyes..."[19] Compare these observations with Lenin's police record and it is clear who Vladimir Ilyich took after.

Released from serfdom and a free man, Nikolai Vasilyevich changed his surname first to Ulyaninov, then to Ulyanov. He soon married Anna Alexeyevna: daughter of a wealthy Astrakhan resident, Alexei Lukyanovich Smirnov, she was born in 1788 and 18 years her husband's junior.

Based on archival research, writer Marietta Shaginyan has suggested that Anna Alexeyevna was not the natural daughter of Smirnov, but was in fact a baptised Kalmyk, rescued from slavery and adopted only in March 1825. There is no indisputable evidence of this theory, especially given that by 1812, the marriage of Nikolai Ulyanov and Anna Smirnova had produced a son, Alexander, who died four months after birth, another son, Vasily, born in 1819, a daughter, Maria, in 1821, Feodosiya in 1823, and finally, in July 1831, a son, Ilya, when his father was already in his 60s.

They settled in Astrakhan in the Volga region, occupying a two-storey brick house with wooden roof on Kazachya Street, in the so-called Kosa district of the city. Anna Alexeyevna's sister Tatyana Alexeyevna Smirnova also lived in the house her whole life and was considered something of a 'godmother'. Nikolai Ulyanov and his sons Vasily and Ilya appear in 1837 conscription lists, denoted as being of *"native Russian origin"*.

After Nikolai Vasilyevich's death, responsibility for looking after the family and raising the children passed to the elder son, Vasily Nikolayevich. Employed then as a clerk for the Sapozhnikov Brothers, a

---

19   Pravda. 1982. 2nd November. For further reading, see: O. Abramova, G. Borodulina, T. Koloskova. Mezhdu pravdoi i istinoi (Ob istorii spekulyatsii vokrug rodoslovnoi V. I. Lenina). Moscow, 1998. pp 78-79.

prominent Astrakhan firm, and having no family of his own, he was able not only to provide for the household, but also to provide an education for the young Ilya.

In 1850, Ilya Vasilyevich graduated from the Astrakhan Gymnasium with a silver medal and enrolled in the faculty of physics and mathematics at Kazan University, graduating in 1854 as a candidate of physical and mathematical sciences and earning the right to teach in secondary schools. Although he was offered the chance to remain with the department of "advancement in scientific study", and despite the insistence of renowned mathematician N. I. Lobachevsky, Ilya Nikolayevich preferred to embark on a career as a teacher.

His first place of work – beginning on 7th May 1855 – became the Institute of the Nobility in Penza. It was a successful time for Ilya Nikolayevich. He was certified as a senior teacher of mathematics for upper grades, and in 1860 was awarded the medal "In Memory of the 1853-1856 War" and received the rank of titular councillor.

In 1860, Ivan Dmitriyevich Veretennikov arrived at the Institute of the Nobility to become the school's inspector. Ilya Nikolayevich befriended him and his wife, and in the same year, Anna Alexandrovna Veretennikova (née Blank) introduced him to Maria Alexandrovna Blank, who had come to spend the winter with her sister. Ilya Nikolayevich began to help Maria Alexandrovna prepare for her teaching exams, while she in turn tutored him in conversational English. The youngsters fell in love, and in spring 1863 became engaged.

On 15th July of the same year, after successfully passing external exams at the Samara Gymnasium, "the daughter of a court councillor, the young lady Maria Blank", obtained the rank of elementary teacher "with the right to teach religious scripture, Russian, arithmetic, German and French." In August the wedding took place, and the "young lady Maria Blank" became the wife of the Court Councillor – a rank bestowed in July 1863 – Ilya Nikolayevich Ulyanov.

Blank's family history was investigated by Lenin's sisters Anna and Maria, and in the Soviet period by Marietta Shaginyan, Alexander Petrov and Mikhail Shtein. Anna Ulyanova records: "Our elders were unable to cast any light on it for us. The surname seemed to us to be of French origin, but there was no information to that effect. I'd personally long suspected the possibility of Jewish heritage, largely as a result of my mother saying that my grandfather was born in Zhitomir, a well-known

Jewish centre. My maternal grandmother was born in St Petersburg and was by heritage a Riga German. But while contact was maintained with my mother and her sister's maternal relatives for some time, nothing was heard of the relatives of her father, A. D. Blank. He'd seemingly broken from them, which drew me to consider a Jewish heritage. His daughter retained no stories of my grandfather's childhood or youth."[20]

In 1932 and 1934, Anna Ulyanova informed Stalin of the results of her investigation, which confirmed her suspicions. She wrote: "The fact of our heritage, as I had supposed before, was unknown in [Lenin's] lifetime... I do not know of any grounds for us, as communists, to remain silent about it now."[21]

"Not a word about it", was Stalin's categorical response. Her own sister, Maria Ulyanova, agreed: "Let it become known in a hundred years or so."[22]

One hundred years have not yet passed; nonetheless, published information now allows us to chart the Blank family tree with relative certainty.[23]

It seems Lenin's great-grandfather, Moshe Itskovich Blank, was born in 1763. He first appears in the 1795 census review, where among the citizens of the town of Starokonstantinov in the Volyn Province he is recorded in entry number 394 as Moishka Blank. How he came to be in those parts remains unknown.

In 1793, Moshe Blank married a 29-year-old local girl, Mariam (Marem) Froimovich. Subsequent census reviews indicate that Moshe Blank was literate in both Yiddish and Russian, owned his own home, engaged in trade and rented five *morgs* of land at the village of Rogachevo, which were planted with chicory.

In 1794, a son, Aba (Abel) was born to him, and in 1799 a second son followed, Srul (Israel). V. V. Tsaplin notes that from the outset, Moshe Blank did not maintain a relationship with the local Jewish community. He was "a man who did not, or was perhaps unable to, find common ground with his kinsmen."[24] In other words, the community had grown to despise

---

20   Otechestvennyye arkhivy. 1992. No. 4. p. 81.
21   Ibid. pp. 78, 79.
22   Ibid. p. 79.
23   See: ibid. pp. 38-46.
24   Otechestvennyye arkhivy. 1992. No. 2. p. 40.

him. After a fire in 1808 that destroyed their home, possibly a case of arson, the Blank family relocated to Zhitomir.

Many years later, in September 1846, Moshe Blank wrote a letter to Emperor Nicholas I which indicates that "40 years previous" he "renounced the Jews", though due to an "excessively pious wife" who had died in 1834, he only adopted the Christian faith and took the name Dmitry on 1st January 1835.

However, this was not the main thrust of his letter: his hostility towards his fellow Jews still in evidence, Dmitry (Moshe) Blank suggested – with a view to assimilation – prohibiting their wearing of native dress, and more importantly, obliging them to pray for the Russian emperor and the imperial family in synagogues.

Interestingly, after the letter was presented to Nicholas I in October 1846, he fully consented to the suggestions of the "baptised Jew Blank", resulting in the prohibition of Jewish dress in 1850, and the introduction of a corresponding prayer text in 1854. Mikhail Shtein, who gathered and carefully analysed the most complete data available on the Blank ancestry, rightly observes that Dmitry Blank's hostility towards his own people "is perhaps comparable only to another baptised Jew, one of the founders and leaders of the Moscow Union of Russian Peoples, Vladimir Gringmut..."[25]

Evidence that Blank had decided to break with the Jewish community long before his baptism is evidenced by the fact that both his sons Abel and Israel were, like their father, literate in Russian, and when a district school opened in Zhitomir in 1816, they were both enrolled and both graduated successfully. From the standpoint of religious Jews, this was tantamount to sacrilege. Nonetheless, belonging to the Jewish faith condemned them to a wretched life within the Pale of Settlement. It was only the events of 1820 that drastically altered the fate of the young men.

In April, a senior official – the senator and poet Dmitry Osipovich Baranov, head of the so-called "Jewish committee" – arrived in Zhitomir on assignment. Somehow, Blank was able to arrange a meeting with him, and asked the senator for his assistance in having his sons admitted to the Medical-Surgical Academy in St Petersburg. Baranov was far from sympathetic to Jews, but this conversion of two "lost souls" to

---

25   *M. G. Shtein.* Ulyanovy i Leniny. Tainy rodoslovnoi i psevdonima. St Petersburg, 1997. pp. 39, 44, 46.

Christianity, then a rare phenomenon, struck him as a noble cause, and he agreed.[26]

The brothers immediately travelled to St Petersburg and filed a petition to the Metropolitan of Novgorod, St Petersburg, Estonia and Finland. They wrote: "Having now settled in St Petersburg and having always had dealings with Christians of the Greco-Russian faith, we wish now to adopt said faith."[27]

The request was granted and on 25th May 1820, both brothers were "shown the light by baptism" by Fyodor Barsov, priest of the church of St Sampson. Abel became Dmitry Dmitriyevich and Israel – Alexander Dmitriyevich. His new name was taken in honour of his godfather, Count Alexander Apraksin, while his patronymic was in recognition of Abel's godfather, the senator Dmitry Baranov.

On 31st June of the same year, on the instructions of the minister for education Prince Golitsyn, the brothers were recognised as "students of the Medical-Surgical Academy", where they would complete their studies in 1824 as "physicians of the 2nd category", receiving as a gift a pocket set of surgical instruments.

Dmitry Blank remained in the capital as a police doctor, while Alexander's first place of practice became the town of Porechye in Smolensk Province, where he served as a district physician. However, in October 1825 he returned to St Petersburg, where he, like his brother, was enlisted in the staff of the capital's police force as a doctor. In 1828, Alexander Blank was promoted to military staff doctor. It was now time to think about finding a wife.

His godfather, Count Alexander Apraksin, was at that time an official on special assignments at the Ministry of Finance, so Alexander Blank, despite his background, could look forward to mixing in respectable circles. It appears that it was in the home of another benefactor, the senator Dmitry Baranov, who was fond of poetry and chess and had hosted Pushkin and much of the rest of "enlightened Petersburg", that he made the acquaintance of the Großschopf brothers, who invited him to their home.

The head of this highly respected household was one Ivan Fyodorovich (Johann Gottlieb) Großschopf, a Baltic German of north German ancestry

---

26   See: ibid. p. 43.

27   *M. G. Shtein.* Ulyanovy i Leniny. p. 10; *O. Abramova, G. Borodulina, T. Koloskova.* Mezhdu pravdoi i istinoi.

whose distant relations included Ernst Curtius, tutor to Kaiser Friedrich III, and whose descendants included Wehrmacht Field Marshal Walter Model.[28]

Ivan Fyodorovich worked as a *konsulent* at the State Collegium of Justice for Livonian, Estonian and Finnish Affairs and rose to the rank of district secretary. His wife, Anna Karlovna – born Estedt – was a Lutheran Swede whose parents were wealthy merchants from Uppsala who had moved to St Petersburg. The Großschopfs had eight children; sons Johann, who served in the Russian army; Karl, a deputy director with the department of foreign trade in the Ministry of Finance; and Gustav, in charge of the Riga customs house. There were five daughters: Alexandra, Anna, Yekaterina (married name – von Essen), Karolina (married name – Biuberg) and the young Amalia.[29]

Having made the family's acquaintance, Alexander Blank proposed to Anna Ivanovna. She had recently graduated from boarding school, spoke a number of languages, and played the clavichord wonderfully. It was her playing that first introduced him to Beethoven's *Moonlight Sonata*, a piece he would grow to love.[30]

Consent to the marriage was obtained and on 9th September 1830, a son, Dmitry, was born (he committed suicide aged 19 in 1850 while a student at Kazan University). On 30th August 1831, a daughter named Anna (married name – Veretennikova) was born, then on 29th August 1832, Lyubov (Ardasheva by her first husband, Ponomareva by her second), on 25th December 1833, Yekaterina (Zalezhskaya), 22nd February 1835, Maria (Ulyanova) and on 24th June 1836, Sofia (Lavrova).[31]

Things initially went well for Alexander Dmitriyevich. As a police doctor, he received 1,000 roubles per year. He was more than once commended for his "efficiency and diligence". However, in June 1831, during the Cholera Riots that took place in the capital, his brother Dmitry, on duty at the Central Cholera Hospital, was brutally murdered by a furious mob. His death so distressed Alexander Blank that he resigned from the police and was unable to practise for over a year. Only in April 1833 did he

---

28 See: *D. Volkogonov*. Lenin. Politichesky Portret. Book 1. p. 52.
29 See: *M. G. Shtein*. Ulyanovy i Leniny. pp. 102, 104, 111.
30 See: ibid. p. 53.
31 See: ibid. pp. 71, 72, 73, 77.

return to work. After passing exams in 1837, he was appointed a medical board inspector and, in 1838, a medical surgeon.

Alexander Blank's own private practice also expanded. His patients began to include members of the nobility. This enabled him to take a good apartment in a wing of a luxury villa on the English Embankment belonging to the emperor's physician and president of the Medical-Surgical Academy, Baronet Sir James Wylie. It was in this apartment that Maria was born, with neighbour Ivan Dmitriyevich Chertkov, equerry to the imperial court and adjutant to Grand Duke Mikhail Pavlovich, becoming little Masha's godfather.[32]

In 1840, Anna Ivanovna fell seriously ill and died, and was buried in the Smolensky Evangelical Cemetery in St Petersburg. Care of the children passed to her sister, Yekaterina von Essen, who had been widowed in the same year. It seems that Alexander Blank had been fond of her for some time: it was no coincidence that he had named his daughter, born in 1833, Yekaterina. They grew closer after his wife's death and in April 1841 Alexander Blank made arrangements for them to enter into a legal union. However, marrying the godmother of one's daughter, or the sister of one's deceased spouse, was not permitted by law. Instead, Yekaterina von Essen became his common-law wife.[33]

That same month they left the capital and the whole family moved to Perm, where Alexander Blank had been appointed inspector of the Perm medical board and doctor to Perm Gymnasium. In March 1843, Alexander Blank took charge of the clinic at the Yugovsky State Factory and from September 1845 was appointed inspector of hospitals in Zlatoust, where he finished his career.[34]

Alexander Blank went down in Russian medical history as one of the pioneers of balneology, treatment by mineral springs. He retired in 1847 with the rank of Court Councillor, which placed him among the minor nobility, and he left the Urals for Kazan Province. With his savings he bought land in Laishevsky District, though much of the funds came from Yekaterina von Essen. They purchased an estate at Kokushkino which consisted of 462 *desyatiny* of land (503.6 hectares), a water mill, and 39

---

32 See: ibid. pp. 20, 75, 76.
33 See: ibid. p. 78.
34 See: Otechestvennyye arkhivy. 1992. No. 4. p. 81.

serfs.[35] On 4th August 1859, the Senate confirmed Alexander Blank and his children's status as hereditary nobles, and they were included in the Kazan Assembly of the Nobility.

Thus Maria Alexandrovna Blank came to be in Kazan, and then Penza, where she met Ilya Nikolayevich Ulyanov.

Their wedding, like those of the other Blank sisters earlier, took place in Kokushkino on 25th August 1863. However, the honeymoon was cut short: on 7th September, Maria's godmother and surrogate mother, Yekaterina von Essen, died at Kokushkino. Only after her burial did the young couple depart for Nizhny Novgorod, where Ilya had been appointed senior teacher of mathematics and physics at the gymnasium.

---

35   See: *I. S. Zilbershtein*. Molodoi Lenin v zhizni i za rabotoi. Po vospominaniyam sovremennikov i dokumentam epokhi. Moscow, 1929. p. 41.

THE SIXTIERS

It is a thankless task, trying to gather the offshoots of the family tree. It satisfies a legitimate curiosity, but explains little.

In practice, drawing out the threads of kinship through the centuries, picking apart one generation from another, it pulls the fate of each from the context of their time, and shifts the focus to factors verging on the genetic. The circumstances and events of each era did influence actions, did determine the destiny of lives, and did define modes of living just as profoundly as familial heritage.

On 19th July 1831, Archpriest Nikolai Livanov baptised Ilya – the second son of Nikolai Ulyanov and his wife Anna – in the Church of Nikola Gostiny in Astrakhan. That same year, Emperor Nicholas I ordered that "under no circumstances are the children of serfs to be sent to schools in which they receive an education that may improve their station."

When Ilya Ulyanov nonetheless graduated from the gymnasium and its director A. P. Aristov appealed to the trustee of the Kazan School District to award a university scholarship to the "gifted boy", he was informed that "coming from a soul-tax paying background" [trans: *proiskhodyashchii iz podatnogo sostoyaniya*] and "belonging to the petty bourgeoisie" [trans: *meshchanskoye sosloviye*] were "insufficient grounds" to qualify for a scholarship. Only assistance from his brother would allow Ilya to complete university.[36]

On 18th February 1855, Nicholas I died. As he wended his way through the lanes of the Arbat, Moscow State University professor and historian S. Solovyov brooded: "I was not saddened by Nicholas I's death, but at the same time felt ill at ease, anxious, apprehensive: what if worse lies ahead? A man released from prison breathes easily in the the fresh air, but where will he be taken next? Perhaps to another, even worse prison."

---

36 See: Y. Yakovlev. Zhizni pervaya tret'. Dokumentalnoye povestvovaniye o sem'ye Ulyanovykh, detstve i yunosti Vladimira Ilyicha. Moscow, 1985. pp. 16, 17, 18.

This bleak inner monologue was interrupted by a passing colleague, Professor T. Granovsky. Solovyov's opening words in place of a greeting were "He's dead." Granovsky's response: "It's no surprise he's dead. The remarkable thing is that you and I are alive."[37]

Alexander II was crowned. N. A. Dobrolyubov wrote in his "Ode on the Death of Nicholas I":

Natural law has deigned it so,
That the times be bound to accustomed fate,
A new tyrant crowned, as the last one goes,
Still a nation strains 'neath a tyrant's weight.

Suddenly, in 1856, like a bolt from the blue, Alexander II announced to the Moscow Governor-General: "It has come to my attention, Sirs, that rumours circulate of my intention to eliminate serfdom. To repudiate such unfounded talk surrounding such a serious subject, I consider it necessary to inform you that I have no such intentions at this time. Of course, Sirs, as you will recognise, the current arrangement for owning souls cannot remain as it presently stands. It is better to abolish serfdom from above than to wait for such time as it begins to abolish itself from below."[38]

Six years after he ascended the throne, after long discussions in the committees of the nobility, in the offices of the bureaucracy, and in the State Council, Alexander II signed the Emancipation Decree to abolish serfdom on 19th February 1861. "Everything that could have been done to protect landowners' interests has been done," he declared with satisfaction. On 5th March, the Decree was published, and all around Russia the church bells rang, with prayers echoing from every pulpit for "Alexander the Liberator".

Few remained sceptical. Recognising Alexander II's achievements, Alexander Herzen recalled the biblical words: "Thou hast conquered, Galilean!" Even the radical Nikolai Chernyshevsky wrote, "The destruction of serfdom blesses Alexander's reign with the highest glory on Earth." However, time was required to truly understand and evaluate what was taking place.

---

37   Ibid. p. 27.
38   Ibid. pp. 19-20.

The reforms indirectly affected the Ulyanovs as well. Alexander Blank's estate, which his daughters and sisters visited every summer, also possessed serfs. However, according to Anna Ulyanova, local peasants bore their landlords no ill will. On the contrary, as a doctor who took in the sick of all the surrounding villages, Alexander Blank enjoyed universal respect. As Anna Uyanova stated, "Kokushkino was an acquired estate and, as such, there could be no such relations between owner and serfs as those which were formed by aristocratic owners who had acquired their serfs as inheritance."[39]

After 1861, reforms were introduced in quick succession. A new impetus for development was felt within industry and agriculture. Unprecedented institutions – trial by jury, rural councils known as *zemstvos* – were introduced. Education allowed society to be more upwardly mobile. Provincial and district school boards were established. Projects for the large-scale creation of public schools were formulated, while great minds such as that of the 'father of Russian pedagogy' K. D. Ushinsky were already dreaming of the elimination of illiteracy in Russia.

"..All Russia," recalled that great rebel Prince Peter Kropotkin, "was talking of education. In the press, in enlightened circles, even in the drawing rooms of the highest society, the ignorance of the people, the obstacles that still stood in the way of those wishing to learn, the lack of schools in rural areas, the antiquated methods of teaching, and what to do to alleviate it all, became the favourite subjects of discussion. A major push for the establishment of Sunday schools began."[40] It was the poet Fyodor Tyutchev who most succinctly encapsulated the spirit of the time: "A thaw!"

If one was to isolate one overarching idea that defined the mindset of the Sixtiers, it would be the recognition of the concept of "public good" as a harmonisation of personal and public interests. It was most fully articulated at the end of the 1860s in the "Historical Letters" of Pyotr Lavrov.

He wrote, "The interests of the individual, when clearly understood, should be put to the realisation of common interests. Genuine social theory requires not the *subjugation* of the social element to the personal, nor the *absorption* of the individual by the collective, but the *fusion* of public and individual interests."[41]

---

39 Otechestvennyye arkhivy. 1992. No. 4. p. 82.
40 Y. Yakovlev. Zhizni pervaya tret'. p. 34.
41 P. L. Lavrov. Istoricheskiye pis'ma. 5th Ed. Petrograd, 1917. p. 88.

Ilya Nikolayevich Ulyanov became swept up in the tide of this 'Great Hope'. In Penza, where he had worked since 1855, a Sunday school had been opened in November 1860, only the 59th in Russia. It had been established "to promote literacy among the artisan and working classes", and in addition to Russian and arithmetic, offered history, geography and the natural sciences. Supplementary to his work at both the boys' and girls' gymnasiums, Ilya Ulyanov began to teach and administrate at the Sunday school as well.[42]

However, times of great frustration followed in the wake of that tide of hope. History had once more confirmed that in conditions of strict governance, where even faint hopes of concession are crushed, dislike towards a regime generally takes on a hidden, latent character. But when concessions are eventually made, such reform cannot alleviate the sheer weight of expectation allowed to accumulate over so long, and discontent spills over. In short, if under "Nicholas of the Stick", no-one had dared utter a breath, then their patience had been exhausted by the time "Alexander the Liberator" took the throne.

The first negative response to the 'Great Reforms' came from the peasants themselves: they felt betrayed, and a wave of riots swept through Russia.

Anna Ulyanova observed, "Upon the liberation of the serfs, my grandfather had advised them to buy out the land, but they did not heed his advice, preferring deeded land instead."[43-44]

Kokushkino avoided any trouble, but in April 1861 in the village of Bezdna, also in Kazan Province, riots broke out and Count Apraksin had around 100 peasants shot in pacifying them. More were killed and wounded in the villages of Chernogai and Kandeyevka in Penza Province, where troops fired on peasants shouting the slogan, "All the land is ours!"

---

42 See: Y. Yakovlev. Zhizni pervaya tret'. pp. 34, 35.

43 According to the Emancipation Decree of 1861, rural communities were afforded the right to buy out their estates and, with the landowner's agreement, plots of land, upon which peasants' obligations to the landowner ceased. Peasants who purchased plots were called "peasant owners". Peasants could also refuse this right of purchase and receive from the landowner a free plot of land to the size of a quarter of a plot, which they had the right to buy out.

44 Otechestvennyye arkhivy. 1992. No. 4. p. 82.

In response, unrest broke out among students at the university and Theological Academy in Kazan. At a service for those killed, organised as an act of defiance by the students, professor of history Afanasy Shchapov, who would later die in exile in Siberia, said that the achievement of the Bezdna peasants was to put paid to the preconception that the Russian people were "incapable of initiating political movements."[45]

Besides the repressions, by summer 1861 the government was devising new "Regulations…" designed to stamp out any university liberties. However, by autumn, as the student year began, mass protest strikes and demonstrations broke out in St Petersburg and Moscow universities. The authorities carried out large-scale arrests, throwing the participants in the Peter & Paul Fortress, expelling them from university, or exiling them to Siberia.

"Where next, you youngsters, who have been locked out of the sciences?" wrote Herzen. "To the people! That is your place, you exiles from science! Show that they will not make clerks of you, but soldiers – not rootless mercenaries, but soldiers of the Russian people."[46]

That autumn of 1861, a proclamation titled "To The Younger Generation" appeared in St Petersburg, composed by *Sovremennik* writer Nikolai Shelgunov. It read: "The sovereign has betrayed the expectations of the people – the freedom he has given is false and not one which the people desired or required. We naturally do not wish for the issue to lead to a violent uprising. But if there is no other way…, we will readily call for a revolution to help the people."[47]

In 1861, the anarchist Mikhail Bakunin fled Siberian exile via Japan and the United States. He wrote, "We understand revolution as the unleashing of what is *presently* referred to as wicked passions and the destruction of what is known *in the same terms* as the natural order."

One must have experienced all the noisy exaltations of liberation and freedom, followed by the utter, brazen betrayal of these hopes, to have comprehended the bitterness felt by the young.

In 1862, the young Pyotr Zaichnevsky, the son of a general, wrote in his proclamation "Young Russia" that only "revolution, a revolution at once bloody and relentless", followed by the dictatorship of a revolutionary

---

45   Krasny arkhiv. 1923. No. 4. p. 409.

46   A. I. Herzen. Sobraniye sochineny: 30 volumes. Moscow, 1958. Vol. 15. p. 175.

47   Istoriya VKP(B). Vol. 1. Issue 1. Moscow; Leningrad, 1926. p. 27.

party which seizes power, was capable of delivering genuine freedom to the people. To this end he was ready to wipe out one hundred thousand landowners and, first and foremost, the "imperial party". "Remember, those who are not with us are against us, and those who are against us are our enemy, an enemy that must be destroyed by all available means."[48]

Ilya Nikolayevich Ulyanov certainly did not share this mentality, and as Anna Ulyanova testifies, disapproved of "all this talk" planting ideas of land redistribution in the peasants' heads.[49] Hating to his core serfdom in all its forms, he, like many other members of that generation of Russian "Sixtiers", firmly believed that after the abolition of slavery, only education and the Europeanisation of Russia would bring about universal prosperity and well-being.

As such, when his students had already begun to contemplate revolutionary terror, Ilya Nikolayevich merely gave himself over with even more vigour to the cause of public education and, in particular, to the Penza Sunday school.

"These people in their sheepskins, their peasant coats, their patchwork Nankeen smocks, with blackened, calloused hands and grimy faces, with a smell and colour that evoke clearly the trade of each," wrote Konstantin Ushinsky at the time, "they come here not for banter or jest, not out of idle curiosity; they have gathered for a cause, a cause for which they have sacrificed hours of each free day of their working week, a cause which to them is not simply of benefit to them, but is in some way sacred, somehow a religious undertaking."[50]

Thus in Penza, the teachers could not be more pleased with their charges, who in their attitude to study far exceeded the students of the gymnasium. However, in 1862, the spotlight fell on them too; on 10th June, a Supreme Order from Alexander II was issued:

"The supervision of Sunday schools and public reading rooms has been insufficient. Recently it has been found that under the plausible pretext of spreading literacy among the people, malicious persons in certain Sunday schools have attempted to advance harmful teachings, seditious ideas and perverse concepts of ownership and irreligion. With regard to the reading rooms, it has similarly been found that these

---

48 Ibid. pp. 27, 28.
49 See: Otechestvennyye arkhivy. 1992. No. 4. p. 82.
50 Y. Yakovlev. Zhizni pervaya tret'. pp. 34-35.

institutions have been used not for the dissemination of useful knowledge, but to instil the same harmful socialist teaching." As a result, the emperor commanded that: "Until the aforementioned schools are reformed on new foundations, all existing Sunday schools and reading rooms are to be closed."[51]

In June 1862, the resultant circular from the Minister of Internal Affairs reached Ilya Nikolayevich, the school closed, and in August of the next year, following their wedding, he and his wife departed for Nizhny Novgorod. The city was large, wealthy, and possessed an entirely different intellectual atmosphere to Penza. Children soon followed. A daughter, Anna, was born on 14th August 1864. A son, Alexander, followed 18 months later on 31st March 1866. However, shortly after, they suffered a bitter loss: Olga, their daughter born in 1868, did not survive her first year, falling ill and dying at Kokushkino on 18th July.

New friends were also made. The young teachers were housed in government-owned apartments in the "red building" situated in the courtyard of the Institute of the Nobility. In the evenings, having put the children to bed, the teachers would gather, converse, and play music together. Ilya Nikolayevich applied himself to his work with the same dedication, and his service continued satisfactorily. In November 1865, he received his first decoration, the Order of St Anna 3rd Class. He began to teach not only at the Institute of the Nobility, but also in the local gymnasium, on forestry taxation courses, and took on private lessons. Whenever he would come home with his wages, Maria Alexandrovna would carefully plan the monthly budget down to the last kopeck. There was a home to build, children to support, and relatives in Astrakhan who needed their assistance. However, even here in Nizhny Novgorod, those years spent in Penza would continue to resonate.

In April 1866, newspapers announced the unthinkable: for the first time in history, revolutionaries had attempted to assassinate a Russian emperor. At around four o'clock in the afternoon of 4th April, Alexander II was returning to his carriage after a stroll in the Summer Gardens when an unknown gunman opened fire with a pistol. However, a peasant standing beside the gunman, Osip Komissarov, managed to jolt his arm as he fired and the bullet missed the emperor. A crowd rushed the gunman and he was knocked to the ground. As they began to beat him,

---

51   Ibid. p. 37.

he cried out, "What are you doing, you fools! I'm doing it for you, for you, for you! For the Russian *muzhik*!"[52]

Prince Peter Kropotkin said: "After the 4th April 1866 shooting, the Third Section became omnipotent. Those suspected of 'radicalism', rightly or otherwise, lived in constant fear. Every night they faced the possibility of being taken for having an acquaintance in common with someone caught up in some political affair, for a harmless letter discovered during a night-time raid, or merely for holding 'dangerous beliefs'. Arrest over a political matter could lead to any number of things: years of imprisonment in the Peter & Paul Fortress, exile to Siberia, even torture in the cells."[53]

In a matter of days, the investigative commission learned that the culprit, the son of a minor nobleman by the name of Dmitry Vladimirovich Karakozov, born in 1840, had lived in Penza until 1860, where he had studied at the gymnasium. Many others from the underground circle organised in Moscow by Karakozov's cousin, Nikolai Ishutin, had also studied there and at the Penza Institute of the Nobility.

For the Ulyanovs, this triggered an agonising series of days as they waited in expectation and fear. They knew both Karakozov and Ishutin, but Ilya Ulyanov did not name either under interrogation. Then his former pupil at the Penza Institute of the Nobility, an N. P. Stranden, revealed during the course of the investigation that he was acquainted with Ulyanov. A letter of recommendation for an application to Moscow University written by Ilya Ulyanov for another of those under investigation was also produced.

In response to an inquiry from the investigative commission about teachers of the Penza Institute of the Nobility and gymnasium who had taught the conspirators, local gendarmes reported that the most "dangerous" and "harmful" individual in a position to influence his charges was a literature teacher, V. I. Zakharov, whom Ilya Ulyanov had not named, despite having recently rented an apartment from him, and from whom he had taken over the running of the Sunday school.

For whatever reason, Ilya Ulyanov was not called for further questioning, and the matter seemed to blow over.

"The sovereign's saviour" Osip Komissarov was enobled and took full advantage of the free vodka offered to him in the taverns, while Karakozov

---

52   Ibid. p. 58.
53   Ibid. pp. 54-55.

was hanged on 3rd September 1866. Ishutin received a gallows pardon, the noose exchanged for a lifetime of hard labour in Siberia, where he eventually lost his mind and died in 1879. Komissarov, in turn, hanged himself in 1892 after an extended drinking session.

Among the multitude of those arrested as either directly or indirectly connected to the case, there were a number of important personages from the capital, and a modest teacher of mathematics and physics from Nizhny Novgorod, who had hitherto done nothing to compromise himself, apparently dropped out of sight of the "ever-watchful eye" of the Third Section.

Life carried on. As before, Ilya Ulyanov set off for the gymnasium every morning, returning late. In the gymnasium attic he built an observatory and set up a telescope. From here, his pupils gazed into the starry evening sky. For the physics classroom he purchased a working model of a steam engine to reassure his students there was no evil forces at work in the "*chugunka*", the railway.

The children, Anna, and Alexander, born four days before Karakozov's attempt on the emperor's life, were also doing well. In July 1867, Ilya Nikolayevich advanced to a new rank, that of Collegiate Councillor, the equivalent of a major on the Table of Ranks. Nonetheless, work at the gymnasium left him dissatisfied, particularly after his experience teaching at the Sunday school. He still aspired to the provision of a truly national public education system. So when his literature teacher in Astrakhan, Alexander Vasilyevich Timofeyev, now an inspector within the Kazan school district, wrote to inform him of a recent vacancy for an inspector of public schools in Simbirsk, Ilya Ulyanov immediately took up the offer.

SIMBIRSK[54]

Ulyanov's appointment was confirmed on 6th September 1869 and the whole family, having moved to Simbirsk, settled on Streletskaya Street, taking a wing of a building belonging to A. I Pribylovskaya. Shortly afterwards, on 10th April 1870 (22th in the Julian calendar), another son, Vladimir, was born. On 16th April, the priest Vasily Umov and deacon Vladimir Znamensky christened the newborn.[55]

At that time, Simbirsk was a quiet provincial town with a little over 40,000 inhabitants, of whom 57.5% were listed as townspeople [*meshchane*], 17% were military personnel, 11% were peasants, 8.8% came from the gentry, and 3.2% - guild merchants and honorary citizens. Accordingly, the city was divided into three parts – the noble quarter, the commercial district, and the district occupied by the townsfolk. The noble quarter boasted kerosene lamps and boardwalks; the townspeople shared their courtyards with cattle which, despite prohibitions, wandered freely around the streets.

Alongside a few small factories and distillers which produced vodka, beer and mead, candlewax, and processed flour, Simbirsk supported both male and female gymnasiums, a military school, a religious school and seminary, *feldscher* and trade schools, a teacher training school for the Muslim Chuvash people, a Tatar madrasa, several parish schools, as well as the Karamzinskaya Public Library, the Goncharov Public Library and, finally, a theatre.

In the summer, the children's mother would take them to their grandfather's *dacha* at Kokushkino. Anna Ulyanova recalled "a tall, thin old man with dark, heavily greyed hair and clear, lively dark eyes, a man who would usually treat us, his grandchildren, kindly, inclined as he was to spoil us. The last summer, I recall my grandfather leading us downstairs to the mezzanine of the house at Kokushkino, where

---

54   Renamed Ulyanovsk in 1924.
55   See: Lenin i Simbirsk. Saratov, 1986. p. 36.

my mother waited to present to him his new grandson, our brother Volodya, born that spring. My grandfather likely inspected the child from a doctor's perspective."[56]

The same summer, on 17th July 1870, Alexander Dimitriyevich Blank died. He was buried beside the grave of Yekaterina von Essen, in the graveyard of the parish church at Cheremyshevo, three *versts* from Kokushkino. One year later, Anna Alexeyevna, their grandmother in Astrakhan and Ilya Ulyanov's mother, also died.

The family, meanwhile, continued to grow. On 4th November 1871, a fourth child, Olga, was born. Nikolai, born the following year, died within a month of birth. Another son, Dmitry, was born on 4th August 1874, followed by Maria on 6th February 1878. With six children, Maria Alexandrovna could afford no thoughts of a 'social life', still less for teaching. After their move to Simbirsk and the birth of young Vladimir, the family took on a nanny, Varvara Grigoryevna Sarbatova, in addition to Nastya, the cook. Considering the Ulyanovs often hosted Maria Alexandrovna's sisters and their children, there was clearly plenty of work for the whole household.

From the outset, Ilya Ulyanov plunged head-first into his new duties. It seemed his dreams were being fulfilled: properly public rural schools to build, expand, and develop curricula and implement the latest teaching and education methods for. However, he faced setbacks from the beginning.

According to all official figures, there existed 460 rural schools in the province. This was taken as an indication of the enlightenment of the local nobility, and Simbirsk was hailed as an example to the rest of the country. However, Ilya Ulyanov's first inspections revealed that only 89 of them were functional. The rest had either never existed at all, or had ceased operation due to a lack of teachers or facilities.[57]

Nonetheless, this disappointment did not quell his enthusiasm for the cause. On the contrary, the middle-aged Ilya, who was no longer in the best of health, demonstrated ample vigour and selflessness to the task at hand. Valerian Nikanorovich Nazaryev, a local landowner and then a well-known journalist, wrote of Ilya Ulyanov: "One would be sitting in a warm room, book in hand, listening to the intolerable howl of a blizzard which has been

---

56   Otechestvennyye arkhivy. 1992. No. 4. p. 82.

57   See: Z. A. *Trofimov*. Dukh revolyutsii vital v dome Ulyanovykh. Moscow, 1985. p. 20.

sweeping the expanse of the steppe and keeping one housebound for three days. Suddenly, from below one's very window, the bell rings. The man of the house hurries to the door to receive this unexpected guest.

'Don't be alarmed, Valerian Nikanorovich. I will thaw out now,' as he huddles into his overcoat. - 'It is Ulyanov, your humble servant. I have been on the road now four weeks.'

Nazaryev sees before him the snow-covered figure of the school inspector, his whiskers hoared by frost and his face blue from cold.

'Ilya Nikolayevich, my God! How wonderful! Come let us warm you and bring the wanderer some comfort.'

Now begins the business of receiving the guest. Ulyanov paces the room continuously, stretching his numbed legs, and strikes up a conversation about school affairs, about his hopes and fears. He continues on this theme through tea, dinner, into evening. One's mind drifts towards thoughts of sleep, yet the inspector carries on talking of school. And the first words with which one is greeted in the morning: "Now, about this school..."[58]

Ilya Nikolayevich himself, with his deep sense of duty, in no way considered himself a martyr. He built schools, procured primers and fuel, selected fresh, young teachers, and worked to improve their salaries. He considered all the burdens of his office the inevitable price he must pay to realise his deepest ambition: to in some way help the people out of their darkness and ignorance.[59]

His efforts were recognised. On 25th November 1871, he was made a State Councillor, and on 22nd December 1872 was awarded the Order of Saint Stanislaus. 1874 would see his career peak: on 11th July, Ilya Ulyanov was made director of public schools for Simbirsk Province, and on 21st December he was awarded his third decoration, the Order of St Anna, 3rd Class. In 1877, he was made Actual State Councillor, an equivalent rank to a general in the Table of Ranks and one that carried with it hereditary nobility. But as his daughter Maria Ulyanova would later write, "For him, it was not titles and decorations that were important to him ... but that his beloved cause, the best possible provision of public education, would flourish, for which he worked neither from fear nor conscience, never sparing himself."[60]

---

58   Y. *Yakovlev*. Zhizni pervaya tret'. pp. 83-84.
59   See: ibid. p. 85.
60   Z. A. *Trofimov*. Dukh revolyutsii vital v dome Ulyanovykh. p. 24.

Meanwhile, his rise in salary also allowed him to realise a long-held ambition. Having occupied six different rental apartments since 1870, he had saved the required amount, and on 2nd August 1878, the Ulyanovs were finally able to put down 4,000 roubles for their own home, a one-storey wooden house with an attic mezzanine on the courtyard side. Behind the courtyard, overgrown with grass and daisies, a beautiful garden extended, with silver poplars, sturdy elms, and yellow acacias and lilacs running the length of the fence.

The rooms were laid out thus: on the bottom floor were Ilya Ulyanov's study, the living and dining rooms, a reception hall for his wife, Maria Alexandrovna, and a separate one with its own entrance for the nanny. On the mezzanine, there were small bedrooms for Alexander, Anna and Vladimir, while the three youngest shared the "children's" room.[61]

"The furnishing were really very simple, such as one would find in the most ordinary households," recalled Anna Ulyanova. "Much was purchased for occasions, there was no specific character to it. There were no portraits or pictures on the walls, and the whole place had something of a puritanical air."[62] However, the home boasted a Schröder grand piano, a fine study and arts library, and instead of paintings, large maps hung on the walls.

Even the earliest memories leave a trace: as well as his father's stories, Vladimir recalled the country tales his nanny Varvara Grigoryevna recounted. Many years later, after his wife Nadezhda Krupskaya began wearing spectacles, he suddenly said:

'Spectacles should be clean. Let me polish them for you. I always polished my nanny's glasses for her.'

'His whole life, he never forgot her,' Krupskaya observed.[63]

He also recalled that despite having barely learned to read, he would make the journey to the Karamzinskaya Library by himself on foot. Geese wandered freely along the route, and young Vladimir would pester them. They would attack, necks outstretched, while he would lie on his back, fending them off with kicks.[64]

---

61 See: Lenin i Simbirsk. pp. 233-234.

62 Z. A. *Trofimov*. Dukh revolyutsii vital v dome Ulyanovykh. p. 25.

63 See: *B. V. Yakovlev*. Stranitsy avtobiografii V. I. Lenina (held in the Russian State Archive of Socio-Political History. Repository 71. Inventory 51. File 94.) p. 42.

64 Ibid. p. 47.

Among the major events of the time, the Russo-Turkish War of 1877-1878 was a period that lived long in the memory. Its twists and turns were a subject of discussion not only among adults, but of the children too. A contemporary and classmate of Vladimir recalled, "Without any newspapers, and having only just learned to read and write, we nonetheless knew a great deal about the heroic exploits of the Russian army, excitedly relaying to one another everything we'd heard, and more of what we'd picked up on the grapevine: the famous crossing of the Danube, the arduous Shipka Pass, the impregnable Plevna... Illustrious names such as Skobelev, Gurko, Radetsky and Dubasov tripped off the tongue, and we would cut out and collect their portraits."

Another memorable occasion was the arrival in Simbirsk of a party of captured Turks. The more militant of 'patriots' were surprised by how the city's residents expressed no particular malice towards the Turks, receiving them "with no great hostility".[65]

Vladimir also well remembered that over the course of the entire war, his beloved nanny, "whose relatives had been called up to the war and a number of them killed, constantly lamented the 'Russian blood spilled in vain for some damnable Bulgar foreigners. And what good do they do us, we who are up to our necks in our own troubles.'" "As I recall," Lenin said later, the views of his nanny "coincided with the attitude of my parents to the war."[66]

The Ulyanovs were not exceptional in this regard. Vladimir Ulyanov's contemporary, Prince Vladimir Obolensky, then resident in Smolensk Province, also recalled his own family "discussing the pilfering of quartermasters, the troops frozen at the Shipka Pass without provision of warm clothing, the way in which Grand Prince Nikolai Nikolayevich (the elder), to surprise the emperor for his name day, stormed the Plevna stronghold in a senseless assault, expending an enormous number of troops in the process, and so on. After this incident, some verse was passed around which began:

One brother to his sovereign sibling gifts,
A name-day pie with human stuffing..."[67]

---

65   A. N. Naumov. Moi vospominaniya: Two volumes. Vol. 1. Paris; New York, 1954. pp. 31, 32.
66   N. Valentinov. Nedorisovanny portret.... Moscow, 1993. p. 410.
67   V. A. Obolensky. Ocherki minuvshego. Belgrade, 1931. p. 42.

If one wished to demonstrate that the main factor in raising children is not pedagogic moralising, nor talks about virtue, still less punishment, but first and foremost a special atmosphere within the family that draws its character from the most important of life's values, values sincerely held by the parents, then a better subject for study could not be found.

What the children garnered from their father was perhaps the most important: the recognition of the absolute value of knowledge and an attitude to work not directed to personal, materialistic gain, but to the common good. The children did not need long explanations of honesty and integrity: Ilya Ulyanov's example was right in front of them. Their mother's attitude towards his selfless devotion to his duty - the cause of public education – further reinforced the impact of their father's example.

Whenever he returned from a trip, the whole family would gather in the living room, and Ilya Nikolayevich would recount his impressions of the peasant way of life he had encountered, of the arbitrary nature of all forms of authority, of the conversations he had overheard and speeches he had witnessed at village meetings. Among other things, this instilled in the children a sense of compassion, and an ability to experience others' woes and misfortunes as they would their own.

In a school essay, Alexander, the eldest son, wrote, "An individual requires the following traits to do good: 1) integrity, 2) a love of work, 3) strength of character, 4) intelligence and, 5) knowledge.

To be useful to society, one must be honest and inclined to hard work, and for this work to produce the best possible results, one requires intelligence and knowledge of the task at hand. Integrity and a sound view of his responsibilities to others should be instilled from an early age, as such beliefs will determine which field of work he chooses, and whether he will be guided in his decision to serve the public good, or follow his own selfish interests."[68] Their father's teachings had not been lost on them.

As for their mother, she offered a very different foundation, one which some biographers of Lenin have sometimes called "German pedantry". In particular, she considered strict routine a vital element of a child's upbringing. The children got up at seven o'clock. They then made their beds. Next, washing and grooming, then breakfast. Afterwards, the older children would be packed off to the gymnasium, though if breakfast had

---

68   *Y. Yakovlev. Zhizni pervaya tret'.* p. 95.

consisted of hot food, a ten-minute wait was required before setting off so as not to catch a cold.

The young ones were also kept busy, first by their mother, Maria Alexandrovna, with reading, writing, foreign languages and music, and later by their tutor, Vasily Andreyevich Kalashnikov, who prepared them for their first year of school.

At lunchtime, the elder children returned from the gymnasium and the whole family sat at the table. Everything was to be eaten up, an instruction Vladimir was happy to fulfil. His appetite as a child was impeccable, and when, under Alexander's direction, the children began to publish a weekly family journal, *Subbotnik*, it was no coincidence that the first pen-name the tubby young Vladimir ever received was *Kubyshkin*, "the round-bellied pot".

At home, the children not only tidied up after themselves. The girls knitted, embroidered, and looked after the boys' clothes: mending, darning and sewing on buttons. The boys, in turn, were expected to fill the water barrels in the garden and help their sisters, mother and nanny carry heavier items. In the summer, when tea parties were held in the pavilion, the children were expected to set the table.

They took their fill of the fruits and berries that grew in the garden, though even in this, discipline and order had their place. Only the already ripened apples that had fallen were to be taken; the rest were for jams for the winter, while only designated strawberry beds were permitted for plunder – the rest were off limits. The cherry tree by the pavilion was only to be touched after 20th July, Ilya Ulyanov's name-day.[69]

However, a system of limitations on conduct and morality could go only so far: when their tutor Vasily Kalashnikov first set foot in the Ulyanovs' home, he found the children resplendent in home-made 'Indian' outfits, brandishing spears and bows, tearing around the courtyard emitting blood-curdling cries and shrieks.

"Children should made a din", Maria Alexandrovna told him in serious tones.

In the far corner of the garden, by the fence, Vladimir and Olga had put together a wigwam. While he went forth hunting, Olga tended the 'fire' and prepared meals. None of the grown-ups were permitted to check up on what went on in this corner.

---

69   See: *Y Yakovlev. Zhizni pervaya tret'.* p. 100; *Lenin i Simbirsk.* p. 231.

After a touring circus had passed through Simbirsk, Olga and Vladimir strung a rope across the barn and, risking a fall, attempted to repeat the feats of the tightrope walkers. Here too, no adults were allowed to interfere.

What surprised the neighbours even more was the fact that the parents were not afraid to admit when they were wrong. "It's now the fashion", they gossiped, "to apologise to the children if needs be … like they'd apologise to adults… The like has never been seen!"[70]

This informal yet wholly natural atmosphere of mutual respect was particularly apparent when the whole family were together. When their father played with them, he would tell the children not only of school affairs and his visits, but of great explorers, the stars and the structure of the universe, or he would read his favourite poetry by Nekrasov and sing Russian folk songs. When their mother played the piano, the house would fill with enchanting music. At Kokushkino, she would lead them on expeditions to the forest, where she knew every trail, and they would pick flowers and collect berries and mushrooms. As Ilya Ulyanov would quip, "If you set them collecting berries, children will not stray far."

It was perhaps during these walks that the children were imbued with an abiding love of the Russian countryside, one that would not be subsumed by the picturesqueness of the Swiss Alps, the stark beauty of Normandy, or the luminous landscapes of Italy.

Maria Alexandrovna's high standards by no means meant that she expected her children to cling to her skirts. During the holidays, she would permit Alexander and Vladimir to disappear for days on boat trips along the Volga.

These voyages stayed with Vladimir his whole life, and years later he would ask Ivan Popov, "Have you been on the Volga? How well do you know it? Not so well? It's wide. A vast expanse… So very wide. As a youth, my brother Alexander and I would take a boat and travel a great distance along it. One would on occasion catch a song float over the river from some unknown location. What songs we have in Russia!"[71]

At Kokushkino, Maria Alexandrovna would let young Vladimir go with the local village children to tend the horses, or to the village and down to the river. Nikolai Veretennikov recalled, "From an early age, Vladimir, myself, and my other cousins loved to paddle in the water. From seven

---

70 Sem'ya Ulyanovykh. 2nd Edition. Moscow, 1986. p. 96.
71 Vospominaniya o Vladimire Ilyiche Lenine. Vol. 3. Moscow, 1960. pp. 115-116.

or eight years old, all of the children were able to swim the breadth of the narrow river, and if you could make it to the opposite bank and back without stopping for a rest, it meant you were swimmer. But swimming lessons did not end there – we were always endeavouring to improve: one had to learn how to float on one's back motionless, to dive head-first, to dive down to the bottom to collect a handful of algae, to jump into the river from the roof of the bathhouse, and to cross the river with your socks or boots in one hand without getting them wet…"[72]

But such fun and games were only permitted as long as they posed no danger.

One of young Vladimir's friends, N. G. Nefedyev, recalled an occasion in Simbirsk when they had gone to the Sviyaga River to fish – one of the group suggested trying a large, water-filled ditch nearby, where he claimed there were fine carp to be caught. They went, but as Vladimir leaned over the ditch, he fell into the water, becoming stuck fast in the muddy bottom, which began to suck him under. "I don't know what would have happened," his friend recounts, "had our cries not been heard by a worker from a local factory who came and dragged Volodya out. After this, we were not permitted to go to the Sviyaga."[73]

The importance of telling the truth was constantly drummed into the children by their parents. This expectation worked its way into everyday life. The eldest, Alexander, adored by his younger siblings, who considered him an absolute authority, expressed this even more categorically by declaring "lies and cowardice" his most hated vices.

Punishment in families of teachers is always an issue. To the end of his days, Ilya Nikolayevich shuddered to recall the attendants in the gymnasium in Astrakhan, where he studied, and at Penza, where he taught, softening birch twigs with steam before administering floggings "for their own good".[74] Later, as director of public schools, Ulyanov was constantly forced to remind his teachers that unacceptable punishments "by rod, forced kneeling, the pulling of hair or ears, striking or kicking and so on are, as punishments, harmful to the well-being of children and encourage a coarseness of temperament."[75]

---

72   *N. Veretennikov.* Volodya Ulyanov. Moscow, 1975. pp. 11, 12.
73   Lenin i Simbirsk. p. 227.
74   Sem'ya Ulyanovykh. p. 26.
75   *Y. Yakovlev.* Zhizni pervaya tret'. p. 118.

Even Lenin's fellow Simbirsk native, the writer Ivan Goncharov, did not escape such harsh punishments, his mother dragging him around furiously by the ears and forcing him to kneel in the corner for hours. At the Ulyanovs', on the other hand, the children faced admonitions, stern conversations, or being packed off to their father's office and impelled to sit in a large leather chair to consider their behaviour.

Meanwhile, elsewhere in Russia, the conversation about corporal punishment, particularly flogging, had acquired a loud political resonance.

From the outset of the 1870s, the "Historical Letters" of Pyotr Lavrov had been widely disseminated among Russia's democratically inclined youth. This eminent Pskov nobleman-cum-revolutionary had written of the sacred 'debt' of the intelligentsia to the people, and of the need to go 'to the people' to repay this debt.

"One had to have lived in the '70s, in that era of going to the people," recalled Nikolai Rusanov, "to have seen all around and feel for oneself the remarkable impact produced by these "Historical Letters"! Many of us, youths at the time, others just boys, would never part with that tattered, well-thumbed little book. It lay by our beds. As we read by night, the warm tears of a lofty enthusiasm, which seized us with a thirst to live and die for our ideals, would spatter the pages…"[76]

Thousands of young people, surrendering everything – wealthy and well-born families, prestigious universities and institutes, and promising careers – went to the people, to the wretched and humiliated. Of these young people, 4,000 were arrested and hundreds were despatched to penal servitude and exiled to Siberia.

Such brute force was met with terror.

On the morning of January 24th 1878, a pretty young woman entered the reception of Fyodor Trepov, governor of St Petersburg. As the adjutant general approached, she opened her handbag to produce a pistol and fired at point-blank range. She was 28-year-old Vera Ivanovna Zasulich, and she had shot Trepov after the governor had ordered the flogging of the student Alexei Bogolyubov, sentenced to 15 years' hard labour for his participation in a demonstration.

Zasulich's trial became a major sensation, discussed and written about across the country. Her lawyer, Pyotr Alexandrov, argued during her defence that the torment inflicted on Bogolyubov constituted a

---

76 *N. Rusanov*. Sotsialisty Zapada i Rossii. St Petersburg, 1909. pp. 227, 228.

disgraceful insult to his honour and dignity. There had been a time, he said, when "the rod reigned everywhere: at school; at village assemblies; the indispensable implement of the landowner's stables; then in barracks, and the police station." But even after the abolition of serfdom, despite the official prohibition of corporal punishment, it remained as a kind of traditional 'memento of Russia'.[77]

Trepov survived his injuries and, on 31st March 1878, a jury acquitted Vera Zasulich. Public opinion was entirely on her side.

Acts of revenge for the death of comrades and outrages committed against individuals continued. As Sergius Stepniak wrote in the pamphlet "A Death For A Death", "We Russians were initially a nation disinclined to political struggle, and still less for violent measures, accustomed to such neither in our history nor in our education. The government has itself dragged us along the bloody path upon which we tread. It is the government who has placed the dagger and revolver into our hands."

When the government appealed to the public to help in combating terrorism, a number of the more liberal *zemstvos* – Tverskoye, Chernigovskoye, Kharkovskoye – turned their criticism on the government and made veiled suggestions about introducing a constitution. As Minister for War Dmitry Milyutin wrote in a diary entry of June 1879, "No-one has faith in the durability of the existing order of things."[78]

---

77   See: ibid. pp. 227, 228.
78   Kratkaya istoriya SSSR. 2nd Edition. Leningrad, 1972. Part 1. p. 285.

SCHOOL

By summer of 1879, the Ulyanov household were preparing for young Vladimir to enter Simbirsk Gymnasium. He was fully versed in the main criteria used to determine 'suitability' – knowledge of "God's Law" and "common prayer", of events from the Old and New Testaments, the ability to read Old Church Slavonic, as well as "dictation without error", recitation of poetry, and the study of elements of speech, declensions, conjugations, and mental arithmetic.

He breezed through the entrance exams held between 7th and 11th August, and was enrolled in the 1st Class "A". On Thursday 16th, the first day of the school year, Vladimir pulled the wide grey trousers over his box-calf half-length boots for the first time, then donned the navy blue, single-breasted coat with its nine silver-plated buttons, the stiff, high collar that buttressed his chin, and the navy cap with silver-plated cap badge, threw a regulation satchel over his shoulder and set off with Anna and Alexander to his first school lesson. Alexander was already in his fifth year, while Anna was in her final year at the Mariinsky Girls' Gymnasium.

His first day was not without incident. During a break, he took his breakfast from his satchel and trustingly handed the packet containing home-made pies to another boy, presuming he would be content taking one. However, the boy "grabbed the entire contents, laughing, leaving Volodya with no breakfast."[79]

The gymnasium was largely disliked by the Ulyanovs as an educational establishment. What Russian gymnasiums had become in the 1870s-80s after the reforms of education ministers Count Dmitry Andreyevich Tolstoy and Ivan Davydovich Delyanov was cleverly portrayed in Anton Chekhov's *The Man In A Case*: "This is not a temple to science, but a directorate of decency, with the sour reek of the police booth." Drills and rote learning were the twin elements that determined the entire educational

---

[79]   A. I. Ulyanova-Yelizarova. O V. I. Lenine i sem'ye Ulyanovykh. Moscow, 1988. p. 43.

process. Everything was strictly circumscribed, from open collars on the uniform, to mischief at break-time, "inappropriate" questioning of teachers, or "poor knowledge of the Gospels". Transgressors were severely punished, in some cases by confinement to a punishment room with bread and water.[80]

However, Vladimir's arrival at school coincided with its reorganisation. Active State Councillor Fyodor Mikhailovich Kerensky had been appointed the gymnasium's director, later writing, "The gymnasium was the poorest performing in the district in terms of pupil underachievement. In the very first academic year after my arrival as director, classical language lessons for seniors were transferred to dynamic teachers with an excellent grasp of the subject, while I took on teaching literature and logic myself. Within three to four years, Simbirsk Gymnasium had earned itself a reputation as the best in the district."[81]

Of course, the general direction of education had not changed in the meantime. In one of his reports to Kazan, Kerensky wrote, "The main focus has been on developing in students a religious sentiment, keeping them away from malign company, and instilling a sense of obedience to superiors, deference to elders, modesty, humility, and respect for others' property."[82]

It was customary in the province to visit friends and colleagues during festivals and holidays. Fyodor Kerensky, who maintained the deepest respect for Ilya Nikolayevich, paid a number of visits to the Ulyanovs. It is therefore more than likely that Alexander Kerensky, future prime minister of the Russian Republic, who had been born in Simbirsk on 22nd April (4th May in the Julian calendar), also crossed the threshold of the Ulyanovs' home.

All his life, Vladimir Ulyanov recalled Simbirsk Gymnasium as an austere, "unloved", even "despised" place. Many years later he would say, "My old school was a school of drills, of learning by rote... It forced people to assimilate a mass of useless, superfluous, defunct knowledge that clogged up one's head..."[83]

However, this did not hinder Vladimir's progression from year to year, gaining certificates of merit or finishing top of his class as he went. In this sense, the eight-year school "ordeal", as Anna Ulyanova put it, became a time

---

80 See: *Z. A. Trofimov. Dukh revolyutsii vital v dome Ulyanovykh.* pp. 34-35.
81 Ibid. p. 35.
82 Ibid. p. 60.
83 *V. I. Lenin. Polnoye sobraniye sochineny.* Vol. 41. p. 303.

of personal growth and character building for all the Ulyanov children, and particularly for Vladimir, as the most lively and expressive child.

As a young child, how one wants to spend one's time and what one is required to do are often one and the same, while what one does not want to do can generally be avoided. Now, however, every day, every hour, he was compelled to busy himself in activities he either disdained, or outright detested.

Lessons began at nine in the morning. However, a quarter of an hour before, all the pupils would gather in the chapel hall for prayers. Three 50-minute lessons, each separated by a short break, would then follow, lasting until 12 o'clock. There would then be a longer break of half an hour for lunch and exercise. Another two lessons would begin at 12:30, ending at half past two. After this, pent up from an almost six-hour school day, the pupils would crowd noisily into the street despite school rules which explicitly stated that students should "go straight home, not as a crowd and not in groups."[84]

His first task was to become accustomed to and develop an aptitude for the systematic nature of the classes: at lessons, he listened attentively to his teachers, and at home repeated the lesson in his textbook or revised previously covered material. Thanks to his fine memory, he got to grips with his exercises quickly.

As for written work, of which there was much, a specific ritual existed for that: all of the children who attended secondary school – namely, Alexander, Anna, Vladimir, and later Olga – would gather round a large table and do their homework under Maria Alexandrovna's supervision. Only after this had been done and checked were they permitted to do anything else. In the morning, before going to school, Vladimir fit in time to go through his lessons once more.

Nikolai Veretennikov recalled one incident, recounted to him by Vladimir: "When classes for new languages began, parallel classes of each grade were combined. The top of the class of one of the parallel classes (something of a Pierrot) asked to copy vocabulary for a German translation.

'And you gave him it?'

'Of course I did… But how can he be top of his class?'

'So you've never once come to class unprepared?'

'Never, and never shall it!', Vladimir snapped."

---

84   Z. A. Trofimov. Dukh revolyutsii vital v dome Ulyanovykh. p. 125.

Veretennikov notes that even then, such short, sharp phrasing was characteristic of him.[85]

All this required not only diligence, full concentration, and enormous patience, but the ability to subdue one's emotions and suppress an entirely natural sense of boredom – in short, the ability to control oneself.

His father and mother nevertheless maintained a suspicion that "it all comes too easily to Volodya" and that he was "not developing an aptitude for hard work".[86] They adopted a more hands-on approach with him, giving him extra assignments. In the senior grades, Ilya Ulyanov would ask Vladimir to give free Greek and Latin lessons three times a week to Nikofor Mikhailovich Okhotnikov, the mathematics teacher of the Chuvash school, to prepare him for university in the space of two years.[87]

Anna Ilyinichna described another rationale for this rigorous system: "It was entirely appropriate for my brother Vladimir, presenting a salutary counterweight to his great self-confidence and continually excellent marks. While in no way weakening his unwavering self-esteem, it certainly knocked the arrogance to which children lauded for their talents are prone..."[88]

The late Yekaterina von Essen had been very fond of repeating a phrase that would live long in the memory of the Blank sisters: "So it must be!" But her "so it must be" had not explained *why* it had to be so. Ilya Nikolayevich, on the other hand, while himself no admirer of the gymnasium, did outline to his children the necessity of the laborious study they endured: the gymnasium was a "necessary bridge" that needed crossed, without which there would be "no access to university".[89]

In a moment of anger, Mikhail Saltykov-Shchedrin had once said of the Minister of Education, Count Dmitry Andreyevich Tolstoy, that he had sent "dozens of young men to kingdom come with his idiot classicism..."[90] This outburst was not without a degree of truth.

Meanwhile, the heir to the Russian Empire, Nicholas Romanov, while two years Vladimir Ulyanov's senior, was in the middle of 13 years of home schooling. The first eight years departed from gymnasium schooling, in

---

85	See: *N. Veretennikov.* Volodya Ulyanov. p. 37.
86	Lenin i Simbirsk. p. 226.
87	See: ibid.
88	*A. I. Ulyanova-Yelizarova.* O V. I. Lenine i sem'ye Ulyanovykh. p. 40.
89	Ibid.
90	*Y. Yakovlev.* Zhizni pervaya tret'. p. 161.

a course designed by court advisor Konstantin Pobedonostsev himself. Latin and Ancient Greek were left out completely; instead, instruction in English, French and German was markedly expanded. Among Nicholas's teachers were a number of renowned academics: Nikolai Beketov[91], Nikolai Bunge[92], César Cui[93], and others. However, the professors were expressly forbidden to put questions to their pupil; as a rule, he never asked his tutors for any deep insight into any subject in any case. As such, his grasp of the sciences remains a mystery.

Over those same eight years, Vladimir Ulyanov was required to engage in a wholly different, 'classical' programme. Classical teaching – Latin and Greek – was delivered in an uncommonly dull manner. It was the scourge of the pupils and the main cause of exam failure, resits, and drop-outs. Both Alexander and his father assisted Vladimir in this area: both had begun to study Ancient Greek themselves, since it had not been taught in the gymnasium at Astrakhan. Vladimir took to Latin quickly, and was so enamoured with it that he was forced to moderate his eagerness so as not to adversely affect his other subjects.[94]

The teachers were, to put it mildly, not thought highly of at all. "The teaching staff," wrote Maria Ilyinichna, "were particularly poor. Some relied on what they could coach by rote, while others approached teaching in a half-hearted manner... This did not inspire a great deal of respect for the teacher."[95]

---

91 Nikolai Nikolayevich Beketov (1st [13th] January 1827, Alfyorievka [Novaya Beketovka], Penza Province - 30th November [13th December] 1911, St Petersburg) – a Russian physical chemist, academic of the St Petersburg Academy of Sciences (1886), pioneer of physical chemistry and chemical dynamics, introduced the basic principles of aluminothermy.

92 Nikolai Khristianovich Bunge (German: Nikolai Karl Paul von Bunge; 11th [23rd] November 1823, Kyiv - 3rd [15th] June 1895, Tsarskoye Selo) – a 19th century Russian statesman, economist, academic and finance minister to the Russian Empire (6th May 1881 – 31st December 1886).

93 César Antonovich Cui (French: César Cui, born Cesarius-Benjaminus Cui; 6th [18th] January 1835, Vilnius – 13th March 1918, Petrograd) – a Russian composer and music critic, member of the Mighty Handful and "Belyaevsky circle" groups of composers, a teacher of fortifications, and engineer-general (1906).

94 See: Vospominaniya o Vladimire Ilyiche Lenine. Vol. 2. Moscow, 1968. p. 230.

95 Ibid. p. 198.

Moreover, any situation to create mischief was seized upon by the pupils, thus beginning a school maxim of "mutual reciprocity."

At one stage Ancient Greek was taught by a relative of Vladimir's, Alexander Ivanovich Veretennikov, a good teacher who marked strictly, but fairly. Gradually, however, he began to develop a severe neurological condition which, according to Vladimir's classmate and future poet Apollon Korinfsky, transformed him into a pitiable, "evangelically relaxed" individual. Here the cruel vindictiveness of schoolboys was fully manifested.

"As soon as he appeared in the classroom," said Korinfsky, "and sat at the deliberately ink-smeared or liberally chalked seat by the lectern, up would rise a loud clatter as all the desks moved as one to obstruct the door. Then the true torment of this miserable man, who could barely move his legs and suffered a nervous collapse at the faintest disturbance, would begin. Chewed paper would be flicked in his face, and his frock coat soiled with all manner of rubbish. 'Hymns to Cholera,' special compositions born of a collective effort, would be sung in all their obscenity. One day, hearing the din and glancing in the classroom, the chaos was observed by the director Fyodor Mikhailovich Kerensky.

"What is this vileness!" he roared. "Performing such cruel tricks on a severely unwell man who must struggle to earn enough for a chunk of stale bread and vital medicines! The whole class, to detention, to the outhouse... with no lunch! All the instigators of this outrage will be named!

Turning to 'Ulyasha', Kerensky looked silently at him before saying:

"I know that you could have played no part in this outrageous delinquency. Gather your books and jotters and go home! I won't require you to point out the instigators."

Ulyanov's faced burned to the tips of his ears and he shouted in a strange voice:

"I cannot leave while all my comrades, the entire class, must sit in detention... allow me to remain with them! I am as guilty as the others."

"I do not believe you, Vladimir Ulyanov! You are not capable of it! You know you could neither be in concert with the instigators nor among the participants of such disgraceful conduct! I repeat, you are free, go home!"

"Indeed I could not!"

Korinfsky concludes: "And after classes, Ulyanov followed his comrades to the school 'dungeon'. We spent three hours there (hungry and almost suffocated by the lavatory stench which penetrated through the cracks in the walls and floor), until nine in the evening."[96]

It was perhaps during one such 'collective action' that Vladimir first tried a cigarette. Years later, while talking to Red Army men furiously puffing rough *makhorka* tobacco, he remarked, "I recall as a schoolboy having smoked so much with some other boys that I became dizzy. I've not smoked since then." There was another reason for his quitting: his mother learned of his habit. She asked him to give up, and, as Nadezhda Krupskaya recalls, Vladimir "never reached for a cigarette from that day hence."[97]

Naturally, other activities also fell victim to his need to concentrate on his studies, particularly in the senior years. For example, Vladimir had learned to skate rather well, but in his senior years, he began to appear at the skating rink all the more rarely. He later told Nadezhda Krupskaya that he would grow tired later in the day and "after skating, the desire to sleep which took hold of me hindered my work, so I gave it up."[98]

A rink on the Sviyaga River, lit in the evenings by kerosene lamps, where the youth of Simbirsk gathered to skate to a military brass band accompaniment, was his favourite spot. He was able to skate the ice run, standing upright as the cadets would. He was also skilled at skating so-called "figures", a source of particular delight for the gymnasium girls.

One of Lenin's biographers, N. V. Valentinov, recalled a remark made by Lenin when in Geneva in 1904: "I was fond of the girls when I was a schoolboy, but now I have neither the time nor the inclination."[99] This "fondness" was of a specific character: his sister Olga introduced him to her friends and he enjoyed helping them with their lessons, but no 'romance' was forthcoming from this. Girls were nervous around him, he was so serious and well-read. Alexandra Shcherbo recalled an occasion when Lenin accompanied her home: "He asked me questions about the teachers in such a serious, direct way that I clammed up and couldn't think of what to say."[100]

---

96 B. V. Yakovlev. Stranitsy avtobiografii V. I. Lenina. pp. 49-50.

97 Rabochiye i krestyane Rossii o Lenine. Vospominaniya. Moscow, 1958. p. 215.

98 Y. Yakovlev. Zhizni pervaya tret'. p. 94.

99 N. Valentinov. Nedorisovanny portret. pp. 65, 68.

100 Sem'ya Ulyanovykh. p. 254.

While he communicated easily with his sisters and cousins, and the cook's daughter Lena, he was especially shy around girls he was not so well acquainted with.

In large families, with cousins as well as brothers and sisters – and the Ulyanovs had 33(!) cousins – the children are often 'self-sufficient'. Their need for company and play is completely satisfied at home. This is possibly why the Ulyanov children, despite being sociable and communicative, rarely made close outside friends. Perhaps this is also why Vladimir did not count any 'soulmates' among his classmates.

In 1918, Apollon Korinfsky wrote: "He initiated friendly relations steadily and consistently, but there was never a time when this progressed to a more intimate level. He was 'ours' to everyone, but never anyone's 'theirs'."[101]

This explains why his classmates' recollections concern only external events, and say little about the formation of his character. But attempts to establish friendships were, as Nadezhda Krupskaya wrote, driven by the fact that "he desperately wanted to speak to someone about the ideas that were forming within him."[102]

The next best student in Vladimir's class was Alexander Naumov. He had joined the third grade from a military school, was a music lover, played the violin, and for six years shared a desk with Vladimir. A few exchanges over break-times indicated to Vladimir that he was not only intelligent, but that the two boys were similar in temperament. They arranged to walk together by the Sviyaga, but conversation did not come easily. Alexander began to talk about career choices, and how best to forge a glittering career and get ahead in life in the fastest way possible. Vladimir grew bored, and made no further attempts to become closer to this "careerist".[103]

Nonetheless, Naumov, unencumbered by thoughts of the 'common good' and the "unpaid debt to the people," did make rather a career for himself. He became a 'land captain' (*zemsky nachal'nik*) and later district marshal of the nobility (*uyezdny predvoditel' dvoryanstva*) in Samara Province. In 1905, he was chosen to be the province marshal of the nobility (*gubernsky predvoditel' dvoryanstva*). He met Nicholas II and in 1908 was

---

101   Vecherneye slovo. Petrograd, 1918. 1st June. p. 3.

102   *N. K. Krupskaya*. O Lenine. Sbornik statei i vystupleny. Moscow, 1979. p. 34.

103   See: *B. V. Yakovlev*. Stranitsy avtobiografii V. I. Lenina. p. 52.

appointed "by imperial decree" to the State Council of Russia. In 1915, he became Minister for Agriculture. Certainly a fine career, and he was a source of pride to his old school. Naumov may have gone further, had the events of 1917 not disrupted his ascent.

Naturally, he disliked Lenin, but in his memoirs, published after his emigration, he wrote: "The central figure among my circle of friends at school was undoubtedly Vladimir Ulyanov, with whom I shared a desk and studied alongside for six years, and with whom I graduated in 1887. Over the course of our period of study together, Ulyanov and I were best in class, he at the top and I second, and when it came time to receive our school certificates, he was awarded the gold medal, and I – the silver.

Short in stature and of a rather heavy build, with slightly raised shoulders and large head rather narrowed at the temples, Vladimir Ulyanov had awkward – I would say – unattractive facial features: small ears, prominent cheekbones, a short, wide, somewhat flattened nose and, on top of that, a large mouth with yellowed, widely spaced teeth. Completely devoid of eyebrows and covered in freckles, Ulyanov had light blonde hair which was long, wispy, soft, slightly curly, and combed back. But all of the aforementioned irregularities were masked by the two round brown coals which burned below his high brow. Talking to him, it was as if his unprepossessing appearance was effaced by the sight of his small but extraordinary eyes, which sparkled with an uncommon intelligence and energy.

In school life, Ulyanov stood out markedly from all of us, his comrades. Neither in junior nor senior classes did he participate in the general high jinks of youth, keeping out of the way and constantly busying himself with either study or writing. Even during break-times, Ulyanov never put down his books, and being short-sighted, would usually stay by the window, lost in his reading. The only thing he acknowledged and loved as a diversion was chess, a game he usually won, even when playing against multiple opponents at once. He was extraordinarily capable, possessed a vast memory, and distinguished himself with his insatiable scientific curiosity and a remarkable capacity for work. I stress, I spent a full six years beside him at school and I do not know a time when Vladimir Ulyanov was short of a precise and comprehensive response to any question, whatever the subject. He was a true walking encyclopedia, a reference book to his comrades and a source of universal pride to his teachers.

As soon as he appeared in class, he was usually surrounded on all sides by his classmates, asking for a translation or for the solution to an exercise.

Ulyanov graciously offered his assistance to all, but it was apparent to me that he did not care for fellows who endeavoured to live and learn off the efforts and intelligence of others.

Ulyanov was by nature a calm and rather good-natured person, but extremely secretive and cold in his dealings with others: he had no friends, was on formal terms with everyone, and I don't recall him allowing himself even a little openness with me. His 'soul' displayed a true 'otherness' and, as such, for those of us who knew him, remained a mystery.

Overall, he enjoyed a great deal of respect and was considered something of a serious-minded authority, but with that, one could not say he was loved – more accurately, he was respected. In addition, his superior intellect and application in comparison to the rest of us was noted in the classroom, although in fairness to him, Ulyanov himself never purposely displayed or emphasised it."[104]

---

104   A. N. Naumov. *Moi vospominaniya*. Vol. 1. pp. 42-43.

1ST MARCH 1881

The traditional gymnasium was clearly no holiday camp. Nonetheless, it was those eight years of study there that gave Vladimir Ulyanov a foundation in a wide range of subject areas, two foreign and two ancient languages, the Russian classics and where he, among other things, learned to write.

From fourth grade, Kerensky permitted students to produce essays on 'free' themes. Some were acutely salutary in nature, for example: "How should children's love for their parents manifest itself?" But mostly, Fyodor Mikhailovich attempted to inculcate in his charges a sense of the beauty of nature. As such, themes such as "A Portrait of Spring", "The Deluge", "The Volga in Autumn", "A Winter's Eve" and so on tended to prevail. Pieces of 'reportage' were also encouraged to develop observational skills: items titled "Market Day in Town", for example. Whatever the theme, Vladimir unfailingly received a "five".[105]

It is unclear whether Kerensky had any specific market day in mind, but had it been that for March 1881, the whole town would have read the following breaking news:

"Today, 1st March, upon the Emperor's return from roll call ... an attempt was made on the blessed life of His Majesty by means of two hurled explosive devices... The second explosion seriously wounded the Emperor. Upon returning to the Winter Palace, His Majesty was received into the Holy Mysteries and fell asleep in the Lord at 3:35pm."

The news was received "in Simbirsk while the market was on, with a large crowd in attendance... The menfolk scrambled to get hold of the first copies of the fateful announcement, paying heaven knows how much money, and taking them home."[106] The following day, rumours began to spread that in one of the villages near Simbirsk, the peasants had refused to attend a memorial service, with the braver among them openly declaring, "Why would we pray for a man who neither gave us

---

105   The highest mark in the Russian education system.
106   *Z. A. Trofimov*. Dukh revolyutsii vital v dome Ulyanovykh. p. 46.

nor wished for us real freedom... Better to pray for the students who want real freedom for us."[107]

The tsar's murder was by no means a complete surprise. 'Open season' had been declared on Alexander II by terrorists of *Narodnaya Volya* [People's Will] for more than two years. In August 1878, they had attempted to blow up the jetty at Nikolaev, where he was due to disembark. On 2nd April 1879, Alexander Solovyov had opened fire on the emperor on Palace Square in St Petersburg. In July, they had prepared another bomb attack in Simferopol, while in autumn the same year, attacks on the tsar's train had been planned for Odessa and Alexandrov. On 19th November an explosion did take place, but it missed the tsar's train, instead derailing that of his entourage which usually followed – on this occasion, they had swapped places as a precaution. On 5th February 1880, the carpenter Stepan Khalturin managed to plant a bomb in the Winter Palace. The main guards' quarters were destroyed, as was the floor of the tsar's dining room, but the emperor was unhurt, having being delayed to dinner. In May, another mine was planted in Odessa. Kamenny Bridge in St Petersburg was also mined in August, as was Malaya Sadovaya Street, a thoroughfare used by the emperor, in January 1881. Each attack was covered extensively by the international, domestic and provincial presses.

One proclamation by the Executive Committee of *Narodnaya Volya* read, "There is no village in the land that cannot count several martyrs sent to Siberia for upholding secular interests or protesting against the administration and kulaks. Of the intelligentsia, tens of thousands stretch in an endless procession into exile, to Siberia, to hard labour, solely for their service to the people... Alexander II is the man most responsible for judicial murder – 14 executions lie heavy on his conscience, the hundreds tortured and the thousands of others who have suffered cry out for vengeance; he deserves death for all the blood he has spilled and the sorrow he has caused."[108]

On 1st March 1881, this came to pass.

Appearing in court, one leader of the *Narodnaya Volya* terrorists, Andrei Zhelyabov, explained why the *narodniki* [Populists, supporters of *Narodnaya Volya* – trans.] had decided to turn to terror: "Those Russians who love the people have not always thrown bombs. There was once youth

---

107   Ibid. p. 48.
108   Ibid. pp. 43-44.

in our actions, rosy-cheeked and starry-eyed, and if that youth has passed, we are not to blame for that. A movement that was completely harmless in its means ... has been broken by the many barriers it has faced in the form of prison and exile. A wholly bloodless movement which rejected violence, which sought not revolution but peaceful means, has been crushed... In accordance with my beliefs, I would have stayed away from such violent struggle, had peaceful means been possible, by which I mean peaceful promulgation of our ideas and peaceful organisation of our supporters."[109]

For the younger Ulyanovs and their close friends, it seems the tsar's murder was not especially affecting. Anna and Alexander Ulyanov had once read a small volume of Nekrasov's poetry in which, over the blacked-out lines of the censor, their father's hand had inscribed:

Go to the fire for your land,
For your creed and for your love,
Go to death unsullied, pure,
You die not light: the cause stays sure,
When through it courses blood...

However, their father had entered these lines as a youth – now, the tsar's murder came as a shock to Ilya Nikolayevich. His children were surprised to see him don his dress uniform and attend a memorial service at the cathedral. "For him, having spent the best years of his youth under Nicholas I, Alexander II's reign, especially at the beginning, was a golden era," wrote Anna Ulyanova. "He was against terror."[110]

Shortly before, in November 1880, he had celebrated 25 years of service, ten of which had been spent in Simbirsk. In that time, he had overseen the construction of 151 schools, and now over 400 public schools were fully functioning in the province. What had been achieved in Simbirsk received justified recognition. On 1st January 1882, Ilya Ulyanov earned his fourth decoration, the Order of St Vladimir, 3rd Class. Alas, Alexander III's ascendency to the throne augured quite different times ahead.

The tone was set by Sergey Rachinsky, a Moscow University professor and former liberal. He believed those in charge of Russian public schools

---

109   Y. Yakovlev. Zhizni pervaya tret'. p. 144.
110   A. I. Ulyanova-Yelizarova. O V. I. Lenine i sem'ye Ulyanovykh. p. 46.

were completely divorced from the people and did not understand their "true needs". Peasants had no cause for the latest pedagogical fads or the questionable truths of the natural sciences. They wanted their children to be able to read the Horologion, the psalter and other liturgical texts, and to sing in the church choir. Given that, he believed that their main instruction should come from a priest.[111]

There were also changes in trends and methods of education, in particular towards the use of corporal punishment. Prince Meshchersky, who considered himself the spiritual mentor to Alexander III, wrote in his newspaper *Grazhdanin* [The Citizen]: "Spare the whip and power is lost. Just as the Russian needs salt and black bread, so also does he require the birch-rod. And if a man is lost without salt, so too are the people without the birch-rod... The rod is required for the people's own benefit."[112]

On the ground, the overtures emanating from above were understood. The wealthy Syzran landowner Dmitry Voyeikov, a friend of the minister Count Tolstoy, speaking at a local district meeting, blamed the public schools for dragging the children of peasants out of their familiar surroundings and educating people who "constitute a threat to the established order".[113]

Inspector of public schools for Simbirsk Konstantin Ammosov wrote to his colleague on 17th March 1882: "Primary public education has almost reverted to the days when it existed more on paper than in reality. It is sad".[114]

Ilya Nikolayevich and his faithful coachman Dunin travelled the length of the province, arguing, pleading his case, writing letters, but he was powerless to stop the advance of the clergy. The number of church-affiliated parish schools grew each year at the expense of the harassed and 'converted' public schools, particularly those for the Chuvash population. Even the provincial authorities were now of the opinion that peasant children should be restricted to strengthening their knowledge of the "word of God and hymns" and their ability to read and use an abacus, and no more.[115]

111	See: Z. A. *Trofimov*. Dukh revolyutsii vital v dome Ulyanovykh. p. 53.
112	Y. *Yakovlev*. Zhizni pervaya tret'. p. 119.
113	Ibid. p. 182.
114	Z. A. *Trofimov*. Dukh revolyutsii vital v dome Ulyanovykh. p. 53.
115	Ibid. p. 56.

On 13th June 1884, the official "Regulations for parish schools" were published, which effectively reinforced the leading role of the clergy in a secular public schooling system. Prince Meshchansky wrote that if the reforms of 1861 had given the Russian his bread and freedom, then now he could finally receive "spiritual" sustenance.[116]

The renowned educator Nikolai Bunakov recalled of this time: "To maintain anything worthwhile under such conditions was impossible: both common sense and basic integrity were forced to exit the scene until more favourable times."[117]

It was a bitter time also for Ilya Nikolayevich, as he began to fear more and more for the future of his children. If he had once loved to talk with Anna and Alexander on socio-political subjects, he no longer "placed any great emphasis on social ideals" with the younger children.[118]

In 1880, Anna had graduated with a silver medal from the Mariinsky Gymnasium and in autumn of 1881 began teaching at an elementary public school. Alexander went to study at St Petersburg University in 1883, having graduated from school with a gold medal. Anna would follow him to the capital to enrol in the philological department of the Bestuzhev Courses [a private, women-only institute of higher education established in 1878 to circumvent the ban on women entering higher education – *trans.*].[119]

However, Ilya Nikolayevich's anxiety for their fate only intensified. Newspapers reported student demonstrations in St Petersburg, Moscow and Kiev. When Anna and Alexander returned to Simbirsk during the summer holidays in 1885, their father decided to speak with his son.

Dmitry Ulyanov recalled: "My father and brother strolled along the main path in the garden. They walked for a long time, speaking in quiet, intense tones. Their faces wore peculiarly serious expressions. At times their voices flared, but they were largely hushed, barely audible. I am sure this conversation was about politics. My assumption was confirmed by my father's words to Anna Ilyinichna upon her departure to St Petersburg: 'Tell Alexander to look after himself, if only for our sake.'"[120]

---

116   Ibid. p. 70.
117   Y. *Yakovlev*. Zhizni pervaya tret'. p. 116.
118   Ibid. p. 153.
119   See: Z. A. *Trofimov*. Dukh revolyutsii vital v dome Ulyanovykh. pp. 51, 65.
120   Y. *Yakovlev*. Zhizni pervaya tret'. pp. 175, 179.

The fact that Ilya Ulyanov was an important government official of the Ministry of Education already meant his children bore a substantial responsibility: he was well-known and his sons and daughters were well aware that they were expected to preserve their father's good name. This required them to learn how to keep a low profile.

These circumstances perhaps go some way to explaining another apparent curiosity:

While Alexander and Vladimir attended Simbirsk Gymnasium, there – as in many other educational establishments in Russia – literature subject to censorship had been published and illegal circles and groups organised.

In 1878 these had been formed in Simbirsk by Kazan University graduate and literature teacher V. I. Muratov. In 1883, an illegal school circle led by Valentin Averyanov, a one-time classmate of Alexander Ulyanov, was formed. The following year, an illegal library at the school was established. With assistance from students of Kazan University, it collected works by Marx, Engels, Lassalle, and other hectographed revolutionary publications.

Rumours about the library reached the gendarmes and Fyodor Mikhailovich Kerensky. After a number of pupils were arrested and house searches conducted in August 1885, events the whole city came to learn of, the contents of the library were confiscated. However, in autumn of the same year, a group of senior school pupils led by Apollon Korinfsky began publishing a handwritten journal titled "Diary of a Schoolboy", which also contained socialist-leaning material.

However, although they were aware of them, neither Alexander nor Vladimir Ulyanov took part in any of these activities. Korinfsky writes that Vladimir, "looked through each of these 'journals' with interest … he would read them, find them interesting, but he never worked with us on a single one of these 'publications.'"[121]

Investigator Zhores Trofimov, having examined the material available, draws the reasonable conclusion that Ilya Nikolayevich, given his dealings with police in an official capacity, probably "spoke with his son Vladimir and warned him of the need to be careful in matters of this kind."[122]

Nonetheless, the atmosphere around Ilya Ulyanov was thickening. Maria Ulyanova wrote: "The authorities had valued him as an efficient and zealous worker, but later began to keep an eye on him, believing that

---

121   Z. A. Trofimov. Dukh revolyutsii vital v dome Ulyanovykh. pp. 86, 118.
122   Ibid. p. 90.

he was not sufficiently harmonising his work with the spirit of the times. He remained in the 1880s a 'Sixtier, an idealist,' incapable of ingratiating himself with the new agenda..."[123]

After Anna and Alexander's departure to St Petersburg, Vladimir became the eldest child in the house, and the drama surrounding his father was to play out in front of him.

At the end of 1885, when Ilya Nikolayevich travelled to Syzran, he was aware that the local provincial assembly had not only expressed its support for the comprehensive development of parish schools and the intensification of 'moral and spiritual' education: the more right-wing *zemstvo* members had also expressed doubt that the current director of schools for Simbirsk Province was up to the task. There was an open vote of no confidence in Ulyanov himself.[124]

"In December 1885, when I was in my third year," wrote Anna, "I arrived back in Simbirsk for the Christmas holidays. I met my father in Syzran as he was returning from another trip around the province, and I rode with him along the way. I recall how much older my father suddenly seemed, and noticeably weaker than he had been in the autumn... I also remember he seemed somewhat depressed, and he relayed to me with sadness that the government was tending towards building parish schools to replace the district schools. It meant his life's work had been in vain. I only later understood how painful it was for my father, and how much it hurried his demise."[125]

They arrived home on 25th December, the day Vladimir, Olga and Dmitry began their Christmas holidays. However, their father was in no mood for Christmas trees or celebrations. Ilya Ulyanov retired to his office and began working on his yearly report for 1885.

New Year passed, and on 1st January news arrived of Ilya Ulyanov's fifth decoration, the Order of Saint Stanislaus, 1st Class, with a moiré ribbon to be worn over the shoulder. On 6th January some of his colleagues visited, and Ilya even danced the polka with Anna. However, an additional piece of news also arrived: education minister Ivan Delyanov had granted Ilya one more year of service, to end on 1st July 1887, instead of the five years he had requested.[126]

---

123   Y. Yakovlev. *Zhizni pervaya tret'.* p. 111.
124   See: Z. A. Trofimov. *Dukh revolyutsii vital v dome Ulyanovykh.* p. 102.
125   A. I. Ulyanova-Yelizarova. *O V. I. Lenine i sem'ye Ulyanovykh.* p. 72.
126   See: *Sem'ya Ulyanovykh.* pp. 75, 100.

On 10th January, Ilya Nikolayevich fell ill. The doctor diagnosed a "gastric condition of the stomach". On 12th January, aged 55, he died of a cerebral haemorrhage in the arms of Maria Alexandrovna, Anna, and Vladimir.

The lengthy obituary published after his funeral stated, "All those who served with the deceased, teachers and pupils of the city's public schools, the vice-governor, the director, and many of the teachers of the gymnasium, the military school and seminary, and all those who hold the memory of the deceased dear (and who in Simbirsk did not know and respect him), as well as a huge number of the public, filled his home and the street outside the deceased's apartment. Senior members of the Simbirsk clergy ... performed a brief lity. The coffin containing the deceased's remains *was carried by his second son* and his close colleagues and friends..."[127]

This sad occasion would be the first mention of Vladimir Ulyanov in print.

---

127   Ibid. p. 76. (Author's italics)

THE MAN OF THE HOUSE

After the funeral and the end of the Christmas holidays, Anna did not return to St Petersburg, remaining at home for almost another two months. Spending a long time in the winter garden, where she was able to 'unburden her soul' in peace, she talked with Vladimir about everyday family affairs and life in general.

As Anna recalled, "He was very negatively inclined towards the school authorities, to the school curriculum, to religion as well, and was not averse to cruelly lampooning the teachers (I took no part in such jokes); in short, he was, so to speak, going through a period in which he was casting off authority, a period in which he as an individual was forming his first negative impressions, as it were... But other than this negative attitude to the things around him – specifically the gymnasium – there wasn't anything especially political about our conversations." She concluded: "Volodya had no defined political opinions at that time..."[128]

On the subject of religion, Nadezhda Krupskaya recalls Lenin's account of an incident that seemingly occurred that winter, when his father was still alive.

Ilya Nikolayevich was telling a visiting teacher that his children were not regular churchgoers. Vladimir, who had been present at the beginning of the conversation, was sent on an errand by his father. Having completed the errand, Vladimir witnessed in passing his father's guest smile and say: "You should beat them." Running into the yard, Vladimir tore the cross from his neck and threw it to the ground.[129]

In the 1922 All-Russian Census Form of Members of the Russian Communist Party (Bol'sheviks), Lenin's response to the question, "Do you have any religious beliefs? If you are a non-believer, at what age did you lose your faith?", was: "No... Aged 16..."[130]

---

128   *A. I. Ulyanova-Yelizarova.* O V. I. Lenine i sem'ye Ulyanovykh. p. 80.

129   See: *N. K. Krupskaya.* O Lenine. p. 34.

130   See: *V. I. Lenin.* Polnoye sobraniye sochineny. Vol. 44. p. 509.

Lev Tolstoy cast off his cross as a 15-year-old.

After Ilya Nikolayevich's death, the family faced immediate difficulties. On 24th April, Maria Alexandrovna asked the school district trustee for financial assistance. "The pension to which I and my children are entitled for my late husband's services will in all likelihood not be received in the near future and in the meantime we must live, pay off the money borrowed for my husband's burial, provide for the children, and support my daughter on her teaching course and eldest son in St Petersburg..."[131]

The district court also dragged its feet. Addressing the court, Maria Alexandrovna wrote, "All property left by my husband is contained in our home and capital of 2,000 roubles held in the Simbirsk public bank..." However, until the court made a decision on her right of inheritance, she was unable to make use of these savings.[132]

Eventually, in May, after a five-month wait, the decision was taken to award the entire household an annual pension of 1,200 roubles.[133]

In May, Anna returned once again from St Petersburg, this time with Alexander. He had not attended his father's funeral: at the end of 1885, he presented his dissertation, "The Segmentation and Sexual Organs of Freshwater Annula", to a panel in the natural sciences department of the Faculty of Physics and Mathematics. It took until February for the panel to announce their decision: Alexander was awarded a gold medal with the inscription "Outstanding". On 8th February, when the medal was presented, the university rector described Alexander as the "pride of the university".

Given that Alexander was kept in the department to begin preparing for a professorship, it was clear he would be expected to become the family's main support. As a result, after some deliberation, the family decided to relocate to St Petersburg. In May, they placed four separate notices announcing the sale of their house and garden, but a suitable buyer could not be found. Later on, they decided, given the high cost of living in the capital, that Vladimir and Olga should remain in Simbirsk until they finished their schooling.

The death of Ilya Ulyanov had also given rise to conflicts within the family. Being now the 'man of the house', the 16-year-old Vladimir began to show obstinacy towards his mother.

131	Z. A. *Trofimov*. Dukh revolyutsii vital v dome Ulyanovykh. p. 128.
132	See: Sem'ya Ulyanovykh. p. 101.
133	See: ibid.

As Anna Ulyanova recalls: "Vladimir was then going through that awkward age when boys become particularly curt and quarrelsome. He'd always been brusque and self-confident, but it became more apparent, especially after the death of his father, whose presence had always kept the boys in check."[134]

Anna shared her thoughts with Alexander and asked him:

"What do you make of our Vladimir?"

"He's certainly a talented fellow, but he and I don't really see eye to eye."

"Why not?"

"Just so."

One day, reacting sorely to the way Vladimir was behaving towards his mother, Alexander spoke out: the brothers were playing chess when their mother, Maria, approached and "reminded Vladimir that he was yet to do something she had asked him to do. Vladimir responded indifferently and made no move to do as he had been asked. Mother was clearly irritated and pushed the issue. Again, Vladimir gave a flippant response and made no move from his seat. 'Vladimir, either you go and do as Mother has requested, or I'm not playing with you any more,' said Alexander calmly, but forcibly enough that Vladimir got up immediately and did as he'd been asked."[135]

The holidays ended, Anna and Alexander returned to St Petersburg, and how the atmosphere in the family developed from there is difficult to determine. At the beginning of March 1887, however, close family friend Vera Kashkadamova called, having rushed over to tell them that a letter had arrived from the capital informing them of the arrest of Alexander and Anna.

The news came as a bolt from the blue to every family member and relative, not to mention Alexander's course-mates and tutors at the university. Since his arrival in the capital in autumn 1883, Alexander – as in Simbirsk – had dedicated all his time to his studies. His friend Ivan Chebotarev wrote: "I took an active part in the Volga Fraternity [*Podvolzhskoye zemlyachestvo*] and from the very outset spoke with Alexander Ulyanov about his joining it, along with his sister Anna, who had come with him. However, there was no inclination on their side. I had the impression they were too 'well bred'

---

134   A. I. Ulyanova-Yelizarova. O V. I. Lenine i sem'ye Ulyanovykh. p. 78.
135   Ibid. p. 79.

for it... They had come to *Piter¹³⁶* only for 'study' and to engage in the 'pure sciences', not 'politics'."¹³⁷

However, the turbulent social atmosphere at the university had gradually begun to affect Alexander. In November 1885, on the poet and satirist Mikhail Saltykov-Shchedrin's name day, Alexander and Anna went along with a deputation of students of the university and Bestuzhev Courses to Saltykov-Shchedrin's apartment to pay homage to the disgraced writer. Alexander then began to attend lectures by the renowned academic Vasily Semevsky on the history of the Russian peasantry, and when in January 1886 the professor was dismissed from the university for arousing "in young minds a sense of resentment towards the past", that is, towards the institution of serfdom, Alexander and another 309 students composed a letter of support for Semevsky and along with Anna visited his flat to complete the lecture series.¹³⁸

On 19th February, the 25th anniversary of the Great Reform, he first took part in a demonstration at the Volkovo Cemetery, where students conducted a memorial service for the "enemies of serfdom" and laid wreathes at the graves of the critic, journalist, poet and revolutionary democrat Nikolai Dobrolyubov and other writers who had supported democratic reform. In March 1886, he joined the student Scientific & Literary Society, where he made the acquaintance of Orest Govorukhin, Iosif Lukashevich, Pakhomy Andreyushkin and Vasily Generalov.¹³⁹ He was elected secretary of the society, but continued to steer clear of illegal organisations.

Orest Govorukhin asserted that in his third year Ulyanov "was still not a part of either revolutionary organisations or self-education circles," and described students who belonged to them as "talking a lot and learning little." When Govorukhin nevertheless broached the subject of joining an organisation, Alexander replied:

"I won't join revolutionary organisations because I have yet to make up my mind on a number of issues that affect me personally and, more importantly, have a societal bearing. I am unlikely to be joining up any time soon."

136	St Petersburg [*trans.*]
137	Sem'ya Ulyanovykh. p. 216.
138	See: Z. A. *Trofimov*. Dukh revolyutsii vital v dome Ulyanovykh. pp. 131, 132.
139	Ibid. p. 135.

"Why not?"

"Because social phenomena are exceedingly complex. If the natural sciences have only now reached a phase of development in which phenomena can be examined quantitatively as well as qualitatively, and are by extension only now becoming genuine sciences, then at what stage are the social sciences? It is clear that issues of a social nature will not be resolved quickly. I am proposing, of course, a scientific solution – no other kind makes sense – but it is the public man that must find a resolution to them. To the benighted, medicines that treat illness seem strange, even nefarious. It is even more strange and nefarious to treat social problems without understanding their causes."[140]

Alexander's formerly all-consuming passion for the natural sciences was now complemented by the same passion for the social sciences. He poured over Marx's *Capital* and *Critique of Hegel's Philosophy of Right*, as well as Georgi Plekhanov's early works *Socialism and the Political Struggle* and *Our Differences*. Gradually he became more inclined towards socialist ideas in their Marxist interpretation.

However, in full accordance with the laws of nature he had studied, which state that small actions can have major consequences, one event radically altered his views, namely the so-called 'Dobrolyubov demonstration' of 17th November 1886.

Mindful of the fact that the demonstration of 19th February had been a success due to a police oversight leading to their arriving late, the student organisations decided to hold the demonstration again, on the 25th anniversary of Dobrolyubov's death. But this time, law enforcement would not be caught napping and as the 1,500 student demonstrators approached Volkovo Cemetery, they found themselves surrounded by a police unit led by the chief of police. After the students made their indignation clear and clashes with police began to flare, the students were permitted to proceed to the grave and lay a wreath. This small victory succeeding in animating the students further, and after holding their demonstration they moved off singing towards Kazan Cathedral in the city centre. However, they were blocked on Ligovsky Prospekt by mounted Cossacks led by General Gresser.[141]

A participant in the procession, M. Braginsky, recalled: "Throughout the demonstration – which lasted from morning to dusk – Ulyanov was

---

140 See: Sem'ya Ulyanovykh. pp. 216-217.
141 See: ibid. p.209.

in high spirits. His mood had reached fever pitch when the huge crowd of demonstrators ... were stopped by a chain of mounted Cossacks ... and the city governor General Gresser appeared. At that moment I was close to Ulyanov, who had been walking arm in arm with his sister Anna the whole time, and his combative disposition was carrying over to everyone..."[142]

The Cossacks, drawing their sabres, surrounded the demonstrators. It was raining, and the sodden and shivering students stood in puddles for hours, exposed to the insults and abuse of the Cossacks as their names were taken, before either being released or arrested. More than 40 were immediately expelled from the capital. It was at that moment, as the euphoria from their victorious procession died down, that Alexander first felt the despair of powerlessness and a wretched, agonising humiliation he had hitherto never experienced.

In his pamphlet "17th November in St Petersburg", written the following day and reproduced as a hectograph, he wrote: "We recall many other such instances when the government has demonstrated its hostility to the common cultural aspirations of society... The brute force on which the government relies we will also meet with force, but a force which is organised and united by an awareness of its spiritual solidarity."[143]

Alexander's views had now solidified. He embraced the central tenets of Marxism and realised that achievement of its ultimate goals and ideals would become possible when society had sufficiently matured. He also recognised that to reach this 'maturity', at least a minimum degree of liberty was required. He came to the conclusion that only terror would impel the government to permit such an 'indulgence' as liberty. When at the end of 1886 the students Pyotr Shevyrev and Orest Govorukhin began to form the core of the terrorist wing of the *Narodnaya Volya* party, Alexander Ulyanov linked up with them and along with Iosif Lukashevich began to produce "throwing devices".[144]

The student Sergey Nikonov recalled: "The idea of killing the tsar was, so to speak, in the air at that time. The political atmosphere had reached such a pitch, and the oppressiveness of Alexander III's

---

142   Ibid.
143   Ibid. pp. 210-211.
144   See: *Z. A. Trofimov. Dukh revolyutsii vital v dome Ulyanovykh.* p. 137.

government so pervading, that many asked themselves: are there not people out there who could take it upon themselves to eliminate a brutal despot?"[145]

Alexander Ulyanov was not the type to wait for someone else to take up that mantle. He had never shied away from his duty. Having decided that 'treatment of social ills' would be administered via a terrorist act, he immediately went into action. With Shevyrev's departure to Yalta, and Govorukhin leaving for Geneva, preparations for the assassination fell largely upon Ulyanov's shoulders. By the end of February 1887, their hit squad (Vasily Osipanov, Pakhomy Andreyushkin and Vasily Generalov) was all set.

At the same time as he was preparing dynamite and giving the assassins their instructions, Alexander continued to attend lectures regularly and conduct laboratory work: it was then that he undertook a new study of the visual organs of a species of worm.[146]

Meanwhile, by October 1886 the entire student group of which Ulyanov was a part had been placed under surveillance, and after Andreyushkin had hinted in a letter to a friend in Kharkov about their intentions, the secret police did not let them out of their sight for a moment. When on 1st March 1887 the would-be assassins emerged onto Nevsky Prospekt to await Alexander III on his way to the Peter & Paul Fortress for a memorial service for his father, they were apprehended. The others were arrested over the following few days.

On 4th March, a short column appeared in print: "On 1st March, at approximately 11am, three students of the St Petersburg University were detained in possession of explosive devices on Nevsky Prospekt. The detainees have declared that they are members of a secret criminal society and a number of shells and bullets examined by experts were discovered to contain dynamite and strychnine."[147]

---

145   Sem'ya Ulyanovykh. pp. 204-205.
146   Ibid. p. 230.
147   Z. A. Trofimov. Dukh revolyutsii vital v dome Ulyanovykh. p. 129.

GRADUATION

When news of events in St Petersburg and the arrest of Anna and Alexander reached Kashkadamova in Simbirsk, she immediately sent for Vladimir at the gymnasium and handed him the letter. He read it through and, as Kashkadamova recalls, "was silent for some time. Sitting before me was no longer the reckless, cheerful boy, but a grown man reflecting profoundly on a grave matter. 'It's a serious business,' he said, 'and might end badly for Alexander.'"[148]

At this time no-one in Simbirsk, including the provincial authorities, was aware of Alexander and Anna's arrest, and certainly nothing of Ulyanov's involvement in any attempt on the tsar's life was known. Neither Vladimir nor Maria Alexandrovna had any suspicion of his key role in organising the assassination attempt, seemingly presuming instead that Anna and Alexander had been picked up at random in a larger wave of student arrests related to the detainment of the terrorists. How it "might end badly for Alexander" was was most likely assumed to be mere expulsion from university.[149]

There was, however, one rather worrying development.

On 3rd March, Matvei Leontyevich Peskovsky, a rather well-known journalist in the capital, delivered a petition on behalf of the Ulyanovs to Department of Police director Pyotr Durnovo: "Ulyanov is a very competent and orderly individual, unsociable to the point of surliness, who has excelled himself in the sciences... Ulyanova is a young lady in the best sense of the word, wholly unfamiliar with anything likely to scandalise a young woman." The most they could be accused of was some accidental "compromising acquaintance", and as such requested their release under his "personal guarantee".

---

148   Ibid. p. 141.
149   Z. A. Trofimov. Dukh revolyutsii vital v dome Ulyanovykh. pp. 142-143.

However, the same day, Peskovsky learned that his request would not be granted and wrote to Simbirsk about what had occurred.[150]

His letter was probably delivered to Kashkadamova on 9th March, and Maria Alexandrovna travelled to St Petersburg, leaving Vladimir in charge of the family. Arriving in St Petersburg on 14th March, she petitioned to see her son. However, it was only after the investigation was concluded on 30th March, with Tsar Alexander III noting on her petition, "Why wasn't she there [for her son] before!"[151], that the meeting was granted. Only when Alexander showed her the interrogation records did his mother grasp the nature of the case and the full extent of Alexander's leading role in it.

The meeting took place on 1st April and lasted two hours. According to his mother's account, "He cried and hugged her knees, begging her forgiveness for causing her such distress, and said that in addition to the duty to his family, he also had a duty to his Motherland. He illustrated to her the downtrodden and disenfranchised state of the Motherland and claimed it was the duty of every honest man to fight for its liberation.

'But such means are dreadful,' his mother retorted.

'But what can one do if there are no other, Mother?,' he responded."[152]

The Supreme Court, which convened on 15th, had finished its deliberations by 19th April: all 14 defendants were sentenced to death. The sentences were then passed to the emperor for ratification, and hope lingered that by petitioning His Majesty, the grim fate that awaited those convicted could be avoided. With this ongoing, the press kept silent about the case.

Maria Alexandrovna was granted another meeting with her son and attempted to persuade him to petition for clemency. Alexander refused. "Imagine, Mother," he said, "two men facing each other in a duel. The moment one has fired, he turns to the other and asks that he does not take his turn to shoot. No, I cannot do that…"

These words, and Alexander's last request – a volume of Heinrich Heine's poetry – were recorded by deputy prosecutor Knyazev, who was present at the meeting. He fulfilled the request, purchasing and passing to the condemned man a collection of Heine's verse.[153]

150	See: ibid. p. 142.
151	See: Y. Yakovlev. Zhizni pervaya tret' p. 222.
152	A. I. Ulyanova-Yelizarova. O V. I. Lenine I sem'ye Ulyanovykh. p. 104.
153	See: ibid. pp. 105, 106.

While this was taking place in the capital, Vladimir was beginning his final exams. On 5th May, he received top marks for his essay "The Tsar Boris", on Pushkin's *Boris Godunov*. On 7th May, he was again awarded full marks for his written Latin. The following morning was his mathematics paper. As Vladimir worked through the exam problems, his brother's execution was beginning in the courtyard of Shlisselburg Prison.

Alexander III commuted the sentences of seven of the condemned to periods of hard labour ranging from ten to twenty years; two – Lukashevich and Novorussky – had their appeals for clemency accepted and instead of the gallows were sentenced to life-long penal servitude, and all were amnestied and freed in 1905. On 8th May 1887, those who had refused to appeal to the emperor for clemency had their sentences carried out.[154]

At dawn, Generalov, Andreyushkin and Osipanov were brought to the gallows. They said their farewells to one another, kissed the cross, and were hanged. When their bodies were brought down, Ulyanov and Shevyrev were brought into the courtyard. A priest came to them. Ulyanov knelt at the cross, Shevyrev refused. Both ascended the scaffold, and in an instant it was all over.[155] No thunder struck, the ground did not open up.

Nikolai Valentinov, who knew the revolutionary milieu of those years well, wrote, "For all his love of chemistry, the natural sciences, and Marx's *Capital*, Alexander was by nature a religious man, one who ached to give up his life for an ideal grounded in love for mankind."[156]

Vladimir remained unaware of the events of that day. On 8th May, he again received another "five" and began studying for his next exam. However, on the morning of 10th May, the executions were officially announced. Notices were posted on virtually every pole in Simbirsk and the public quickly learned what had taken place. Maria Ulyanova recalled, "I was too young to understand the full horror of what had happened, and was, as strange as it seems, more struck by how Vladimir seemed:

---

154   According to the version of events Mikhail Shtein describes in his book *Ulyanovy i Leniny: semeinye tainy* (Olma Media Group, 2004), Alexander did in fact file a petition under pressure from relatives and out of sympathy for his mother, but it was rejected.

155   See: *N. Valentinov. Nedorisovanny portret...* p. 424.

156   Ibid. p. 425.

hearing him speak so sorrowfully of his brother, I began to absorb the gravity of events."[157]

Despite the news, on 12th May, Vladimir excelled in his algebra and trigonometry paper, as he did with his written Greek the following day. On 22nd May, his oral exams began, and Vladimir gained top marks for history and geography. That evening, his mother and Anna returned to Kokushkino after departing St Petersburg under police supervision.

His mother was in a terrible state, so it was left to Anna to recount to him all that had happened. The only thing Kashkadamova recalled Vladimir saying: "Alexander could not have acted any differently – he had to do what he did."[158]

His exams nonetheless continued: 27th May, Scripture knowledge, 29th – Latin, 1st June – his Greek oral exam, and finally, on 6th June, oral arithmetic, algebra, geometry, and trigonometry. Only a handful of students received top grades in the final exams: Vladimir Ulyanov, and those bidding for the silver medal, Alexander Naumov and Alexander Pisarev.

Vladimir's graduation certificate boasted 17 subjects at top grade – the only subject he fell short in, logic, for which he received the second highest mark, had been taught in the seventh grade by Fyodor Kerensky. The ongoing situation could have served as grounds for denying him the gold medal, but this did not come to pass: on 10th June, the Pedagogical Council decided "to award Ulyanov the GOLD MEDAL". This was also an acknowledgement of Vladimir's efforts throughout those eight years, having been top of his class in each grade, and a recognition of the work of his father, for whom the teachers maintained a deep respect. Whatever the reasoning for the award, the medal served as a passport to university.

Nonetheless, Simbirsk 'society' turned its back on the Ulyanovs. Those who had up until then sought out introductions and social engagements with the family of the director of schools now lowered their eyes on meeting, then whispered behind their backs, close friends included.

The young schools inspector Ivan Vladimirovich Ishersky spent a decade working with Ilya Ulyanov. He had maintained a reverent respect for his senior and his family; as their guest, his fine voice would accompany Maria Alexandrovna's piano playing through a repertoire of sentimental

---

157   Z. A. Trofimov. Dukh revolyutsii vital v dome Ulyanovykh. p. 149.
158   N. Valentinov. Nedorisovanny portret... p. 428.

romances. Each time he would proclaim earnestly: "Oh, it's the simplest thing to sing when I have such wonderful accompaniment!"[159]

Now, having inherited the post of director of public schools, Ishersky no longer had time for any of the Ulyanovs.

Olga Ulyanova wrote in one letter that on one occasion, she and her friend Nina Strzhalkovskaya had gone to the post office and run into some of their former schoolteachers there, the same ones that had awarded her the same gold medal for her achievements as had been awarded to Vladimir. "They greeted Nina, but didn't seem to notice or recognise me," she wrote bitterly.[160]

In this regard, the Simbirsk public were akin to that in the capital. St Petersburg University rector and professor of police law Andriyevsky, the same man who in February 1886 described Alexander Ulyanov as "the pride of the university", wrote on 6th March 1887 that he was "an intolerable disgrace", and in an address to the emperor he cast "before Your Majesty feelings of faithful fidelity and fervent love," in order to maintain the monarch's goodwill towards the university.[161]

Hence Vladimir did not need long to ruminate over where to study and what to choose for a profession: he selected Kazan University, located as it was in the school district in which his father had worked. As for which faculty to enter, this was also a straightforward decision – he chose law, in order to work outside state institutions now shut off to him as the brother of a "state criminal", and to practise a freer profession, as a lawyer in a private attorney's office.

However, his choice was not born out of purely pragmatic considerations. Vladimir told his cousin Nikolai: "These are times in which one must study legal science and political economy. Perhaps in different times I would have chosen different sciences…"[162]

There was no longer any cause to remain in Simbirsk, and on 30th May 1887, an announcement appeared in the Simbirsk Provincial News: "Owing to departure, house with garden for sale, grand piano, furniture. Moskovskaya Street, Ulyanov residence." This time the house, garden and

---

159	See: Y. Yakovlev. *Zhizni pervaya tret'* p. 229.
160	*Sem'ya Ulyanovykh*. p. 257.
161	See: Y. Yakovlev. *Zhizni pervaya tret'* p. 216.
162	R. I. *Nafigov*. …*I stal ubezhdennym marksistom*. Kazan, 1995. p. 57.

furniture were sold quickly.¹⁶³ Immediately after the sale, the family left for Kokushkino.

Besides his graduation from school, that summer of 1887 marked another important event in Vladimir's life: what might nowadays be called his 'rediscovery' of Nikolai Chernyshevsky's *What Is To Be Done?*

The execution of Vladimir's brother, in addition to the personal turmoil wrought by the loss of a loved one, had given rise to further questions: How and why had he chosen such a dangerous path? Out of a sense of duty to the people and to the motherland? Indeed, this was sacred and incontrovertible! His father's experiences had illustrated that hopes for the gradual reform and enlightenment of Russia were an illusion in the present circumstances. But did duty to the motherland necessarily involve dynamite and mercury fulminate?

The summer before, Alexander had been dissecting worms, an activity that had disgusted Vladimir. He had seemed so absorbed in science that nothing else around him seemed to matter. But Alexander had also been reading a great deal. Vladimir recalled his brother's excitement upon reading Chernyshevsky's novel. Vladimir had tried to read it in school, but it had not left much of an impression on him then. He now decided to try again. This time, he was left stunned.

In 1904, he told his distant cousin Maria Essen, "I read *What Is To Be Done?* five times in one summer, finding new and exciting ideas each time." Nadezhda Krupskaya confirms that he knew the novel in the "minutest detail" and down to its "finest points".¹⁶⁴

On one occasion in the same year, Nikolai Valentinov casually remarked in Vladimir's presence on the subject of *What Is To Be Done?*: "You wonder how people could be taken in and carried away with such a thing. It's difficult to imagine anything more feeble, primitive and simultaneously pretentious."¹⁶⁵

Hearing this, Lenin "leapt up with such rapidity that the chair screeched from under him. 'Can you account for what you are saying?' Lenin snapped. 'One cannot call *What Is To Be Done?* feeble and primitive. It has made revolutionaries of hundreds of people… Take my brother, for example: it did for him what it did for me. It rocked me to my core.

---

163   See: Y. Yakovlev. Zhizni pervaya tret' p. 235.

164   N. K. Krupskaya. O Lenine. p. 92.

165   N. Valentinov. Nedorisovanny portret… p. 495.

When did you read it? There is no point when you're still wet behind the ears. Chernyshevsky is too complex, too rich in ideas, to be understood and appreciated at a young age. I tried to read it when I was around 14 – I skimmed it, which proved a waste of time. But when my brother was executed, I decided to read it properly, knowing that Chernyshevsky's novel was one of his favourite works, and I dedicated not days but weeks to it. Only then did I realise the depth to it. It is a work that energises you for life.'"[166]

The main conclusion Vladimir drew from the novel was that in Russia, "every right-thinking and truly decent person must become a revolutionary..."[167]

With that, Vladimir Ulyanov's youth came to an end.

---

166   Ibid. p. 496.
167   Ibid. p. 500.

PART TWO – BROTHER OF A HANGED MAN

KAZAN

In July 1887, the Ulyanovs moved to Kazan. On 29th July, Vladimir applied for admission to the law faculty of the Imperial Kazan University. However, the rector was all too aware of the Ulyanov name and the admission request was met with the instructions: "Defer until further credentials received". These credentials were sent for in Simbirsk, and Vladimir's fate now rested on testimony from Kerensky.

His response was confidential, and neither Vladimir nor his family and friends could have known what it contained. However, Fyodor Mikhailovich Kerensky demonstrated decency, if not courage, in writing on 10th August, "neither at the gymnasium nor elsewhere did Vladimir, either in word or deed, elicit a negative opinion from governors or teachers. Ulyanov's education and moral development were scrupulously overseen by his parents… Religion and mental discipline lay at the core of his upbringing."

Kerensky did not touch on the obligatory questions regarding his attitude to "social issues" and "perverse schools of thought"[168], concluding, "Looking more closely at his family life and Ulyanov's character, I was compelled to notice in him an unnecessary aloofness and reluctance to interact even with those he was familiar with, and a general unsociability outside of the gymnasium."[169]

"Religion and mental discipline", coupled with this "reluctance to interact", put the university at ease. On 13th August new instructions appeared on Vladimir's application: "Admit". That day, Vladimir became a student and made a further request: to be exempted from tuition fees.

---

168   Z. A. Trofimov. Dukh revolyutsii vital v dome Ulyanovykh. p. 152.
169   Ibid.

The faculty supported his application and on 8th September, the university board included him in a list of those "of Orthodox faith" in need of a bursary "on grounds of poverty, final year marks, and school reference." On 12th, the list was ratified by higher authorities. However, it appears that Ulyanov was eventually turned down when it reached St Petersburg: apparently, for Ministry of Education officials, memories of his brother were still too fresh.[170]

Alexander Ulyanov's shadow would long stalk Vladimir. In the eyes of the authorities, it served as a warning and a reminder of "a most dangerous state criminal", grounds for heightened suspicion and a constant expectation of the unorthodox or "grievously revolutionary" when extant within the student body. Having escaped the confines of the gymnasium and its incessant supervision of pupils, and now flushed with his first taste of student freedom, Vladimir found himself having to absolve himself of such overinflated concerns.

Immediately after enrolment, Vladimir signed a declaration in which he, in accordance with the rules, pledged "not to be a member of, and not to participate in, any societies such as, for instance, regional fraternities [*zemlyachestva*] or similar, ... nor even to join legal organisations without the prior approval of the nearest authority in each instance..."[171] Nonetheless, the tumultuous atmosphere among the student body on campus drew Vladimir into far more than his studies and no declaration would stop him from joining the fraternities.

At this time eight illegal fraternal circles were operating at the university, enjoying enormous influence among the students. They maintained communication with similar societies in St Petersburg, Moscow, and other university towns, and ran libraries that held banned literature. The largest among them was the Simbirsk fraternity, in which Vladimir was active. He was immediately selected as its representative on the Council of Fraternities at the university.

Also active in the fraternity were individuals already known to the police, L. Bogoraz, and S. Polyansky; students of the Veterinary Institute, I. Voskresensky, K. Vygornitsky, and A. Skvortsov; as well as social democrats expelled from St Petersburg, A. Abramova and Y. Belova. Vladimir's association with them was immediately noticed by

---

170   See: *R. I. Nafigov. ...I stal ubezhdennym marksistom.* p. 64.
171   *V. I. Lenin i Tatariya.* Kazan, 1964. p. 30.

police. "The department places particular importance", it reported to the provincial gendarmerie, "in the relationship of Bogoraz and Skvortsov with Voskresensky, Konstantin Vygornitsky and Vladimir Ulyanov, particularly the last two, given Vygornitsky's closeness to and relationship with the state criminal Andreyushkin, who was executed along with Vladimir Ulyanov's brother in the case of 1st March 1887."[172]

It was at this time – in June – that the Minister for Education, Ivan Delyanov, issued a circular that went down in history as the Cookwomen's Children Circular, which drastically increased university tuition fees and curtailed access for children of the "lower classes". At the same time, regulations were approved which deprived universities of any residual autonomy and prohibited meetings, gatherings, and any student organisations. Meanwhile, the role of the 'student inspectors', regulatory officers who essentially policed the student body with powers of surveillance and investigation, was significantly expanded.

Protests against these 'innovations' began in Russian universities at the outset of the academic year, with unrest spreading to Kazan by November. On 5th November, the students boycotted ceremonies for the university's jubilee year. In the following days, under the guise of attending dance evenings, they gathered in apartments to discuss how to proceed with further actions, and prepared pamphlets and petitions demanding democratic reform in the universities. Vladimir Ulyanov was in attendance at a number of these meetings as representative of the Simbirsk fraternity.

Maxim Gorky, who was working in Kazan at that time, penned a collective portrait of local students in *My Universities*: "A noisy crowd of people living in state of anxiety for the Russian people, ever fearful of Russia's future. Always inflamed by what the papers were saying, the ideas they had wrought from newly devoured books, and events in the life of the town and university, they would clamour together in the evenings ... from every street in Kazan for fierce debate, and hushed whispers exchanged in corners. They would bring with them thick tomes and, jabbing fingers at the pages, would roar at one another, asserting whichever truths within that had taken their fancy... I recognised I was looking at people who were ready to change life for the better, and although their sincerity was subsumed by the turbulent flow of words, it did not drown therein.

---

172   Krasny arkhiv. 1934. No. 1. p. 65.

I often felt that my dumb thoughts resounded in the students' words, and I was as thrilled by these people as a prisoner by the promise of freedom."[173]

On 28th November, a letter from Moscow arrived in Kazan with news of a massacre of Moscow students that had taken place between 23-25th November. Passions boiled over at this point. The final wording of a petition was agreed on 3rd December, with a demonstration planned for the following day.

One police report stated: "Vladimir Ulyanov, two days before the demonstration was due to take place, gave us reason to suspect he was planning something nefarious ... he has been leaving his house and returning bringing items for others, and generally behaving secretively..."[174]

On 4th December, towards 11am, groups of students began to gather in the lobby, cloakroom and smoking room of the university. At around 12 o'clock, with a cry of "to the gathering, comrades, to the gathering!" they went round the lecture halls, bringing everyone to the assembly hall. The doors had been barred, but they broke through, and the protest began. A large group of students from the Veterinary Institute were also in attendance.

Present was Yevgeny Chirikov, later a writer, who described the prevailing mood among those gathered: "I have not forgotten how I felt. My entire soul quivered at the onrush of a singular sense of my citizenhood, and burned with a desire to perform some manner of heroic civic deed. As soldiers entered and demanded we leave under threat of bullets, we did not blink, but stayed put! Gone was the logic of reason – only the logic of the heart remained."[175]

When the rector Kremlev appeared, he was handed a petition, which began with the words, "What gathers us here is nothing less than an awareness of the impossibility of the conditions imposed upon life in Russia, and student life in particular, as well as our desire to draw society's attention to these conditions and present to the government the following demands..."[176]

---

173   *M. Gorky*. Sobraniye sochineny: 30 volumes. Moscow, 1951. Vol. 13. pp. 535-536.

174   *R. I. Nafigov*. ...I stal ubezhdennym marksistom. p. 93.

175   *Y. Chirikov*. Tsvety vospominany. Sobraniye sochineny. Vol. 13. Moscow, 1915. pp. 48-49.

176   *R. I. Nafigov*. ...I stal ubezhdennym marksistom. p. 100.

The gathering ended at around four o'clock. However, by then, the informants among them had taken enough notes to provide a list of practically everyone present. On the back of their report, which described the "instigators", a university trustee wrote to Minister Delyanov that on 4th December, Vladimir Ulyanov had "rushed to the assembly hall as part of the first group, and along with Polyansky, was the first to dash through the second floor, crying out and waving his hands, as if to incite others; leaving the meeting, he handed back his entrance card".[177]

Upon returning home, Ulyanov wrote to the rector: "Considering it impossible to continue my education at the university given the present conditions of university life, I have the honour to request kindly that Your Excellency make the proper arrangements for my withdrawal from the student body of the Imperial Kazan University."[178]

That request was dated 5th December 1887. On the night of 5th, he and 40 other students were arrested and detained in a holding prison.

Y. Foss, a participant in the demonstration, wrote, "Despite the prison smocks we wore, the fact that most of us had not eaten in over 24 hours, ... and the swarms of parasites on the bunks, a feeling of joyful, merry excitement prevailed among the youth, as they composed appeals 'for freedom' in prose and poetry, sang revolutionary songs and simple student refrains, relayed to one another the myriad events of the previous days, and so on. Vladimir Ulyanov was silent, deep in concentration the whole while, and took no part in the general merriment. Someone had the idea to survey his fellow prisoners on what their plans were upon release. When it came to the student Ulyanov's turn, ... he, after a short pause, seemed to awake from his reverie and, smiling gently, said: 'I'll have to think... For me it's the path trodden by my older brother'... Immediately, the laughter and noise in the cell died down. Everyone was left mortified and embarrassed by this simple, unaffected response."[179]

In seeking conclusions on what determined Vladimir Ulyanov's path in life, a number of authors have been inclined towards the most simple interpretation: vengeance for his brother's execution. But is it

---

177   Ibid. p. 104.
178   Ibid.
179   See: *I. Kondratyev*. Lenin v Kazani. 2nd Edition. Kazan, 1962. p. 64; Pervaya tyurma // Ogonek. 1926. No. 11.

sufficient to assume that such a decision is merely the consequence of an individual's personal circumstances?

Who did Sofia Perovskaya, daughter of the St Petersburg governor-general, have to avenge? Or the Oryol nobleman and son of a general, Pyotr Zaichnevsky? Or Mikhail Bakunin, who came from a long line of Tver nobility? Hence, there must have been other motives besides the purely personal for the path they chose. And given that those in question were for the most part educated people, it is beyond doubt that some of this motivation stemmed from the intellectual trends of the time, and the thoughts and ideas that prevailed in society; indeed, since Pyotr Lavrov wrote of his duty to the people in 1868, the notion of their liberation had dominated among the progressive intelligentsia.

On Sunday 6th December, the first batch of prisoners was released and expelled from Kazan. A crowd gathered in front of the police station greeted them with applause and cheering, and sledges laden with gifts. "...society," wrote Olga Ulyanova to a friend, "is sympathetic to the students: in the first few days of arrests and expulsions from Kazan they were sent 300 roubles, along with fur coats and scarves, since many students had nothing in which to travel. The ladies of Kazan sent them tobacco and cigarettes, while the students of the gymnasium, particularly those from the 1st Gymnasium, gave them all the money they had, those that had them handed over their watches, and some, even their fur coats."[180]

On 7th December, Vladimir was released. He was also instructed to leave Kazan, to return to Kokushkino, where his older sister Anna had also been residing under strict police monitoring since 23rd July 1887. That evening, he left Kazan on a covered sled, accompanied by his mother and sister Maria. They were escorted all the way to the city limits by a police officer to make sure the expulsion order was carried out.

In 1887, there were 918 students enrolled at Kazan University. 256 of them took part in the demonstration; of those, 164 were removed and expelled.[181]

---

180 I. *Kondratyev*. Lenin v Kazani. p. 57.
181 See: *R. I. Nafigov*. ...I stal ubezhdennym marksistom. pp. 60, 110.

KOKUSHKINO

At Kokushkino, Vladimir settled in one wing of the house, taking a corner room with north-facing windows. The room contained "a wooden-framed trestle bed, a bookshelf on the wall, a simple wardrobe, two or three chairs, a folding stool, and a table. A carpenter's bench stood by the door: it was to set to be removed, but Vladimir said to leave it, as he could use it to stack books on..."[182]

The future remained uncertain. On the advice of his family, it was decided that in time he would have to seek re-entry to Kazan University, or enrol in a different Russian university. In the meantime, Vladimir could play to his heart's content on the old billiard table in the largest room of the wing, or read, go on walks, stroll in the forests that surrounded the house, or go hunting. However, neither billiards nor hunting seemed to satisfy him.

Initially, he was in a state of agitation, as if reliving all that had occurred; Anna Ulyanova described him as in "a heightened frame of mind". "With great zeal" he set about composing a detailed account of the student demonstration in a letter to a friend. Vladimir – as is often the case – was now finding the very words that had remained unspoken at the time. He paced around the room, and, "with obvious relish", as Anna wrote, read out "the sharp epithets that he had bestowed upon the inspector and the other powers that be".[183]

But the letter was never sent, and his excitement passed as the January frost descended. Vladimir instead immersed himself in reading.

In winter 1904, Vladimir told Vatslav Vorovsky, "I don't think that at any other point in my life, even while in prison in St Petersburg or in Siberia, did I read as much as I did in the year following my expulsion from Kazan to the village. I read non-stop from early morning till late at night.

---

[182]   A. Ivansky. Molodoi Lenin. Povest' v dokumentakh i memuarakh. Moscow, 1964. p. 416.

[183]   Vospominaniya o Vladimire Lenine. Vol. 1. pp. 24-25.

I read for university courses, presuming I'd soon be allowed to return to university. I read a wide range of fiction, and I was particularly fond of Nekrasov, my sister and I competing to see who could memorise more of his poetry, and how quickly. But most of all, I read the articles published in *Sovremennik*, *Otechestvennye Zapiski*, and *Vestnik Evropy*. Those contained the best and most engaging material on social and political issues published in the preceding decades.

My favourite author was Chernyshevsky... I read Chernyshevsky with pencil in hand, taking excerpts and making summaries of what I'd just read. The notebooks in which all this was chronicled I kept for a long time. Chernyshevksy's encyclopedic knowledge, the clarity of his revolutionary stances, his merciless polemical talent – it swept me away... There are musicians who are said to have perfect pitch, and there are those whom one can say possess a perfect revolutionary instinct. Marx was one of those, and Chernyshevsky another."

These views he shared in winter 1904, but in Kokushkino in the winter of 1887/88, Vladimir was not yet giving much thought to Marx: "In those old magazines I had, there may have been articles on Marxism, by Mikhailovsky or Zhukovsky, for instance. I cannot say with any degree of surety whether I read them or not. One thing is certain ... they did not catch my attention, although thanks to articles by Chernyshevsky, I became interested in economic issues, particularly those dealing with rural life in Russia.

My first introduction to philosophical materialism came about through reading Chernyshevsky. It was he who first revealed to me Hegel's role in the development of philosophical thought, and it was from him that my understanding of dialectical method developed, as a result of which Marx's dialectics became more straightforward to absorb. I read Chernyshevsky's splendid essays on aesthetics, art and literature from cover to cover... I devoured all of Chernyshevsky's articles on the peasant question, his notes on the translation of Mill's political economy... It was excellent preparation for a later transition to Marx."

But as Krupskaya rightly noted, it was *What Is To Be Done?* that Ulyanov particularly adored, "despite its artless, naïve structure".[184] "Before I became acquainted with the works of Marx, Engels and Plekhanov", Lenin told Vorovsky, "the *overwhelming* influence on me was Chernyshevsky

---

184   Ibid. p. 600.

alone, and that began with *What Is To Be Done?* Chernyshevsky's greatest service was not only to demonstrate that every truly right-thinking and decent person must become a revolutionary, but even more importantly: what kind of revolutionary he should be, which principles he should follow, how best to strive for his ends, and which ways and means he must employ to ensure their realisation."[185]

According to Chernyshevsky, one cannot find true peace of mind when one does not acknowledge the inseparability of one's own interests from those of society, if one's soul does not share in the fate of one's homeland, when one insulates one's life from the common experience of the people and removes oneself from the cares of society. For as Chernyshevsky believed, a life removed from such concerns was at best "spitefully vulgar, wantonly vulgar, and in either case, pointlessly vulgar".

Was this the sense that Vladimir derived from the novel? It appears so, as many years later, he evaluated his own efforts against these criteria and wrote that his life had become first and foremost a battle against vulgarity – vulgarity in his own life, the vulgarity of politicians, and the vulgarity of opportunism. As a consequence, he harboured a "hatred for vulgar people..."[186]

A number of historians, in analysing the scope of the 18-year-old Vladimir's reading, have sought to uncover the 'devil's seed' that would manifest itself 30 years later in the "bloody and ruthless dictator". They have sought evidence of this in Chernyshevsky's writing: "Great men, perhaps because of their greatness, strike when the iron is hot... Suvorov and Napoleon, indeed, every great commander since Alexander the Great, were renowned for their pitilessness in achieving victory... We do not wish to arbitrate on whether military victories are virtuous things or not, but be decisive – before going to war, *have no pity for the people*."

Another passage runs: "A political leader must be decisive, and once his goal is determined, pursue it ruthlessly to the end." However, in his preface and commentary to his translation of Georg Weber's *Basic World History*, Chernyshevsky rejects despotic rule over the people and makes plain his opposition to militarism and "the admiration of the malign and glorification of the wicked". He argues that world history testifies to the

---

185   N. *Valentinov*. Nedorisovanny portret.... pp. 499-500.
186   V. I. *Lenin*. Polnoye sobraniye sochineny. Vol. 49. p. 340.

fact that violence, even when successful in its aims, has consequences for those who commit it.

The German tribes who conquered the Roman Empire paid an excessively heavy price, with many wiped out in the process. Genghis Khan's Mongols who invaded Europe lost a large part of their force in their conquest of Russia, with those who remained crushed by resurgent Russian forces. Similarly, the Spanish forces who devastated the West at the height of their powers eventually went to ruin and half starved to death. Finally, the illustrious French, who conquered Europe under Napoleon, but were finally defeated in 1814 and in subsequent years suffered devastation and national humiliation.

Chernyshevsky's principal conclusion formulated explicitly in opposition to Russian autocracy was that by no measure did all means achieve their goal, and by the middle of the 19th century, "even the Turkish government has ceased attempting to improve the lot of its subjects by committing violence against them".[187]

Life in the meantime continued as usual. Vladimir Ulyanov had not given up on the idea of continuing his education and on 9th May 1888, Vladimir and Maria Alexandrovna sent two petitions to St Petersburg: his to the education minister Delyanov, and his mother's to the director of the Department of Police. Both contained a request that "the former student Vladimir Ulyanov" be permitted to re-enroll at Kazan University.

Both petitions were rejected and a trustee of the Kazan school district clarified that a brother of the executed criminal of the state Alexander Ulyanov "could not be considered a morally or politically trustworthy individual".[188]

On 15th July, Maria Alexandrovna petitioned Count Durnovo, but on this occasion the Department of Police turned down the request, believing it too soon to allow Vladimir Ulyanov's readmission to Kazan University.[189]

At the end of August, Delyanov came in person to Kazan, and on the 31st Maria Alexandrovna was able to hand him another petition personally, requesting Vladimir be permitted into any Russian university. "My son," she wrote, "is the only support to me in my old age, and to three younger

---

187   *N. G. Chernyshevsky*. Polnoye sobraniye sochineny. Vol. 11. pp. 287-288; *G. Weber*. Basic World History (Russian translation). Vol. 10. Moscow, 1888. p. 37.

188   Krasnaya letopis' 1924. No. 1. p. 55.

189   See: *R. I. Nafigov*. ...I stal ubezhdennym marksistom. p. 128.

children who, since his death, are without a father who gave 30 years of service to the Ministry for Public Education..." She did not have to wait long for a response. By the next day, the minister made his decision: "There is nothing that can be done for Ulyanov."[190]

Later, on September 6th, Vladimir composed a new petition addressed to the Minister of Internal Affairs: "In order to earn a livelihood and support my family, I require access to higher education as a matter of urgency, and having no possibility of obtaining it in Russia, I humbly request that Your Excellency permits me leave to go abroad for admission to a foreign university."[191]

However, Vladimir was refused again. Moreover, on 19th August, by order of the administrative department of the office of the Ministry of the Imperial Court, his name was included in a classified register listing individuals permanently barred from public office.[192]

When considering which factors shaped the young Vladimir Ulyanov, it is clearly insufficient to look merely to the materials he was reading and his circle of acquaintances – the actions of the authorities themselves must be taken into consideration. Later, in relation to the student unrest of 1901, Lenin would write: "There is a striking disparity between the modesty and innocuousness of the students' demands and the alarm of a government which acts as if the axe was already hacking at the pillars of its rule."[193] Similarly, after the Kazan University demonstration of 1887, the authorities left the protesters with virtually no alternatives. Their own callous, officious stupidity, which left lives in tatters, only succeeded in breeding more sworn enemies.

However, resistance to the regime was not a road that guaranteed Vladimir a rosy future. His brother's execution was warning enough. After all, the most benign, well-intentioned instances of 'going to the people', even those that did not end in arrest and exile, would only lead to frustration at the waste of effort and futility of outcome. Vladimir knew this from practical experience.

In the summer of 1888, his cousin Anna Ivanovna Veretennikova came to Kokushkino in the final stages of tuberculosis. She had come to

---

190	Ibid.
191	*V. I. Lenin*. Polnoye sobraniye sochineny. Vol. 1. p. 553.
192	See: Vladimir Ilyich Lenin. Biograficheskaya khronika. Vol. 1. p. 38.
193	*V. I. Lenin*. Polnoye sobraniye sochineny. Vol. 4. p. 392.

visit frequently in the preceding years, and had also visited Simbirsk, and Vladimir had always listened attentively to her stories. Like the heroine of *What Is To Be Done?*, Vera Pavlovna, Anna Ivanovna was one of the first female physicians in Russia. She had turned down an offer to work in a hospital in St Petersburg in order to work as a country doctor in the remote Belebei district of Ufa Province. She had plunged herself into her work, so as to ease her debt to the people.

"I was given a great deal to think about by the terrible amount I was confronted with during my service in the *zemstvo*", Anna Ivanovna had told him. "The door to my cabin was open from morning till late. The chronically ill came to me with festering sores, caries, chronic ulcers, syphilis and diseases of the eyes. Every day, a man of around 30 to 40 suffering from fever would come and request the bitter medicine. That's what they called quinine. But one member of the local district council said – and these are his precise words – that expensive medicines like quinine were 'harmful to a peasant, as he is by nature crude, and the cruder and, more to the point, cheaper the medicine administered to him, the more beneficial it would be for him.' Doctors had neither medicine nor instruments and, like many rural public servants, received no salary for months on end."[194]

---

194   Y. *Yakovlev*. Zhizni pervaya tret'. p. 46.

A MUDDLED PAPER

In early September, the Ulyanovs returned to Kazan as a family: Maria Alexandrovna's pleading had worked, and their exile was over. They settled in a two-storey extension of the Orlova mansion on Pervaya Gora Street in Arsk Field. "The apartment is large, bright, recently decorated, and comes with a neat little garden," Olga Ilyinichna wrote to a friend. There were two kitchens – one on the ground floor, another on the first. Vladimir took the extra kitchen on the ground floor, as it was more secluded and suited to working than the upstairs rooms. Newspapers were piled on the unused range, which effectively functioned as a second table.[195]

However, Vladimir had little inclination for study at that time. At the beginning of October, he had received official notification that he had been refused permission to travel abroad to continue his education, and was in no mood to delve into textbooks. Nonetheless, after his enforced exile at Kokushkino, Kazan itself seemed like Paris.

An opera and ballet troupe under the direction of conductor Alexander Orlov-Sokolovsky came to the city, boasting among its ranks the renowned soloist and dramatic tenor Yulian Zakrzhevsky, who had performed on stages in Moscow, Warsaw, Venice and Prague. He was an idol to young people, particularly students, who would literally carry him on their shoulders after performances and, on one occasion, actually unharnessed his horses and pulled his carriage round the dark streets themselves.

After his return from Kokushkino, Vladimir also began to attend a chess club in Kazan. He had learned to play chess around the age of eight or nine, playing with his father and older brother, and since Ilya Nikolayevich consistently outplayed the brothers, they developed a good grounding in the game and eventually began to defeat not only their friends, but their father as well.

---

195   See: *R. I. Nafigov*. ...I stal ubezhdennym marksistom. p. 141.

His younger brother Dmitry, himself an avid chess player, wrote, "...his [Vladimir's] main interest in chess was the challenge of playing the right move to extricate himself from a difficult, occasionally seemingly hopeless situation; winning or losing in and of itself did not especially concern him. The better moves of his opponent pleased him more than the weak ones."[196]

Over the years, his interest in chess gradually waned, replaced by other concerns. In any case, it seems he was an adherent to Moses Mendelssohn's view that chess is too serious to be a game, too much of a game to be serious. Back in Kazan, meeting old university friends and making new acquaintances, Vladimir flung himself wholeheartedly into the tumult of student life.

Major changes had taken place within the student milieu during those months spent in Kokushkino. Alongside the fraternities, there began to emerge groups whose purpose was to foster political self-development and cultivation among students. Such groups were still dominated by various strains of populism and the *Narodnaya Volya* movement. However, a new trend – Marxism – was beginning to make its presence felt, and the name most associated with it was that of Nikolai Yevgrafovich Fedoseyev, one of the first in the Volga region to declare his adherence to Marxism. It was Fedoseyev who arranged a programme of study for the self-development groups that examined Marxist literature, reviews and essays dedicated to the history and socio-economic development of Russia.

Among Vladimir's new acquaintances was Maria Pavlovna Chetvergova (née Orlova), the widow of a staff captain. Despite already being in her 40s, as a veteran *Narodnaya Volya* member, she was held in high standing among the youth. A *Narodnaya Volya* group formed around Chetvergova, affiliated to the so-called Sabunayev organisation.

Fedoseyev's student self-development groups also made use of Maria Pavlovna's apartment on Staro-Gorshechnaya Street.[197] Vladimir would also look in at the apartment, whose owner shared his love for Chernyshevsky. They would while away the hours discussing his articles, dissecting the subtlest of nuances in one or other of his ideas. Lenin later told Nadezhda Krupskaya, "I know of no other person with whom discussing Chernyshevsky would be as pleasant or illuminating."[198]

196	Vladimir Ilyich Lenin v Samare. p. 25.	
197	See: *R. I. Nafigov*. ...I stal ubezhdennym marksistom. p. 160.	
198	*N. Valentinov*. Nedorisovanny portret... p. 460.	

It was in her apartment in the winter of 1888-89 that he heard a talk by a student, Mikhail Mandelshtam, on Marx's *Capital*.

Karl Radek recalls how, "during our walks by the deep blue Aare River in Bern in 1915, if Vladimir was in a pleasantly reflective mood, he would talk at length about his revolutionary youth". On one occasion, Radek wrote, "Ilyich found himself at a *Narodnaya Volya* group meeting. There he heard mention of Marx for the first time. A student, Mandelshtam, a future Constitutional Democrat, was delivering a paper in which he expounded the views of Emancipation of Labour. The paper was really rather muddled, but nonetheless Vladimir, as if peering through fog, saw potent revolutionary theory within. He got hold of the first volume of *Capital*, and a new world opened up to him…"[199]

Of course, Vladimir had heard mention of Marx as a schoolboy, and again as a student. He had seen his brother with a copy of *Capital*. However, Vladimir had paid little attention to the name back then. Now, after his time spent reading in Kokushkino, the paper clearly left an impression.

Mandelshtam, himself exiled from Kazan after the December demonstration of 1887, recalled it thus: "From winter 1888-89, I began illegal forays into Kazan and resumed activities with the groups I had been involved with. I now dedicated more attention to political economy, and it was in my focusing on introducing the audience to the works of Marx that my lectures during this time particularly deviated from those previous.

My main audience was made up of students from Kazan University, and some from the Veterinary Institute, but occasionally young people whose surnames I did not know would attend. In Kazan at that time, there were a number of groups who were only vaguely aware of each other's existence. But within the groups themselves – to maintain secrecy – there was an arrangement whereby members' surnames were not known to each other… Only [later] did I learn that Lenin was among my listeners in that secret circle in Kazan in winter and spring of 1888-89."[200]

Mandelshtam was not afraid to be self-critical: "Lenin was right to call my lecture 'muddled'. Aside from the fact that Russian Marxism

---

199 K. B. Radek. Iz rasskazov tov. Lenina o yego vstuplenii v revolyutsionnoye dvizheniye // Rabochaya Moskva. 1924. No. 92.

200 I. S. Zilbershtein. Molodoi Lenin v zhizni i za rabotoi. pp. 205-207.

was in its infancy at the time, I could not help but continue to reflect the ideology of *Narodnaya Volya* in my Marxism... We had no programme, no leadership, and no literature. We had to ... do it our own way."²⁰¹

Organisationally, Vladimir was neither a part of Mandelshtam's group, nor that of Chetvergova. He continued to work independently, engaging with those who, like him, were wrestling with Marxist theory. On this basis, he developed a circle of comrades, and Anna Ulyanova confirms that "this circle had no leader: it was young people seeking their own path entirely independently".²⁰²

Vladimir studied the 1872 Russian edition of *Capital*. He and his sister Olga read *The Poverty of Philosophy* in French, but for the most part he was required to translate Marx and Engels from the original German. However, reading individual works did not provide an overall sense of Marxism as a whole. At this point, that winter of 1888/89, he came upon the programme drawn up by Fedoseyev.

Such programmes were in those years themselves a distinct and highly respected art form among revolutionaries. The *narodniki* [populists] were the first to begin composing them. These were lists – frequently annotated in detail – covering a variety of subjects including philosophy, political economy, history, and natural history, as well as fine literature; the intention was to develop not only a scientific, but also a social and ethical 'comprehensive world view'.

Marxist programmes of this kind were devised in many cities at this time, including St Petersburg, Kiev, Tambov and Chelyabinsk.²⁰³ In the Volga region, the "Kazan Programme", compiled by Fedoseyev in autumn 1888, became the most well-known.²⁰⁴ Towards the end of his life, in winter 1922, Lenin would write: "For the Volga region and a number of areas in central Russia, the role played by Fedoseyev was of immense importance and there is no doubt that his audience's conversion to Marxism can in no small measure be attributed to the immense influence

---

201   M. L. Mandelshtam. 1905 god v politicheskikh protsessakh. Zapiski zashchitnika. Moscow, 1931. p. 15.

202   Deyateli SSSR I revolyutsionnogo dvizheniya v Rossii. Entsiklopedichesky slovar' Granat. Moscow, 1989. p. 501.

203   See: *N. Valentinov*. Nedorisovanny portret... p. 491.

204   See: *R. I. Nafigov*. ...I stal ubezhdennym marksistom. p. 156.

of this unusually talented and remarkably dedicated revolutionary."[205] That being so, it becomes apparent why Lenin always addressed the 17-year-old Fedoseyev respectfully by his name and patronymic.

There was another individual involved in the development of the "Kazan Programme": the writer and statistician Pavel Skvortsov[206], a pioneer of Russian Marxism and the first to throw down the gauntlet to the populist *narodnik* movement in the press.

Analysing *Capital* became a genuine passion for Skvortsov. He knew "whole pages almost by heart and would spend hours making charts based on the formulae Marx outlines…"[207] Researcher G. L. Beshkin, who met Pavel Skvortsov in 1929, wrote: "He came to Marx as if to the revealed truth of the Gospel."[208] It was Skvortsov who assisted Fedoseyev in obtaining a deeper understanding of Marxist theory.

In 1904, as Lenin was telling young Bol'sheviks of how he had "begun to turn to Marxism after developing an understanding of the first volume of *Capital* and Georgi Plekhanov's *Our Differences*," he was able to say precisely when: "Early 1889, January".[209]

In Kazan, the sense of epiphany towards this 'great truth' deeply affected Vladimir. Anna Ulyanova wrote, "I recall that in the evenings, when I went down to talk to him, he would relate to me with great passion and enthusiasm the basic principles of Marxism and the new horizons they opened up."[210]

This sentiment, 'emotional' as well as 'rational', remained with Lenin his whole life. In winter 1917, he wrote to Inessa Armand: "I am still 'in love' with Marx and Engels, and will not hear them denigrated lightly. No, these are men of substance! We must learn from them. They must remain our foundation."[211]

---

205 *V. I. Lenin*. Polnoye sobraniye sochineny. Vol. 45. pp. 324-325.

206 Proletarskaya revolyutsiya. 1923. No. 8. p. 58.

207 *N. Valentinov*. Nedorisovanny portret… pp. 481-482; Proletarskaya revolyutsiya. 1923. No. 8. p. 58.

208 Nizhegorodsky krayevsky sbornik. Vol. 2. Nizhny Novgorod, 1920. p. 199.

209 *N. Valentinov*. Nedorisovanny portret… p. 186.

210 Vospominaniya o Vladimire Ilyiche Lenine. Vol. 1. p. 26.

211 *V. I. Lenin*. Polnoye sobraniye sochineny. Vol. 49. p. 378.

SAMARA

Vladimir's new connections and contacts did not go unnoticed by the police. Secret surveillance intensified and the Provincial Gendarme Administration identified him as someone "acquainted with suspicious persons" and " individuals considered politically unreliable". He was also noted for his "Marxist leanings".[212]

As a rule, Vladimir did not invite his new acquaintances home, recognising he was being followed. He also wished to avoid giving his mother any cause for alarm, though she quickly realised her son was again in peril.

In January 1889, the family purchased a *khutor* smallholding near the village of Alakayevka in the Bodganovskaya parish of Samara county and Province. This necessitated spending all the money raised from the sale of their home in Simbirsk, plus a portion of their savings.[213]

By buying the *khutor*, Vladimir's mother secretly hoped that, should he not be permitted to continue his education, he would be drawn towards running the farm, an occupation which would both provide a source of income for the family, and distract him from "undesirable company".

Nonetheless, in April 1889, Maria Alexandrovna made another attempt to obtain permission for Vladimir to travel abroad to continue his studies. He underwent a medical examination and on 29th April was issued certification, signed by Kazan University professor Nikolai Kotovshchikov, to the effect that he was suffering from a stomach ailment which required alkaline water treatment abroad. A corresponding application for a foreign passport was lodged with the governor. On 14th June, the application was met with a categorical rejection: "Such treatment is available in the Caucasus".[214]

---

212 R. I. *Nafigov*. ...I stal ubezhdennym marksistom. pp. 144, 161.
213 See: *I. S. Zilbershtein*. Molodoi Lenin v zhizni i za rabotoi. p. 210.
214 Vladimir Ilyich Lenin. Biograficheskaya khronika. Vol. 1. p. 41.

However, he did not receive the refusal in Kazan: on 3rd May, the family had moved to Alakayevka, which proved timely, as searches and arrests began in the city that same month. On 13th July, Nikolai Fedoseyev was arrested in the village of Klyuchishchi, followed by a number of members of the circle that frequented M.P. Chetvergova's apartment.[215]

Fedoseyev would languish in jail for more than two years. Lenin later wrote: "In spring 1889 I departed for Samara Province, where at the end of summer 1889 I learned of the arrest of Fedoseyev and some other members of the Kazan circles – including the one in which I had been active. I suspect I could easily have been arrested as well, had I remained in Kazan that summer."[216]

This suspicion was probably justified: if Vladimir had managed to avoid arrest, he had not escaped police surveillance. Samara gendarmes reported to the Department of Police that, "on 4th of this May, Anna Ulyanova, daughter of an Active State Councillor and currently subject to open police monitoring, came to a *khutor* near the village of Alakayevka… She arrived along with her mother, her sisters Olga and Maria, and brother Vladimir, currently under covert surveillance, as well as the former student and son of a peasant, Mark Timofeyevich Yelizarov, an individual of doubtful political reliability. Yelizarov has been entrusted by the Ulyanovs to run their affairs and manage the farm."[217]

Mark Timofeyevich, with his greater experience, did indeed take over the running of the smallholding. Moreover, he then became a full member of the Ulyanov family. Having met Alexander and Anna in the Volga fraternity while studying in St Petersburg, he began a relationship with Anna, and now they had decided to marry. On 28th July, Vladimir served as a witness at their wedding in the neighbouring village of Trostyanka.

Initially, they did in fact attempt to farm, buying a cow, a horse – Bulanka – and sowing wheat, buckwheat, and sunflower. However, their efforts ended in failure, and the following year they put the land out for rent.[218]

---

215 See: *R. I. Nafigov*. …I stal ubezhdennym marksistom. p. 155.
216 *V. I. Lenin*. Polnoye sobraniye sochineny. Vol. 45. p. 324.
217 Krasnaya letopis'. 1925. No. 2. p. 150.
218 See: ibid. p. 160.

Nonetheless, for the next four years, Alakayevka became a permanent and much loved 'summer residence'. While steppe dominated the local landscape, Alakayevka marked the starting point of the so-called Muravelny Forest, which was abundant with wild raspberries. Beyond that stretched the Gremyachy Forest, offering good hunting.

They lived in an old, one-storey wooden house, which backed onto an overgrown, neglected garden that tapered steeply down to a brook. A ten-minute walk from the house was a pond by a mill where they would go to swim.

Each had their own corner of the garden. It was, the Ulyanovs would say, "Olya's maple tree", and indeed Olga would often be found under the tree with a book. Anna preferred a little avenue formed by birch trees. In the shade of some old lime trees was where Vladimir installed his 'office': a table knocked together from planks planted in the earth, along with a bench and a horizontal bar. Here he whiled away the time with his books: in the morning, he studied university courses, and after lunch, political material and literature. It was at this time he developed his habit of walking while working, mulling over what he had read, before suddenly returning to his 'office' 10-15 paces away.

In the evenings, they would set up the samovar on the porch, light a kerosene lamp and either read – occasionally aloud – or sing songs. It pleased Maria Alexandrovna to see how calm and harmonious things were, and that Vladimir, despite all the refusals, was taking his university exam preparations seriously.

But their mother's hopes that retreat to the backwoods of Samara would insulate Anna and Vladimir from "undesirables" were dashed. Alakayevka as a location had long been flagged by the police, since three *versts* from there [approximately two miles – *trans*.], on 100 *desyatinas* of land, a student commune had been established at the *khutor* of Sharnel.

A former student of Kazan University, expelled for his involvement in rioting, Dmitry Goncharov hailed from the same region as the Ulyanovs, and had known Ilya Ulyanov well. He began to pay the Ulyanovs visits. He introduced Vladimir to a fellow commune member, the *narodnik* Alexei Preobrazhensky.[219] When, on 5th September, the Ulyanovs moved

---

219   See: Vladimir Ilyich Lenin v Samare. pp. 158-160.

to the city of Samara from Alakayevka, the number of such acquaintances began to grow daily.

Samara had become a favoured resettlement destination for many prominent exiled *narodniki* after their sentences were completed. There were also many *narodnik* youth in the city, students expelled from universities for their participation in disorder.

The Ulyanovs were warmly received into this environment. A. I. Samoilov, a broadly liberal-leaning land captain, wrote upon meeting Anna and Vladimir of the immediate impression they made on him, stating that "this impression was perhaps reinforced by the halo of martyrdom placed by the intelligentsia upon the recently-executed Alexander Ulyanov at the time, and this had been naturally expanded to include his family."[220]

Vladimir enjoyed especially good relations with veterans of prison and hard labour: he listened to their stories of the *narodniki* and *Narodnaya Volya* members, of methods of revolutionary struggle and maintaining secrecy, and of trials and prison conditions. If they began to grumble about "young Marxists", accusing them of artificially implanting a "European doctrine" on Russian soil, Ulyanov would state his case while remaining careful not to insult the 'old hands'.

It was easy to have some sympathy for them: it was at this time that the moral authority of the *narodnik* cause was being severely tested.

Native Samaran Matvei Semenov, a former student of the Petrovsky Agricultural Academy and someone who already had experience of 'going to the people', arrest and exile, wrote that by the end of the 1880s, the *narodnik* movement "no longer garnered much enthusiasm among its followers". Alexei Preobrazhensky wrote: "By this time, I had already become sufficiently frustrated by the peasantry's natural inclination towards communist ideals and, as far as my judgement stretched, maintained no illusions or preconceptions about the peasantry." Semenov's references to "a vague sense of dissatisfaction" and his view that they were, "in effect, standing at a crossroads", offer a reasonably accurate impression of the mood among radical youth.[221]

Vladimir Ilyich made contact with leading figures in Samara immediately after arriving from Alakayevka. Alexei Sklyarenko had already served a one-year sentence in Moscow's Butyrka Prison and Kresty in St

---

220   *I. S. Zilbershtein*. Molodoi Lenin v zhizni i za rabotoi. p. 227.
221   See: Vladimir Ilyich Lenin v Samare. pp. 42, 43, 161.

Petersburg. Apollon Shukht, the son of a major-general and a former pupil of the Tsarskoye Selo Gymnasium, was found to be indirectly involved in Alexander Ulyanov's case and sent to Western Siberia for three years, before being resettled in Samara subject to police monitoring. Wilhelm Buchholz, a Prussian subject and student of St Petersburg University, was expelled from the capital for taking part in student disorder in 1887.[222]

Vladimir Ulyanov could count among his acquaintances both the offspring of wealthy Samara merchants – young people drawn to Sklyarenko – and representatives of the creative professions, people who generally had no dealings at all with the "young Marxists".

However, he avoided the rowdy student gatherings (which included endless political chatter as well as dancing), as they would almost invariably descend into heavy drinking sessions. At this time, Vladimir began to exhibit a clearly defined trait which Matvei Semenov describes: "Even to a young Vladimir Ilyich, all kinds of Bohemianism and intellectual slovenliness was foreign, and in his presence, those of us in his circle would buck up our ideas, as it were... Frivolous conversation and crude jokes were impossible when he was around."[223]

Wilhelm Buchholz wrote of the group: "Since these meetings did not have any defined revolutionary intention, one could not consider them 'revolutionary circles'. It was more of a 'self-development' circle, typical of the time. The large majority of the membership had until shortly before considered themselves staunch *narodniki*. Now, they were gradually mastering a new theory which to them seemed to point the 'true way'."

Compared to the others, Vladimir was already a more 'rounded' Marxist. However, as Buchholz writes, "he gave no impression of being a comrade who wanted to assume the role of leader, or stand out in any way at all... Nor did he try to present himself as a better Marxist than others."[224]

He and his new friends began to meet semi-regularly, discussing the issues that interested them and the new books they had read. Initially, they decided to follow the "Kazan programme", which began with the study of ethics. At one meeting in spring 1890, which took place on a

---

222   See: *I. S. Zilbershtein*. Molodoi Lenin v zhizni i za rabotoi. pp. 240, 241; Vladimir Ilyich Lenin v Samare. p. 102.

223   Vladimir Ilyich Lenin v Samare. pp. 60, 101.

224   *I. S. Zilbershtein*. Molodoi Lenin v zhizni i za rabotoi. p. 243.

boat on the Samara River, Buchholz delivered a talk on "The Foundations of the Ethical Teaching of Good". A debate ensued between him and Vladimir as to whether such a thing as absolute good existed "for any circumstance in life and at any point in time", as Vladimir framed the questioned. The way in which he employed dialectics to dissect seemingly commonly-held notions left a strong impression on those present.[225]

They usually met in Sklyarenko's rented apartment. They would also go to the Strukovsky Gardens, where the Marxists had commandeered their own bench.[226] However, Sklyarenko, who they nicknamed "Doctor of Beerology", loved to drag his friends to the famous pavilion of the Zhigulyovskoye Brewery, picturesquely situated on the steep banks of the Volga. "All sorts came there, it was quite the scene: the merchant, the grain broker, the goods carrier [*kryuchnik*], the greaser [*maslenshchik*], the ferryman, the vendor, the local council employee, the carter, a gaggle of civil servants, the *raznochinets* intellectual, and your typical Samara rowdy – it was an endless kaleidoscope of people of all backgrounds..."[227]

As evening fell, fires were lit on the steps down to the river – then the boatmen, porters and mill workers would take their half-bottle of vodka, watermelon, dried fish and boil up some chowder. Matvei Semenov recalled: "Around such working folk, one could sit and strike up a conversation with any passer-by."[228]

On one occasion, Vladimir decided to join them. Recalling Vladimir Ilyich, Karl Radek writes with characteristic humour: "He got talking to one labourer, expounding his theories to him. The labourer had had a little to drink and was somewhat maudlin, and was gratified to hear the way in which Ilyich spoke of politics, exploitation and oppression. Vladimir Ilyich invited him back to his apartment to read to him the contents of some or other pamphlet. They drank some tea, Ilyich read the pamphlet to him, then went to another room for something. When he returned, the object of his propagandising was nowhere to be seen. Before he had time to consider this unexpected outcome of his going to the people, he noticed that, along with the humiliated and insulted one, his coat had also vanished."[229]

---

225   Vladimir Ilyich Lenin v Samare. pp. 63, 142.
226   See: ibid. p. 73.
227   Ibid. pp. 141-142.
228   Ibid. p. 40.
229   Rabochaya Moskva. 1924. No. 92.

On 28th October 1889, Vladimir once more wrote to Delyanov, the education minister. Again, he requested permission to sit exams as an external student of any Russian higher education institution, since he was "in urgent need of an occupation that would allow [him] to support his family": "I have had ample opportunity to witness the immense difficulty, if not impossibility, of finding employment when one has not received a specialised education."

The minister sent the request to the Department of Police and received the following reply from Durnovo, its director: "Noted as having dealings with politically unreliable persons." Annotating Ulyanov's letter with the words "a malign individual", Delyanov refused the request and at the end of December 1899, Samara police forwarded the refusal to Vladimir.[230]

At this point, Maria Alexandrovna made a desperate move. In May 1890, she travelled to St Petersburg, where she lodged at petition with the Department of Police and requested an audience with the Minister for Education. The letter she wrote to him on 17th May has been preserved: "It is agonising to watch my son as his best years fruitlessly disappear… I beg Your Excellency to release my son from the punishment that he has been under for so long, a punishment that basically forbids him, as one whose working capacity stems pre-eminently from his intellect, from seeking so much as private tuition… Such an aimless existence with nothing to occupy oneself cannot help but exert the most pernicious influence on a young person, - it will almost inevitably lead to thoughts of suicide… In other words, I am beseeching you to preserve my son's life…"

On 19th May, Delyanov proffered his resolution: "The University Commission may provide access to exams." At the end of July, permission was granted for him to sit his exams as an external student of St Petersburg University.[231]

In August 1890, Vladimir and his sister Olga travelled to St Petersburg. Olga enrolled in the higher Bestuzhev Courses, while Vladimir enquired about procedures for sitting his exams.

Sitting exams as an external student presented significant difficulties. Besides the fact that a high number of 'unreliables' featured among this cohort, their professors were concerned that their knowledge would

---

230   See: *I. S. Zilbershtein*. Molodoi Lenin v zhizni i za rabotoi. pp. 228, 229, 233.
231   See: ibid. pp. 247-249.

be too superficial. Towards externals, "professors were particularly mistrusting and prejudiced, demanding more of them and pushing them further than the regular students; moreover, externals were unfamiliar with the practices of the institution, and were expected to do considerably more work to get the same results as the regular students. Externals very rarely received good grades in exams."[232]

On 4th April 1891, having completed a preliminary written paper on criminal law and paid 20 roubles to the exam board, Vladimir Ulyanov was permitted to sit the exam on the history of Russian law. The subject of the exam: the status of *kholop* feudal bondsmen within the *Russkaya Pravda* legal code, and *kholops* of all categories during the Muscovy period. His grade: "very satisfactory", the highest mark. His public law exam took place the following day: the estates of the nobility and peasant self-governance. Again, he received the highest mark. "The exams are proving to be very easy... He is going for dinner each day..." Olga Ulyanova wrote to her relieved mother on 8th April.

His political economy and statistics exams took place on 10th April, with questions on forms of labour remuneration and the German statistician and political scientist Hermann Conring. The following week, he sat his exam on the encyclopedia of law and the history of legal philosophy; the topic – Plato's writings on law. On the 24th April, Roman legal history; the subject – laws enacted by elected rulers. In each subject, he received the highest grade, and with that the spring term came to a close.[233]

At the same time, Olga was also undergoing exams in algebra, geometry, chemistry, and physics at the Bestuzhev Courses. In free moments, the siblings would go on walks around the capital together. Spring came late that year, and they would stroll along the banks of the Neva and watch the ice drifts, discussing their plans for the summer. Olga intended to visit Alakayevka with a friend after the exams were over.

However, at the end of April, she suddenly fell ill with typhoid fever. Initially, the doctors predicted a full recovery, but typhus is a complicated beast. Vladimir immediately called for his mother in Samara. On 8th May, four years to the day since the execution of Alexander, Olga died in the arms of her mother and brother. On 10th May, "a wet and windy Petersburg day," she was laid to rest.

| 232 | Krasnaya letopis'. 1925. No. 1. pp. 139-142. |
| 233 | See: ibid. |

Zinaida Nevzorova-Krzhizhanovskaya recalled, "I gently led Olya's mother by the arm. Vladimir Ilyich supported her by the other arm... Burying Olya, a wonderful 19-year-old girl, a fine mind only just beginning to display its brilliance, and a dear friend whose death seemed such an absurdity, was unbearable. It was insufferable to see her mother as she passed silently behind the coffin. I knew of the blows that had rained down one after the other upon her splendid grey head: the passing of her husband, the terrible end of her eldest son Alexander, and now the sudden death of a daughter... It was too much for one person to take. She went along softly, in silence, as tense as a violin string, her lips pressed tightly together. And none of us said a word."[234]

Around nine years later, at one of the most dramatic junctures in his life, as his relationship with Plekhanov seemed frayed to breaking, Lenin would write: "'It is as if we are going to a funeral,' I said to myself. And indeed, we walked as if we were following a coffin, in silence, eyes lowered, laid to the very lowest degree by the absurdity, savagery and senselessness of our loss... There was a sense of disbelief (the precise sense of disbelief one experiences when the death of a loved one is still raw)... It was at times so hard that it seemed I might weep...One is brought to tears most easily at funerals when words of condolence and despair are uttered..."[235] Such words could only have been written by someone who had experienced the pain and sorrow wrought by the untimely loss of a loved one.

The new exam session began in September with a law written paper, and oral exams on criminal law and the tenets of Roman law. His third and fourth exams followed in October: civil and commercial law, alongside legal procedure. The fifth and six covered police and financial law, and church and international law followed in November. He was awarded top grades for his written and oral exams once again, and received the best marks overall of the 134 students sitting.

On 15th November 1891, the Exam Board for law at the University of St Petersburg awarded V. I. Ulyanov a first-class degree, equivalent to the earlier degree of bachelor of law.[236]

---

234   Molodaya Gvardiya. 1924. No. 2-3. pp. 33, 34.
235   V. I. Lenin. Polnoye sobraniye sochineny. Vol. 4. pp. 346-347.
236   Krasnaya letopis'. 1925. No. 1. p. 141.

FAMINE

In 1891, famine struck Russia. Although it only affected 17 provinces across the Volga and Black Earth [*Chernozem*] regions, with a population of around 30 million people, the famine was a manifestation of a deeper national crisis, comparable in severity only with defeat in the Crimean War.[237]

The wheat harvest had yielded half of what had been produced in previous years, themselves exceptionally lean ones. Given that the crop failure coincided with the complete collapse of the peasant economy, suffering as it was from lack of land, suffocating rents, excessive taxation, and redemption [*vykup*] payments, the famine was a result not only of weather conditions, but of the socio-economic processes taking place in rural Russia since 1861.

The worsening food situation, clear from the beginning of summer 1891, called for a vigorous response from the government. Instead, the bureaucracy did everything in its power to silence and downplay the suffering of the population. Interior Minister Durnovo's suggestion that the government restrict the free trade and foreign export of grain, and form with immediate effect a single government body for its purchase, had been rejected by the Council of Ministers so as not to adversely affect exporters – gentlemen landowners.[238] Alexander III himself rather bluntly stated: "*I have no starving people*, there are only those affected by a bad harvest!" It was as if the famine itself had been declared illegal. The catchphrase doing the rounds ran: "*A bad harvest is decreed by God – famine is decreed by the Tsar!*"[239]

Meanwhile, the most alarming reports were emerging from the provinces. A priest in Buzuluk County in Samara Province wrote to his diocese committee to inform them that "hunger has reached desperate

---

237   See: *N. P. Sokolov*. Golod 1891-1892 godov i obshchestvenno-politicheskaya bor'ba v Rossii. Abstract of dissertation in support of candidature for doctorate in historical sciences. Moscow State Historico-Archival Institute. Moscow, 1987. pp. 3, 10.

238   See: ibid. pp. 11-12.

239   *V. A. Obolensky*. Ocherki minuvshego. p. 197.

levels in [the] parish. By August, the population was living on the last remnants of a meagre harvest, and by the start of September were selling their livestock for a pittance to feed themselves. Since the second half of September, there has been literally nothing to eat. Exhausted by hunger, people trail from house to house begging for charity and returning to their families empty-handed: charity is no longer being offered." In Ryazan Province it was reported that "people are eating orache plants in the absence of bread, but these too have almost run out and there is almost a year to go, a terrible, hungry, and cold one. No potatoes, no cabbage, no cucumber; nothing with which to feed the cattle, no fuel, neither chaff nor straw, nowhere even to beg... The situation is hopeless... 'Better to die,' many are saying..."[240]

Only when it was beyond doubt that a catastrophe had unfolded did the export of grain abroad cease, though the whole matter of providing food aid to the starving provinces was turned over by the government to local *zemstvos*, which had neither the means nor the necessary grain reserves. It was decided to provide assistance to the starving population in two ways: to issue grain for infants and the elderly wherever possible, and to those fit to work – those between the ages of 15 and 55 – food would be issued in lieu of earnings for labour provided to a series of public works being coordinated by the governors.

However, as a result of organisational incompetence and plain embezzlement, the projects to which the treasury had allocated ten million roubles were unsuccessful: less than a third of the funds assigned to the peasantry as wages reached them, the rest having been pilfered by state officials and contractors.[241]

The issuing of food grants ended equally lamentably. According to preliminary estimates, 300 million roubles were required to fund serious famine relief efforts. The government assigned 48 million roubles, but had only released 20 million before winter set in. Similarly, the *zemstvos* did not always dispose of their grants in the best interests of the peasantry. On receiving the grants, artful *zemstvo* members would hand over food supply procurements to grain-trading speculators. Even in April 1892, when grant provision was at its peak, this were reaching a mere 11.8

---

240   G. V. Plekhanov. Sochineniya. Vol. 3. pp. 314-315.
241   N. P. Sokolov. Golod 1891-1892 godov i obshchestvenno-politicheskaya bor'ba v Rossii. p. 12.

million people, approximately a third of those affected.[242] Mortality in all affected provinces rose to an average of 28% in 1891-1892, reaching as high as 56% in Samara Province.[243] Even graver outcomes were avoided thanks to the import of flour, with shipments beginning to arrive in the province from the United States in spring 1892, and the financial assistance offered by English Quakers brought to Samara by Count P. A. Geiden and Princes Pyotr and Pavel Dolgorukov.[244]

None of this in any way dissuaded tender-hearted *zemstvo* officials from rewarding each other handsomely for their efforts. Plekhanov writes: "The grants, trimmed down to a few ounces per person; the flour, unfit for consumption; the furs, carriages, decorations, pensions and loans the *zemstvo* officials handed out to one another – it was all the most callous, shameless mockery of the starving, combined with the most unabashed predation."[245]

It was clear the bureaucratic apparatus was unable to deal effectively with the food crisis. Moreover, the activities of governmental and *zemstvo* food agencies – given the scale of corruption – reeked to high heaven. As a result, from summer 1891, civil society began to develop responses separate from and almost counter to 'official' aid channels.

These were begun by Lev Tolstoy, who – in spite of his opposition to charity – created free soup kitchens for the hungry in Tula Province. Initially, the government was strongly opposed to such public initiatives, this opposition encouraged by the most reactionary elements of the nobility. Even the renowned lyric poet Afanasy Fet stated that peasants required no charity, since "their only banes are laziness and their tendency for drunkenness". But as public aid became more widespread despite official resistance, Alexander III published a rescript in the name of his son and heir on 17th November 1891. Therein, he publicly admitted the "failure of the wheat harvest" and established a "Special Committee", headed by the future Tsar Nicholas II, but guided primarily by regional governors,[246] to manage all matters concerning public welfare. However, such committees

---

242 See: ibid.
243 See: ibid. p. 13.
244 See: *V. A. Obolensky*. Ocherki minuvshego. p. 209.
245 *G. V. Plekhanov*. Sochineniya. Vol. 3. pp. 331.
246 See: *G. V. Plekhanov*. Sochineniya. Vol. 3. pp. 324, 337; *N. P. Sokolov*. Golod 1891-1892 godov i obshchestvenno-politicheskaya bor'ba v Rossii. p. 14.

were often formed not to provide aid to the hungry, but to guarantee "reasonably-priced" food for those peasants engaged in the excavation works that had been orchestrated by the governors.

By this time, the relationship between liberal *narodniki* and Marxists was strained to breaking, not only as a result of the discordance between the tenets of *narodnik* populism and Plekhanov's Emancipation of Labour group, but in the Russian provinces as well. When, as during the famine, these disagreements moved into a real-world footing, this mutual antagonism began to take on more drastic forms.

Pretexts for the developing conflict were given by a group of exiled Orenburg students identifying as Marxists – they had been outspoken in their criticism of youth activists who had gone to starving rural areas "to feed the peasantry", since, in their view, doing so would "obstruct the development of capitalism". Meanwhile, the June 1892 edition of *Russkaya Mysl* featured an article by Nikolai Mikhailovsky which accused Marxists of preaching the *need* for "separating the producers" (the peasantry) from their "means of production" (the land). Sergey Krivenko claimed in one of his own articles that all that was required to achieve the Marxist 'ideal' was "to open the taverns" everywhere as they were more capable than anything else of proletarianising the rustics. And while philosophical and theoretical arguments had failed to capture the imagination of the public, now the talk across Russia was that Marxists "had *no love* for the simple peasant" and "*rejoiced* in the ruin of the rural way of life".[247]

The Marxist position at the beginning of 1892 was outlined by Georgi Plekhanov in his essays "The All-Russian Ruin" and "On the Tasks of Socialists in the Struggle against Famine". As he wrote, it was unfair to judge the young volunteers who believed it was possible to "empty the deep, boundless sea of the people's suffering with a teaspoon". "These people are fearlessly performing their duty as they see it. Are we going to fall in behind them?" No! Socialists must push on and direct their efforts towards fighting the causes of the calamities the people endured.[248]

If the government and bourgeoisie had bread and money for a system of charity that merely created the illusion of assistance, then socialists only had their *word*. They were unable to feed the starving, but they were in a position to denounce government policy, and expose kleptocratic officials

---

247 Vladimir Ilyich Lenin v Samare. p. 171.

248 See: *G. V. Plekhanov*. Sochineniya. Vol. 3. pp. 359.

and the swindlers who fed off human misery. Socialists were obliged to further the *development of class consciousness* among the working masses and the peasantry and facilitate the correct understanding of the causes of the current famine, so that the people would be in a position to "wrest their fate from the hands of tsarist officials", win their political rights, and above all else, gain universal direct suffrage. Only a *zemsky sobor* [the peasant term for a country-wide elected assembly – *trans*.] convened under such conditions was capable of forming a government able to satisfy the people's need and "give the Russian farmer the opportunity to sow *bread*, and not *famine*." It was with this aim that the social democrats would seek "*the complete expropriation of major landowners* and the conversion of land *into public ownership*." If the peasantry chose to divide it among their communities - "I see no harm in that". Russia, Plekhanov concluded, "will save herself by way of revolution".[249]

Plekhanov's rallying cry was heard by Vladimir Ulyanov and his friends in Samara, where he would later write a significant portion of his work "What the 'Friends of the People' Are and How They Fight the Social Democrats". In it, Ulyanov would defend the need to protect the interests of the peasantry, writing, "Social democrats will demand in the most vigorous terms the immediate return of land taken from the peasantry and the complete expropriation of landowners' estates – those strongholds of feudal institutions and traditions." The nationalisation of the land that Plekhanov referred to would, in Ulyanov's view, create the democratic grounding for the elimination of peasant disenfranchisement and oppression by landowners and officials.[250]

---

249   Ibid. pp. 415, 420, 422, 423.
250   See: *V. I. Lenin*. Polnoye sobraniye sochineny. Vol. 1. p. 295.

SELF-DETERMINATION

Many years later, in spring 1920, completing a questionnaire on when precisely he embarked on revolutionary activity, Lenin would write, "1892-93... Samara... Illegal group of the s-d [social democrats]..."[251]

This was not because that year marked the completion of his conversion to Marxism, but because political passions aroused by the events surrounding the famine of 1891-1892 had forced the young Marxists to break cleanly from the rest of the Samara intelligentsia.

They knew now who their enemies were: firstly, it was the well-fed liberal establishment who, when not carving out careers for themselves, were ostentatiously demonstrating their "love for the people", a fashion that had carried over from previous years as a signifier of good taste. Alexei Belyakov recalled that, despite the innumerable masses of poor and the daily newspaper reports of horror in the starving regions, liberal society continued in the usual routine "observed in Samara before the days of famine. Balls, concerts, and dance evenings went on as usual," with the only concession being that they were now laid on "for the benefit of the starving".[252]

It was such caustic observations of Samara life, alongside absurd accusations of the Marxists' desire to "ruin the peasant", that forced Vladimir Ulyanov and his colleagues to state their position publicly.

This was no easy task. As Lenin wrote, many of those who embarked on the path of revolutionary struggle in the 1880s "had begun to consider revolution as members of *Narodnaya Volya*. Almost everyone in their early youth worshipped these heroes of terror."[253] The beginning of the 1890s was, as Anna Ulyanova-Yelizarova recalled, "a time when Mikhailovsky, V. V. [Vasily Vorontsov] and other *narodniki* enjoyed great authority, when the glow from *Narodnaya Volya* still burned brightly and the light of the

---

251   Ibid. Vol. 43. p. 417.
252   Vladimir Ilyich Lenin v Samare. p. 133.
253   *V. I. Lenin*. Polnoye sobraniye sochineny. Vol. 6. p. 180.

social democrat message was only just sparking into life – especially in particularly agricultural provinces such as the Volga region – while the young people who carried this message were viewed as overly bumptious youths. With Samara being the first staging post on the return journey from Siberia, the former exiles – those being monitored or their close relations – that made up progressive provincial society at that time chose either to dismiss the views of such boys, or come down on them hard."[254]

Harsh words did not frighten Ulyanov and his friends in the least. They were types who were, so to speak, never short of a comeback. Vladimir Ulyanov, Alexei Sklyarenko and their contemporary Isaak Khristoforovich Lalayants, exiled from Kazan to Samara in 1893 and immediately bestowed with the nickname "Columbus" due to his patronymic, never turned down an opportunity to cross polemical swords with any opponent, whatever their standing.

Lalayants recalled, "Soon people in the city would refer to us exclusively as a trio, adding to that some epithet or another depending on how the speaker considered us 'ideologically'. Our trio ... was extremely tight-knit and we always appeared and 'performed' together."[255]

The general tone of the discussions Ulyanov conducted could vary greatly. As Matvei Semenov recalled, "There were sharp distinctions in the way he spoke to people: with those comrades he considered like-minded, he argued gently, joking good-naturedly, and would try all sorts of ways to show them their error and make it clear to them. But as soon as he spotted that his opponent was of another persuasion, an unapologetic and obstinate *narodnik*, for example, his polemical fire became merciless. He attacked his enemy at his weakest points and held little back in the phrasing he employed."[256]

No-one was spared in the heat of debate. As one Samara native remarked, when the youth grow tired of those venerable intellects whose ideas dominate, they have no hesitation in "consigning the old gods to the dump" with a characteristically youthful single-mindedness.[257]

---

254 Stary tovarishch Alexei Pavlovich Sklyarenko (1870-1916). Collection of essays. Moscow, 1922. pp. 21-22.
255 Proletarskaya revolyutsiya. 1929. No. 1. p. 45.
256 Vladimir Ilyich Lenin v Samare. p. 62.
257 Ibid. p. 97.

This jarred with the 'veterans' and Vladimir "made no apologies for biting attacks on such recognised pillars of public opinion as Mikhailovsky, V. V., Kareyev and others... The more established strata of progressive society looked on him as an extremely capable but overly arrogant and scathing young man. Only in youth circles, among future social democrats, did he enjoy unfettered respect."[258]

"In a general organisational sense," wrote Isaak Lalayants, "we did not present ourselves as any kind of *circle*; we did not arrange regular fixed gatherings of this 'circle', and no regular activities were conducted by Vladimir Ulyanov or any of the rest of us in it. It was simply a small group of very close, like-minded friends who came together in the sea of dissident intelligentsia that surrounded us."

As before, they would meet at Ulyanov's home, or more commonly at Sklyarenko's, and as Lalayants recalled, at times "we simply went somewhere out of the city, to the Annayevskoye Kumis-Cure Institute, for example, or straight to the ferry docks on the banks of the Volga, where we were able to discuss the subjects of interest to us over a tankard of Zhigulovskoye beer in a relatively tidy and comfortable corner of some modest dockside tavern...

While generally in agreement with each other over the... [main – *author*] issues, we occasionally disagreed in our understanding of some or other of the finer points, giving rise to fierce disputes from time to time, until through detailed dissection of a subject we would come to complete unanimity..."[259]

Of course, meetings conducted over a glass of beer were not the friends' main activities. Arguing over whether social democrats "loved" the common man or not also produced little of worth. Thinking radicals among the youth of the day were far more interested in the debate that raged over Russia's paths of development, an argument Georgi Plekhanov had evolved from the writings of V. V. and Nikolai-on [Nikolai Danielson]. Delving into this debate required a thorough mastery of the regional statistical data upon which *narodnik* theorists had based their conclusions both on the unique nature of peasant society and on the futility of seeking a capitalist approach to Russia's development. Hence, the response had to be to employ the same weapons: facts and figures, not affirmations of "love for the peasant". The result was a craze for statistics among young Marxists.

---

258   Ibid. p. 8.

259   Proletarskaya revolyutsiya. 1929. No. 1. pp. 47-49.

In addition to the *zemstvo* data, which Vladimir Ulyanov was able to gather from libraries, he began to call in on I. M. Krasnoperov, head of the statistical bureau of the provincial *zemstvo* authority [*zemskaya uprava*] and publisher of its reports on the status of the rural economy of Samara Province. Alexei Sklyarenko got a position as a *zemstvo* clerk, allowing him to conduct surveys on behalf of *volost* administrations, travel to villages to attend hearings, and receive those who had come to the city to submit petitions and complaints.[260]

However, the more Vladimir Ulyanov immersed himself in the data, the more confounded he became by the limited information contained in the *zemstvo* reports. The artificial division of particular elements of the peasant economy, while offering interesting material for analysis, hindered opportunity for an overarching political and economic investigation of the processes taking place in the Russian countryside.

Then, some time at the beginning of 1893, Vladimir came across a sizeable monograph titled *The Southern Russian Peasant Economy* by V. Y. Postnikov, published in Moscow in late 1891, in the so-called "Samara schoolboys' library".[261] Despite the seemingly tedious nature of the subject matter, the book made a great impression on Vladimir, and he would later describe the work in reverential terms as "one of the most remarkable phenomena in our economic literature of recent years..."[262]

Working as an official administering state-owned land in Taurida Province, Postnikov had painstakingly gathered and processed a range of data for a number of counties in Taurida, Kherson and Yekaterinoslav Provinces, offering the fullest picture of the progressive disintegration of the traditional village community or commune [believed by *narodniki* to be a primitive form of peasant communism – *ed.*]. In its place, the Russian peasant village was becoming increasingly stratified.

He divided the population of the peasant community into three groupings according to degrees of self-sufficiency and means of agricultural production.

The first group were well-off peasant families. They made up around 20% of the inhabitants of the countryside. The second group were medium-scale farmers, making up around 40% of the rural

---

260   See: Vladimir Ilyich Lenin v Samare. pp. 44, 74.
261   See: ibid. p. 50.
262   *V. I. Lenin*. Polnoye sobraniye sochineny. Vol. 1. p. 5.

community. The third group were poor peasants – around 40% of the rural population.

The main source of income for this third category was through the sale of their labour, which they offered to the large farm enterprises of the first group, who were unable to manage the land on their own. The situation for those medium-scale farmers of the second group was precarious and unstable, since they were only capable of sowing enough – that is, the very minimum – to fulfil the modest requirements of their family and cattle.

Postnikov did not limit his book to ascertaining wealth disparity among peasants. By analysing the relationship between the rural poor and their rich masters, he concluded that the "bitter struggle" was not one of "community traditions and the growth of individualism in rural life, but a simple struggle of economic interests, which can only end disastrously for one section of the population, due to the current shortage of land," inasmuch as "all that is ineffectual in an economic sense must be cast out of peasant agriculture one way or another sooner or later".[263]

The same idea was echoed in the October 1890 edition of the respected journal *Vestnik Evropy*: "In many places, a new kind of serfdom has been established. It is not the landowners who rule, but the tavern owners, the kulaks and bloodsuckers, the coarse, semi-literate vultures who reduce the people to ruin with a ruthless consistency."[264]

N. Valentinov believed that Postnikov's book had a great influence on Vladimir Ulyanov: "'I leapt with joy,' wrote Herzen upon discovering Feuerbach. Perhaps Ulyanov had a similar response upon reading Postnikov. Eureka! He had found what he was searching for, the perfect complement to Marx and Plekhanov, despite Postnikov having nothing to do with Marxism."[265]

While preparing a detailed summary of Postnikov's book for the Samara-based social democrats, Ulyanov translated its most impressive numerical data into the language of political and economic analysis. Hence, the quantitative differences between the peasant strata became qualitatively voiced, revealing the commercialisation of agriculture and the further deepening of disparity within the community as capitalist exchange took hold.

---

263   V. Y. Postnikov. Yuzhno-russkoye krestyanskoye khozyaistvo. Moscow, 1891. p. XXXII, 368.

264   G. V. Plekhanov. Sochineniya. Vol. 3. p. 347.

265   N. Valentinov. Nedorisovanny portret... p. 472.

In 1892, opposing attempts by the *narodniki* to introduce ethical categories to the analysis of socio-economic relations ("worthy of sympathy – unworthy of sympathy", "liked – disliked") Georgi Plekhanov wrote: "The scientific study of social phenomena requires a great deal of composure and, where possible, even a cold dispassion. But this can only serve to create a solid grounding for the passionate actions of a selfless political fighter..." In other words, the logic of investigation was not to be ancillary to emotions; instead, emotions were to be governed by the precepts of logic.[266]

Ulyanov fully agreed that it was necessary to establish only those objectives that were grounded in reality and abandon any wishful thinking. "The first duty of those who wish to seek 'the path to human happiness,'" he wrote, "is not to undermine oneself, but to have the courage openly to acknowledge the actuality of things."[267] Vladimir valued Postnikov's book primarily for the view of reality it presented, which was not an imagined picture of Russian rural life. Nonetheless, he was wholly unable to suppress an emotional response and remain a cold pragmatist.

A number of Russian and foreign biographers have somewhat clumsily attempted to lay bear the 'Lenin phenomenon' by identifying the one text responsible for forging his system of beliefs. It is a simple enough narrative: he works through Chernyshevsky, moves on to Nechayev and Tkachev, is captivated by what he discovers there, and draws inspiration from their views on the objectives and means of struggle and, more broadly, the purpose of life.

Nowadays, such examples – individuals inspired by a single text – are not countenanced: one could spend one's entire life reading dull pamphlets on 'scientific communism' and suddenly come across Hayek, see a new world open up, and immediately become an ardent liberal. While such a scenario is certainly possible, it is also likely that, in time, such an individual would eventually find a second, third or fourth such life-changing text.

This simple narrative does not hold water as far as the young Ulyanov is concerned, since we know not only his range of reading, but also the spectrum of society with whom he interacted. He was taken neither by Nechayev nor Tkachev. He certainly was by Chernyshevsky and Marx. Evidently, at least two conclusions should be drawn in this regard: firstly,

---

266   See: *G. V. Plekhanov*. Sochineniya. Vol. 3. p. 360.

267   *V. I. Lenin*. Polnoye sobraniye sochineny. Vol. 1. p. 403.

that his system of beliefs was formed over a relatively extended period, and secondly, that this process was not defined by the books he read alone.

Vladimir Ulyanov, despite his youth, was a worldly young man whose understanding of the problems of the Russian rural experience was not solely based on literary sources and statistical directories. As a child in Kokushkino, he would hear the grievances and complaints about lack of land, excessive taxes and unscrupulous levies in the languid tales of Karpei the hunter, the simple yarns of the carters Roman and Uncle Yefim, and in everyday conversations with the local peasant children with whom he played jacks and tended the cattle. In Alakayevka, village talk revolved around the same issues. Now, alongside feelings of sympathy and compassion, it aroused in Vladimir a deep interest in the study of the peasant economy and way of life.

His sister Anna recalled: "Vladimir Ilyich garnered a great deal from the direct contact he enjoyed with peasants in Alakayevka, where he spent three to four months a year for five summers... Having grown familiar with the general state of the peasantry through speaking with peasants, Ilyich made efforts to learn still more from them, rather than do much talking himself – he did not go about expressing his own beliefs, at any rate."[268]

At Sharnel farm, Vladimir Ulyanov made the acquaintance of some peasant 'troublemakers' who were being persecuted by the authorities as sectarian dissenters for framing their protest in clever arguments about how to "live in God". Moving them away from religious issues to more worldly problems was not easy, given that their main concern was "how to contrive a simple faith, free from deceit, that could bring together all people as one family?" But as Ulyanov was a patient listener and it was clear he posed no threat, they also opened up about the 'secular', and the conversation evolved towards more general interests and enjoyments.[269]

12 years later, Ulyanov would have grounds to recall these conversations.

In 1905, the nationwide peasant movement put forward a seemingly strange slogan - "God's land!" How the liberal press railed against such ignorance and savage country superstition! But they had missed the point – the real meaning behind the slogan was clear to any peasant: if the land was God's, then it could not remain the property of landowners

---

268   Vladimir Ilyich Lenin v Samare. p. 10.

269   See: ibid. pp. 102, 112, 113, 162, 163.

and must be returned to the people. "The land belongs to God," said the peasantry, "and we are the tenants of God."

It is consequently no wonder that Ulyanov was fond of repeating Marx's view that the peasant possessed both superstition and sense, and those Samara 'peasant troublemakers' had helped him to see the truth in this.

Conversations with rural 'parasites' also provided interesting food for thought. In May 1890, during one of his boat trips along the Volga, Vladimir spoke to a local merchant, one P. Nechayev, in the village of Yekaterinovka. Nechayev was convinced that the impoverishment of the bulk of the Russian peasantry had not descended from the heavens or been ordained by God, but was the result of "human stupidity and life itself". When Ulyanov's *narodnik* travelling companions objected, citing the positive influence of the peasant commune system and cooperatives, Nechayev merely roared with laughter: communes were good only for chasing arrears – a boon of collective responsibility – and for carousing, provided it didn't end in a punch-up. "For serious work, for the economy, they're good for nothing."[270]

Anna Ulyanova-Yelizarova recalled another incident: "He got most of his material from the stories of Mark Timofeyevich Yelizarov, who came from peasant stock in Samara Province and maintained close connections with those from his village. He also met Mark's older brother, Pavel Yelizarov, a so-called 'wealthy' peasant [*kulak*] who had grown rich by renting imperial lands and re-leasing it to peasants. The most popular figure in the village, he was elected onto the local council. Like the rest of his ilk, he strove to accumulate capital and get in with the merchants, which he eventually did. I remember my surprise at how long and with what enthusiasm Vladimir was able to talk with this semi-literate kulak to whom principles were alien, and it was only later that I understood that he was using him to obtain information about the condition of the peasantry, about the divisions among them, and about the views and aspirations of the economic elite of the village. As ever, he laughed infectiously at the stories of the merchant, who was thrilled with the attention he was receiving and greatly impressed by Vladimir Ilyich's intellect. But what he did not grasp was that often Vladimir was not laughing at how cannily the village merchants were conducting business,

---

270   Ibid. pp. 103, 104.

but at the *narodniki* and their naïve faith in the solidity of the peasant way of life and commune system."

Anna Ulyanova-Yelizarova's reflections on this incident are noteworthy: "During these conversations, what manifested itself was Ilyich's characteristic ability to speak to any audience and to elicit from each person that which he required; and his ability to stay grounded, to remain unencumbered by theory, and to look soberly at life around him and tune in to its resonance."[271]

This "resonance of life" had, along with the scent of new-mown hay and fresh milk, remained with him from childhood, and alloyed by the academic knowledge he had garnered, precluded Vladimir Ulyanov from indifference to the ruin of millions of Russian peasants. His mind strove to find a way to solve problems using means which were as painless as they were beneficial to the peasant worker.

The experience of European countries offered enough evidence that a striking disparity among rural populations in certain historical circumstances was inevitable. It was to this experience that, generally speaking, Marxists looked. However, there were alternative experiences. In his search for a way to, as Plekhanov stated, "prevent the expropriation of the peasantry as anticipated by Engels," Ulyanov looked to the American experience, where free farming on open land provided a different solution to the problem of capitalist development in agriculture.

In his early works, written while still in Samara, Ulyanov formulates the idea of the expropriation of the landed estates and the nationalisation of land, measures which would provide the democratic groundwork for "*agrarian relationships*" to prosper and an improvement in the welfare of the general population.[272]

Another fundamental conclusion that Ulyanov drew in his works was that Marxist theory "only provides general *guiding* principles which will *in their detail* apply differently to England than to France, to France differently than to Germany, and to Germany differently than to Russia".[273]

---

271 Ibid. p. 9.

272 V. I. Lenin. Polnoye sobraniye sochineny. Vol. 1. pp. 299, 300.

273 Ibid. Vol. 4. p. 184.

WARD NO. 6

As far as the provincial gendarmerie were concerned, any educated person was obliged, in accordance with the Table of Ranks, to be on record as belonging to either the military or civilian categories of service. As such, the Russian intelligentsia, in order not to attract suspicion, always strove to combine the most disruptive social activism with service to the state. After gaining his degree, Vladimir Ulyanov faced the same issue.

On 4th January 1892, the attorney Andrei Nikolayevich Khardin filed a request with the Samara district court, stating, "Vladimir Ilyich Ulyanov ... has stated his desire to act as my assistant attorney," and consequently, he – Khardin – requested Ulyanov be recognised as such. The request was granted on 30th January, but as he was missing a character reference, certification of his right to practise was delayed until July. Nonetheless, Ulyanov began work on 1st March,[274] and his mother made him a gift for the occasion.

Having worked his way up the ranks, Ilya Nikolayevich had had a dress coat made for formal visits requiring such attire. Such trips were few and far between, and after his death this virtually brand-new coat was left hanging in the wardrobe. It was now dusted off and tried on and, having been a little too large for Ilya, turned out to be a perfect fit for Vladimir. Now, during appearances at the district court, he would go adorned each time in this unfamiliar new garb.[275]

His first defence case, heard on 5th March 1892, was that of the peasant Vasily Mulenkov, charged with "blasphemy" under Article 180 of the Penal Code. According to Article 180, "words blasphemous in nature, or which denigrate the saints of the Lord, or which censure the faith or the Orthodox church," even if uttered "with no intent to offend sanctity, but merely as a result of misguidance, ignorance, or drunkenness", were invariably and

---

274 See: *I. S. Zilbershtein*. Molodoi Lenin v zhizni i za rabotoi. pp. 283, 285, 291.
275 See: Proletarskaya revolyutsiya. 1924. No. 3. p. 107.

without exception to be punished by prison. Ulyanov succeeded in having the sentence reduced.

On 11th March, Ulyanov represented Mikhail Oparin and Timofei Sakharov, peasants from the village of Berezovy Gai, charged with breaking into the coffers of a wealthy local man by the name of Murzin after being caught in the act. Their guilt was beyond doubt, but once again, their lawyer managed to have the punishment mitigated.

On 16th April, the case was heard of the peasants Ilya Uzhdin, Kuzma Zaitsev and Ignat Krasilnikov, farmhands in the village of Tomashev Kolok. They had attempted to steal bread from the granary of the kulak Kopyakov and were apprehended at the scene of the crime.

On 5th June, the peasant M. S. Bambukov appeared before the court; on 9th June, it was the turn of peasants P. G. Chinov, F. I. Kukleyev and S. Y. Lavrov.

Case followed case. Ulyanov successfully gained an acquittal on three counts of petty theft for a desperately impoverished peasant, and succeeded in having the 13-year-old farm worker Stepan Repin released from prison and acquitted. Of 18 cases in which Ulyanov provided representation, he was successful in almost every one – either beating the prosecution's indictment, or reducing the scale of punishment demanded by the prosecution.[276]

There were occasions when Ulyanov refused to take a case. Faina Wetzel recollects him refusing to defend the interests of a wealthy grain trader, Fyodor Krasikov, who was brazenly cheating peasants.

"We'd be raking in money with a shovel!" senior advocate Yashchenko implored his young colleague.

"I have no desire to defend a blatant thief," Ulyanov replied sharply, flatly refusing to "accept stolen money for representation".[277]

There was one instance when he refused to defend a client as the court was already in session. On 15th September 1892, the case was heard of the Samara tradesman Gusev, on trial for beating his wife with a whip. When, after hearing the powerful testimony of his wife, Gusev's guilt was proven beyond doubt, Ulyanov refused to make a plea for leniency.

---

276 See: *V. K. Shalaginov*. Zashchita poruchena Ulyanovu. Novosibirsk, 1970. pp. 253-263; *A. Y. Arosev*. Materialy k biografii V. I. Lenina. Moscow, 1925. pp. 24-26.

277 *I. B. Sternik*. V. I. Lenin – yurist. Tashkent, 1969. p. 84.

On 19th September of the same year, he succeeded in having one case dismissed altogether. The trial was under way of a peasant from the village of Svetlovka, Filipp Laptev, who had been accused of disobeying and insulting his father. The punishment was potentially fairly severe, but under the pretext of calling an additional witness, the hearing was delayed and Ulyanov was able to reconcile father and son: the son made a formal pledge that he was committed to obeying his father, and the trial was discontinued.

Such incidents from his time in legal practice stayed with Vladimir Ulyanov. In *Casual Notes*, written in winter 1901, he presents a picture of the courtroom as it was:

"There is the village elder – I'm thinking here of the provincial court – ill at ease in his simple country attire, not knowing what to do with his pitch-stained boots and peasant hands, timidly raising his eyes to His Excellency, the chairman of the chamber, sitting at the same table. Here is the town mayor, a rotund merchant, breathing heavily in his awkward dress uniform and chain round his neck, trying to follow the lead of the man beside him, the head of the nobility, a groomed gentleman of aristocratic sensibilities in courtly garb. Next, the judges, those who had passed through the full bureaucratic gamut, true *dyaks*, greyed by service… How could such an atmosphere fail to dispel the desire to speak in even the most eloquent of lawyers, and not remind him of the old adage, 'Do not cast your pearls before…'?"[278]

In April 1893, he turned 23, and Vladimir was growing increasingly troubled by the thought that time was marching on, and this was far from his best use of it. Khardin, who was closely monitoring the work of his assistant, believed that with time Ulyanov would develop into an outstanding civil lawyer. In the meantime, he confined him to petty criminal cases to gain both judicial and life experience.

Of course, perhaps he could expect more serious and high-profile cases in a year or two. And were he content to observe the run-of-the-mill vagaries of life, even minor cases would offer a wealth of material on the ways of a provincial town. But for an individual establishing himself as a social and political activist, this would not suffice: another 'year or two' of the judicial routine could well drive him mad.

His situation brings to mind the conversation between Olga and Irina in Anton Chekhov's *Three Sisters*:

---

278   *V. I. Lenin*. Polnoye sobraniye sochineny. Vol. 4. p. 409.

"My head aches constantly and I catch myself thinking like an old person. It is really as if, over these four years of service in the gymnasium, my youth and vigour have been seeping from me in drops with each passing day. There is only one dream that grows and deepens…"

"Going to Moscow. Selling the house, settling matters here and then back to Moscow."

"Yes, to Moscow, and with haste."

Even better, Ulyanov would have added, to Petersburg.

Perhaps his were merely literary reminiscences. Far from it… "From the distant provinces," wrote Vera Zasulich in her memoirs, "Petersburg seemed a laboratory of ideas, a centre for life, of action and activity, and those youth who wished to devote themselves to revolution, or as Chernyshevsky put it, to devote themselves to 'deed'… rushed [there]…"[279]

It was at this time that St Petersburg was emerging as the centre of a nascent mass proletarian movement which, according to the firm conviction of the Marxists, would be the one to liberate Russia. In early 1891, during a shipbuilders' strike at the New Admiralty plant, M. I. Brusnev's social democrat group, who enjoyed relatively extensive ties with workers in the capital, established a relationship with the strikers. Vladimir was still in Samara at that point, but by the time the writer and Sixtier Nikolai Vasilyevich Shelgunov died on 12th April, Ulyanov had already arrived in St Petersburg.

Shelgunov's articles on workers' issues were greatly influential at the time, and his funeral was transformed into a political demonstration. Students predominated, but gymnasium pupils and apprentices from the technical schools were also in attendance, along with public figures such as Nikolai Mikhailovsky. However, most unexpected was the appearance of dozens of workers. Among the multitude of wreaths was their metal one decorated with dark green oak leaves and a ribbon with the inscription: "To the one who showed the way to freedom and brotherhood." After the reactionary 1880s, this was effectively the first public political protest.

Despite the funeral having been authorised, police blocked the procession, forcing demonstrators off the main streets and clearing the wreaths. Police informants lurked in the crowd. Nonetheless, the workers refused to hand over their wreath and at the gates of Volkovo Cemetery

---

279   *N. Valentinov*. Nedorisovanny portret… p. 471.

it was taken by the gymnasium pupils, among them the lean, bespectacled Yuliy Tsederbaum: "I peered eagerly at the faces of the workers, studying these unfathomable representatives of the true people. Every one seemed impressive to me, particularly their 'leaders', both the older and younger."[280]

Two weeks later, on 1st May 1891, the first May Day in Russia took place in the Nevskaya Zastava district. Police were unable to disperse the crowd, and the speeches made there by workers Nikolai Bogdanov, Fyodor Afanasyev and Yegor Klimanov were copied by hectograph and widely shared among democrat supporters.

A few years later, Vladimir Ulyanov would become acquainted with many of the students and workers who took part in Shelgunov's funeral and that first May Day, including Yuliy Tsederbaum, who became more widely known under the pseudonym L. Martov. However, in April 1891, Vladimir was preparing for his latest exam, pouring over dense textbooks on the philosophy of law. On 1st May, he was in Alexandrovskaya Hospital, sitting at the bedside of his dying sister Olga.

No-one could reproach him for this – he was where he should be. Nonetheless, he was evidently aware that something significant – truly historic – was taking place so close by and he was not a part of it.

Why, then, did he not remain in St Petersburg in 1891 after passing his exams, instead returning to Samara and remaining there for another year and a half? Anna Ulyanova-Yelizarova writes: "I can answer that question: he stayed for his mother."

The grief from the loss of her eldest son was overwhelming, but she did not let it overwhelm her – she summoned enough inner strength, masking her tears and anguish as best she could, to be there for her children more than ever before. After the death of her husband it was left to her alone to care for them. In the year Vladimir graduated from university, the family had been struck by another tragedy: the death of his sister Olga from typhoid fever. Vladimir was the only one who was there for his mother at her most difficult time, and it was he that brought her home to Samara. He saw the courage she displayed in the midst of this latest blow – but despite her efforts to overcome her grief, his mother naturally suffered greatly. The only thing that alleviated her sorrow was the proximity of her remaining children to her. Vladimir remained at home in Samara for another year.[281]

---

280   Y. Martov. Zapiski sotsial-demokrata. Moscow, 1924. p. 63.
281   A. I. Ulyanova-Yelizarova. O V. I. Lenine i sem'ye Ulyanovykh. p. 128.

Once more, the days dragged on, as court sessions, visits to Khardin and, less frequently, to other colleagues, alternated with youth gatherings and his study of Marxist and other literature.

However, as Anna Ulyanova-Yelizarova wrote of her brother, "Samara could not provide scope for his activities, and gave too little sustenance to his intellect. He had already consumed as much of the theoretical study of Marxism as was available to him in Samara. He had begun to apply Marx's methods to an examination of the Russian experience... And he had already plundered Samara's city library – a good library by provincial standards – of everything of consequence."

In other words, his period of 'self-development' had come to an end. The three friends, Sklyarenko, Lalayants and Ulyanov, now fully identified as Marxists and social democrats. Now they were eager to act, but there was nothing for them to throw their efforts into in Samara at that time.

Vladimir made attempts to expand his circle of contacts. He corresponded with Fedoseyev, sending his detailed analysis of Nikolai-on's *Essays on Our Post-Reform Social Economy*, published at the start of 1893, to him in Vladimir Prison. He sent Pyotr Maslov, at that time in a settlement in the Uisky district of the Urals, a thorough analysis of the works of V. V. on the development of capitalism in Russia. But the friends' main efforts were concentrated on gaining a foothold in the press.

Vasily Vodovozov had, thanks to his connections, managed to have an article titled "Public works in Samara", which dealt with corruption within the regional administration during the famine, published in the St Petersburg-based *Yuridichesky Vestnik* No. 3 for 1892. For provincial Samara, this was something of a coup.

In 1893, Sklyarenko made advances with an article that appeared in the *Samarsky Vestnik* on the influence of the famine on the stratification of the peasantry, utilising data on the distribution of cattle among households. However, when Alexei Preobrazhensky offered the same paper a similar article on the desperate plight of the peasantry, he was turned down. The manuscript was left annotated with the censor's hand: "We have God!" "We have the Tsar!" "We have the Motherland!" Vladimir advised Alexei to send the article to the capital, to one of the large-volume journals, but the censors had learned to spot seditiousness behind columns of dry numbers.[282]

---

282   See: Vladimir Ilyich Lenin v Samare. pp. 57, 75, 161.

In December 1892, the relatively moderate *Yuridichesky Vestnik* was closed down for publishing a similar column by Pavel Skvortsov. Editors were on their guard. V. M. Lavrov, editor of *Russkaya Mysl*, wrote to Anton Chekhov, "Now, when the censor pricks up his ears and flashes his adder eyes at us, his basilisk's stare, I fear whatever knavery might follow."[283] Consequently, when Vladimir Ulyanov sent his article on Postnikov's book to *Russkaya Mysl*, he received a polite rejection.[284]

This offered little encouragement and, as Lalayants writes, from early 1893 Vladimir began to completely eschew "the wider public, in particular the young intelligentsia," with their endless bickering over wording, their dances, and their drinking sessions.[285] It was at this time that Sklyarenko and Lalayants first began to call Lenin "the old man" [*starik*].[286]

When one ruminates on the changing mindset of one's subject and no clear conclusions come to mind, their reaction to a book may offer oblique indications of their developing attitudes.

At the start of 1893, it appears Vladimir got hold of the November 1892 edition of the journal *Russkaya Mysl*, with contained Anton Chekhov's latest work, *Ward No. 6*. The story caused a storm in the press. The democratic-leaning intelligentsia greeted it enthusiastically: Ilya Repin wrote to Chekhov, "How grateful I am to you… Such a terrible force of feeling this piece stirs up!" Nikolai Leskov noted: "*Ward No. 6* depicts in miniature our collective ways and natures. *Ward No. 6* is all around us. It is Russia…"[287] Among other things, the Russian intelligentsia saw in the story a condemnation of the philosophy of inaction and accommodation with the prevailing evil.

The story made a truly profound impression on Ulyanov. Anna Ulyanova-Yelizarova recalled, "I still remember talking to Volodya about Chekhov's new story, *Ward No. 6*, which had appeared in one of the journals that winter. Describing the talent exhibited in the tale, and the strong impression it produced – Vladimir adored Chekhov – he summed

---

283   A. P. Chekhov. Sobraniye sochineny in eight volumes. Moscow, 1970. Vol. 5. p. 523.

284   See: Proletarskaya revolyutsiya. 1929. No. 1. p. 248; N. Valentinov. Nedorisovanny portret… p. 472.

285   See: Vladimir Ilyich Lenin v Samare. p. 171.

286   See: Krasnaya letopis'. 1926. No. 6. p. 26.

287   A. P. Chekhov. Sobraniye sochineny. Vol. 5. p. 522.

up his feelings thus: 'When I finished the story last evening, an uncanny sensation immediately overtook me and I found I could not remain in my room, so I got up and went out. I felt as if I was trapped in Ward No. 6 itself.' This was late in the evening. Everyone had gone off to their corners and were already asleep. There was no-one he could share his feelings with.

Volodya's words lifted a curtain on his state of mind: for him, Samara had already become a Ward No. 6: he was as desperate to get away from there as Chekhov's unfortunate patient had been, and had resolved to make his break with it..."[288]

As it happened, events transpired of their own accord. In June 1893, his younger brother Dmitry passed his school exams and it was decided that he would enrol at Moscow University. Consequently, the family found themselves relocating to the city. Vladimir was the only exception.

Anna Ulyanova-Yelizarova writes: "He did not want to be based in Moscow, where the whole family had gone with my younger brother Dmitry for his enrolment at Moscow University... St Petersburgers called Moscow a big village at that time – there was much of the provincial in it in those years, and Vladimir had had his fill of the provinces. He had decided to move to a more lively, intellectually stimulating, revolutionary centre – Piter. However, his inclination to seek contact with workers and engage fully in revolutionary activity meant he preferred to be there by himself, without his family members, whom he may have incriminated."[289]

On 24th April and 12th May, Vladimir defended his final court cases, after which he departed for Alakayevka. On 23rd July, an agreement was drawn up for the sale of the *khutor* and mill. On 12th August, he returned to Samara and four days later filed a request with the Samara District Court "pursuing registration as assistant district attorney in the jurisdiction of the St Petersburg Judicial Chamber," and requested he be certified in the same position he had held in Samara.

On 18th August, he received certification and by 20th Ulyanov had left Samara. Travelling via Nizhny Novgorod, he made his way to Vladimir, where Nikolai Fedoseyev was due for release from prison.

Nikolai Sergiyevsky, on meeting Ulyanov at the station, recalled: "At the appointed hour I arrived at the station and spying the almost empty cafeteria ... I immediately spotted a short man by the pre-agreed table

---

288   A. I. *Ulyanova-Yelizarova*. O V. I. Lenine i sem'ye Ulyanovykh. pp. 129-130.
289   Ibid. p. 130.

who matched the description of V. U. I quickly approached and said the codeword. V. U. responded, snatched his bag and without another word made towards me...

At first, we walked in almost complete silence... I observed him with curiosity. He was short, rather on the slight side, diffident, neat and, one could say, decently though unpretentiously turned out, with nothing about him that would pique the curiosity of the locals. I liked this camouflage. Everything was the same as it is now – that reddish spade of a beard, his moustache then untrimmed, a Tatar's narrowed eyes and that remarkable skull, (which could only be his – seven or eight years later and I instantly recognised V. I. the moment my eyes landed on that skull) not yet bald, but much thinned. The wiliness of expression that I detected later on, after his exile, was then not in evidence. It was in all likelihood yet to develop. Cautious, inquisitive of his surroundings, observant, and reserved, despite the feisty nature I had detected in his correspondence, V. U. was the exact opposite of Nikolai Fedoseyev. Well, I thought: if the fiery, reckless Fedoseyev falls in the fight, then this is a man who will see to it that the common enemy falls first."[290]

No meeting with Fedoseyev took place on this occasion: he was eventually released from prison a month later. Consequently, Ulyanov left Vladimir the same day and arrived in Moscow on 26th August.

By 31st August, he was in St Petersburg.

---

290   Fedoseyev Nikolai Yevgrafovich. Odin iz pionerov revolyutsionnogo marksizma v Rossii. Collection of memoirs. Moscow; Petrograd, 1923. pp. 98-99.

PART THREE – THE LEAGUE OF STRUGGLE

IN THE CAPITAL

For a young man arriving in the capital from the provinces, St Petersburg can often be overwhelming. Such was the case for 17-year-old Gleb Krzhizhanovsky, who came to the city to enrol at the Technological Institute. "At first," he recalled, "I was overcome by the gloomy grandeur of the city. The stone hulks of the buildings, the granite and marble of its palaces, the mighty black band of the Neva, the splendour of its European shops, the blue beams of electric light on the magnificent avenues, and the morose factory lanes and alleys on the outskirts, teetering on the marshy turf, sinking in the unhealthy, damp gloom.

Petersburg at that time was a city made execrable by triumphant Tsarism. The crack squads of burly policemen [*gorodovye*] who mooched at every intersection, the no less well-fed figures of the portly precinct officers, the distinctive tattoo of the drums and screech of the marching pipes which accompanied the numerous columns of troops marching continuously every which way, the 'colour' of the bureaucracy and upper ranks cutting a dash on Nevsky Prospect's wide promenades, and the swarms of spies scurrying about in the hazy fog of St Petersburg's boundless streets..."[291]

However, there is no evidence to suggest the city left such a dismal impression on Vladimir Ulyanov. Firstly, he was 23, not a 17-year-old. Secondly, he was fulfilling a dream by escaping the dusty Samara he so disdained and now, for the first time, he was left to his own devices. Finally, this was not his first time in the city – previous visits had brought exam success and fostered new acquaintances in the capital.

---

[291] *G. M. Krzhizhanovsky.* O Vladimire Ilyiche (Address delivered at a memorial evening to V. I. Lenin, 3rd February 1924). Moscow, 1933. pp. 28-29.

Of course, his mind went back to the spring of 1891, when he had strolled along the banks of the Neva with his sister Olga, watching the ice drifts. That same spring, he had buried her. Hence, one of his first acts, after taking a flat on Sergiyevskaya Street, was to visit Volkovo Cemetery. Olga's grave had been well kept: "It is all safe – both the cross and the wreath," he wrote to his mother.[292]

Despite the hectic nature of his initial settling in, by 3rd September he was already registered as assistant attorney to one of Khardin's good friends, the renowned advocate Mikhail Filippovich Volkenshtein. Now, attired in his father's dress coat, he would go regularly to the Council of Advocates for the St Petersburg District Court on Liteiny Prospekt for legal consultations and court appointments. In the Legal Calendar for 1894, his name and address appear on page 276 of a register listing advocates practising in the capital.

Gradually, daily life began to take shape. He would take dinner with the Chebotarevs, close friends of the Ulyanov family. On the advice of his mother, Vladimir began to keep a record of his spending.

On 2nd October 1893, Vladimir moved to Yamskaya Street, where he wrote to his mother: "It seems I've finally found myself a decent room: there are no other tenants, the landlady's family is small, and the door from my room to their hallway is sealed so the sound is muffled. The room is clean and bright. The walk is good – I am pleased I am so close to the centre (15 minutes on foot to the library, for instance)."[293]

Having settled in the capital, Vladimir immediately set about establishing contact with illegal social democrat groups. He went to Tsarskoye Selo to visit the family of Apollon Shukht after the birth of his daughter, Anna, who many years later would become a famous violinist. At her baptism on 24th October 1893, the register of the Tsarskoye Selo Church of the Life Guards of His Majesty's 1st Infantry Battalion records "assistant attorney Vladimir Ilyin Ulyanov" as her godfather.

Meanwhile, a letter of recommendation from social democrats in Nizhny Novgorod to their St Petersburg-based compatriots arrived. At the end of September, Ulyanov handed the letter to first-year student Mikhail Silvin, known to the Nizhny Novgorod contingent for his activities in Pavel Skvortsov's circle.

---

292   *V. I. Lenin*. Polnoye sobraniye sochineny. Vol. 55. p. 1.
293   Ibid.

"In the letter he gave me, which I read immediately," writes Silvin, "the Nizhny Novgorod contingent recommended I treat Vladimir Ilyich with complete trust and made reference to Alexander Ilyich. That was more than enough... After destroying the letter, I sought out Herman Krasin that same day and informed him of the interesting new arrival, insisting they meet. The name 'Ulyanov' impressed him, but I was told that we would discuss it."[294]

Herman Krasin, like his brother Leonid, had at one time been a member of the Brusnev social democrat organisation. After it was broken up between 1891 and 1892, Herman was exiled to Nizhny Novgorod. However, upon his return to the capital, he had managed to form a new group, made up of students from the Technological Institute, which included Stepan Radchenko, Pyotr Zaporozhets, Vasily Starkov, Gleb Krzhizhanovsky, Anatoly Vaneyev, Alexander Malchenko, Yakov Ponomarev, Mikhail Nazvanov, and others. Ties with workers who had been part of the Brusnev circles were also renewed.

Their activities were – for the time – effective, and the 'longevity' of the group was largely down to the strict secrecy which Zaporozhets enforced. Consequently, each newcomer was treated with extreme caution. Receiving word from Silvin that "the brother of A. I. Ulyanov" wished to join the organisation, Krasin and Radchenko visited him at home: "Let's go and give him the once over," Krasin had said.

In his early recollections, Krasin notes, "We appeared at Vladimir Ilyich's with the intention of getting to know him and conducting a casual assessment of the firmness of his Marxist principles."[295] While Ulyanov not only held his own during this examination, but, according to Krasin, turned it back on his examiners, the 'technologists' remained ambivalent in their impressions of him. The stumbling block lay in his attitude to *Narodnaya Volya* terror, since Ulyanov "expounded ... the belief that, as a point of principle, social democracy does not renounce terror as a method of struggle".

As Starkov wrote, "To us, raised on the articles of Plekhanov, which sharply criticised the programme and tactics of *Narodnaya Volya*, for whom terror was a cornerstone, and having personally crossed swords with

---

294   M. A. Silvin. Lenin v period zarozhdeniya partii. Vospominaniya. Leningrad, 1958. p. 41.

295   Stary bol'shevik. Moscow, 1933. Corpus 2 (5). March-April. p. 188.

Narodnaya Volya members on a number of occasions, such ideas seemed heretical."[296]

Ulyanov's "unusual position" on this issue had been in evidence back in Samara in his debates with Lalayants, who had written of "a certain sympathy within Vladimir Ilyich towards *Narodnaya Volya* terror". It had also been noticed by those in Nizhny Novgorod, who recalled Vladimir's discussions with Skvortsov on the "acceptability of a Marxist programme of terror as a means of struggle".[297] And now Herman Krasin and some of the other 'technologists', suffering from what Gleb Krzhizhanovsky described as a "crippling elementary pedantry," again decided to "thoroughly interrogate Vladimir Ilyich in regard to his views on terror, and I do recall a few experts among our number, although they ought to have acknowledged the soundness in Marxist terms of his views on terror, drawing attention to the fact that our new friend's temperament was, in this regard, too 'hot-headed and insufficiently reliable'..."[298]

Krzhizhanovsky believed that Ulyanov's attitude to *Narodnaya Volya* terror "stemmed directly from family tragedy, from the heroic image of his brother, which unlike us tied him to the traditions of the heroic revolutionary struggle that had come before".[299] In contrast, Lalayants – the first to challenge Ulyanov over the issue – wrote unequivocally that "Vladimir Ilyich's attitude to terror was in no way a direct consequence of his brother Alexander Ulyanov's influence on him".[300]

Lalayants clearly had a greater understanding of matters than Krzhizhanovsky, since to remain faithful to Marxism in this regard meant assessing the value of any method of struggle in its 'historical' context: that is by taking into consideration the historical period and conditions of the struggle itself.

It is also worth noting that Vladimir Starkov's reference to Plekhanov, who he alleged inculcated in them a principled aversion to terror, is groundless. In *Our Differences*, Plekhanov plainly stated that

---

296   Krasnaya nov'. 1925. No. 8. p. 111.

297   Proletarskaya revolyutsiya. 1929. No. 1. p. 49; Krasnaya nov'. 1924. No. 5. p. 102.

298   *G. M. Krzhizhanovsky*. O Vladimire Ilyiche. p. 31.

299   Ibid.

300   Proletarskaya revolyutsiya. 1929. No. 1. p. 49

"propaganda among the workers does not preclude the necessity of terrorist struggle". The Emancipation of Labour group's own programme also stated that social democrats "will not baulk at so-called terrorist activities if they prove necessary to the interests of the struggle".[301]

This issue will resurface in later chapters, but in the meantime, it is should be noted that neither then nor later did Ulyanov conceal his attitude to the tactics of *Narodnaya Volya*.

He wrote, "They have demonstrated great sacrifice and have astonished the world with their heroic terrorist methods of struggle." In terms of practical results, "Their immediate aim of igniting a people's revolution has not been achieved and would not have been achieved." But in conditions where there were no masses upon which to rely, when it seemed that the country – like the despotic kingdoms of Eastern antiquity – existed in a historical vacuum, the very act of open protest and struggle, even in isolation, took on great significance. "There is no doubt," Lenin wrote, "that these sacrifices were not made vain, and there is no doubt that they have contributed – directly or indirectly – to the subsequent revolutionary development of the Russian people."[302]

Many years later, Leonid Krasin wrote, "Marx remarks somewhere that, given competing trends of thought, the ideological disposition and standpoint of the newer tendency is often defined as a negation of the ideas and perspectives of its predecessors. And in seeking to avoid any similarities to these, the 'youngsters' often go much further down roads they would not otherwise have gone in the absence of such disagreement and internal struggle."[303] This strikingly acute observation is worth returning to in any evaluation of the attitudes of both Lenin himself and his opponents.

Vasily Starkov writes that he did not recall "how reconciliation came about" in the debate surrounding the use of terror, but one way or the other, the 'technologists' accepted Vladimir Ulyanov into their midst. However, this is not to say that their attitude to him improved immediately. Mikhail Silvin recalled, "The impression he made on me, and I suspect others, was initially quite a mixed one. His person, unprepossessing and at first glance

---

301   O. V. Budnitsky. Terrorizm v rossiiskom osvoboditelnym dvizhenii: ideologiya, etika, psikhologiya (vtoraya polovina XIX – nachalo XX v.). Moscow, 2000. pp. 266, 267, 268.

302   V. I. Lenin. Polnoye sobraniye sochineny. Vol. 30. p. 315.

303   Proletarskaya revolyutsiya. 1923. No. 3. pp. 4, 5.

rather ordinary, did not make much of an impact on us, but with each passing day every one of us found ourselves involuntarily peering ever more closely at this strange individual. It seemed he was sizing us up at the same time..."[304]

Initially, the age gap was what most likely hindered any speedy rapprochement. Four or five years does not seem such a gulf, but when you are a 19-year-old first-year student, as was Silvin, and Ulyanov a 24-year-old assistant attorney, the difference is rather more significant. Nonetheless, as Silvin himself wrote, this began to change "reasonably quickly".

They met weekly in the apartment of a student from the Technological Institute. Respect for his grasp of Marxist theory grew with each meeting. In those years, as Leonid Krasin noted, something of a theoretical superficiality existed among democrat youth, who believed there was "nothing to be gained from pouring over books, [considering it] sufficient to read through a few articles by Herzen and Chernyshevsky, work one's way through Lavrov's *Historical Letters*, and if one had also happened to have read a pamphlet by Lev Tikhomirov, then one's theoretical training as a revolutionary could be considered complete and one could and should proceed immediately to practical action".[305]

Such 'set texts' also existed among student social democrats: the first volume of Marx's *Capital*, a few articles by Engels, Kautsky, Bebel and Plekhanov, and that was sufficient. So when Ulyanov spoke of having worked his way through the Marxist canon and other literature with the aid of abridged summaries while in Samara, the 'technologists' decided to adopt the same method.

Herman Krasin was tacitly acknowledged as the group's leader, and he offered "to present at the next meeting an abstract on the market," choosing Nikolai-on's (N. F. Danielson) *Essays...* as the study subject.[306] Exploring the process of 'capitalisation' of the entire peasant economy, Danielson had argued that the poverty of the peasantry curtailed the internal market and thus deprived capitalism of its bedrock. Its only support was the protectionist policy of the government. Without such a policy, capitalism and with it the 1.5 million people of the Russian proletariat would inevitably be doomed to degradation.

304	Proletarskaya revolyutsiya. 1924. No. 7 (30). p. 68.
305	Ibid. 1923. No. 3. p. 4.
306	*M. A. Silvin*. Lenin v period zarozhdeniya partii. p. 46.

The authority Danielson commanded from having been the first to translate Marx into Russian, his enormous breadth of knowledge, and the wealth of statistical material in his possession made him a formidable opponent. But Herman Krasin was in no way fazed. Referencing Marx's analysis of capital circulation outlined in Vol. 2 of *Capital*, and the theory of the faster growth of the constant part of capital relative to variable, Krasin logically demonstrated that the development of capitalism is immanent to the process of producing the means of production for the means of production.

Since he was a poor orator, he wrote out the full text of the report he was to deliver in a notebook, the pages folded so that half was taken up by a margin. He gave the text to Vladimir Ulyanov, who used this margin to scribble his own notes on the text. However, Herman did not pay these much heed, convinced as he was of the irresistibility of his own arguments.

The meeting took place in early November 1893 at the home of Zinaida Nevzorova, and with Krasin as recognised leader of the circle speaking, a decent-sized audience had gathered. Krasin read out his prepared piece, which was perfectly sensible and correct and faithful to Marx, but what did anyone need with such veracity? Ulyanov made that apparent as soon as he got up to add his own commentary on the text.

It had been obvious from the outset that neither Herman nor the majority of those present knew anything "of Russian agriculture, of the many shapes and forms in which capitalism has embedded itself at the core of the lives of the people". Without any reference to Marx, Ulyanov appealed to his colleagues to eschew models and abstractions and instead view the reality of Russian life critically. Danielson was wrong, not because he contradicted Marx, but because his conclusions had no bearing in reality.

"He spoke for a long time," writes Mikhail Silvin, "with his usual finesse, trying not to offend the speaker, but the latter felt crushed, as we all did...

'We shouldn't concern ourselves with markets,' Vladimir Ilyich concluded, 'but with the organisation of a worker's movement in Russia. The markets are our bourgeoisie's concern.'"[307]

This meeting is described in detail by Sofia Nevzorova, who had arrived to visit her sister in St Petersburg the day before: "I vividly remember our small, elongated room, with its one window, green couch and two bunks. On the couch by the table sat a striking new face. Vladimir Ilyich was then

---

307   *M. A. Silvin*. Lenin v period zarozhdeniya partii. pp. 48, 49.

only 23. The light from the lamp illuminated his large, high crown, with licks of reddish hair around an already prominent bald patch, his lean face sporting a small beard. He read out his response to Herman Krasin's article from a notebook. Opposite him on a bunk sat Gleb Krzhizhanovsky, as tense as an arrow, the others gathered round in a circle on chairs..., while by the stove stood the tall, high-browed Herman Krasin, his arms behind his back. To the side, a samovar bubbled away on a table laid with glasses, bread and butter. I was on serving duty. Vladimir concluded his reading. A heated debate began. Herman Krasin tried to explain himself, while Gleb Krzhizhanovsky mainly stood fuming. V. I. remained quiet, listening attentively, flashing his sharp, derisive, searching gaze from one to the other. Finally, he took the floor, and silence descended. Everyone listened with an unusual attentiveness as V. I. refuted Krasin and some of the others who had challenged him. I no longer recall his arguments, but I have a strong memory of how incontestable they were. It was the first time in my life I had seen V. I. He immediately introduced something fresh, bright, vivacious, and irresistible. I, a raw provincial type, was left dazed by that evening..."[308]

The evening marked a turning point, both in attitude towards Vladimir Ulyanov, and in the existence of the group itself.

---

[308] Proletarskaya revolyutsiya. 1930. No. 1 (96). p. 86.

INITIAL RECOGNITION

Vladimir went to be with his family in Moscow for Christmas. They had been apart for four months, the first such long separation, and there was much to catch up on around the Christmas table. But as ever, other meetings were soon being arranged.

At the same time, Maria Golubeva-Yasneva, an acquaintance from Samara exiled to Tver, arrived illegally in Moscow. Upon meeting a *Narodnaya Volya* member with whom she had had dealings in the past, she was invited to a clandestine, 'invitation-only' gathering set to take place in the home of a liberal-leaning bookshop owner by the name of Zalesskaya on Vozdvizhenka Street. Initially, Vladimir did not want to go with her, but later acquiesced. By completely different channels, Mark and Anna Yelizarov also received invitations to the same gathering.

On 9th January, in Zalesskaya's large three-room apartment, they ran into each other completely unexpectedly. "The 'select invitees'," recalled Anna Ilyinichna, "turned out to be a whole procession of people. Secrecy was such that when it transpired there were two entrances to the building, or two apartments at the same address – I don't recall exactly – many initially tried the wrong one, before making a noticeable display of finding the correct door. Given also that these were furnished lodgings for students, at that time the element most inclined to revolutionary activity, they effectively served as a duty station for all manner of infiltrators, and one must acknowledge that a less clandestine evening could not have been organised. But what other options were there?! More upstanding citizens were at that time too careful to give over their homes to larger gatherings. As always and everywhere, youth is fearless..."[309]

Whatever lecture began proceedings prompted the 'Jacobin' Maria Golubeva to curse quietly: "What was the point of gathering an audience in all this secrecy only to listen to talks about pharmacies and libraries!"

---

[309] N. Lenin. (V. Ulyanov). Sobraniye sochineny. Vol. 1. Moscow, 1924. pp. 704-705.

However, as Ulyanova-Yelizarova writes, afterwards commenced "debates which quickly grew heated, especially after Vladimir Ilyich began to contradict one especially avowed *narodnik*, a short, thickset fellow with balding blond hair whom the young people deferentially treated as something of a guest of honour".

Standing among the crowd of young people in the doorway to the next room, Ulyanov began by firing off a few ironic remarks, before taking the floor and "with all the ardour of youth" launching into a critique of *narodnik* doctrine. The thickset, balding, blond-haired fellow with the red beard turned out to be none other than Vasily Pavlovich Vorontsov, the famous V. V. He began his response to Ulyanov, "putting it to him," as Viktor Chernov writes, "like a knife to the throat, so to speak: 'Your positions are without evidence, your assertions unfounded... Demonstrate to us that you have grounds to make such claims; show us your analysis of the facts and figures of reality."[310]

Back in Samara, Vladimir had delivered a number of papers on V. V.'s book *The Fate of Capitalism* in Russia, and later written an article titled "The Grounds of the Narodnik Movement in the Works of V. V." Consequently, as Anna Ulyanova-Yelizarova writes, "the patronising attitude and scholarly objections of the more senior fellow did not trouble my brother. He began to back up his views with similarly scholarly evidence and statistics, pouncing on his opponent with another wave of sarcasm. The whole gathering turned into a duel between these two representatives of 'fathers and sons'. Everyone present, especially the younger ones, followed the exchange closely. The *narodnik* began to climb down, clamming up, before meekly retiring. The Marxists among the young people assembled celebrated victory."[311]

There is nothing over-effusive in this assessment of Vladimir's *first public performance*. An agent of the secret police, naturally present at this 'secret gathering', also reported that Ulyanov defended his views "with full knowledge of the facts".[312] What the agent was unaware of was its comical conclusion: as he was in the entrance hall preparing to leave, Ulyanov asked Golubeva the identity of the man he had argued with. On hearing it was

---

310   Ibid. Vol. 1. pp. 705-706.

311   Ibid. Vol. 1. p. 705.

312   Krasny arkhiv. 1934. No. 1. p. 76.

V. V. himself, he became deeply embarrassed and bristled that he had not been warned in advance.³¹³

After this episode, Ulyanov immediately became known in Moscow's radical circles and according to Golubeva, "the name of this 'St Petersburger' who had so soundly licked V. V. was suddenly on everyone's lips".³¹⁴

News of his debate with V. V. reached St Petersburg too. When he returned to the capital a few days later, his friends beseeched him to offer a response to an article by Mikhailovsky, directed against Marxists, which had appeared in *Russkoye Bogatstvo*.³¹⁵

This experience of arguing with V. V. demonstrated that the papers he had delivered in Samara had not lost any of their 'deadly force' and Vladimir decided that it would be no bad thing to update and modify the content and have them published, at least as hectographs. It needed to be done quickly with other affairs to one side, particular his work as an advocate. Naturally, the question arose – how would he make a living?

Practising as an assistant attorney did not bring in an especially impressive salary. Immediately after his registration with the St Petersburg Attorneys' Office, the Department of Police had quickly made their colleagues in the capital aware of "Ulyanov's unreliability". There was consequently little cause to expect major, high-profile cases that would offer career advancement. Nonetheless, he continued to go to Liteiny Prospekt for legal consultations and represented a few minor criminal cases as a court-appointed attorney, i.e. without receiving a fee. Vladimir once lamented to Mikhail Silvin that his attorney's fees were barely enough to cover the costs of accessing documents for conducting cases.³¹⁶

It appears he discussed this with his mother in Moscow, learning in the process that the family was relatively stable financially. There were the savings left from Ilya Nikolayevich's death and the sale of Alakayevka, as well as the pension which Maria Alexandrovna, her son Dmitry, a first-year student in the medical faculty of Moscow State University, and her daughter Maria, a fifth-year gymnasium pupil, were still receiving. Moreover, her son-in-law Mark Timofeyevich Yelizarov had acquired a high-paying job in the administration of the Kursk Railway. This taken

---

313   See: *Y. Martov*. Zapiski sotsial-demokrata. p. 271.
314   *N. Lenin. (B. Ulyanov)*. Sobraniye sochineny. Vol. 1. p. 706.
315   See: *M. A. Silvin*. Lenin v period zarozhdeniya partii. p. 70.
316   See: ibid, p. 69; Proletarskaya revolyutsiya. 1924. No. 3. p. 107.

with the money Maria Alexandrovna was paid by her sister for her share of the land inherited from their father's estate at Kokushkino allowed the family to offer assistance to Vladimir.[317]

Now, Ulyanov's appearances at the District Court became much rarer, as he spent almost all day, every day in the Public Library, browsing the most recent literature penned by the ideologues of liberal *narodnik* populism.

A first edition of his work titled "What the 'Friends of the People' Are and How They Fight the Social-Democrats (A Reply to Articles in *Russkoye Bogatstvo* Opposing the Marxists)" was completed in April 1894. This edition was entirely dedicated to a criticism of Nikolai Mikhailovsky. In May, work was completed on a revised second edition, the 'hero' of the piece on this occasion being Sergei Yuzhakov. By the middle of June a third edition was written, which looked at the works of Sergei Krivenko.

"What the 'Friends of the People' Are..." gained an audience not only in St Petersburg, but also in Vilnius, Penza, Vladimir, Kiev and Chernigov.[318]

The title of the piece stemmed from an old edition of *Otechestvennyye Zapiski* for 1879, whose editorial ran: "Recently one literary donkey kicked out at *Otechestvennyye Zapiski* for its *pessimism towards the people*, as he put it ... and suddenly out of thin air appeared such a multitude of defenders of the people that we, truly, are impressed that they have so many allies. Serenading the peasantry and getting 'doe-eyed' over them is not the same as expressing love and respect, in exactly the same way that pointing out their problems in no way equates to treating them with hostility."[319]

Vladimir Ulyanov discussed a unique characteristic of this 'love' and 'hostility' in "What the 'Friends of the People' Are...": that by appealing to "paternal ideals", liberal *narodniki* were attempting to appear more spiritually elevated and radical than the social democrats. Certainly, there was a whole epoch of the liberation movement during which, according to Kautsky, "every socialist was a poet and every poet was a socialist," when it was faith in the peasant revolution and the communal structure of Russian life that inspired and elevated Russian youth towards heroic struggle with the government. "You cannot accuse the social democrats," Lenin wrote, "of being unable to appreciate the immense historical achievements of these,

---

317   See: *V. I. Lenin*. Polnoye sobraniye sochineny. Vol. 55. p. 2.
318   See: *N. Lenin. (B. Ulyanov)*. Sobraniye sochineny. Vol. 1. pp. 692-693.
319   *V. I. Lenin*. Polnoye sobraniye sochineny. Vol. 1. p. 354.

the best people of their time, and of not holding a deep respect for their memory. But I ask you: where is this faith now? It is no longer there..."[320]

"The countryside has long been stratified and split. Along with it, there has also been splintering in the old Russian peasant socialism, replaced on the one hand by workers' socialism, on the other, by degeneration into vulgar [*poshly*] petty-bourgeois radicalism."[321]

It should be noted that this work features a large amount of invective language, one of the most oft-repeated examples being the word "*poshlost* [vulgarity]".

It is nowadays construed unambiguously: as something coarse, vulgar, morally low, even sordid. However, in the past, as the lexicographer Vladimir Dahl notes, the adjective "*poshly*" indicated that which is old, long-standing, stemming from older times. Only in the second half of the 19th century did the word acquire a different meaning: something common, born out of habit, tired and hackneyed.

Towards the end of the 19th century, the world was entering a new era. Many older concepts were losing their meaning; and not merely concepts – many intellectuals and political figures would long continue to attempt analyses of this new reality as they had previously, using old tools and long-established, stale truths. This also explains why words such as "*poshly*" and "*poshlyaki*", those who personified this 'vulgarity', began to be heard in a completely different way.

Offering Marx a patronising pat on the back for the 'meticulousness' of his research and expansive 'erudition', the *narodniki* mocked the social democrats for their apparent overestimation of the value of his conclusions in a Russian context. The Marxist vision of Russia's future was, as Mikhailovsky asserted, untenable, since it did not stem from Russian realities, but from the projection on Russia of "Hegelian triads" and "abstract historical schemata".[322]

A different path was required for Russia: it must take all that was good of the Middle Ages and supplement this with the good that capitalism could undoubtedly offer, while marrying Russia's patriarchal character to Western enterprise and enlightenment. Further down the line, it would be necessary "to demonstrate that this theoretical structure can accommodate

---

320 Ibid. Vol. 1. pp. 261, 271.
321 Ibid. Vol. 1. p. 272; see also pp. 242, 261, 265.
322 See: ibid. Vol. 1. pp. 163, 164, 195.

'human nature' and steer towards the 'correct path' a government which had thus far led the country in the wrong direction.[323]

"Not a single Marxist," responded Ulyanov, "has ever seen in Marx's theory any universally valid philosophical-historical framework… Naturally Marxists adopt from Marx's theory only those valuable devices without which it would be impossible to understand societal relations; consequently, the yardstick for their evaluation of such relations lies … in how closely it matches reality."[324]

Lenin had also written, "Social democrats will demand in the most vigorous terms the immediate return of land taken from the peasantry and the complete expropriation of landowners' estates – those strongholds of feudal institutions and traditions…"[325] Evidently, Marxists were far from 'pessimists' in regard to the future of the peasantry.

However, the main political task of the social democrats, as Vladimir Ulyanov frequently repeated, was to AWAKEN THE CONSCIOUSNESS OF THE WORKER and facilitate the conversion from "smouldering discontent" and "dumb despair" towards reasoned protest, and from senseless revolt and isolated strikes to a conscious and organised struggle for the liberation of all working people. "The basis for this undertaking is the common belief among Marxists that the Russian worker is the only natural representative of the whole of the toiling and exploited population of Russia."[326]

The conclusion of the work reads almost prophetically: "The social democrats focus all of their attention and all of their efforts on the working class. When their leading representatives have mastered the concepts of scientific socialism, the notion of the historical role of the Russian worker, and when these ideas are widely disseminated and organisation among the workers solidifies… – then the Russian worker, rising as the vanguard of all democratic forces, will overthrow absolutism and lead the RUSSIAN PROLETARIAT (alongside the proletariat of ALL NATIONS) along the direct route of open political struggle to the VICTORIOUS COMMUNIST REVOLUTION."[327]

---

323   See: ibid. Vol. 1. pp. 139, 157, 191, 192, 197, 199, 248, 262, 273, 342.
324   Ibid. Vol. 1. pp. 195, 197.
325   Ibid. Vol. 1. pp. 299-300.
326   Ibid. Vol. 1. pp. 241, 301, 309-310.
327   Ibid. Vol. 1. pp. 311-312.

Ulyanov's "What the 'Friends of the People' Are and How They Fight the Social-Democrats" made a profound impression on the readers of the time. Many years later, Yuliy Martov wrote, "...the pamphlet ... exuded a genuine revolutionary passion and plebeian rawness reminiscent of the democratic disputes of the 1860s. Despite its rather heavy-handed articulation, poor structuring, and disjointed, underdeveloped ideas, the pamphlet exhibited a literary talent and the mature political thinking of an individual made in the mould of a party leader. I was intrigued by the personality of the author, but at that time the level of secrecy was so high that I was unable to discover anything... Only subsequently, a year later, did I hear the name V. I. Ulyanov."[328]

---

328   *Y. Martov*. Zapiski sotsial-demokrata. pp. 239-240.

THE MARXIST SALON

Ulyanov's efforts at formulating common objectives for workers' socialism in Russia in "Friends of the People..." caught the attention of social democrats across the country. As Marxism became more fashionable, Vladimir Ilyich found himself invited to a so-called Marxist salon shortly after his pamphlet was published as a hectograph.[329]

The salon had initially formed around Alexandra Mikhailovna Kalmykova. A *Narodnaya Volya* member in her day, she later established close ties with Plekhanov's Emancipation of Labour. Now aged 46, her late husband D. A. Kalmykov had been a senator and she was herself a woman of some means, owning a book depository and shop that was often visited by St Petersburg social democrats, to whom she would provide material assistance. It was in her apartment that, "young people interested in Marxism would gather of an evening and take tea..."[330]

It was Peter Struve who ruled the roost in this 'salon'. Grandson of the famous astronomer and founder of the Pulkovo Observatory, and son of the governor of Irkutsk, Astrakhan and later Perm Provinces, he was in the process of completing his studies in the law faculty of St Petersburg University. After the death of his father in 1889, Peter lived with Kalmykova as something of an adopted son. Despite the 21-year age gap, they had in fact become lovers. While the relationship was carefully concealed, Alexandra Mikhailovna openly assisted him in any way she could.[331]

Struve had garnered attention in late 1893 after publishing a piece titled "On the question of capitalist development in Russia" in a German social-democratic publication. The other main figure in the salon was Mikhail Tugan-Baranovsky, five years Struve and Ulyanov's elder. In 1894, Tugan-Baranovsky defended his master's thesis "Periodic crises in England" at

---

329   See: Krasnaya letopis'. 1925. No. 2 (13). pp. 144-145.
330   Ogonek. 1926. No. 17.
331   See: Russkaya kultura XX veka na rodine i v emigratsii. 1st Edition. Moscow, 2000. p. 10.

Moscow University, framing his conceptualisation of crises in Marxist economic terms and utilising the analysis Marx developed in the second volume of *Capital*.

Another key member of the Marxist salon was Alexander Potresov, the son of a general. He was a natural sciences graduate and had completed two courses in the law faculty of St Petersburg University; by 1892 he was in contact with Emancipation of Labour. Other regulars at the salon included engineer Robert Klasson, architect S. M. Serebrovsky, and the students Y. P. Korobko, Klobukov, Korsak, and others. A young teacher, Nadezhda Krupskaya, was also a frequent visitor, as was Ariadna Tyrkova. Besides the Kalmykova apartment, there were sometimes gatherings at Klasson's home on Bolshaya Okhta Street, but most meetings and discussions took place at the apartment of Tugan-Baranovsky, whose wife Lidiya Karlovna, the daughter of a celebrated cellist and director of the St Petersburg Conservatory, was renowned for her hospitality.

Ariadna, a writer, left vivid accounts of these gatherings:

"We would drink tea and gossip about the *narodniki*, arguing ceaselessly. Refreshments were simple: sandwiches with sliced sausage and cheese, sometimes jam and biscuits...

It was at Lidiya's that I first met P. B. Struve... There was some sparring going on at the table over Nordau's sensational book on degeneration. Many believed that Nordau was guilty of exaggeration... Suddenly, a young man with a red beard burst like a tempest into the conversation. He brushed the long, carelessly combed red locks from his large ears, and tugging at them with both hands as if trying to wrench them off, cried loudly:

'There is no such thing as degeneration? Look at me, look at my ears!'

How many times later, over far more serious issues, would I hear that strangled voice, that impassioned, abrupt speech, in which such profound, occasionally prophetic discourse merged so curiously with sudden, hysterical outbursts. Struve, like Tugan, made no effort to mind his manners and did not consider it necessary to do so. This was a common trait among the intelligentsia. The fashion of the '60s for simplifying one's life had not passed... Struve also had scant regard for the sentiments of others. He would occasionally pay attention to their ideas, but their tastes, habits, and feelings were of little interest to him."[332]

---

332   A. V. Tyrkova-Williams. To, chego bol'she ne budet. Paris, 1954. pp. 231-233.

The reputation of the Marxist salon, and of Struve in particular, grew markedly after Alexandra Kalmykova had his book *Critical Remarks on the Subject of Russia's Economic Development* published in St Petersburg in September 1894. Kalmykova wrote that the print run was relatively small – 200 copies – but as it had been published legally, it sold out immediately. The concluding words of *Critical Remarks*, on the need to cancel out the outdated ramblings of the *narodniki*, recognise "our lack of culture", and "learn from capitalism", went into wide usage, becoming formulas repeated almost by heart.

The popularity of Struve's book, along with the fashion for Marxism itself, can be understood only in the context of the circumstances of the time. Despite the disillusionment with and degeneration of the *narodnik* movement, it had remained since the 1860s a kind of 'moral maxim' which defined many of the values held by the intelligentsia.

Meanwhile, the development of capitalism, with its demand for 'intellectual labour', opened up new opportunities for intellectuals, not only in the traditional and relatively low-paid fields of education and public health, but also on the boards of major banks, joint-stock companies, and the new giants of industry.

Tempting as it may have been to become an establishment intellectual – like those in Europe – it smacked of a betrayal of those principles of love for the people and simple living which had been professed, albeit at times in words alone, in the 1860s-1880s. But, of course, the intellectual could not commit a base act without first attributing to it the highest of motives. Peter Struve's book addressed just this issue: once progress is bound up with the development of capitalism, once *narodnik* theories prove unworkable, then every intellectual who desires the best for Russia not only can, but must, serve those driving this progress.

In any event, Struve's book heralded something of a honeymoon period for so-called 'legal Marxism' when, as Lenin later wrote, "everyone became Marxists en masse, Marxists were courted and indulged, and publishers revelled in the remarkable sales of Marxist books".[333]

Shortly thereafter, under the pseudonym Beltov, Plekhanov published *The Development of the Monist View of History*, which gave enormous impetus to the spread of Marxism in Russia. Lenin was particularly enthusiastic about it, if only briefly.

---

333   V. I. Lenin. Polnoye sobraniye sochineny. Vol. 6. pp. 15-16.

In April 1895, 2,000 copies of the collection *Materials for a Characterisation of Our Economic Development* was printed by a publishing house in the capital – a fairly large print run for the time. It contained two articles by Plekhanov (under the pseudonyms D. Kuznetsov and Utis), articles by Ulyanov (as K. Tulin), Struve, Potresov, P. Skvortsov, V. Ionov, and a translation by Klasson of Eduard Bernstein's extensive essay on the recently published third volume of Marx's *Capital*. The collection therefore represented the first 'union' of emigrant, underground, and legal Marxist strains.

However, the St Petersburg censors were on the alert. They were particularly outraged by the article attributed to Tulin, being as it was an explicit programme for Marxists. The print run was speedily confiscated and burned. Potresov was only able to save 100 copies, which were distributed around Marxist groups in the capital, the provinces, and abroad.

AWAKENING

Having obtained a copy of the collection in Zurich that May, Pavel Axelrod read it from cover to cover. Later he recalled: "I was drawn by the lengthy article by K. Tulin, a name which was new to me. I was most impressed by the article. Tulin was presenting here a criticism of the *narodnik* movement and Struve's *Critical Remarks*. It was pieced together rather clumsily, perhaps even carelessly. But therein one sensed the temperament and the combative spark; one sensed that for the author, Marxism was no abstract doctrine, but an instrument of revolutionary struggle."[334] Despite having become one of his most vocal opponents by the time he wrote these recollections, Pavel Axelrod grasped the essence of the young Ulyanov's work.

One of the main accusations Ulyanov levelled at Struve was the abstract nature of his analysis of the Russian reality, since it completely ignored the specific socio-economic relationships characteristic of Russia.[335] This primarily related to passages which glorified the "utility" of capitalist progress *"in a general sense"*.[336]

There was no disputing that Russia was chronically backward. It was a matter of fact that capitalism brought with it progress. After all, no-one could deny that even the most rickety puffer boat would lighten a man's burden more effectively than barge-hauler's straps. All that was quite true. Moreover, Ulyanov demonstrated that the *narodnik* desire to "arrest capitalism in its medieval forms, which united exploitation with fragmented, technically antiquated production" only multiplied the suffering of the workers. "We must therefore desire not to delay the development of capitalism, but hope for the opposite: its full development, to the point of its demise."[337]

---

[334] Perepiska G. V. Plekhanova i P. B. Axelrod. Vol. 1-2. Moscow, 1925. Vol. 1. p. 269.

[335] See: *V. I. Lenin*. Polnoye sobraniye sochineny. Vol. 1. pp. 445, 485.

[336] Ibid. Vol. 1. p. 496.

[337] Ibid. Vol. 1. pp. 497, 510, 511.

Within those programmes of the old revolutionary *narodniki,* the Marxists supported broadly democratic, progressive provisions such as the "extension of peasant land ownership", "self-governance", "free and broad access to education for the people", the creation in rural areas of "technical and other schools", the elevation of small-scale farming "by means of cheap credit, improved technology, regulation of distribution, et cetera". "The more decisive reform is in Russia," the more "economic development" in the nation will be advanced, the "higher the standard of living" for the worker will be, the more developed his needs will become, thus "accelerating and facilitating his independent thinking and activites".[338]

The who, how and when of implementing such reform was still to be resolved. Liberal *narodniki* presumed the present government and state were capable of delivering it.

Such an understanding of the issue, wrote Ulyanov, "really only signifies the 'innocence' of the kind of academic daydreaming that renders the arguments of the *narodniki* fit only for parlour talk".[339]

Marx, Ulyanov writes, was correct in saying that even the most modern state was an organ of class domination. It remained a governing authority, separated from and acting in opposition to the people. Accordingly, the bureaucracy, in which the fullness of real power was concentrated, expressed completely different class interests. As such, no amount of preaching by liberal professors espousing the most "modern moral ideals" would force it to relinquish its own selfish interests. The only force capable of making that happen was one which opposed the present state, a force drawn from "the intellect of those upon whom change depends," i.e. the working masses themselves. Ulyanov concludes, "Use class against class... This is the only, and therefore most direct, 'path to human happiness'..."[340]

This proclamation of the "intellect" of the masses was greeted with derision, even guffaws of Homeric laughter, by the liberal public. The 'benightedness' and 'sufferance' of the Russian peasant was not merely a constant source of comment, but also the basis for the belief that any change in Russia must be 'top down'. This was why they spoke of the peasant's "sacred duty of toil, passed down from father and grandfather, a duty manifested in the sweat on his brow to earn his bread," not once

---

338 Ibid. Vol. 1. pp. 385, 530, 531.
339 Ibid. Vol. 1. p. 532.
340 Ibid. Vol. 1. pp. 370, 438, 439, 528.

considering – as they were in the West – "the right to work," or "the right to rest from the overwork which cripples and breaks him".[341]

"The Economic Content of Narodism" is written in a relatively calm style. Only occasionally does it break out not merely in a passion, but in something of a fury, when it warns that the patience of the people is not eternal, that the more heinous the outrage committed on the person, the worse the retribution will be, given the inevitability of conflict; "the struggle is already under way, but blindly, unconsciously, unguided by ideas". How well concepts of liberation were received, how successful an undertaking "enlightening the mind" and "providing ideological substance to the ongoing struggle" would be, depended on what form the process of awakening the individual within the downtrodden and persecuted worker would take.

This came as no surprise to readers: they knew that the workers' strikes of the 1880s and early 1890s had often been characterised by violence and excess. There had been smashing of machinery and factory premises. The Hughes Strike of 1892 was still fresh in the memory: it had ended in a terrible massacre, as troops opened fire on miners. There, despair and a desire for vengeance had manifested itself in savage form in response to the inhuman conditions faced by the workers. From a historical perspective, the strikes represented the beginning of protest, the loss of the age-old faith in the inviolability of the orders which kept them down, a breaking with servility. They gave rise to the sense that collective resistance was essential. In other words, it was the first steps, albeit primitive, ugly ones, in the awakening of consciousness.[342]

There are provisions in Marxism that have taken the character of axioms, not because they require no further proof, but because they provide the basis for its entire world view. Such 'axioms' are often forgotten by those who consider themselves Marxists. One such provision is the understanding that the people cannot merely be an object of benevolence from on high, but that the liberation of the workers should be an undertaking of the workers themselves.

This was an idea continually reinforced to the young Marxists by Plekhanov, who wrote that were it won *in this way*, the happiness of

---

341 Ibid. Vol. 1. p. 420.
342 Ibid. Vol. 4. pp. 292, 294, 295.

the people would not only be far more fully realised: it would also be considerably *more enduring*.[343]

Ulyanov fully shared this position. But putting revolutionary ideas into practice "requires an enormous amount of groundwork..." In the meantime, Russian social democrats should for the foreseeable future consider the only measure of the success of their efforts to be "not the formulation of advice to 'society' and 'state', but the extent to which [their] ideals are disseminated within a particular social class..."[344]

---

343   G. V. Plekhanov. Sochineniya. pp. 402-403.

344   V. I. Lenin. Polnoye sobraniye sochineny. Vol. 1. pp. 408, 533.

NIKOLAI PETROVICH

The literature which examines the first steps of the Russian proletarian movement often gives the impression that the appearance of workers' circles was due solely to the radicalising influence of the radical intelligentsia. Paradoxically, this was also the impression of the gendarmerie, who were convinced that "student socialists" were leading lost lambs astray and inciting them to rebel. In reality, the process of developing proletarian consciousness and activism was a far more complex one.

The 1880s are sometimes referred to as the "dead" decade: a decade of decline and regression, in which everything and everyone seemed stuck in a kind of stalemate. However, it was at precisely this time that, invisible to the naked eye, the forces which in the 1890s would provide the impetus for the rapid revival of the economy and public life were maturing.

There was little change in the terrible working and living conditions of the Russian worker. Semi-literate and not long arrived from the countryside, he lived a monotonous, bleak, semi-animal existence. And though even in this "dead" decade not a year passed without spontaneous strikes breaking out, it seemed to many that the worker would never be free of his cursed bondage and be in a position to improve his lot. Only a few realised the need for change and tried to elevate themselves through books and study. Then, in the 1880s and 1890s, new motivations emerged beside the purely human and personal.

The upturn in industrial production dramatically increased the demand for skilled workers. This was met to some extent by inviting foreign craftsmen and workers, but more shrewd employers recognised that such personnel could be trained domestically. This led to the foundation in some plants and factory quarters of a range of general and trade schools.

The appearance in industrial plants of literate, highly-skilled workers immediately placed them at the centre of factory life. A certain K. S---ky gave his impressions of some advanced metalworkers in St Petersburg: "These are independent-minded, intelligent people with relatively good incomes… They are at the very least a bracket of the workforce able, to some degree, to live free of desperate hardship – the constant toil aside, of course. They are in a position to take apartments, albeit cheap ones, once they started a family. Their wives are free to busy themselves with housework. They may boast a hearth and home, things that many other types of worker must do without. Working in the mechanical industries, despite the demands it places on him, should instil in a man a desire for individualisation. There should be space for imaginative thought: the worker should use his head, and think while working... In their mode of speech, even in the very language they use, there is almost no distinguishing them from our intelligentsia. In my view, they are of more interest, as they are fresher in their assertions, and their beliefs, once embraced, are more firmly held. In recent times their moral sense has been growing in that most Russian of ways – not by the day, but by the hour..."[345]

Nikolai Dementyevich Bogdanov, who formed a self-education circle for his comrades in railyard workshops in 1886, wrote: "To be an organiser of the working class, one must first of all be honest in all one's dealings; second, one must be a good comrade; and finally, a well-informed person to whom questions can be directed. This is why one must educate oneself and study."[346]

But even workers such as these often lacked the knowledge to be able to lead lessons, which as a result brought them into contact with the radical intelligentsia. This was the impetus behind the foundation of Dmitry Blagoev and Pavel Tochissky's circles in the 1880s and the Brusnev groups of the early 1890s. These circles maintained contact with the Technology Institute social democrat group of which Vladimir Ulyanov was a member. Alongside these 'technologists', who had begun to be referred to as the "old men", other younger students of the Technology Institute, people such as Illarion Chernyshov, Yevgeny Bogatyrev, Sergey Muromov, Friedrich Lengnik, the dentist Nikolai Mikhailov and others, also emerged.

Vladimir Ulyanov intimated his desire to work with the circles immediately after becoming acquainted with the 'technologists', but only in late autumn 1893 did Herman Krasin introduce him to Vasily Andreyevich Shelgunov, a radical St Petersburg proletarian via whom both *narodniki*

---

345 See: article by I. S. Rozental' in the collection: Rossiisky proletariat: oblik, bor'ba, gegemoniya. Moscow, 1970. pp. 147-148.

346 Ot gruppy Blagoyeva k "Soyuzu bor'by" (1886-1894) Collection. Rostov-on-Don, 1921. p. 40.

and Marxists had established contact with workers' circles back in the 1880s. It seems Ulyanov was only allocated his first groups in spring 1894: after the main core of the *Narodnaya Volya* group, yet another youth association, was betrayed by the police spy Kuzma Kuzyutkin and arrested on 21st April 1894, there was an immediate need to fill the gaps. When Shelgunov received a request from workers in the Petersburg and Nevskaya Zastava districts, he sent Ulyanov.

The 22-year-old Vladimir Knyazev, a technician in the New Admiralty port whose apartment was used as a meeting place by representatives of the workers' circles, recounts: "At the appointed hour, there was a knock at my door. Opening the door, I saw a man of around 30, with a small, reddish beard and piercing eyes hidden under a cloth cap, wearing an autumnal coat with the collar turned up... Overall, I was wholly unable to place his background from his appearance."

However, his début proved to be a success: "Approaching those gathered, he introduced himself, took the seat offered him, and set forth a schedule for the work we had come to do. He spoke earnestly, with clarity and thoughtfulness. Those in attendance listened attentively. They answered the questions he asked: who worked at which factory, how advanced the factory's workers were, what views they held, whether they were capable of grasping socialist ideas, what the workers' main concerns were, what they were reading, and so on." When the session was over and Ulyanov left, the others in the circle surrounded Knyazev: "Who was that? He speaks so well..." But beyond the understanding that their lecturer was to be addressed as Nikolai Petrovich, Knyazev knew nothing.[347]

A few months later, when given the address of an experienced lawyer by the name of Ulyanov for help with an inheritance issue, Vladimir Knyazev was stunned to arrive for the appointment and find his Nikolai Petrovich resplendent in top hat, coat and tails.[348]

During the summer, classes were usually halted, as many of the student agitators were from outside of the city and returned home for the holidays. As the workers joked, "the revolution has gone to her *dacha*".[349] On 14th June,

---

347   See: Vospominaniya o Vladimire Ilyiche. Vol. 2. p. 39.
348   See: Ob Ilyiche. Sbornik statei, vospominany, dokumentov. Leningrad, 1924. pp. 112-115.
349   Ot gruppy Blagoyeva... p. 57.

Ulyanov also left for Podolsk, where Maria Alexandrovna was renting a *dacha*. His entire summer was taken up with issues surrounding the publication of "Friends of the People...", meetings with Moscow-based social democrats, a translation from German of Karl Kautsky's pamphlet on the Erfurt Programme, and other matters, and Ulyanov only returned to St Petersburg on 27th August.

In the meantime, all the talk among the workers had been of this 'Nikolai Petrovich', with representatives of the Petersburg and Vyborg districts of the city, as well as Vasilyevsky Island and Kolpino, gathering in Vladimir Knyazev's apartment. Ulyanov's fame had spread rather widely, and Shelgunov promptly offered him Nikita Merkulov and Ivan Babushkin's workers' groups in Nevskaya Zastava.

The impression Ulyanov made on this new audience was more than favourable. In his memoirs, written in 1902, Babushkin recalled: "We began lessons on political economy and Marx. Our lecturer expounded his knowledge verbally, without any notes, often attempting to elicit objections from us, or trigger a debate, and then, once this was provoked, he would compel one participant to demonstrate to the other the validity of his point of view on the question at hand. Thus our lectures became lively, engaging affairs... We very much enjoyed the lectures and marvelled continually at our lecturer's sharpness of mind." Between themselves, the workers would sometimes refer to him as "baldy", but usually jokingly added that "his oversized mind has caused his hair to fall out".[350]

Ulyanov began to conduct lessons in other groups and eventually "by the winter of 1894 the most valuable worker contacts in Nevskaya Zastava had transferred to V. I. Ulyanov's group..."[351]

The nature of the lessons themselves also changed. Many of the workers, despite their youth, carried a wealth of life experience and were 'individualised' enough to be of interest not merely as students, but as peers. The workers possessed a knowledge and experience of everyday proletarian existence that Ulyanov lacked, and he began to divide lessons into two parts: initially, it was theory, most often Marx's *Capital*, and later they would begin a conversation "on the topics of the day. This was the most animated part of the session," writes Nadezhda Krupskaya.[352]

---

350   Vospominaniya I. V. Babushkina. Leningrad, 1925. pp. 14, 51.
351   *K. M. Takhtarev*. Rabocheye dvizheniye v Peterburge. p. 39.
352   Tvorchestvo. 1920. No. 7-10. p. 4.

Vasily Shelgunov, who would look in on Ulyanov's lessons to, in his words, "rest his soul," recalled that "in these early workers' circles – where more often than not he found himself talking not of political economy or important issues of state but of a worker's home life, of how his wife and family were, how she viewed his absence when he went to the meetings, how he was getting on with his foreman, what his biggest concerns in the factory were – he took it all on board so simply, so effortlessly..."

If Vladimir Ulyanov had gone on to become a writer, these conversations would no doubt have made fine source material for vivid tales or sketches from a worker's life. Had he become a historian or economist, then he could easily have written something similar to Tugan-Baranovksy's 1898 book *The Russian Factory in Past and Present*. But he had chosen a different path, and the more he worked with these circles, the more dissatisfied he became with the results.

The circles were able to influence dozens of workers, helping them develop both culturally and politically, and introduce to them all the subtleties of the theory of struggle. However, at the same time, hundreds of thousand of proletarians were spending all their free time in taverns and remained hostile to any 'rabble-rousing'. Konstantin Takhtarev wrote, "No wonder ordinary workers referred to the workers in the circles as heathens and shunned them, saying 'Those who abjure God and the Tsar, what can they tell us!' Clearly, much more preliminary preparatory work was required to bring the grey working masses into a state of consciousness..."[353]

Looking at the experience of other nations, it was clear that it would take a mass proletarian movement to draw such workers into conscious struggle in defence of their own interests.

Eight years later, in *What Is To Be Done?*, Ulyanov would write: "I worked in a circle that set itself very broad, all-encompassing tasks – each of us in that circle suffered agonies from the realisation that we were mere apprentices at such a historic moment, when we could have been able to say, to paraphrase the famous epigram, 'Give us an organisation of revolutionaries, and we will turn Russia upside down!'"[354]

There was a feeling in many industrial centres that it was time to shift towards towards mass agitation and in October 1894 Yuliy Tsederbaum

---

353   *K. M. Takhtarev*. Rabocheye dvizheniye v Peterburge. p. 31.
354   *V. I. Lenin*. Polnoye sobraniye sochineny. Vol. 6. p. 127.

(Martov) arrived in St Petersburg with the manuscript for a pamphlet titled "On Agitation", which he presented to local social democrats.[355]

On 20th October 1894, Emperor Alexander III died.[356]

He died in his chair on the terrace of the Livadia Palace in Crimea. That morning he had said to his wife, "I feel the end approaching." In the two hours before his death, he had called his successor to him and ordered him to sign an accession manifesto there and then. "Certainly, Papa," was the reply.

Nicholas II was 26 at the time, the 18th tsar of the Romanov dynasty. As ever in Russia, not only during a royal accession, but with any transfer of power, there was – particularly in liberal circles – a period of hope that positive change from on high would be forthcoming.

In the meantime, the social democrats, who were "zealously engaged in economic agitation," as Ulyanov puts it, had nonetheless missed the beginning of the unrest which flared over Christmas in the Nevsky Zavod (Semyannikov) plant, when salary payments were delayed by a number of days. This was the second or third such delay and the owners had decided that the workers could wait once more. This time they would not.

During a shift handover on 23rd December, when the morning shift were still at their stations and their evening replacements were just arriving, with around 3,000 men congregated in the factory, groups of youths began blocking Shlisselburgsky Prospekt with passing sledges and halted the streetcars. A riot began: the gatehouse, office and factory shop were smashed up, workshop windows broken, and the manager's accommodation set ablaze. 200 Cossacks, police and the fire brigade, who sprayed workers with freezing water from their hoses, arrived to quell the disorder. The riot was halted, but the factory workers did not disperse. Cossacks were sent after the factory clerks, who had fled in terror, and brought them back on sledges; it was late at night by the time it was left to gendarmerie officers themselves to hand the workers their wage packets.

When after these events Vladimir Ulyanov visited Ivan Babushkin's circle, which included some Nevsky Zavod workers, he berated them at length for not having been present.

A few days later, Gleb Krzhizhanovsky wrote up and printed in hectograph form a leaflet which, besides calling workers to the organisation,

---

355   See: Y. Martov. Zapiski sotsial-demokrata. pp. 236, 239.
356   See: Rabochaya gazeta. 1926. 22nd January.

explained that spontaneous riots were not only pointless, but damaging: "Let us take our example. We could have said beforehand that destroying the owners' property would only lead to quicker police interference, the workers being shut up, and the affair ending in the way that it did. We all know that the factory owners, the police, and the entire authority of the state are all together and all against us."[357]

Soon news arrived from circle members of trouble brewing in the New Admiralty port. In January 1895, the port commander General Verkhovsky effectively extended the working day when he cancelled the 15-minute 'grace period' at the start of the shift and cut 15 minutes from the lunch break. The general did not finish there: on Monday 6th February, he moved the shift start time by half an hour and cut another 15 minutes from the lunch break.

This time the social democrats would not be caught napping. By 7th February, a leaflet titled "What should the dockworkers seek to achieve?" had been prepared, which set out a list of demands. That day, as a witness recounts, "a section of the workers arrived at work in accordance with the old schedule. They were not let in. The gates were locked and they were required to pay a fine for the period of the day they had not worked. There were around 100 such late arrivals. The workers asked the guards to admit them, but were refused. At that point, they broke through the gates and entered the workshops. There they appealed to their fellow workers to drop their tools, which they quickly did. The administration just as quickly called for a detachment of city and district police headed up by a superintendent [*pristav*]. The usual procedure followed: "So, it's a riot you want!", followed by a volley of abuse appropriate for the occasion. To this, the workers responded that they had no wish to quarrel, and the superintendent calmed down. Each answered that they were not thinking of 'rioting', but sought only for the conditions of employment agreed by the administration upon their hiring to be adhered to... One worker, speaking on behalf of his comrades, explained the situation in a thorough and reasoned manner and laid out their demands. An attempt was made to apprehend him, but this was successfully resisted by the body of workers acting as one in coming to his aid. At one o'clock in the afternoon, the factory hooter sounded to return to work, but this had the opposite effect.

---

357   Listovki peterburgskogo "Soyuzu bor'by za osvobozhdeniye rabochego klassa". Moscow, 1934. p. 1.

It was the same story the following day. The workers maintained exemplary discipline. It was clear someone who knew how to control the movement was in charge. On Wednesday the same story repeated itself again.

On the Thursday the administration itself halted work for the rest of the week on the pretext of celebrating the upcoming Shrove-tide festival, but by Monday of the first week of the fast, the workers were arriving for work with their old conditions restored. Victory was theirs, and at a state-run factory, no less. A new mood took hold among the workers in the circles. This was a turning point. There was a sense, growing ever stronger, that the truly conscious worker should be closer to life around him, should more actively address the needs and demands of the working masses, and confront the daily violation of human rights..."[358]

---

[358] *K. M. Takhtarev*. Rabocheye dvizheniye v Peterburge. pp. 42-43.

LEADER OF THE PETERSBURG SDS

With the coronation of Nicholas II, the nation looked forward to positive change.

Prince Vladimir Obolensky recalled: "It was said that he (Nicholas II) left the Mariinsky Palace without any escort and returned after buying cigarettes at a tobacco kiosk. This scene, remarkable in Russia, was witnessed by many passers-by on Nevsky Prospekt and rumours immediate spread around the city of the extraordinary simplicity and openness of the young monarch."[359]

However, this period of hope and anticipation did not last long. His mother, the Dowager Empress Maria Feodorovna (née Princess Sophie Frederikke Dagmar) had often warned her son: "Your grandfather got it into his head to liberalise, and they blew him up. Your father did not allow any of this liberal stuff and, thank God, he died a good Christian."[360]

The emperor heeded her advice. At a reception at the Anichkov Palace on 17th January 1895, he announced to representatives of the *zemstvos*, cities and estates: "Let it be known that I … will preserve the foundation of our rule as firmly and steadily as my cherished late father." As to the timid calls for a role for 'society' in the governance of Russia, the emperor responded by dismissing them as "empty dreams".[361]

The speech had been composed by Konstantin Pobedonostsev, and Nicholas II slipped his copy of it, printed in large letters, inside the Astrakhan hat he held in his hand. The Tver *zemstvo* delegate A. A. Savelyev recalled, "I saw clearly that after each utterance he would glance down into the hat, just as we had done in school when we were unsure of the lesson."

The emperor spoke in a raised voice and his wife, who at the time spoke poor Russian, asked her lady-in-waiting, "Has something happened? Why

---

359   *V. A. Obolensky.* Moya zhizn'. Moi sovremenniki. Paris, 1988. p. 131.
360   *M. K. Kasvinov.* Dvadtsat' tri stupeni vniz. Moscow, 1987. p. 76.
361   Istoriya KPSS. Vol. 1. p. 185.

is he shouting?", to which her lady-in-waiting replied loudly enough for those present to hear, "He's telling them that they're imbeciles."[362]

It eventually emerged that the whole episode of the emperor appearing on Nevsky Prospekt without an escort was pure myth. Vladimir Obolensky wrote, "It appears that it was not Nicholas II buying himself cigarettes on Nevsky Prospekt, but his cousin, the future George V, who could have passed for his twin."[363]

Meanwhile, on 26th April 1895, a strike began at the cotton mill of the Bolshaya (formerly Korzinkinskaya) Works in Yaroslavl. As was customary, the police had arrested the 'ringleaders'. When a crowd of workers attempted to free their comrades, soldiers of the Fanagoriisky Regiment were given the order to open fire. Three people were killed, and 18 injured. Nicholas II noted on a report of the incident: "Very satisfied with the calm and steadfast conduct of the troops during the factory disturbances."[364]

Vladimir Ulyanov did not hear of these events, as he had left the country on 25th April.

His travel passport, which had been refused so many time before, was finally issued on 15th March 1895. The Petersburg social democrats had agreed at the start of the year on the necessity of travelling to Switzerland to establish direct contact with Emancipation of Labour. There had been no discussion over which of them was to go: by that time, Ulyanov's status as leader was clear.

How and why had this role become his? Within a bureaucracy, a leader is appointed – a straightforward enough process. In a democratic system, he may be elected, although in such a circumstance 'informal leaders' may also emerge. But in the revolutionary milieu of the time, leaders were neither designated nor elected. They became such on the strength of their knowledge, their experience, and – mostly importantly – their personal authority.

Alexander Potresov did not immediately recognise the primacy of Ulyanov's knowledge and experience. But 32 years later, he would write: "No-one else could galvanise with his designs, impress with his will, and command with his personality as he could." Nor did anyone else possess

---

362   M. K. Kasvinov. Dvadtsat' tri stupeni vniz. p. 77.

363   V. A. Obolensky. Moya zhizn'. Moi sovremenniki. p. 131.

364   Rabocheye dvizheniye v Rossii v XIX veke. Sbornik dokumentov i materialov. Moscow, 1961. Vol. 4. Part 1. p. 81.

"the knack that Lenin had for hypnotising others – a mastery over them, I would say... Only Lenin represented that most singular of individuals, particularly rare in Russia – a man of iron will and irrepressible energy, who fused a fanatical belief in the movement and the task at hand with an equal faith in himself."

"We recognised him as our leader unanimously, unequivocally and implicitly..." wrote Mikhail Silvin. "His primacy was based not only on his overwhelming authority as a theorist, his vast knowledge, his extraordinary capacity for work, or his intellectual superiority – to us he possessed great moral authority as well..."[365]

Thus, it was authority of knowledge, intelligence, work ethic, and morality that was the determining factor; no other sources of leadership existed in such a setting. But Struve did not see it this way, and if Potresov was unable to see Ulyanov's superior knowledge, then Struve refuted outright any moral superiority.

"In his dealings with people," he wrote, "Lenin exuded real coldness, contempt, and severity. It was clear to me even then that these unpleasant, even repellent traits of Lenin's were the basis for his strength as a politician: his focus was only on the goal to which he was firmly and steadfastly striving. Or, rather, his mind did not fix on one goal in the distance, but on ... an entire chain of them. The first link in this chain was gaining power within the narrow circle of his political friends. Lenin's harshness and severity became apparent to me almost from the beginning, from our first meeting – they were psychologically inseparable, both instinctively and consciously, from his irrepressible desire for power."[366]

This assessment has been enthusiastically adopted by modern critics of Lenin, not only for its simplicity: it has proved particularly attractive for the way that it invokes the experience of the 1990s, when the motivation for political involvement lost all substance and seeking power for personal enrichment became the norm.

However, the character references offered by Potresov and Struve seem to reflect not so much their actual impressions and observations of the 1890s as they do the later political conflicts that took place in the following decades. This is particularly underlined by the recollections of Yuliy Martov.

---

365   Proletarskaya revolyutsiya. 1924. No. 7 (30). p. 75.

366   *P. Struve*. Moi vstrechi i stolknoveniya s Leninym // Novy mir. 1991. No. 4. p. 219.

In his memoirs, written in 1919, he recalled: "[Ulyanov] had not yet developed, or at least did not exhibit, that confidence in his own strength – not to mention historical mission – which became more apparent later in his life... The pre-eminent position he enjoyed within the social democrats as part of the 'old men' [*stariki*], and the attention his first literary literary works attracted, was not enough to elevate himself in his own mind too much above those around him... V. Ulyanov was still at a stage when a man of great calibre, and aware of the fact, seeks in his interactions with others more opportunities to learn than to instruct. In his personal interactions there was no trace of the self-assurance visible in his first literary endeavours, especially his criticism of Struve... He dealt with his political opponents with a large dose of modesty." Martov makes another noteworthy comment: "I never observed any elements of personal vanity in Ulyanov's character."[367]

Konstantin Takhtarev, one of Ulyanov's ideological opponents, also tried to be objective in his assessment, writing: "I cannot say whether Vladimir Ilyich was intent on leading those in his circle, or set on becoming head of the movement, from the very beginning... My own view is that in most instances he began to lead his comrades and those around him not out of a desire to be foremost within his group necessarily, but because he was always moving ahead of them, showing them the road by example, and inadvertently became the one they followed."[368]

Of particular interest in this respect are the views of the main workers of influence, who were not only entirely independent in their judgements, but could also – on the strength of their life experience – sense from a distance a man on the make, not to mention the slightest hint of "coldness, contempt, and severity" towards others.

Shelgunov's characterisation of Ulyanov reads: "There were many good people among the revolutionaries at that point, but no-one was more plain in his dealings with others than Ulyanov." This is a view shared by Matvei Fisher, a worker at the Siemens & Halske plant who had passed through *Narodnaya Volya* and Marxist circles and was from 1901 active in the English workers' movement, only returning to Russia 20 years later. In his recollections of Ulyanov and the 1890s, he wrote: "Outwardly, there was nothing that particularly marked him out from the rest of the

---

367   Y. Martov. Zapiski sotsial-demokrata. pp. 270-271.
368   K. M. Takhtarev. Rabocheye dvizheniye v Peterburge. p. 167.

revolutionary intelligentsia, ... but there was a distinction in his bearing towards others. He was not aggressively assertive, and caused no offence, did not boast, nor did he flaunt his attainments. He knew just the way to approach a person so as to make him feel, without him even realising it, enough at ease that he would comfortably open his soul, sure in the belief that he would have all his questions answered."[369]

If such testimonies seem somewhat fawning, their authors can hardly be accused of insincerity. At any rate, these opinions offer grounds to cast doubt on Struve's suggestion of "coldness, contempt, and severity" towards others, accusations which could certainly be more properly applied in the fierce political struggle of later years.

Potresov's 1927 portrait of Ulyanov could also be viewed in the context of these later conflicts: "He was only young on his passport. Looking in his eyes, one would not have given his age as anything less than 35-40. A wan face, the baldness spreading across his entire head, leaving only strands of growth around the sides, a thin, reddish beard, and cunning, rather furrowed eyes which squinted narrowly at those he was speaking to, and a hoarse, aged voice... In my recollection, there was nothing youthful about the young Lenin. I was not the only one to pick up on this – the others who knew him had similar impressions. There was a reason ... he was called 'the old man', and as we often joked, even as a child, Lenin was probably as 'old' and bald as he seemed to us in '95."[370]

Contrast this with Gleb Krzhizhanovsky's view: "The Old Man nickname was in sharp contrast to the youthful vivaciousness and energy which burst forth from him." Or Herman Krasin's reflections: "We were met by an unusually lively and cheerful individual... He possessed a boundless sense of humour and an infectious laugh which would bring him to tears."[371]

Whether "he exuded coldness and contempt", as Struve claimed, or as Krasin suggests, he was "an unusually lively and cheerful individual", Ulyanov was nonetheless recognised as leader by both the intellectuals of the Technological Institute and leading St Petersburg workers.[372]

---

369   Ob Ilyiche. Sbornik statei. Moscow, 1930. pp. 124-125.

370   Istochnik. 1993. No. 4. pp. 20-21.

371   Gorkovskaya Pravda. 1955. 22nd April; Moskovsky stroitel'. 1940. 21st January; Stary bol'shevik. 1933. Collection 2 (5). p. 188.

372   Proletarskaya revolyutsiya. 1924. No. 3 (26). p. 103.

By early 1895, their illegal St Petersburg organisation was already in regular contact with social democrat groups in Moscow, Nizhny Novgorod, Ivanovo-Voznesensk, Kiev and Vilnius. It was now time to establish direct links with the most significant formation of social democrats abroad – Geneva-based Emancipation of Labour.

With Ulyanov now in possession of a travel passport, on 25th April, having barely recovered from a severe bout of pneumonia, he left the country.

IN DISTANT LANDS

He experienced no issues crossing the border, despite an order from the Department of Police to "arrange careful surveillance of Vladimir Ulyanov's activities and dealings abroad".[373] However, he immediately faced problems with the language. It became apparent that the German he had been taught by Yakob Mikhailovich Shteingauer at school, adequate as it was for reading literature, bore no resemblance to that spoken by Austrians and Germans.

On 2nd May, during a stopover in Salzburg, Ulyanov wrote to his mother: "I have proven to be quite *schwach* (weak), and have the greatest difficulty in understanding Germans – more accurately, *I do not comprehend them at all*. (I do not understand even the simplest of words – that is without mentioning their strange pronunciation and the rapidity of their speech.) I will approach the conductor with a question, he will respond, but I won't understand him. He will then repeat himself more loudly. I still won't understand, and he will then grow impatient and depart. Despite such embarrassing fiascos, I am not losing heart and am quite enthusiastically mangling the German language."[374]

His next letter was sent after having reached Switzerland. "The scenery here is magnificent. I am constantly in awe of it. The Alps and lakes began immediately beyond the German station from which I wrote to you, and it proved impossible to tear myself away from the carriage window..."[375]

He obtained Plekhanov's address from relatives of Robert Klasson in Lausanne and then travelled to Geneva, where the two met for the first time. Plekhanov made an immediate impression on him: Ferdinand Lassalle's remark about the "physical force of the mind" instantly sprang to Ulyanov's mind.

373	Krasny arkhiv. 1934. No. 1 (62). p. 79.
374	V. I. Lenin. Polnoye sobraniye sochineny. Vol. 55. p. 7.
375	Ibid. Vol. 55. p. 8.

To say that Ulyanov treated him with the degree of reverence due to a man Russian Marxists viewed as something of a patriarch would not be entirely correct. It was more like the *'youthful adoration'* of his younger days. Georgi Valentinovich was like a spiritual guide to him, one who had in part inspired his path in life. There was a direct thread running from him to the men who had become idols to the revolutionary generation – Marx and Engels. This in itself aroused a kind of spiritual awe. Some years later, Ulyanov would write frankly about his "immense love for him", stating that he and his friends "loved Plekhanov ... and like a loved one, forgave him everything, closing [their] eyes to every shortcoming..."[376]

However, none of this was in evidence at that first meeting. Yevgeny Sponti, who had arrived in Switzerland some time earlier and was present at their meeting, wrote that Ulyanov "was very reserved ... [and] behaved with great dignity," and, most likely as a result of nerves, "said little, or rather nothing more than the conversation demanded".[377]

During the meeting, Ulyanov presented Plekhanov with a copy of "What the 'Friends of the People' Are..." Plekhanov "took a cursory glance at the pamphlet and remarked, 'Yes, it seems like a serious piece of work.'"[378] He was perfectly polite and cordial, but Ulyanov reported to his sister Anna that "there was certain coolness" about him. This was not down to any specific issue with Ulyanov, but was rather a manifestation of his usual habit of maintaining a certain distance with people, even those with whom he was friendly, never mind the endless procession of young Russians that continually sought him out.

This is reminiscent of Maxim Gorky's experience: "When I was 'led' to Plekhanov, he stood with his arms folded, looking at me sternly and with a bored air, like a teacher who has long grown weary of his duties looks at his latest pupil."[379]

Lunchtime arrived, but Plekhanov did not offer Ulyanov and Sponti anything, as his wife was away. Instead, he recommended an inexpensive restaurant, and they set off. For Ulyanov, this was his first experience of restaurant dining abroad, and as is often the case with Russians, it did not pass without incident. Sponti writes, "Unfamiliar with the foreign

---

376	Ibid. Vol. 4. p. 344.
377	Zapiski Instituta Lenina. III. 1928. pp. 71-73.
378	Ibid.
379	*M. Gorky*. Sobraniye sochineny. 30 volumes. Moscow, 1952. Vol. 17. p. 7.

menu, Lenin and I took our hats after the second course and, much to the amusement of the waitresses, made attempts to pay the bill without realising the meal was not yet over."[380]

Plekhanov sent Ulyanov to see Pavel Axelrod in Zürich for more substantive talks with Emancipation of Labour. While the reverence he felt for Plekhanov somewhat paralysed Ulyanov, he detected something of his late father Ilya in Axelrod, and they immediately formed a warm friendship. They spent a week in the village of Affoltern, an hour's drive from Zürich, and Axelrod recalls them spending "whole days together" walking in the surrounding countryside, climbing "the hills around Zug, constantly immersed in discussion of matters of great concern to us both".

They talked mostly about the content and form of the work that social democrats were undertaking. Throughout their conversations, Axelrod continually returned to the same idea – that it was time to form a party. Each time congresses of the International gathered, Plekhanov and his colleagues would receive their mandate from a rather disparate collection of groups. The Fourth Congress of the Second International was approaching in the summer of 1896, and Axelrod proposed that if the relationship between the St Petersburg contingent and the workers was as solid as Ulyanov had suggested, then it was necessary to form an organisation and name it, by way of an example, "The League for the Emancipation of Labour".[381]

Lenin did not need to be convinced of the necessity of forming a party. A year before their meeting in Switzerland, writing in "What the 'Friends of the People' Are...", he had argued that such a step was a priority.[382] There was no further debate: they agreed to establish regular correspondence and begin producing an illegal newspaper for St Petersburg workers, while in Switzerland they would launch a non-periodical collection edited by Axelrod under the title *Rabotnik* [The Worker], which would feature material sent from Russia.[383]

The meeting had been an enormous success. Many years later, Axelrod wrote, "These conversations with Ulyanov were a truly

---

380   Zapiski Instituta Lenina. III. 1928. p. 73.
381   Perepiska G. V. Plekhanova i P. B. Axelrod. Vol. 1. pp. 273, 274.
382   V. I. Lenin. Polnoye sobraniye sochineny. Vol. 1. p. 304.
383   See: Perepiska G. V. Plekhanova i P. B. Axelrod. Vol. 1. pp. 265-275.

wonderful time for me. I now think back on them as one of the brightest, happiest periods in the existence of Emancipation of Labour."³⁸⁴

"Ulyanov, while undoubtedly gifted and assured in his views, showed a willingness to examine his own ideas, and to study and learn from those of others. He showed not the slightest hint of conceit or vanity... He conducted himself purposefully, seriously, yet modestly at the same time."³⁸⁵

From Switzerland, Ulyanov travelled to Paris. On 8th June, he wrote to his mother: "I received your letter just before setting off for Paris... I'm only beginning to get my bearings in Paris... It is enormous, and so widely spread out that the outlying districts (in which one often finds oneself) bear no resemblance to the centre. There is a pleasant air to the city – wide, bright streets, many of them boulevards, and plenty of greenery; the people seem wholly at ease, so much so that it initially took me aback, used as I am to St Petersburg's stiffness and severity. I will need a few weeks to properly absorb it."³⁸⁶

Ulyanov was there to meet with Paul Lafargue. As a gifted proponent of Marxist ideas, a leading figure in the socialist International, and Marx's son-in-law, he was awe-inspiring to any socialist, never mind one as young as Ulyanov. But for Plekhanov and his colleagues, of more importance was the opportunity to 'present', as it were, a representative of Russian social democracy with connections to the nascent proletarian movement. When the visit took place, it was no coincidence that Lafargue was most interested in what Russian socialists were doing on the ground.

Yuliy Martov reports Ulyanov's account of the meeting thus:

"What do you do in these circles?" asked Lafargue. Ulyanov explained that, after introducing the subject in popular lectures, the most capable workers would study Marx.

"And they read Marx?" Lafargue asked.

"They do."

"And do they understand it?"

"They do."

---

384   Ibid. p. 271.
385   Ibid. pp. 270, 271.
386   V. I. Lenin. Polnoye sobraniye sochineny. Vol. 55. pp. 8, 9.

"Here you are mistaken," concluded the waspish Frenchman. "They understand nothing. Here, after 20 years of the socialist movement, no-one understands Marx."[387]

Alongside his visit to Lafargue, Ulyanov also made time to go to the Bibliothèque Nationale. There he compiled a list of books on the Paris Communards, some published as early as 1871: André Léo's *The Social War*, Benoît Malon's *Third Defeat...*, *Social Antagonism* by Adolphe Clémence, Jules Guesde's *Red Book on Rural Justice*, and Lissagaray's *Eight May Days on the Barricades*. These he read, and also produced a summary of a book by Gustave Lefrançais.[388]

He only took notes on its early sections, as he did not want to spend the hot summer days cooped up in a library. He wrote later to his mother: "I spent only a month in Paris, and did little there, spending most of my time scurrying round the 'sights'."[389] He visited Communards' Wall in the Père Lachaise cemetery, the Museum of the 1789 Revolution, the Grévin Waxworks Museum, the Ménagerie du Jardin des Plantes, and the Jardin du Luxembourg. He walked every back street and lane on which the Paris workers had erected their barricades. Later, Vladimir Bonch-Bruevich recalled: "Vladmir Ilyich was extremely fond of recounting the events of the Paris Commune, which he was able to do quite from memory. He knew which battles took place where, who had been killed, and which figures had covered themselves in glory. He so enjoyed speaking of those days that it almost felt that we ... had been present when the great battles of the Parisian proletariat had been fought not so long ago."[390]

It is likely that Ulyanov intended to go from Paris to England for a meeting with Friedrich Engels. A year before, Plekhanov had introduced Alexander Potresov to Engels in London, and now he was able to do the same for Ulyanov. This meeting was to be the culmination of his travels abroad. However, it emerged that Engels had suffered a sharp decline in health and any visit became impossible.

From Paris Ulyanov returned to Switzerland. On 18th (6th) June, he wrote to his mother: "I have been all over and now find myself ... at a Swiss health resort: I have decided to use this opportunity to properly address a

---

387   Y. Martov. Zapiski sotsial-demokrata. p. 266.
388   See: Inostrannaya literatura. 1957. No. 4. pp. 7-17.
389   V. I. Lenin. Polnoye sobraniye sochineny. Vol. 55. p. 74.
390   B. V. Yakovlev. Stranitsy avtobiografii V. I. Lenina. pp. 157-159.

(stomach) condition which has been bothering me, not least because this resort's specialist was recommended to me as an expert in the field. I have been here for some days now and feel quite well; the *pension* is splendid and the treatment is apparently doing the trick, so hopefully I will be able to move on from here in 4-5 days. Life here is, it turns out, very expensive; treatment even more so, so I've already gone over my budget and no longer expect to get by on my current funds. If at all possible, send me another hundred or so roubles..."[391]

The Russian police were keeping a close eye on his international correspondence, so it is difficult to say for certain whether Ulyanov actually visited the resort or not – most likely, he did not. It is certainly a fact, albeit one missed by the compilers of Lenin's biography, that he travelled from Paris to Geneva, then on to the remote village of Ormône, in the company of Plekhanov, Alexander Voden, and the newly arrived Alexander Potresov.[392]

Here, below the snowy alpine slopes, Potresov writes that they spent all their time "on walks, talking continuously as we went".[393] And although both the scenery and the company were excellent, Ulyanov was seemingly ill at ease. Firstly, he felt a certain inhibition around Plekhanov, and, secondly, their endless conversations were to him too reminiscent of genteel salon talk.

Plekhanov was certainly a refined individual, with mannerisms more akin to those of an aristocrat. With his phenomenal erudition and, as Potresov notes, "his all-encompassing range of interests, which fuelled the consistently vivid and gifted workings of his mind," Plekhanov was a fount of ideas. "As if from a bottomless well of wisdom, one could draw ideas and insights [from him] on the most varied fields of human knowledge; talking with him was a lesson, not only on politics, but on art, literature, theatre and philosophy..."[394]

But whatever the subject of discussion, as soon as it touched on Russia, Plekhanov totally transformed: "He would light up when he spoke about it..."[395]

---

391   *V. I. Lenin*. Polnoye sobraniye sochineny. Vol. 55. pp. 9-10.

392   See: *S. V. Tyutyukin*. G. V. Plekhanov. Sud'ba russkogo marksizma. Moscow, 1997.

393   Istochnik. 1993. No. 4. p. 22.

394   Ibid.

395   *S. V. Tyutyukin*. G. V. Plekhanov. Sud'ba russkogo marksizma. p. 131.

During these conversations, talk had turned to "What the 'Friends of the People' Are...", which Ulyanov had written under the pseudonym Tulin. Having written of the need "to lead all democratic forces" in the struggle against absolutism, Ulyanov found he faced no fundamental objections to this, Axelrod noting that Plekhanov "recognises the correctness of the Group's point of view on this issue".[396]

In the second half of July, Ulyanov travelled to Berlin. On 10th August, he wrote to his mother: "I do not know if you received my last letter, which I sent from here around a week ago... My arrangements here are very adequate: a few steps away is the Tiergarten (a splendid park, the largest and best in Berlin), the Spree, in which I bathe daily, and a metropolitan railway station. Here the railway traverses the entire city (below the streets): the trains depart every five minutes, so I am finding travelling around the 'city' very easy (Moabit, where I am staying, is actually considered a suburb).

The language is the only wretched thing: my understanding of spoken German is incomparably worse than my French. I find German pronunciation so alien that I cannot even discern the content of public speeches, despite understanding virtually everything in such addresses on first hearing while in France."[397]

In his next letter, Ulyanov writes: "I feel very well – it must be that regular routine (I had had enough of moving from place to place, and had not been eating properly or regularly enough as a consequence), the bathing and so forth, adhering as I am to the doctor's instructions, are having their effect..."[398]

Documents and memoirs show that he was kept busy in a number of ways while in Berlin: in the reading room of the Prussian State Library he studied the newest Marxist literature on a daily basis, and he attended a number of workers' meetings, hearing a lecture on the German social democrats' agrarian programme. He also met up with an old friend from Samara, Wilhelm Buchholz, through whom he met Vilnius-based social democrats, making arrangements to establish links between there and St Petersburg.

Meanwhile, sad news arrived of the death on 24th July (5th August) of Friedrich Engels, for whom Ulyanov composed an obituary.

---

396   Perepiska G. V. Plekhanova i P. B. Axelrod. Vol. 1. p. 272.

397   *V. I. Lenin.* Polnoye sobraniye sochineny. Vol. 55. p. 11.

398   Ibid. p. 12.

In early September, he was visited by one of the German Social Democratic Party's leaders, Wilhelm Liebknecht. To facilitate the meeting, Plekhanov had written to him: "I am recommending to you one of our finest Russian comrades. He will be returning to Russia... He is going to relay to you a matter of great importance to us. I trust that you will do everything in your power for him."[399] The matter he wished to discuss was the possibility of having illegal literature published in Germany and ferried into Russia. On 7th September, Vladimir Ulyanov re-entered Russia quite legally by passenger train as it crossed the border at Verzhbolovo Station.

His yellow suitcase, fitted with a double bottom filled with illegal printed material, had been expertly put together by the Germans. The chief of the border post reported to the Department of Police that nothing suspicious had been found during a most careful inspection of Ulyanov's luggage. Spies established that he had bought a ticket to Vilnius, but failed to find any further trace of him there.

---

399 Vladimir Ilyich Lenin. Biograficheskaya khronika. Vol. 1. p. 105.

THE BIRTH OF A PARTY

Ulyanov detailed his further movements in a letter to Axelrod: "I was initially in Vilnius. I spoke with people there about the collection. The majority agreed that it is time for a publication of this kind and promised their support... They said that we should assess whether it fits with the tactics of agitation and tactics of economic struggle. I stressed that that was really up to us.

I was later in Moscow... There have been huge *pogroms* there [arrests – author], but it seems there are still enough people around for our work to continue. We have received some material from there, namely an account of some of the strikes... We will get that to you...

...Give me more details about the collection: what material we already have, what is planned, when the first issue will be published, and what exactly we need for the second... We'll likely send some money..."[400]

There is something unusual, both in tone and content, in this correspondence. Earlier, his letters had been to family and friends, or to acquaintances near and far. In them he would share his thoughts, put forth arguments, or express his wishes. But in this letter, he is for the first time *reporting on* work accomplished. It was the first time he considered himself part of what was for him something significantly greater, in which relationships were built not on personal friendships, but on their belonging to a *common cause*.

To this end he had taken on certain obligations which had necessitated this dangerous journey across Russia. This new style of communication was in no way a burden to him. It is with obvious enthusiasm that he waxes in his letters to Zürich about paper and ink for printing press, channels of communication, secret meetings, and methods of correspondence. He writes that India ink requires "the addition of a small quantity of potassium dichromate ($K_2Cr_2O_7$): that way it won't wash off," and that when sending correspondence in the bindings of books, "one must use a very watery

---

400   V. I. Lenin. Polnoye sobraniye sochineny. Vol. 46. pp. 8-9.

paste: no more than a teaspoon of starch (potato starch, not wheat, which is very strong) to a glass of water."[401]

Ulyanov returned to St Petersburg on 29th September. By the following week he was already taking steps to unify autonomous social democrat groups in the capital.

By the middle of November, this task was complete. In attendance at the meeting where this unification was formalised were the core of the 'old men': Vladimir Ulyanov, Anatoly Vaneyev, Pyotr Zaporozhets, Gleb Krzhizhanovsky, Alexander Malchenko, Yakov Ponomarev, Stepan and Lyubov Radchenko, Mikhail Silvin, Vasily Starkov, Zinaida Nevzorova, Apollinariya Yakubova and Nadezhda Krupskaya. Yakov Lyakhovsky, V. M. Trenyukhin, and S. A. Gofman were present from Martov's group, along with Martov himself. These 17 individuals would form the spine of the organisation in the city. In the event of any disaster befalling them, V. K. Seryozhnikov, A. I. Shestopalov, and I. Smidovich were nominated as replacements, as were Fyodor Gurvich-Dan, Boris Goldman-Gorev and M. A. Luria from Martov's group.[402]

The organisation's members were assigned to districts. Ulyanov, Krzhizhanovsky, Vaneyev, Starkov and Martov made up the 'Central Group', which would direct the organisation as a whole. Ulyanov was also appointed editor of the publications they intended to produce, while Stepan and Lyubov Radchenko took on responsibility for security and financial matters. Ponomarev was put in charge of equipment, and Krupskaya was tasked with maintaining communication with the workers through the night school that she ran. Naturally, this division of responsibilities was all rather provisional, but Martov rightly considered these to be the first steps in the foundation of a party.[403]

One significant issue remained unresolved: the installation of workers within the governing Central Group. In 1894, the so-called Central Workers' Group, headed by Shelgunov, had been formed from the most influential workers in the various city districts. It functioned as a bridge between the social-democratic intelligentsia and workers' circles. However, as a shift to direct action was taking place in the factories, a young

---

401   Ibid. Vol. 46. p. 10.

402   See: *Y. Martov*. Zapiski sotsial-demokrata. pp. 271-272; *M. A. Silvin*. Lenin v period zarozhdeniya partii. p. 103.

403   See: ibid.

generation of activists had emerged alongside the veteran workers' circle members. The question was now: who to draft into the Central Group? According to his biography, Ulyanov met frequently with Boris Zinoviev, Vasily Shelgunov and Ivan Babushkin at this time. However, a decision was not forthcoming. Martov writes, "Eventually, giving vent to our frustration at what we considered to be the obvious difficulties of the situation, we decided in the meantime not to cut through the tangled knot and support a 'bicameral' governing and workers' centre, which in practice would be merely consultative, and allow ourselves more time to seek an alternative structure for the organisation."[404]

This was really not the time to be engendering internal conflict: a wave of strikes was reverberating around St Petersburg and social democrat representatives were skilfully steering the protests in a more constructive direction, distributing leaflets and proclamations among the workers. At the beginning of November, weavers at the Thornton factory struck, followed by workers at the Laferme cigarette plant, and only an increase in workers' earnings brought the strikes to a halt. Concessions from the administration also ended a three-day strike by shoemakers of the Skorokhod factory.

A few days later, more leaflets appeared at the Putilov Works. The mimeograph was working flat-out, while the illegal printing press was also operating at full capacity, producing 3,000 copies of Ulyanov's pamphlet "Explanation of the Law on Fines Imposed on Factory Workers".

Upon receiving a copy from St Petersburg, Plekhanov and Axelrod were glowing in their assessment. Ulyanov replied: "Your ... reviews of my literary endeavours ... are greatly encouraging to me. There is nothing more I could have wished for ... than the opportunity to write for the benefit of the workers."[405]

Comparing "What the 'Friends of the People' Are..." or "The Economic Content..." with "Explanation of the Law...", it may appear that they are written by entirely different authors. The earlier works are full of Ulyanov's reflections on complex philosophical and economic problems. Here, the talk is of fines and damages.

This is not simply a journalistic aptitude for adapting to a new subject by using alternative jargon and professional vernacular. To represent the interests of others, one must first learn to understand them. At Kokushkino

---

404   Ibid. p. 274; cf. Ot gruppy Blagoyeva. pp. 57, 58.
405   *V. I. Lenin*. Polnoye sobraniye sochineny. Vol. 46. p. 12.

and Alakayevka Ulyanov had witnessed the lives and heard the language of the Russian peasantry. Now he was familiarising himself with *working-class* existence, which had its own specialised vocabulary of factory life. St Petersburg would mark his first exposure to this new stratum of society.

The success of the leafleting indicated that a common language had been found between the working masses and the social-democratic intelligentsia.

Takhtarev writes, "The leaflets, and the concessions that followed, had rather a magical effect on the workers: it created an energy, and a belief in their ability to fight, a belief in the impact of large-scale action and in the strength of unity. The unification of workers in St Petersburg's various districts and efforts to create a common organisation continued. The mood among organised workers was especially buoyant. Finally, a means to utilise the strength, education and knowledge they had accumulated while their activities had been confined purely to the circles."[406]

It was this unification of social democracy and the proletarian movement that was the decisive step on the way to founding a party that would "lead the proletarian class struggle ... without resorting to any kind of conspiracy, instead drawing its power from the *unification* of the socialist and democratic struggle as a single, indivisible class war waged by the proletariat of St Petersburg".[407]

Heated debate still continues around when the League of Struggle for the Emancipation of the Working Class was so named, and by whom. However, it is a point of fact that the first time that title appeared on a leaflet was on 15th December 1895.

On 6th December, preparations for the first issue of the newspaper were completed. In agreement with the *Narodnaya Volya* group, it was named *Rabocheye Delo* [Workers' Cause]. During the meeting which took place in Radchenko's apartment, Ulyanov opened by saying, "I consider my position as editor sovereign," thus eliminating the need for any further debate on the content of articles already agreed upon by the authors and editors.[408] The composition of the first issue was confirmed: there were to be four articles by Ulyanov, including a leader which called on the Russian proletariat to fight for its political freedom. The remaining articles were

---

406   *K. M. Takhtarev*. Rabocheye dvizheniye v Peterburge. p. 51.
407   *V. I. Lenin*. Polnoye sobraniye sochineny. Vol. 2. p. 460.
408   *M. A. Silvin*. Lenin v period zarozhdeniya partii. p. 106.

to be written by Martov, Krzhizhanovsky, Vaneyev, Silvin, Zaporozhets and others.

In the evening, they decided to attend a traditional students' charity ball, held in the hall of the Assembly of the Nobility. It is worth noting that these balls held a special place among the activities of the social democrats. Before the balls, the student body elected a number of committees, including an artistic committee, which invited renowned actors, and a dance committee, completely dominated by the more affluent students, the so-called *belopodkladochniki* [literally, those in white-lined tunics – *trans*.].

The finance committee was, as a rule, run by *narodniki* or social democrats. They picked the most attractive female students to sell – at quite absurd prices – entrance tickets (at least 10 roubles), flowers (25 roubles for a buttonhole bouquet) and champagne (up to 100 roubles a glass). The proceeds went to pay for tuition and for assistance to poorer students. Only a small percentage went to fund student organisations, occasionally ending up in the hands of the illegal ones.[409]

Surveillance was intensifying from day to day. By now, it was easy to spot. Ulyanov bought himself a new coat and changed address. Clearly applying the principle of taking the fight to the enemy, he moved to 61 Gorokhovaya Street, immediately beside the secret police [*okhranka*].

That December, he wrote to his mother, "I am living simply. I am not especially pleased with my room – primarily due to the prissiness of the landlady; secondly, it has become apparent that I am separated from the neighbouring room by a thin partition wall and I hear everything, so am required at times to escape the strains of the balalaika with which my neighbour likes to entertain himself... By Christmas, when the lease runs out on my room, it will not be difficult to find another. The weather here is particularly fine, and my new coat has proved just right for the season."[410]

On 8th December, Ulyanov held another editorial meeting of *Rabocheye Delo*. However, in the early hours of 9th December, arrests began. Vasily Shelgunov, Nikita Merkulov, Ivan Yakovlev, Boris Zinoviev, Pyotr Karamyshev and other workers were held. From among the ranks of the 'old men', Anatoly Vaneyev, Pyotr Zaporozhets, Gleb Krzhizhanovsky, Alexander Malchenko and Vasily Starkov were taken in. Late on 9th December, Vladimir Ulyanov was arrested too.

---

409   See: ibid. p. 133.

410   *V. I. Lenin*. Polnoye sobraniye sochineny. Vol. 55. p. 14.

PART FOUR – PRISON & EXILE

SOLITARY CONFINEMENT

How many revolutionaries were broken by the solitary confinement, punishment cells, blunt-witted wardens and monotony of the tsarist prison? It was not the paucity of the rations, nor the rock-hard prison bunk that wore them down. It was the isolation and apparent hopelessness. Prison tested the limits of revolutionary romanticism: often, such sentiment failed to endure, dashed instead against those bleak walls.

The St Petersburg Remand Prison on Shpalernaya Street was typical of a Russian prison. Cell No. 193, where Ulyanov was held, was a standard isolation cell: six paces from door to window. Those stories the Samara veterans had told him of prison survival, conduct in interrogations, and the rules of the 'clink' were to prove invaluable.

The first weeks were especially tough: back in November, when Maria Alexandrovna and Anna Ilyinichna had visited from Moscow, he had asked his sister, in the event of his arrest, "not to allow his mother to trouble herself by coming to Petersburg".[411] She fulfilled this request and now the time passed without visits or parcels, with no knowledge of who else had been arrested or what was happening on the outside.

Unlike the criminal prisoners, who were permitted regular courtyard exercise, organising noisy games and interacting as much as they pleased, political prisoners were held in isolation. Barred windows were installed in a deep recess just below the ceiling. For a fit person it was just about possible to reach the window by standing on the slop pail, stretching to his fullest extent, and grasping the bars. There, for the few seconds his strength held out, he would catch a glimpse of the prison yard, with

---

411   Proletarskaya revolyutsiya. 1924. No. 3. p. 107.

its slatted enclosures for solitary exercise, which Vladimir Ulyanov immediately christened "*spazieren*-pens".[412] But neither observation of this kind nor tapping on the walls in prison code offered up any information.

His first interrogation took place on 21st December. When questioned by Lieutenant Colonel Klykov of the Special Gendarme Corps, and A. Y. Kichin, deputy prosecutor of the St Petersburg Appellate Court, Ulyanov responded: "My name is Vladimir Ilyich Ulyanov. I am not guilty of membership of the social-democratic party, nor of any other party. I know nothing about the existence at the present time of any anti-government party. I do not participate in anti-government agitation among the workers... I do not wish to talk about my acquaintances for fear of compromising anyone by my association with them."[413] It would appear both sides drew adequate conclusions from the interrogation. The interrogators, recognising there was little to be gleaned from interviewing their man at the present time, decided that they would have to wear him down. Ulyanov in turn realised that they did have some evidence against him and consequently the investigation could take some time.

If it was to be an extended 'stretch' – as Ulyanov suspected it would be – there were at least three problems to solve. Firstly, regular contact with the outside world had to be established. Secondly, he must work out how best to fill up his days. Thirdly, he had to maintain his own health so as to avoid the usual bedfellows of solitary confinement, namely mental breakdown and tuberculosis. This required as many visits and parcels as he could get, and the opportunity to obtain books and food beyond the prison rations; i.e. he would have to make full use of his 'rights' and elicit from the prison authorities as much in the way of amenities as was afforded a person on remand.

It would be his first Christmas and New Year alone. There would be no amusing gifts, Christmas trees, or feasts with the family. Instead, he looked forward to conversations with the prosecutor. A. Y. Kichin, a man who had distinguished himself even within the judiciary for his reactionary views, and was renowned for his malicious attitude towards political prisoners, considering each to be something approaching a personal enemy.[414] There

---

412 See: *M. A. Silvin*. Lenin v period zarozhdeniya partii. p. 165.
413 *V. I. Lenin*. Polnoye sobraniye sochineny. Vol. 46. pp. 443, 444.
414 See: *Y. Martov*. Zapiski sotsial-demokrata. p. 300.

are no transcripts of his interrogation of Ulyanov. However, Ulyanov knew the laws and rules of prison. It was fruitless to attempt to intimidate or debate with him. Kichin was also aware that M. F. Wolkenstein, Ulyanov's boss and a renowned lawyer in the capital, and V. O. Lyustikh, chair of the St Petersburg Council of Attorneys, had expressed a desire to put up bail for Ulyanov, so discussions with the prosecutor ended favourably.

On 2nd January 1896, Ulyanov wrote to Alexandra Chebotareva, with whom he had been boarding, to pass on the following to his 'acquaintances': "Literary activities are permitted to prisoners – this was something I made a point of discussing with the prosecutor, though I was aware of this beforehand (these are permitted even to convicted prisoners). He also confirmed to me that there are no restrictions on the books that are permitted. One is able to return them later, so one can make use of libraries. In this regard, the situation is good."[415]

Meanwhile, it appears the issue of how best to occupy his time was already resolved. He states in a letter, "The plan I am working on has taken up much of the time since my arrest, and the further I go with it, the more engaged I become. There is one specific economic question that has occupied me for a while (on the sale of domestic manufactured goods), and I have selected some literature, worked out my approach, and even written a little... I have no wish to give up on this work, and now, it seems, I am presented with a choice: either write it in here, or abandon it altogether."[416]

The letter came with an extensive bibliography attached, the main body of which did indeed relate to the work he was planning. However, the list also contained entries of a completely different kind: by interspersing real authors and works with clearly invented ones, he was employing a cipher to enquire about the fate of his comrades.

From 9th January, a month after his arrest, he was permitted packages and visits from his family. His sister Anna arrived from Moscow and he received parcels from friends and family withheld from him over the Christmas period.

Maxim Gorky once wrote, "Every Russian who has done a month in prison or a year in exile as a 'political' considers it a sacred duty to gift Russia a memoir of his suffering."[417] Ulyanov's letters from his time on remand

---

415   V. I. Lenin. Polnoye sobraniye sochineny. Vol. 55. p. 15.
416   Ibid. Vol. 55. p. 15.
417   M. Gorky. Sobraniye sochineny. Vol. 17. p. 24.

are the very opposite of this, treating his experiences in prison first and foremost with humour.

On 12th January, Ulyanov wrote to his sister Anna, "I received the provisions you sent yesterday, while just before you someone else brought in all manner of things for me to eat, so I am gathering quite the stockpile: I could, for example, begin a roaring trade in tea, but I doubt they'll let me, as I would no doubt emerge victorious were I to go into competition with the racket here."[418]

Two years later, when his younger brother Dmitry was jailed, Ulyanov wrote to his mother, "It is a bad sign that he has managed to grow portly after only two and half months. First of all, is he observing a diet in prison? I dare say he isn't. In my view, that is essential while he is there. Secondly, is he exercising? It appears not. That is also vital. I can say, at least from my own experience, that it was a great pleasure and of enormous benefit to exercise before bed *every day*."[419]

Five years later, when his younger sister Maria was imprisoned, he wrote to her, "How are you getting on? I hope that you have established the regular routine that will stand you in such good stead in solitary confinement. I wrote to Mark today outlining to him in some detail how best to institute a 'routine': as far as mental activity is concerned, I recommended translating back and forth, i.e. a written translation from a foreign language into Russian, then from the Russian translation back into the foreign language. My experience of this demonstrated to me that this is the most effective way of learning a foreign language. In terms of physical exercise, I strongly recommended to him, and repeat to you, daily callisthenics and body rubs. In solitary confinement, this is vital.

...I also advise you to properly apportion out your reading of the books you have, so as to vary them: I remember very well that changing one's reading or activity – from translation to reading, from letter-writing to exercising, from serious literature to fiction – helped immensely... After lunch, in the evening, I recall *regalmässig* [regularly] turning to fiction as a means to relax, and I have never relished it as much as I did in prison."[420]

A record of the fiction works he so "relished" in solitary confinement has not survived, but we do know which books Anna and Potresov brought

---

418　*V. I. Lenin*. Polnoye sobraniye sochineny. Vol. 55. p. 17.
419　Ibid. Vol. 55. p. 72.
420　Ibid. Vol. 55. pp. 208, 209.

from the university library, Academy of Sciences and Free Economic Society. These are primarily dense (and dull!) collections of statistics from various provinces, statistical surveys of Russian industry, plant and factory indices, books on peasant farming, economies and communities, economic reports from provincial councils, and so on.

He spent a large part of his time pouring through material of this kind. By January 1896, he had made his decision on whether or not to write the book. He told Anna, "I sleep around nine hours a night, and dream of the various chapters in this future book."[421] Meanwhile, he had also begun translating regularly from German.

In January Anna spent a short time in St Petersburg, staying for around a month. Only in May, after his mother and sisters had settled in a *dacha* near the capital, did those few summer months become "paradise" for Ulyanov: his mother Maria Alexandrovna and sister Maria would come for half-hourly private visits on odd Mondays, while on Thursdays, he would talk with Anna through a double grille during general visiting hours. She brought him books and coded messages from outside, and three times a week he received food parcels prepared by his mother which allowed him to stick to the strict diet he had been prescribed by doctors. For a fee, Ulyanov was also permitted to receive meals, mineral water and milk.[422]

Modern critics of Lenin are wont to sneer: bought-in meals, mineral water and milk – this was more a sanatorium than a prison. But these are the judgements of people who have never been within 100 paces of a prison and consider all of its ills to stem exclusively from the quality of the food. However, inmates suffered from more than lousy prison slops.

Mikhail Silvin wrote to his fiancée while held in solitary remand, "It is difficult to cope with the despondency – the same walls, the same grime, the same racket, while all the time the weather drifts towards autumn, the days grow shorter, the heavy sky hangs as a dank, dreary, smothering mantle, and the rain batters monotonously against the roof and windows, reverberating in my soul with the sombre thought: 'I will be the end of you, I will be the end of you...'"[423]

Did Ulyanov suffer any of the 'mood swings' that so many prisoners have described, or was he made of sterner stuff? This question is answered

---

421	Ibid. Vol. 55. p. 18.
422	See: Proletarskaya revolyutsiya. 1924. No. 3. pp. 111-112.
423	See: *M. A. Silvin*. Lenin v period zarozhdeniya partii. p. 164.

by Nadezhda Krupskaya: "However much Vladimir Ilyich was in possession of himself, whatever efforts he made to build a routine, it is clear he suffered attacks of prison melancholy."[424] He made allusions to this himself in a letter to his younger sister: "Sometimes drops in mood – changeable as it is in prison – stem from simple fatigue brought on by the monotony of the experience, or the monotony of the work, and varying it is enough to bring oneself around and regain command over one's nerves."[425] This does not indicate that he never suffered from mood swings; rather that he was prepared to employ any means to overcome them and never relayed, either to his family or to his comrades, "his suffering".

Nonetheless, there were grounds enough for his nerves to be tested. The dentist Mikhailov was offering the gendarmes a wealth of information, although they were finding it difficult to make much use of it. Firstly, they could not expose their stool pigeon. Secondly, Mikhailov only had third-hand knowledge of the activities of the 'old men' – he had not been allowed any closer to them. Those arrested continued to employ a tactic of denial during interrogations, completely refuting any of the charges levelled against them. This principle was only abandoned when it could alleviate the plight of a comrade.

However, the situation soon worsened. The prosecutor Kichin turned out to be quite a crafty psychologist. While he was unable to get anything from the 'old men' and veterans of the workers' circles, long questioning of the young leader of the Putilov Works strikers Boris Zinoviev proved more productive. He fell prey to what Martov called "the lure of political vanity".[426]

Kichin was generous with his flattery, marvelling at Zinoviev's talents and intellectual development, and made one simple request: for Zinoviev to clarify why such an outstanding proletarian leader was getting mixed up with intellectuals. In the end, Zinoviev cracked. Initially, he spoke only of the plight of the working class and of the tasks facing the movement. Then he began to talk about his participation in the organising of strikes. He then outlined how propaganda work was carried out and how he had 'used' the intellectuals for the purposes of the movement. Boris was

---

424 Vospominaniya o Vladmire Ilyiche Lenine. Vol. 1. p. 221.

425 *V. I. Lenin.* Polnoye sobraniye sochineny. Vol. 55. p. 209.

426 *Y. Martov.* Zapiski sotsial-demokrata. p. 301.

neither a traitor nor a stool pigeon, but his sincerity and volubility in face of such experienced investigators had devastating consequences.

"However it came about," writes Martov, "the result of this 'partisan' policy, as Zinoviev himself later called it by way of a defence, was that his admitting to associating with us at meetings destroyed our entire system of defence, built as it was on persistent rebuttal of the details uncovered by surveillance or the slanders of traitors."[427]

This all necessitated a new way of colluding and the close coordination of their statements, feasible now that communication among the prisoners had been established. Signalling between cells and floors through tapping out the basics of prison code on the walls, practised since the earliest days of their arrest, was not a particularly sophisticated method and precluded much in the way of serious discussion. The general visiting hour took on an important role in conveying important information. Unlike private visits, at which a gendarme was always present, the general visiting hour "allowed one to say much more: there was one warder to a row of cells, so it was possible to speak more freely. My brother and I employed pseudonyms that we had agreed upon in coded letters… We naturally included a host of foreign words when we spoke in Russian", Anna wrote.[428]

After the initial visits, she began to pass important information to relatives visiting other prisoners and arranged with them which books the prison mates should request from the prison library. The appointed title would have barely discernible marks highlighting individual letters on the pages, allowing the reader to assemble a message. It was in this way that Ulyanov corresponded with Krzhizhanovsky, Starkov and Silvin.

As regards contact with the outside, alongside the 'marked' books returned to the library every Thursday, simple cryptography was also employed. Anna Ulyanova-Yelizarova wrote, "Of course, there was no way of getting hold of any chemical agents in prison. But Vladimir told me of a children's game shown to him by his mother: writing in milk so it can be viewed later under the light of a candle or lamp. He received milk every day, and began fashioning miniature ink wells from lumps of bread, into which he would pour a few drops of milk, before using it to write between the lines of whichever book had been offered up for the purpose." Were a warden to peer through the spy hole, the ink well was hastily popped into

---

427   Ibid.
428   Proletarskaya revolyutsiya. 1924. No. 3. p. 111.

the mouth. In the time it took to write a single message, at least half a dozen would have to be despatched in this way.[429]

Communication with the outside broke the isolation which was so carefully cultivated by the gendarmes and was an enormous source of moral support to the prisoners. But their long-term fate also depended on the 'outside'. If the organisation proved able to continue its activities, then this would go some way to lifting suspicion from its imprisoned leadership. Those social democrats who had survived the first wave of arrests on 9th December 1895 were well aware of this. On 15th December, around 20 of them met in a deacon's office on Aptekarsky Island.[430]

First of all, they selected a new central leadership, consisting of Stepan Radchenko, Silvin, Martov and Lyakhovsky. Former applicants and new members were also inducted.

There were two tasks at hand: firstly, to demonstrate that the arrests in no way impacted on the activities of the group; and secondly, to advertise that the main perpetrators of the unrest at the plants remained at large and mass agitation at factories and works was continuing.

Both tasks could be achieved by the speedy release and distribution of flyers. Silvin writes, "A proclamation addressed to all St Petersburg workers, likely written by Krzhizhanovsky before the arrests and kept by a comrade in manuscript form, was read and approved for publication then and there. Then Martov read a draft appeal to the workers on the subject of the arrests, which was also passed with no amendments." It was decided both proclamations should be published in the name of the League of Struggle for the Emancipation of the Working Class.

---

429   Ibid. pp. 115, 116.

430   See: *M. A. Silvin*. Lenin v period zarozhdeniya partii. p. 119; *Y. Martov*. Zapiski sotsial-demokrata. pp. 290-291.

THE HYDRA OF REVOLUTION

The appearance of the proclamation "From the League of Struggle for the Emancipation of the Working Class" caused a sensation. Making reference to the unrest in the Thornton, La Ferme and Putilov factories, the leafleting campaign that had made "the capitalists' hair stand on end", and the arrests of 9th December, the proclamation announced that "leaflets are appearing as before, garnering support wherever they are read, while their distributor, the League of Struggle for the Emancipation of the Working Class, remains intact and will continue its activity".[431]

Takhtarev writes, "This proclamation created quite a stir within circles of power. It gave the impression that the security department and the gendarmerie had blundered and missed those they should have arrested in the first place. It created a real scandal."[432]

A new round of arrests followed, and on the night of the 4th to 5th January 1896, Martov, Lyakhovsky, and Ponomarev were taken in, along with the workers Babushkin, Lvov, Shepelev, and others. However, following the arrests, a new League of Struggle central leadership was formed in a matter of days. This included Radchenko, Silvin, Krupskaya, Gurvich and Gofman, with districts being reassigned to their respective new charges.[433]

There was no longer any shortage of manpower. Martov writes, "The brilliant début of our League marked an overdue turning point for revolutionary youth, and dozens of students, college girls and intellectuals began to offer the League various types of assistance; the organisation soon found itself besieged by a multitude of groups who wanted to work with us... As a result, there was no shortfall in either funds or technical capabilities."[434]

431	*K. M. Takhtarev*. Rabocheye dvizheniye v Peterburge. p. 53.
432	Ibid. p. 54.
433	See: *M. A. Silvin*. Lenin v period zarozhdeniya partii. pp. 129, 130.
434	*Y. Martov*. Zapiski sotsial-demokrata. p. 303.

"The League's name rung round all of St Petersburg, and talk raged in every factory about the leaflets. In those plants where no-one had links to the League, the workers prayed to the gods that they would somehow be infiltrated by 'students' and their leaflets." As soon as the leaflets appeared, "all manner of important figures would descend on the factory. The factory inspectorate and a gendarmerie colonel would carry out their investigation in full view of the workers, trying the foetid, unboiled water in the tanks, testing the weights, checking the scales, measuring lengths… In short, the impact was enormous. There was a buoyancy of mood among the workers, especially given that any obvious signs of malpractice had already been concealed by the time all this shaking down would take place."[435]

League members gave Ulyanov regular updates about all of their activities. Anna Ulyanova-Yelizarova recalled, "He was informed about the leafleting and other underground publications in letters from the outside; they expressed regret that he had been unable to compose the leaflets himself, as he had wanted to be the one to write them."[436]

He began to develop themes for flyers in his letters to the outside: capitalist profits and workers' earnings; eight-hour working days; and so on.[437] When the need arose to outline the basic principles of the Russian social democrats, at the request of his comrades he set enthusiastically to work composing a programme.[438]

By early 1896 Ulyanov had put together this draft programme, composing it in milk between the lines of a book. In the summer of 1896, he added an explanation to the programme which, together with the draft, formed a single work.

The development of capitalism in Russia, it read, would not lead to the creation of a society for the common good, but the opposite. "In Russia, an entire class of major financiers, manufacturers, railway owners, merchants and bankers has emerged, an entire class of people living on the income generated by capital… The luxury and extravagance apparent in all these classes of the wealthy has reached an unprecedented scale,

---

435   *K. M. Takhtarev. Rabocheye dvizheniye v Peterburge.* p. 55.

436   Proletarskaya revolyutsiya. 1924. No. 3. p. 115.

437   See: *Vladimir Ilyich Lenin. Biograficheskaya khronika.* Vol. 1. pp. 123, 126, 127.

438   See: *K. M. Takhtarev. Rabocheye dvizheniye v Peterburge.* p. 85.

and their princely palaces and luxurious manor houses now line the main streets of large cities."[439]

Meanwhile, conditions continued to deteriorate for workers. "The emancipation of the workers should be a matter for the workers themselves." The task of the social democrats was "...to side with the workers' movement, offer enlightenment to it, and assist the workers in a struggle that they are already beginning to lead by themselves".[440] This 'enlightenment' would only be possible "through the development of workers' class consciousness, by facilitating their organisation, and by identifying the goals and objectives of the struggle".[441]

The immediate task of the organisation was to attain political freedom, which first of all meant universal and direct suffrage, the convening of a *zemsky sobor* to draft a constitution, guaranteeing the freedom to strike and the right to form unions, ensuring freedom of the press, recognising equality of the citizenry before the law, guaranteeing freedom of worship, the equality of all nationalities, freedom of trade, employment and movement, instituting the abolition of passports, and recognising the right to prosecute any official in a court of law.[442]

In his solitary confinement, pacing the six steps from door to window, Ulyanov perhaps had a more elevated sense of the human desire for liberty and the need to maintain one's dignity. This may in part explain why the rights and freedoms of the working person were so carefully outlined in his draft programme. It was particularly important that precisely these concepts began to set the tone of the leaflets published by the League of Struggle in spring 1896. This appeal to the importance of human dignity would not go unanswered.

Things continued as before, with the future auguring nothing out of the ordinary. However, in May, Russia and beyond was shaken by the events of the Khodynka Disaster.

In accordance with the laws governing the manifesto on accession signed by Nicholas II on 20th October 1894, a coronation ceremony was scheduled to take place in Moscow in May 1896. Alongside the official ceremonies, balls, concerts, banquets and dinner parties, the extensive

---

439	*V. I. Lenin.* Polnoye sobraniye sochineny. Vol. 2. p. 89.
440	Ibid. Vol. 2. pp. 101-102.
441	Ibid. Vol. 2. p. 84.
442	Ibid. Vol. 2. p. 85.

programme arranged for the three weeks of festivities included a public festival on Khodynka Field on 18th May, at which the tsar was to distribute gifts.

The vast space that served as a training field for a Moscow-based garrison had become pitted all over with trenches, breastworks, ditches and hollows. There had been no attempt to fill these in, and now 400,000 bags containing rolls, sausage, gingerbread, sweets, nuts and commemorative enamelled mugs bearing the emperor's initials had been prepared.

From the evening of 17th May and all through the night, hundreds of thousands of people rushed to Khodynka. There was no stewarding in place, and when the gift bags began to be handed out, a crush started to build. As people began to fall into the ditches and hollows, the cries of those being trampled caused a panic.

Lev Tolstoy and Maxim Gorky have both written about Khodynka, as have dozens of Russian and overseas journalists, but even they have admitted that putting the full horror into words is impossible. Official figures put the dead at 1,389, with another 3,000 seriously injured. The total number of those injured and maimed ran to the tens of thousands. "I was left revolted by the news," the tsar wrote in his diary.[443]

Nonetheless, it did not stop the sovereign from spending the evening of the 18th May at a ball in the French embassy. The 100,000 roses imported from Provence, a luxury silver service sent from Versailles, and the 7,000 guests who enthusiastically welcomed him somewhat assuaged his sense of revulsion. While soldiers were piling corpses on wagons at Khodynka, the royal couple were dancing a quadrille to universal applause.[444]

From 14-16th May, all Russian factories and plants halted production while the official coronation festivities were ongoing. On 17th May, work resumed as normal. By the next day, rumours were beginning to circulate about the Khodynka Tragedy. State festivities continued, but St Petersburg textile workers were in no mood to participate, not least because they were losing out on earnings as a result. On the 23rd May, workers at the Kalininskaya Mill went to the office to demand pay for the 'coronation days'. By this time, such a demand was tantamount to a political act in itself. But fearing scandal at such a historic time, the management paid out. Then the workers began to demand pay for the extra minutes they

---

443   M. K. Kasvinov. Dvadtsat' tri stupeni vniz. pp. 90, 93.
444   See: ibid. p. 94.

were working daily as a result of their machinery being started up earlier than the appointed time.

The next day, they began striking. On 27th May, the textile workers returned to work, but at lunchtime resumed their strike. They were joined by other St Petersburg factories and mills. By this stage, around 30,000 workers were on strike.[445]

Approximately 100 representatives from these plants assembled in Yekaterinhof Park to draw up their demands. These were passed to the League of Struggle and by 30th May, a flyer titled "What the Workers of the St. Petersburg Cotton Mills Demand" was being circulated.

On 1st, 3rd, 4th, 5th, 9th and 10th June, the flyers were reprinted, sometimes two to three times a day. They were addressed not only to the strikers, but to the workers of those enterprises who were not on strike, with an appeal to donate money in support of the textile workers. Almost every proclamation advised the workers to remain peaceful and abstain from rioting or disorder, since it would only be of benefit to the police. The self-possession of the workers astounded everyone.

Silvin writes, "The strike came about not at the initiative of the League of Struggle, but was organised entirely by the workers themselves, spearheaded by groups who travelled from one factory to another..." But the tsar's officials rightly noted that "the speed at which the disorder spread ... the unanimity of the demands ... and the extraordinarily calm demeanour of the masses during this unrest all pointed to the fact that the strikes were the result of groundwork laid through criminal agitation of the workers".[446]

At that time, Silvin continues, "our comrades were working tirelessly, not only distributing leaflets, meeting with individual workers in taverns, cemeteries, parks and the like, but also going in amongst the workers themselves, dressing in smocks and sometimes blackening their faces with soot, to their impromptu gatherings and meetings... The work went well; there was an effective union between our League of Struggle and all those groups who had hitherto worked independently."[447]

Not a single line appeared in the Russian press about the strikes. But everywhere, in bureaucratic circles and fashionable salons, in taverns and on the streets, it was the only topic of conversation. At the request of the

---

445 See: *K. M. Takhtarev*. Rabocheye dvizheniye v Peterburge. pp. 61-63, 73.

446 *M. A. Silvin*. Lenin v period zarozhdeniya partii. pp. 142, 143.

447 Ibid. p. 142.

League, Potresov wrote the appeal "To Russian Society", which called for donations, and characterised the strikes as "the desire to advance from the mire of stagnation; it is the cresting wave of the conscious and awakening masses, destined to sweep away our common foe – the autocracy".[448]

The press in Britain, France, Germany, Austria and Switzerland offered particularly detailed accounts of the strikes. In Britain, the Society of Friends of Russian Freedom, headed by émigré *narodniki*, began requesting donations. British trade unions answered their call.

The money collected was sent to Russia, along with a letter of solidarity on behalf of British workers signed by the leaders of UK-based socialist parties and trade unions. Later, the League published this letter, along with a reply penned by Potresov, as a leaflet.[449]

On 10th June, the city administrator, Major General Kleigels, as if borrowing the methods of the League, had leaflets pasted around factory quarters demanding the end of the strikes, promising workers that "grievances levelled in accordance with the law will be heard as a matter of urgency." However, these exhortations had no effect.[450] At that point, police and Cossacks moved to the factory perimeter. Only on 18th June did the strike begin to subside. "The workers all returned to their stations, *but no longer were they the same people that had left them*. Over the course of the strike, the workers had faced the government head on, and the confrontation would not be forgotten. Both the government's 'exhortations', underpinned by threats, and the harsh treatment it meted out to peaceful strikers, produced a real revolution in the minds of even the least class-conscious and most downtrodden of workers, forcing them to consider who their real friends and advocates were, and who they should regard as their oppressors and enemies... If before only a few dozen had given it any thought, now thousands were growing curious."[451]

On 15th (27th July), the IV Congress of the International opened in London. For the first time, the Russian delegation was made up not of émigrés, but by representatives of the actual proletarian movement. Alongside Plekhanov, there on a mandate from the League, and other members of Emancipation of Labour, three acquaintances of Ulyanov also

---

448	Ibid. p. 144.
449	*K. M. Takhtarev*. Rabocheye dvizheniye v Peterburge. pp. 71, 75.
450	Ibid. pp. 71, 76.
451	Ibid. p. 72.

travelled to the congress: Buchholz from Berlin, and Struve and Potresov from St Petersburg. The congress delegates offered a rousing welcome to the young Russian social democrats.[452]

Ulyanov had received regular information about the strikes from Anna, so was aware of the nature and scale of the movement. It was as if the same situation that occurred in 1891 was repeating itself. Somewhere nearby, *History* itself was marching on with heavy gait, and circumstances – this time imprisonment – were keeping him isolated from events. However, there was no cause to reproach himself: his role in what was happening on the outside was evident, a charge his opponents – not then, and not later – were unable to refute.[453] And since, as Martov noted, Ulyanov was not blighted by "personal vanity",[454] he was far less concerned with how the accolades were shared.

Another episode, largely overlooked, took place on the eve of the textile workers' strike. Martov writes, "Wild scenes, perhaps triggered by the news emerging from Moscow about Khodynka, were witnessed on the streets of St Petersburg during the coronation festivities, particularly in the factory quarters: drunken youths, hoodlums for the most part, caused a series of riotous incidents which necessitated the cessation of the festivities."[455] In the June edition of *Russkoye Bogatstvo*, Mikhailovsky wrote angrily, "One is forced to consider the question of our attitude to the people as a whole, and to their spiritual life in particular." In other words, the sentimental "love for the people" that several generations of Russian youth had been raised to profess was gradually being replaced in the minds of the liberal intelligentsia by a pathological dread.

To suggest that Mikhailovsky rejected out of principle any form of popular protest would be untrue. It was a *principle* he supported, but on the proviso that that protest be organised and disciplined, and clearly define the aims and objectives of the movement. This was evinced by the German model, in which a resolution is taken, the workers gather and form up in columns, they hoist their slogans and banners, and their appointed leaders stand at the head of them with band in tow. This was an orderly, civilised, and hence effective way of doing things. It was therefore

---

452 See: Perepiska G. V. Plekhanova i P. B. Axelroda. Vol. 1. pp. 141-142.
453 See: *K. M. Takhtarev*. Rabocheye dvizheniye v Peterburge. pp. 168, 169.
454 See: *Y. Martov*. Zapiski sotsial-demokrata. p. 270.
455 Ibid. p. 305.

necessary to educate the workers, elevate their consciousness and degree of organisation *first*, and only *then* could action be undertaken.

At the same time as Mikhailovsky was publishing his article, Ulyanov was putting the finishing touches to a pamphlet on the strikes from his prison cell. In contrast to Mikhailovsky, who emphasised the need for education before action, Ulyanov believed that in the Russian context it was pointless to wait when self-education circles, Sunday schools and specific texts and lectures to assist the people in reaching the requisite level of class consciousness and organisation already existed. Even the smallest forays into such activity could be ruthlessly suppressed. The experiences of his father had demonstrated this to him in childhood.

Meanwhile, the experience of the 1890s had shown that nothing had such a powerful organisational and educational influence on the working masses as active struggle itself, particularly when it took the form of strikes.

"Striking teaches the workers to understand where the power of the owner class is centred, and where that of the workers is concentrated; it teaches them to think not only of their own bosses and immediate comrades, but of all bosses, and of the entire capitalist class and working class as a whole..."[456]

It was the act of striking that awakened in strikers a sense of dignity and the desire to resist evil and injustice. This purely moral aspect of the struggle was of greatest interest to Ulyanov.

During the summer strikes of 1896, the workers themselves would occasionally take up the pen if theirs was a factory that the League of Struggle's proclamation had not reached. "We will come together, brothers, in one spirit and fight steadfastly for the improvement of our lot," read one flyer. "Comrade workers! Take a look at yourselves. Were you to meet a foreigner of equal station to yourself, you would immediately be compelled to admit that you are savages in comparison to him... They do not spend their resting hours as we do, wallowing in filth, in torn clothing outside taverns and inns, they do not resort to foul oaths or thrashing their comrades, as the Russian *muzhik* does, but instead gather together to talk of improvement; or when he wants to enjoy himself, he cycles, thus boosting his muscle power at the same time... They were also oppressed by their masters, but thanks to their keen

---

456 V. I. Lenin. Polnoye sobraniye sochineny. Vol. 4. pp. 294, 295.

apprehension succeeded in improving their lot long ago... So we, brothers, shall help each other while this strike lasts."[457]

It was fruitless to wait for the working masses to become a 'civilised' proletariat, shunning 'violent incarnations' of the movement and baulking at 'excesses'. It was necessary to go to the masses, educate the workers, learn from their victories and defeats, and most importantly, make every effort to lead them in organised, considered action.

If any canons existed in the train of political thought that would later become known as Bol'shevism, then that would be considered one of the most significant. More than two decades later, Lenin would write, "That communists condone spontaneity is a lie ... communists believe – quite rightly – that it is their duty *to be with the struggling masses* of the oppressed rather than standing waiting timidly to the side as do the heroes of the petty bourgeoisie. When the masses are struggling, mistakes within the struggle are inevitable: communists, recognising these mistakes, articulate them to the masses, strive to correct them, and fight tirelessly for the victory of consciousness over spontaneity, *but remain with the masses.*"[458]

He wrote these words in 1919, but what he was writing in prison was equally as explosive, and was in fact putting him at some risk.

His solitary confinement cell endured regular 'shakedowns' and the gendarmes ransacked not only his belongings, but also examined all the papers and books in the cell. During visits, Anna often warned Ulyanov that "they will give you hard labour for having the audacity to write illegal pieces in prison". Ulyanov was aware of this and it most probably weighed on his mind, but in response to his sister only laughed, "I'm in a better position than the rest of the citizens of the Russian Empire – they cannot arrest me any more."[459]

---

457   *K. M. Takhtarev*. Rabocheye dvizheniye v Peterburge. pp. 64, 65.

458   *V. I. Lenin*. Polnoye sobraniye sochineny. Vol. 38. p. 393.

459   Proletarskaya revolyutsiya. 1924. No. 3. p. 117, 118.

BY IMPERIAL DECREE

After a three-month trip around Europe, Emperor Nicholas II returned to St Petersburg on 19th October 1896. He was tanned, fresh-faced and there was no more talk of Khodynka in his presence. As the new year approached, the tsar wrote in his diary, "May God grant that the next year, 1897, passes as favourably as this one."[460]

But as soon as the New Year came, more unpleasantness reared its head. The St Petersburg textile workers' strikes of the previous summer, which had caused such a sensation around Europe, had come to a halt on 18th June, partly as a result of notices posted in the factories on 15th June by order of finance minister Sergey Witte. These had promised to consider the demands of the strikers and shorten the working day. However, six months on, there were no indications that any improvements were forthcoming.

In December the League of Struggle issued a leaflet, referencing the minister's promises, that called upon the workers to continue the fight. "Factory owners and the government," it read, "will fulfil our demands only under constant pressure from our forces. You will not get far on such nags without using a whip."[461]

Immediately after New Year, on 5th January, representatives from a number of factories and plants gathered to reassert their demands of the summer and declare a general strike for 7th January.[462]

However, on 3rd and 5th January, factory owners and inspectors had met with Witte, who asked the city administrator Kleigels whether he could force the workers back to work. Kleigels replied: "If the workers were crowding the streets and disrupting peace and order, then I could deal with them. If they stay in their homes, there's nothing I can do about them." Then Witte asked the factory owners if they were prepared to offer concessions. Most owners of the major concerns responded positively, and

---

460   *M. K. Kasvinov.* Dvadtsat' tri stupeni vniz. p. 99.
461   *K. M. Takhtarev.* Rabocheye dvizheniye v Peterburge. p. 87.
462   See: ibid. pp. 89, 91.

a decision was taken to inform the workers that their demands were to be partially fulfilled, the working day shortened to 11 hours, and that the Senate would consider a new factory act, which would eventually be issued on 2nd June 1897.[463]

By placing the 'labour question' on the agenda, the government was in effect legitimising its very existence. It also somewhat changed attitudes towards the labour movement, and to some extent its organisers. As it turned out, the January strike had a very positive impact on the fate of the 'old men' as well.

Martov writes, "We suddenly learned that the long years of exile we initially faced had been ameliorated by the higher authorities and replaced by considerably shorter sentences, while for a section of the workers, exile in far-flung locations had been commuted to police supervision outside the capital... Instead of the expected eight-ten years in Eastern Siberia, six of the League's members (Ulyanov, Krzhizhanovsky, Lyakhovsky, Starkov, Vaneyev and I) received three... The workers were dealt with even more mildly: some were exiled to Arkhangelsk Province, while others were packed off out of the city under police supervision." When they began to investigate why such 'indulgences' had been afforded them, officials "justified this change in our fates by saying that the social democrats were merely waging an economic struggle, not a political one".[464]

There were genuine grounds for such seemingly absurd reasoning.

In intellectual circles, particularly among radical youth, the fashion for Marxism was continuing to snowball. Those for whom it was merely a passing trend had long decided on their idols. As Boris Gorev writes, if yesterday's adoring female students had flocked around Mikhailovsky or Yuzhakov, then it was now Struve and Tugan-Baranovsky who "became the authorities upon whose word, to use the phrasing of the time, the girls hung, and whom they followed in herds at all the student balls and functions".[465]

These balls and functions, so steeped in the alluring spirit of 'oppositionism', were popular with the famous lawyers, artists and writers of the day. Martov's sister Lidia Tsederbaum recalled that in November

---

463 See: ibid. pp. 90, 94.

464 Y. Martov. Zapiski sotsial-demokrata. pp. 314, 315.

465 B. I. Gorev. Iz partiinogo proshlogo. Vospominaniya. 1895-1905. Leningrad, 1924. p. 12.

1896, she invited a young Fyodor Shalyapin, then singing with a leading private opera, to a charity ball organised by women students.

Vladimir Obolensky recalled, "Speeches by the young Marxists, particularly Peter Struve, were met with loud applause, despite using such intricate language that he rendered himself incomprehensible to the majority of the audience. His delivery was also poor – he struggled to find the right words and would pause in the wrong places. It should be said that at this time, the Russian intelligentsia had no experience of public speaking whatsoever, and most were poor orators."[466]

In autumn 1896, a legal Marxist newspaper called *Samara Vestnik* appeared, and began publishing material by Russian Marxists. The paper had readers in St Petersburg, Moscow, and other Russian cities, as well as London, Paris, and as far away as the Sandwich Islands. Keeping up with a growing trend, the magazine *Nauchnoye Obozreniye* [Scientific Review] began publishing pieces by Marxists. Even the liberal-populist *Russkaya Mysl* offered space to Plekhanov and Struve. In early 1897, with assistance from Alexandra Kalmykova, Struve and Tugan-Baranovsky bought over the St Petersburg magazine *Novoye Slovo* [New Word], putting prominent Marxist writers onto its staff, among them Ulyanov.

Meanwhile, Ulyanov and his comrades were set for release from prison.

It is easy to sneer at the officials who believed that the social democrats were not waging a 'political struggle', but whatever the reasoning, their sentences were reduced. On 29th January, after a report by his humble servant State Secretary Muravyov, the Minister for Justice, His Majesty the Emperor ordered a resolution of the "present investigation by administrative order", rather than by trial. 65 individuals involved in the League of Struggle case found the location and length of their exile to be less severe than expected.

Moreover, writes Martov, "our relatives conceived the daring idea of petitioning for us to be permitted to go into exile as free passengers at our own expense, rather than as part of a prison transport. Having attained this for only a select few individuals, among them Ulyanov, they were still able to win a hitherto unheard-of concession for the majority of the others, namely four days of freedom to settle their affairs before departing into exile."[467]

---

466   V. A. Obolensky. Moya zhizn'. Moi sovremenniki. pp. 133, 140.
467   Y. Martov. Zapiski sotsial-demokrata. pp. 315-316.

On 14th January, Ulyanov and his comrades were released. They were given until evening on 17th January to leave the capital, leaving them three days. Two of these evenings were spent in Radchenko and Martov's apartment, in meetings which lasted well into the night and which were attended by both old and new members of the League of Struggle. Members of the new central leadership felt it was proper to report on the activities of the past year. In addition to this, Gorev writes that "I pointed in my report to emerging differences within the League and the bias towards a peculiar 'democratism' and 'workerphilia' [*rabochefil'stvo*], and it was these issues which elicited the most discussion, even a degree of hot temper".[468]

The background for the disagreement lay in the fact that during the arrests of 1896, police had seized the former leaders and advanced workers who had received training in the circle schools. This coincided with the rapid growth of a strike movement which had drawn in less cultivated strata: "A mass of workers that had seemed to us more 'grey' than it was in reality..."[469]

Five years later Ulyanov recalled, "A sharp difference of opinion emerged between the 'old men' (the 'Decembrists', as St Petersburg social democrats called them by way of a joke) and a few of the 'young' members ... and a heated debate ensued... The 'old men' believed that we first of all needed to consolidate the League of Struggle into a revolutionary organisation to which a variety of workers' funds [*kassy*], student activist circles, and so on must be subordinated."[470] Takhtarev did not agree and made an issue of the necessity of expanding their organisational base by creating workers' funds and mutual aid funds in factories with the purpose of uniting the working masses as one whole, without stratifying them into the 'conscious' and the 'grey'. In this regard, he admonished the League as "undemocratic" and insisted on the need to abandon the old centralist structure and co-opt workers into the central leadership, thereby eliminating the "barriers" separating them from the social-democractic intelligentsia.

Referring to the argument, Ulyanov makes a significant observation: "It goes without saying that those arguing, far from considering this

---

468   B. I. *Gorev*. Iz partiinogo proshlogo. p. 37.

469   M. A. *Silvin*. Lenin v period zarozhdeniya partii. p. 139.

470   V. I. *Lenin*. Polnoye sobraniye sochineny. Vol. 6. p. 34.

disagreement the beginning of a split, conversely regarded it as isolated and incidental."[471]

During the meeting the possibility of forming an accord with the newly resurrected *Narodnaya Volya* came under discussion. Gorev writes that in this instance Ulyanov "demonstrated the hard-bitten political nous in appreciating the strengths of others that was so characteristic of him. 'Once they have a printing press,' he said, 'there will be much they can dictate to us, and much that we would have to go along with.'"[472]

Martov recalls, "Alongside these discussions, we also needed to have something of an in-house meeting to have it out with B. I. Zinoviev over his 'partisan' actions under interrogation. The conversation became especially heated, as Zinoviev, rounding on the poorly formed nature of our organisation, stubbornly defended his right to interact with the gendarmerie in whichever way he considered most useful for advancing the social aspirations of the nascent workers' movement in the eyes of the authorities. Of course, he did not convince us, and we informed him we were reserving the right for the party to instigate a formal investigation of his case…"[473]

After the meeting in Martov's apartment had concluded and the others had left, Ulyanov and Martov continued their discussion into the night, perhaps for the first time enjoying something of a heart to heart. Martov's brother, V. O. Tsederbaum (V. Levitsky) wrote: "He stayed the night with us so he could have time to talk alone with Yuliy, for whom he evidently had a great deal of affection and respect. They did not even retire to bed, talking until morning instead. That night probably marked the beginning of the close personal relationship that developed between them…"[474]

The three-day period the Department of Police had permitted Ulyanov to gather his things expired. However, Maria Alexandrovna, citing her deteriorating health, managed to receive permission for Vladimir to travel to Moscow for two days. On 17th February he left St Petersburg with his mother and sister.

---

471   Ibid. Vol. 6. p. 34.

472   *B. I. Gorev*. Iz partiinogo proshlogo. p. 38.

473   *Y. Martov*. Zapiski sotsial-demokrata. p. 318.

474   *V. Levitsky (V. O. Tsederbaum)*. Za chetvert' veka. Revolyutsionnye vospominaniya. Moscow, 1926. p. 51.

Ulyanov arrived in Moscow on 18th February and decided to give up the right to travel independently to his place of exile that he and Yakov Lyakhovsky had been afforded. He intended to allow himself to be taken into custody, await his St Petersburg comrades in a transit prison, and go with them in a prison transport. That same day, Maria Alexandrovna – "very much against her will," as Anna Ulyanova-Yelizarova writes – submitted the necessary request.

Anna wrote, "Vladimir Ilyich did not want to enjoy a privilege not afforded to his comrades. I remember that it greatly upset my mother, for whom Volodya's permission to travel at his own expense was the greatest consolation... A. Kalmykova had even offered the funds for it. My mother refused assistance, having me relay to Kalmykova that she should give the money to those in more need, such as Krzhizhanovsky, and that she would offer the funds to Vladimir Ilyich.

And now, after our mother had expressed how important it was for her that he had been permitted to travel at his own expense, after she had heard the words of a former exile: 'I could do exile again, but not the transport,' Vladimir was now refusing this hard-earned privilege and voluntarily returning to prison."[475]

In anticipation of his arrival at Butyrka Prison, the transit point through which the St Petersburg contingent would be passing, Vladimir Ulyanov visited Rumyantsevskaya Public Library. There he gathered materials for the book he had begun while still on remand. He was partly drawn there for other reasons as well. Anna Ulyanova-Yelizarova writes, "Having grown used to the regular, settled activities that had maintained his balance of mind in prison, he did not wish to give them up suddenly and immediately sink into nervous inactivity, overexposing himself to the stimuli around him after the involuntary quiet and monotony of the remand prison. It was perhaps completely instinctive for him to immerse himself for a few hours each day in the silence and solitude of the library hall. For all his *sangfroid*, he must have felt the frayed nerves of one emerging from a long period in prison, and would not have wished to needlessly overload them any further."[476]

However, Ulyanov's intentions, such a cause of distress to his mother, were destined to remain unfulfilled. On the morning of 22nd February, he

---

475   Proletarskaya revolyutsiya. 1924. No. 3. p. 121; Vospominaniya o Vladimire Ilyiche Lenine. Moscow, 1989. Vol. 1. p. 86.

476   Vospominaniya o Vladimire Ilyiche Lenine. Vol. 1. p. 88.

was summoned by the Moscow secret police [*okhranka*], and as three days had passed instead of the allotted two, he was presented with a choice: he could either be arrested on the spot, imprisoned, and sent on a prisoner transport alone without being allowed to wait for his comrades, or he could set off for exile by himself that same day. For Vladimir, there was nothing more to be done except obtain a certificate of passage and submit notice of his departure.

At the height of the Shrove-tide festival, when all respectable families were gathered together at the table, the Ulyanov family – Maria Alexandrovna, Vladimir, Anna, Maria and Mark Yelizarov – hastily assembled and set off from Moscow Kursky Station for Tula. There they bade farewell to Vladimir; from there, in accordance with his certificate of passage, he was to continue alone.

However, his solitude did not last long. On the same train was the 40-year-old Krasnoyarsk doctor Vladimir Krutovsky. The train was extremely crowded and stuffy: either a carriage had been uncoupled in Moscow for repair, or, as was common, too many tickets had been sold. Whatever the circumstances, even coupé-class carriages were mobbed. Having embarked at Tula, Krutovsky noticed a young man "of relatively slim, short stature, with a small wedge of a beard and of a very lively and animated disposition, who was continually quarrelling with the railway representatives about the dreadful overcrowding on the train and demanding they couple an extra carriage…"

Krutovsky himself was one of those intellectuals who in such situations preferred not to involve himself. As the Russian saying goes, "one will not break an axe butt with a lash": nothing he could say would alter the situation. Initially, the young man's bullishness merely amused Krutovsky. However, he found himself becoming impressed by the way he pressed the railway staff more and more vigorously. Gradually, other passengers began to take his side. When by Samara the local railway officials found themselves surrounded by a crowd, with Ulyanov urging them to "attach another carriage and do something about this overcrowding," the station master turned to the yardmaster and cried, "Damn him! Couple a carriage."[477]

Krutovsky introduced himself to Ulyanov and when the extra carriage was coupled and the other passengers offered Ulyanov, as instigator of the

---

477   Proletarskaya revolyutsiya. 1929. No. 1 (84). pp. 91-96.

protest, his own two-berth compartment, Ulyanov invited Krutovsky to join him. From Samara, they travelled together.

It seems Ulyanov was able to meet with one of his old acquaintances while halted at Samara, as back in the carriage he laid out before his travelling companion a full complement of the Marxist-leaning *Samarsky Vestnik*. Since Krutovsky was an avowed *narodnik* sympathiser, the newspapers incited a heated discussion. Krutovsky writes, "We argued on this basis all the way to Krasnoyarsk... At times it led to fiery exchanges, but it would all resolve it peacefully, and we would settle down to tea or reading."[478]

Barren, desolate steppe rolled past the windows of the carriage from Chelyabinsk all the way to Novosibirsk (then still the village of Krivoshchekova). "Neither dwellings nor towns," Ulyanov wrote to his mother, "the very occasional village, the odd forest, but otherwise nothing but steppe. Snow and sky – and this for three days."[479] But as often happens on trains, the bleak landscapes were alleviated not only with tea, but by long conversation. During that week-long journey from Samara to Krasnoyarsk, they talked more about what awaited Ulyanov in Siberia than they did about Marxism and the *narodniki*.

As he wrote to his mother, "I met the very same *Arzt* [German: doctor] on the train that Anna went to in St Petersburg. I learned a number of useful things from him about Krasnoyarsk, and so on... As a result of my conversations with the *Arzt*, I have had a great deal explained to me (albeit roughly), and feel very calm as a result: I have left my nervousness in Moscow. The cause of it was the uncertainty of my situation, nothing more. Now that uncertainty is greatly reduced, and I feel well."[480]

This marked improvement in his mood was down to the advice the worldly Vladimir Krutovsky had given him. Setting off from Moscow, Ulyanov had presumed that upon reaching Krasnoyarsk he would travel on by rail to Kansk, and from there, donning a sheepskin coat, boots, and a fur hat, would continue on horseback to Irkutsk, location of the residence of Goremykin, governor-general of Eastern Siberia.

However, Krutovsky believed that he should not go beyond Krasnoyarsk. He knew the governor well – he was an extremely cantankerous individual and Krutovsky was sure that dealings with him would not end well for

---

478   Ibid. pp. 93, 94.
479   *V. I. Lenin*. Polnoye sobraniye sochineny. Vol. 55. p. 23.
480   Ibid. Vol. 55. pp. 23-24.

Ulyanov. Back in St Petersburg, Krutovsky had advised Anna Ulyanova-Yelizarova to write a request that Vladimir be exiled to Krasnoyarsk, or in the south of Yenisei Province. The letter had been sent on 22nd February, meaning he must remain in Krasnoyarsk and await a response. There he should also undergo a medical assessment to obtain a certificate affirming his weak health and recommending exile in the Minusinsk district, then half-jokingly referred to as the "Italy of Siberia".

The plan seemed entirely feasible, and now even the view out of the window no longer seemed so desolate. Vladimir wrote to his mother, "I'm told that further on we'll first see taiga, and then, from Achinsk, the mountains. That said, the steppe air is particularly fine: it makes breathing easy. The frost is heavy: more than 20 degrees, but is far more tolerable than in Russia... The Siberians say that this is down to the 'softness' of the air... This sounds quite plausible."[481]

---

481   Ibid. Vol. 55. p. 23.

'CIVILISED' EXILE

Late in the evening of 4th March 1897, Ulyanov's train pulled into Krasnoyarsk. He took a small but reasonable room with full board for 60 kopecks per day in a two-storey wooden house belonging to Klavdiya Popova, the widow of a civil servant, who rented her residence to political exiles. The following day he hurried to the Yenisei Province administration and discovered that no specific instructions had been received concerning his case. It appeared that his mother's petition had been ignored and, in accordance with the conditions of his certificate of passage, he would need to drag himself the 1,000 *versts* to Irkutsk.

However, as chance would have it, while at the provincial administration Ulyanov also discovered that the governor himself, infantry general Alexander Goremykin, had been in Krasnoyarsk since 2nd March. On Krutovsky's advice, he penned an appeal: "I have the honour to request kindly of Your Excellency that I am permitted to remain in the city of Krasnoyarsk pending allocation of a place of residence. Mindful of my weak health, I request that I am allocated a place of residence within Yenisei Province and, if possible, in Krasnoyarsk or Minusinsk District."[482] It is not known whether or not the governor read Ulyanov's appeal. However, the fact that it was submitted, and indeed backed by a medical certificate, was to prove very significant.

Long days of waiting followed – for formal notification from the governor, and for the arrival of his comrades, following on in a prison transport 'at the state's expense'.

There was a large contingent of exiles in Krasnoyarsk, the bulk of which comprised of *narodniki* and *Narodnaya Volya* members. Of the few Marxists there, Ulyanov was most familiar with Pyotr Krasikov. His grandfather, a Minusinsk Cossack, had been a protopriest in Krasnoyarsk and Pyotr himself had been banished from St Petersburg back to his place of birth as a result of his acquaintance with Plekhanov in Geneva, and

---

482 *V. I. Lenin. Polnoye sobraniye sochineny.* Vol. 46. p. 451.

for spreading social democrat propaganda among students of the capital's university.

In order to gather additional material for the work he had begun in prison, Ulyanov, after seeking advice from Krutovsky, visited the renowned library of the merchant bibliophile Gennady Yudin, which was situated in the Krasnoyarsk suburb of Tarakanovo.

"I go to the library every day, and as it is situated two *versts* from the city's outskirts, I am required to travel around five *versts* – about an hour's journey," he wrote to his mother on 15th March. "I very much enjoy the walk, although it often leaves me very drowsy. It turns out there are far fewer books on my subject in the library than one might have thought, considering its size, but there is at least some of use to me, and I am very glad that my time here will not be entirely wasted. I also visit the municipal library: I am able to browse newspapers and magazines there; they arrive on 11th of the month, and I still cannot get used to such late 'news'."[483]

Ten days later, he writes to his mother: "Life goes on as before, I wander over to the library, I stroll around the outskirts on walks, I visit friends, and I sleep enough for two – in short, everything is quite satisfactory." He talks again of these walks in his next letter: "The city's outskirts, running along the river Yenisei, remind me of both the Zhiguli mountains and the views in Switzerland: I have recently made a number of excursions (the days have been very warm here and the roads have dried out) which I thoroughly enjoyed..."[484]

As it turned out, the tedious wait for both a reply from the governor and the arrival of his comrades came to an end almost simultaneously. On 4th April, Lyakhovsky sent a telegram from Irkutsk to inform Ulyanov, Krzhizhanovsky and Starkov that they had been "assigned to Minusinsk District". On the same day, his friends from the League of Struggle arrived in Krasnoyarsk by mail train.

Contrary to expectations, their trip had not been too gruelling. Firstly, they had not gone by the usual route taken by exiles, the notorious *Vladimirka*, but had travelled along the new Trans-Siberian Railway – the exiled party, escorted by a gendarmes colonel, had travelled the distance in particularly quick time by bypassing all of the intermediate stages.

---

483   Ibid. Vol. 55. p. 26.

484   Ibid. Vol. 55. pp. 28, 31.

Martov wrote, "The journey in a separate car, lasting ten days, was relatively comfortable."[485]

When the train stopped, Vladimir Ulyanov and Krzhizhanovsky's sister Antonina rushed to the carriage and "exchanged handshakes and breathless questions" with the new arrivals through the open windows. The colonel, jumping down from the carriage to carry out a ceremonial debrief to local authorities, was furious. "Draw your swords!", he commanded, and the guards began to drag the convicts away from the window. However, as Martov writes, "The station gendarmes had the sense to grab Ulyanov and his companion quite literally by the collar and in full view of us drag them off to a room somewhere.

The scene made quite an impression on our little travelling companion, the four-year-old Valya Yukhotskaya… When they began to take us from the carriage … and a gaggle of officials and senior officers approached us, surrounded by an escort with swords drawn, the little girl, looking directly into the eyes of our portly colonel, said in a loud and furious voice, 'We will hang you!'…

All the sheen slipped from this very proper and perfumed ex-guardsman… 'And we will hang you too,' he growled, and abruptly lost his composure. We found this amusing, and everyone broke into laughter."[486]

The fate of the new arrivals was decided relatively quickly. By order of the governor-general, they were to be sent to their places of exile after the winter, once navigation became possible along the Yenisei. Krzhizhanovsky and Starkov were to go to Minusinsk District, Lepeshinsky to Yenisei District, while Martov and Vaneyev would be sent to far-flung Turukhansk.

They were released from transit prison on 23rd May, and, like Ulyanov, were given certificates of passage on 24th. However, before leaving, the friends managed to stage, as Martov put it, "something rather daring" in prison.

Nikolai Fedoseyev had been taken from the Butyrka prison in Moscow to Krasnoyarsk, and from there was supposed to continue on to Irkutsk Province. Learning that Ulyanov was in the city, he asked the St Petersburg contingent if they could arrange a meeting with him. They had made attempts to meet before, in the Volga region and in Vladimir, but these had not been successful. Finally, another opportunity had arisen.

---

485   *Y. Martov*. Zapiski sotsial-demokrata. p. 334.

486   Ibid. pp. 334-336.

Martov writes, "We had not been given our belongings when we came out of prison, so the following day we returned to the prison storehouse with a cart to collect them, the driver accompanied by Ulyanov ... posing as the cart's owner. Dressed in a fur coat, Ulyanov's merchant appearance looked every part the liveryman, and the guards let us through: in the storehouse we demanded that the warden summon Fedoseyev, as the 'senior' of the political prisoners, for the return of our property. Thus, while we carried out and loaded up our possessions, Ulyanov and Fedoseyev were able to talk, to the great embarrassment of our 'enabler', who despite recognising that he had been duped, did not want to create a fuss."[487]

On the morning of 30th April, the vice-governor raised the navigation flag and the captain of the *St Nikolai* sounded the horn. The city's churches responded with the peal of their bells. The ship slowly pulled off from the dock. "Today", wrote Anatoly Vaneyev to his relations, "I saw off three comrades assigned to Minusinsk District (navigation to Minusinsk is now open). They departed in good spirits... One – to the village of Shushenskoye, the other two – to Tesinskoye..."[488] Gleb Krzhizhanovsky's mother, Elvira Rosenberg, also travelled with Ulyanov, Starkov and her son.

It was noisy and crowded on board the ship. This first voyage carried merchants and gold producers, teams of raftsmen and quarry workers, monastic novitiates, miners and gold prospectors.

Towards evening, the ship moored at the Skit jetty close to the monastery at the mouth of the Filaretov creek. As tradition dictated, the entire crew, led by the captain, went to the monastery to offer a prayer for "those who sail and those who journey" and left the passengers clustered round camp fires on the bank: the respectable folk of the first and second-class cabins round one, the artisan miners round another, and the monastic novitiates round a third. The exiles had to make themselves comfortable a little way from the rest. The ship's canteens supplied plenty of drinks and snacks for this 'picnic', so no-one was bored. The 'prisoners of the state' also kept themselves entertained .

It was the night before May Day. While in Butyrka prison, Gleb Krzhizhanovsky had translated into Russian the Polish song *Warszawianka* by Wacław Święcicki. With the holiday almost upon them, they performed it for the first time on the outside. Its lyrics: *"But we hoist proud and bold/*

---

487   Ibid. pp. 336-337.
488   *B. Yakovlev*. Lenin v Krasnoyarske. Moscow, 1965. p. 143.

The banner of struggle for the workers' cause/ The banner of the great struggle of all peoples/ For a better world, for a sacred freedom," could not have better matched the mood. There, by the light of the camp fire, they saw in May Day. In the morning, they climbed the steep cliff overlooking the mouth of the Shumikha, opening up before them views of the Biryusinsky and Divny Mountains, and once more sang the *Warszawianka*. Then, on the pier at the Biryusinsky flood plain, the three friends helped the crew and artisan miners load logs aboard and the *St Nikolai* set off again downstream.[489]

The revelry which had begun on the upper and lower decks on the first day continued into the next. The prayer offered at the monastery to "protect and deliver from every wicked disposition of enemies seen and unseen" kept the travellers soundly for four days. On the fifth day the water level in the river dropped and the *St Nikolai* ran aground at Sorokinskiye Razboi. This meant engaging a wagon and, in accordance with their certificates of passage, continuing on dry land. The road largely ran through the mountains, firstly across the Turan ridge, and then over Tepsei mountain. On the steep climbs, the friends would get out the wagon and push, despite having clothing and footwear wholly unsuitable for the task. As Ulyanov later wrote, "It is a good thing the weather was fine – had it rained..."[490]

Somewhere along the way the travelling companions shared a curious exchange. Gleb Krzhizhanovsky was recalling the words of the famous Prussian-born surgeon Theodor Billroth: "Sound health manifests itself in a clarity of emotional expression." Ulyanov immediately seized on this: "Precisely so. When the healthy individual wishes to eat, then he is truly hungry; when he needs to sleep, he cares not how soft the bed is... And if he develops a hatred, then that is also a very real one..." As he glanced at Ulyanov, flushed by the wind, eyes gleaming, Krzhizhanovsky thought, "You are the very image of such a healthy individual."[491]

Late in the evening of 6th May, they reached Minusinsk. They spent the night with another exile, Yefim Bragin. In the morning, they reported to the district police captain Mukhin, a despotic and boorish man. Bragin recalls, "We entered. Sitting on the chair was a menacing official, twisting

---

489   See: ibid. p. 148.

490   V. I. Lenin. Polnoye sobraniye sochineny. Vol. 55. p. 37.

491   Vospominaniya o Vladimire Ilyiche Lenine. Five volumes. Moscow, 1969. Vol. 2. p. 12.

his whiskers and glaring at us like he wanted to eat us. Naturally, we took a seat as well...

'I demand you stand!' barked this Zeus in a police uniform, 'This is a public office.'

'But you yourself are sitting, Captain!'

So we did not stand either."[492]

Having left a request with the officer to "allocate an allowance as prescribed by law for upkeep, rent and clothing," and having been instructed to depart Minusinsk the following day, the friends visited the renowned regional museum and library established by a local pharmacist, Nikolai Martyanov.

Here they met some of Minusinsk's exile community: Feliks Kon, sent there after ten years of hard labour, Arkady Tyrkov, exiled permanently to Siberia for his part in an assassination attempt on Alexander II, and others. Yefim Bragin, who had now had a chance to observe Ulyanov closely, noted that "among his own he loved to joke and was lively and good-natured. With those unfamiliar to him, in wider company, he was the opposite: withdrawn, cautious and restrained."[493]

Now travelling alone after his companions departed for the village of Tesinskoye, Ulyanov left Minusinsk by wagon along the Uryankhai trail in the early hours of 8th May. Covering 55 *versts*, he arrived the same day in Shushenskoye, or as he wrote, "'Shu-shu-shu', as I'm calling the place of my eventual repose."[494]

In one of his first letters to his mother from there, he wrote, "Shu-shu-shu is not a bad little village." On another occasion he wrote, "The village is a sizeable one, comprising a number of rather dirty, dusty streets – everything is as one would expect. It is a steppe village – there is nothing in the way of gardens or flora. The village is surrounded ... in manure, which here is not used on the fields, but dumped immediately outside the village, so to leave one must always have to navigate through a fair amount of it. Running immediately alongside the village is the little Shush river, which is very shallow at the moment... A *verst* and a half or so away is the 'forest', as the peasants grandly call it, though this is in fact a wretched, heavily felled little wood in which barely a shadow is cast... The mountains ... are around

---

492   B. Yakovlev. Lenin v Krasnoyarske. pp. 158-159.

493   Ibid. p. 157.

494   V. I. Lenin. Polnoye sobraniye sochineny. Vol. 55. p. 34.

50 *versts* from here, so can only be glimpsed when the clouds are not obscuring them ... exactly as Mont Blanc can be seen from Geneva."[495]

From the moment it became clear that Ulyanov faced Siberian exile, Maria Alexandrovna had intended to go after him, as Krzhizhanovsky's mother had. However, Vladimir had delayed her decision under various pretexts. When he arrived in Shushenskoye, he had immediately written: "I am so settled here (and certainly better than the rest of my comrades) that there are no grounds to upset my mother, and as regards a summer holiday, I also think that going abroad would offer a far more agreeable rest than here, given you would have to journey several thousands *versts* by all manner of means."[496] He repeated his argument from one letter to the next, until in June Maria Alexandrovna and his sister Maria went abroad instead.

His claims that he was perfectly comfortably settled were not overstated. On the recommendation of a local clerk, he had taken up residence with a peasant, Apollon Zyryanov. Initially he shared a room with his hosts, until they offered him a small private room with a bed, table, corner cupboard, and – somewhat at a squeeze – four chairs. All horizontal surfaces with the exception of the bed he immediately covered in books and papers.

Books were his main preoccupation. "I am surprised," he wrote to his mother in that first letter from Shushenskoye, "that you have not written a word about sending me the rest of the books. It would be regrettable if they have not been sent yet…" He sent an additional list of the newspapers and journals he required to continue the large work on markets he had begun in prison. Learning the books had been posted to Krasnoyarsk, he lamented: "I was under the impression they were already on their way. I'd better find out when they are to reach Krasnoyarsk. Perhaps not until the end of the summer!"[497]

In the meantime, he set about making himself at home. "He often ate with us," recalled Zyryanov, "in the peasant way, from a common pot, joining in the conversation with loud, infectious laughter. A very earnest fellow was Vladimir Ilyich, and a cheerful one."[498]

---

495   Ibid. pp. 47-48.
496   Ibid. p. 40.
497   Ibid. pp. 35, 39.
498   Lenin v Shushenskom vstrechaet XX vek. Dokumenty. Pisma. Vospominaniya. Moscow, 1980. p. 50.

"Vladimir Ilyich's 'salary' – the maintenance money afforded to exiles – got him a clean room, food, and his laundry washed and mended", says Krupskaya, "for which he believed he was paying too much. Lunch and dinner was certainly simple fare – one week they slaughtered a sheep for Vladimir Ilyich and fed him on mutton day after day until it was all eaten; once that was gone, they bought meat for the week and a maid prepared cuts of it in the trough where feed for the cattle was stored, and this also did Vladimir Ilyich for a full week. However, there was plenty of milk and rye cakes [*shan'gi*]..."[499]

'Full board' with Zyryanov did not come with any frills, but it did relieve him of many of life's daily concerns. "...it is high time to leave the habits of the capital behind: here they are entirely out of place and one must accustom oneself to the local ones", Ulyanov wrote to his mother. "It feels like I am already reasonably well adjusted; only when it comes to shopping do I still think as a St Petersburger at times: when one can simply pop into the shop and pick up what one wants, so to speak..."[500]

Shushenskoye was a relatively large village: 257 households with 1,382 residents. It had its own *volost* administration, one church, four merchant stores, two taverns, and one elementary school with one teacher for 30 pupils. It was to him that Ulyanov first went in an attempt to "strike up an acquaintance", as Krupskaya recalled, "but nothing came of it. The teacher was more drawn to the local aristocracy: the priest and a pair of shopkeepers. They spent their time on cards and drink. The teacher had no interest whatsoever in issues of a social nature."[501]

Some local Jews, shopkeepers by the name of Matov who had their own pretensions to intellectualism, offered their introductions, but as Krupskaya wrote, they fostered in Ulyanov "a special antipathy due to their obtrusiveness".[502] Relations were better with another shopkeeper, Ioanniky Zavertkin. Ulyanov often visited him for ink and other writing materials, and occasionally helped him with his book-keeping.[503]

---

499 Vospominaniya o Vladimire Ilyiche Lenine. Five volumes. Moscow, 1984. Vol. 1. p. 226.

500 *V. I. Lenin.* Polnoye sobraniye sochineny. Vol. 55. p. 55.

501 Vospominaniya o Vladimire Ilyiche Lenine. Vol. 1. p. 224.

502 *V. I. Lenin.* Polnoye sobraniye sochineny. Vol. 55. p. 404.

503 See: Rabochaya Moskva. 1924. 2nd February.

With Stepan Zhuravlev, the *volost* clerk, on the other hand, he became genuinely friendly. Krupskaya writes, "Vladimir said of him that he was by nature a revolutionary, a protestant. Zhuravlev spoke out boldly against the wealthy and would not suffer any injustice."[504]

Ulyanov also became friends with two exiled workers in the village. One of them, a a later arrival, was a worker from the Putilov Works, a Finn by the name of Oskar Engberg. The other was a Pole, a hatter from Łódź called Jan Promiński, exiled with his wife and five children. The three formed, as Ulyanov joked, "a little International". He quickly began to include requests in his correspondence with family: "Promiński's children have nothing to read. I have even considered this: subscribing to the magazine *Niva*. It would be an amusement for the Promiński children (pictures daily), and for me – Turgenev's collected works, which *Niva* is offering as a bonus, in 12 volumes. And all of this for seven roubles with shipping!"[505]

Early on he also befriended some local hunters, who began to take him on long expeditions, hunting rabbit, duck and grouse and sharing with him their plethora of hunting yarns about the bears, deer, and even wild mountain goats. He often went to nearby spots to hunt small game with his new friends. He wrote to his mother, "For the most part I go with Promiński; I take my host's dog, whom I have trained to accompany us, and who possesses some (albeit limited) hunting abilities. I have got myself my own dog – I obtained a puppy from an acquaintance here and I hope by next summer to have reared and trained it: I just don't know how much of a dog it will turn out to be, whether it has the nose. I have no eye for that..."[506]

And so the days went on, seeing out the sentence handed down to him by imperial decree. The most painful period of adjustment passed relatively quickly. "In the early days of my exile," he wrote to his younger sister, "I decided not to so much as look at a map of European Russia and Europe: one had such a sense of bitterness when one spread out those maps and contemplated all those black dots. Now, it is nothing, I have grown used to it..."[507]

By 17th August 1897 he was writing to his mother, "There is really nothing to say about myself. My letters are short as life is much too

---

504   Vospominaniya o Vladimire Ilyiche Lenine. Vol. 1. p. 225.
505   *V. I. Lenin*. Polnoye sobraniye sochineny. Vol. 55. p. 80.
506   Ibid. pp. 36, 39, 54.
507   Ibid. p. 107.

monotonous: I have already described all my external surroundings; on the inside, one day differs from the next only in the fact that I read from one book one day, another the next; one day I set off right out of the village, the next I go left; one day I am busy with one piece of work, the next another... I am of course in perfect health..."

When at the end of September Ulyanov spent a few days in Tesinskoye, contrasted with the ailing and overstrained Gleb Krzhizhanovsky he seemed a picture of health. "Here too everyone has noticed that I have put on weight over the summer and am tanned, the very model of a Siberian. That is what hunting and country life means! In one stroke all my Petersburg ailments have been put to one side!"[508]

---

508   Ibid. Vol. 55. p. 54.

THE WEDDING

At the start of winter Apollon Dolmantyevich Zyryanov began to notice a change in his tenant's mood: "He had little to say, and his laughter and joking ceased."[509]

That summer, Krzhizhanovsky's sister Antonina had come to visit Vasily Starkov, and on 30th July, they had married, with Vladimir serving as best man. At the end of the summer, Anatoly Vaneyev was joined by Dominika Trukhovskaya, who had visited him as his 'bride' while he was still in remand prison. News also arrived from St Petersburg of Struve's happy family life: after a dramatic split from Kalmykova, he had married Nina Gerd on 1st May 1897.[510] Tugan-Baranovsky, meanwhile, married her friend Lida Davydova.

The sagacious Zyryanov began to tease Ulyanov: "Is it worth getting upset over this? There are plenty of brides in the village…"[511] But Ulyanov and Krzhizhanovsky, who was also beginning to show some strain, did not react to the joke. They were both waiting for someone: Gleb for Zinaida Nevzorova, and Vladimir for Nadezhda Krupskaya. Both women expected to be exiled after their remand, at which point they could begin pushing for what is now referred to as 'reuniting families'.

Ulyanov most likely met Nadezhda Krupskaya at Klasson's 'salon for Marxists' in early 1895.[512] She was born on 14th (26th) February 1869 and was a year older than Ulyanov. Her father, Konstantin Krupsky, came from a family of impoverished noblemen from Vilna [today Vilnius] Province – graduating from Mikhailovsky Artillery School and Military Law Academy, he had risen to the rank of major. Her mother,

---

509 Krasnoyarsky Rabochy. 1941. No. 17. 21st January.
510 See: R. Pipes. Struve: Liberal on the Left, 1870-1905. Harvard, 1970. p. 171.
511 Sovetskaya mysl'. Ustyug. 1926. 23rd March.
512 See: Tvorchestvo. 1920. Nos. 7-10. p. 4.

Yelizaveta Vasilyevna, who had earned a diploma as a home schooling teacher, occasionally worked as a domestic tutor.[513]

In *My Life*, Krupskaya wrote, "There was much discontent among the officer class at that time. My father read a lot, did not believe in God, and was familiar with the socialist movement in the West. While my father was alive, revolutionaries were forever visiting our home (initially nihilists, then *narodniki*, then *Narodnaya Volya* members); as to what extent my father participated in the revolutionary movement, I cannot say. He died when I was 14..."[514]

After his death in February 1883, his wife and daughter continued to live in St Petersburg on a modest pension. However, thanks to the assistance provided by her late father's brother, Active State Councillor Alexander Krupsky, Nadya was able to afford a place at the prestigious Princess Obolenskaya private gymnasium. Her closest friends, Ariadna Tyrkova and Nina Gerd, daughter of the school's director, came from relatively wealthy families and when they visited the small, modest apartment in which Nadya lived, they witnessed the 'orderly poverty' so characteristic of the low-income intelligentsia of the time. "I wondered how she and her mother could exist at such close quarters," Ariadna wrote.[515]

Tyrkova continues, "Nadya's mother kept the small, sparsely furnished apartment in good order, creating a comely homeliness as she bustled around in a warm and welcoming fashion, pouring us tea with delicious home-made jams and stuffing us with home-made buns. With her plain, dark dress and smoothly combed blonde hair, she resembled a nun. I enjoyed her gentle, attentive gaze and the way she listened to our chatter as it flitted from complicated ideas about universal welfare to childish laughter, something she readily echoed. I liked that in every room there was a lamp burning before an icon. The rooms were small, but the icons were large, much larger than we had at home... Nadya Krupskaya and her mother radiated onto me a good-hearted friendliness and warm calm."[516]

---

513 See: *B. Sokolov.* Armand i Krupskaya. Zhenshchiny vozhdya. Smolensk, 1999. pp. 9, 10, 21.
514 Ibid. p. 19.
515 *A. Tyrkova-Williams.* To, chego bol'she ne budet. p. 214.
516 Ibid. pp. 112-113, 114.

Her friends were tactful enough, but this did not stop Nadezhda from developing certain complexes. She later referred to them as her "fear of people", or more precisely, "rabid shyness" ("I am suddenly and unexpectedly overcome by a rush of the most rabid shyness – I find myself completely tongue-tied… It is an excruciating sensation and one of which it is difficult to divest myself…"[517])

Meanwhile, the girls were growing up. Tyrkova writes, "My girlhood had passed. I had admirers. Poetry was written for me. Nadya would occasionally hear the gushing comments of the young men, strangers to us, as we walked along the street. They did not surprise or offend me. I would make it my task to carry on with such a detached, impenetrable expression that it would appear I had heard nothing… This amused Nadya. She was much taller than me. Tilting her head slightly to one side, she would look down on me from above, her plump lips breaking into a smile… Nadya knew nothing of such temptations. In her girlhood there were no flirtatious games, no exchange of cues, of glances and smiles, and certainly no stolen kisses. Nadya didn't skate, didn't dance, didn't go on boats, and spoke only with her girlfriends at school or with her mother's elderly acquaintances."[518]

Nadezhda graduated from school with a gold medal and was moved into an eighth 'teaching' grade. In 1887, having received a diploma as a home schooling teacher in Russian and mathematics, she went to work in the Pospelova School, where girls were taught to sew. In 1889 she entered the Bestuzhev Courses, where she met an old friend, Olga Witmer, who introduced her to the Technology Institute Marxists.

Later, in a letter to Maria Alexandrovna, she talked about this period in her life: "I remember how much to-ing and fro-ing I did in those years. I had set myself on becoming a school teacher, but was unable to find a position and looked to the provinces. Then, when the Bestuzhev Courses began, I enrolled there thinking that I would now be taught all those subjects which had interested me, so when they began lecturing me on other things entirely, I dropped the courses. In short, I was thrashing about helplessly. Only at the age of 21 did I hear of such a thing as the 'social sciences': up until then serious reading had for me been the

---

517   V. I. Lenin. Polnoye sobraniye sochineny. Vol. 55. pp. 419, 426.
518   B. Sokolov. Armand i Krupskaya. pp. 29-30.

natural sciences or history, throwing myself one minute into something of Rossmässler's, the next into a history of Philip II of Spain..."[519]

Having dropped out of the Bestuzhev Courses, Nadya entered service with the Chief Directorate of Railways, but also began to teach geography at a workers' school in Nevskaya Zastava three evenings a week.[520] Extremely shy around people unfamiliar to her, the school quite literally transformed her. She was respected and loved by her students, and her shyness and stiffness vanished of their own accord. Her friend Ariadna noticed that as soon as Nadezhda began to talk about the school, she would literally "blossom". "Her kind blue eyes would gleam... I was so pleased for her."[521]

It was at that same workers' school in 1894 that she first heard about the newcomer from the Volga. By this time, Ulyanov enjoyed extremely good relations not only with the 'technologists', who made up the backbone of the social democrat organisation in St Petersburg, but also with the female students [*kursistki*] who worked in the workers' school and were active in the League of Struggle.

After their meeting at Klasson's apartment, he had accompanied her home. They talked, and then began to meet more and more often. Eventually, he began dropping in on her at home on Staro-Nevsky Prospekt as he returned from his activities with the workers' circles.

Ariadna Tyrkova soon noticed that something was going on with Nadya. Initially she did not respond to her questioning, instead merely blushing. "Nadya had very white, delicate skin, but the colour which took from her cheeks to her ears, chin and brow was a soft pink. She wore it well..." Gradually, though, the friends got talking, and all became clear. "By now, Nadya's life was defined by, and brimming with, the ideas and sensibilities destined to hold dominion over her from early youth to the grave... These ideas and sensibilities were inextricably linked to one who had possessed her just as completely... Nadya spoke about him sparingly and unwillingly. I never gave her the slightest indication that I could see she was head over heels in love with him... I was happy for Nadya that she was experiencing something great and intense."[522]

519	V. I. Lenin. Polnoye sobraniye sochineny. Vol. 55. p. 172.
520	See: B. Sokolov. Armand i Krupskaya. pp. 21, 30.
521	A. Tyrkova-Williams. To, chego bol'she ne budet. p. 189.
522	Ibid. pp. 192, 194.

Krupskaya herself wrote, "At that time I was in love with the school and I would have gone without bread if it meant I could talk about the school and the students... One must say that the workers held their teachers in great esteem: the sombre guard at Gromov's timber yards telling his teacher with face beaming about the birth of a son; the consumptive textile worker wishing for her a dashing suitor for having taught him to read and write; the toiling religious dissenter searching for God his whole life who wrote contentedly that only on Holy Week had he learned from Rudakov (another pupil in the school) that there was no God and how easy things had become as a result... The tobacco worker, debased with drink every Sunday and so heavy with the reek of tobacco that one's head span when you leant over his exercise book, who wrote in scrawled hand, missing out the vowels, that they had found a three-year-old girl in the street and had taken her in to live within their team, that they had had to hand her over to the police, and what a pity this was; the one-legged soldier who came and told you that the Mikhail who had spent a year with you learning to read and write had suffered a rupture at work and died, but in his final moments had thought of you, bade you to remember him, and wished us long lives..."[523]

Ulyanov listened attentively to these stories while Krupskaya's mother Yelizaveta Vasilyevna laid on a fine lunch for them, something of a boon for a bachelor such as Ulyanov.

However, as Krupskaya writes, "Ilyich expected a rejection of the usual intellectual pursuits of the time – calling in on one another, inconsequential conversation, 'over-chatting', as we used to say. Here Ilyich was maintaining certain revolutionary traditions. ...Ilyich berated our young people for calling in on each other. Zinaida Pavlovna [Nevzorova] recalls having gone over with a friend to Ilyich's, who lived close by, under no particular pretext, and not finding him at home. In the evening, at almost 12 o'clock, the doorbell rang. It turned out to be Ilyich himself, who had just come from Nevskaya Zastava, tired and sporting a somewhat pained expression. He began to ask in anxious tones what had happened, why they had come, and upon hearing that they had not called in for any particular reason, that they had simply stopped by, he grumbled angrily, 'Not very clever,' and departed. Zinaida told me how taken aback they were."[524]

---

523   Vospominaniya o Vladmire Ilyiche Lenine. Vol. 1. pp. 213-214.
524   *N. K. Krupskaya.* O Lenine. p. 118.

There was generally no indication that any marriage proposals were in the offing at this stage. However, there was certainly a degree of mutual affection. While in solitary confinement, Ulyanov had made a request of Krupskaya: each day, when being taken to the yard, he was able to catch a glimpse of a sliver of pavement on Shaplernaya Street from a window in the prison hallway. Krupskaya writes, "He came up with a plan that we – Apollinariya Alexandrovna Yakubova and I – would come and stand on that piece of the pavement at the appointed hour, and he would see us. For some reason Apollinariya was not able to go, but over a number of days I came and stood on that spot for some time."[525]

While in prison, Ulyanov wrote one of his 'chemical' letters to Krupskaya declaring his love. By now it was clear to Anna Ulyanova-Yelizarova, who at that point was not especially fond of Krupskaya, that "Nadezhda would likely go all the way to the end (by then it was clear where it was leading) and he would not be alone" going into exile.[526]

Now he waited patiently while Krupskaya was in custody. Only in May 1897, after becoming settled in Shushenskoye, did Ulyanov ask his sister to relay "my regards" to Nadezhda, and send a photograph "in exchange for one of me".[527] However, by the end of the year, as Zinaida Nevzorova was handed a sentence of three years in exile and began making efforts to be transferred to Minusinsk district to be with Gleb Krzhizhanovsky, Ulyanov was beginning to grow nervous. "It is quite possible," he wrote to his sister Maria, "that Nadezhda Konstantinovna will come to me as well: this will probably be decided quite soon, and may even have been decided by the time you read this letter."[528]

It seems he sent a lengthy letter to Krupskaya that summer. Unfortunately, its contents have not survived. However, Vera Dridzo, Nadezhda's secretary in the 1930s, recalled the details of the episode.

"Arriving in Shushenskoye, where he was to serve his exile, Vladimir Ilyich wrote a long letter, again in 'chemicals', to Nadezhda Konstantinovna, calling her to him and asking her to be his wife. In her reply she wrote, 'Well, wife it is, then'. Why would Nadezhda Konstantinovna offer Vladimir Ilyich such a response?"

---

525   Vospominaniya o Vladmire Ilyiche Lenine. Vol. 1. p. 221.
526   Proletarskaya revolyutsiya. 1924. No. 3. p. 119.
527   *V. I. Lenin*. Polnoye sobraniye sochineny. Vol. 55. p. 42.
528   Ibid. pp. 59, 65.

Dridzo continues, "People are different and express their feelings in different ways. Some express minor sentiments grandly and noisily, with lofty words, while others do not know how to express their deepest, strongest feelings. Nadezhda Konstantinovna was the latter kind of person. She loved Vladimir Ilyich deeply, and was aware of how he felt towards her, but because of her shyness, awkwardness, and aversion to grand words, this was the form her response to him took."[529] As soon as she learned her sentence – three years' exile in Ufa Province – Krupskaya made a request to be sent to Siberia, to Yenisei Province, to wed Vladimir Ulyanov.

While awaiting their brides, Gleb Krzhizhanovsky and Vladimir Ulyanov decided to see in the New Year together. Gleb arrived in 'Shushu' on 24th December and all other matters were set aside. In the mornings, Vladimir would drag the heavy-sleeping Gleb into the yard and begin wrestling, an activity which would descend into good-natured cavorting in the snow drifts. "We are living very well," wrote Ulyanov to relatives, "and going on many walks, thanks to the weather remaining for the most part very warm... We hunt eagerly ... though very unsuccessfully. Such is hunting in the winter! The walks are pleasant at least."[530]

Their keenness for walking was also driven by the inclination among the male members of the Zyryanovs, their hosts, to drink heavily at holidays and compel their 'dear guests' to join them. Ulyanov writes, "Holidays in Shu-shu-shu were quite the thing in those days, and I didn't notice those ten days passing. Gleb particularly enjoyed Shu-sha... The Sayan Mountains enthralled him, especially on clear days when the light was good. Gleb has now become a great lover of singing, so my silent rooms were greatly cheered by his arrival, and have again fallen into silence with his departure. But he has no sheet music and songs." Recalling evenings at Alakayevka, he wrote to his mother: "We had, I think, a lot of such material (from back when we would also have something of a sing)... It would be good to send it to him: he would be delighted... Gleb's health improved somewhat while with me thanks to a proper routine and plenty of walks, and he left greatly heartened."[531]

It seems those "silent rooms" were once more beginning to evoke a melancholy in Ulyanov, and on 8th January 1898 he sent a telegram to the

---

529   V. Dridzo. Nadezhda Konstantinovna. Moscow, 1969. p. 54.

530   V. I. Lenin. Polnoye sobraniye sochineny. Vol. 55. p. 64.

531   Ibid. pp. 66, 67.

director of the Department of Police: "I have the honour of requesting permission for my bride Nadezhda Krupskaya to transfer to the village of Shushenskoye." On 24th January he wrote to his mother, "Nadezhda Konstantinovna has been assured her three years in Ufa Province will be commuted to two years in Shusha and I am awaiting her and Yelizaveta Vasilyevna. I am even arranging accommodation – a neighbouring room in the same quarters. An amusing competition has arisen with the local priest, who is also asking the owner for the room. I am protesting and insisting that they await final clarification of my 'family' circumstances."[532]

But January came and went, then February, and then March, as all the while this 'family' question was passed from one rung of the police to the next. In April, as a result of ice movements on the Yenisei, communication with the rest of Russia was cut completely for two to three weeks. Consequently, Nadezhda and Yelizaveta Vasilyevna's arrival in Krasnoyarsk on 1st May, and then in Shushenskoye on 7th May aboard the first steamer (which could bring them only as far as Sorokin Razboi) came as a complete surprise.

Krupskaya writes, "We arrived in the village of Shushenskoye, where Vladimir Ilyich was living, at dusk; Vladimir Ilyich was off hunting. We disembarked and were led to the cabin. In Siberia – in Minusinsk district – the peasants live in a very orderly fashion, floors covered in colourful homespun rugs, walls whitewashed and garlanded with fir. Vladimir Ilyich's room was, though small, equally tidy. My mother and I were given the rest of the cabin by the owners. The cabin was crowded with members of the host family and neighbours and we were diligently examined and questioned." They took a shine to Nadezhda Krupskaya, impressed by her affability, her 'city' dress, her large eyes – as yet unaffected by Graves' disease – and especially her long, thick braid.

They decided to play a trick on Vladimir Ilyich. As he was returning home from his hunt, he spotted light coming from his window; his host, Apollon Zyryanov was outside waiting for him and told him that a very drunk Oskar Engberg had come and kicked up row, throwing his books around. Ulyanov rushed to the porch, at which point Nadezhda appeared.[533]

In the year since their first meeting, it appears they had not once spoken face to face of their feelings. The two 'chemical' letters Vladimir

---

532   Ibid. Vol. 55. p. 69.

533   See: Vospominaniya o Vladmire Ilyiche Lenine. Vol. 1. pp. 223, 224.

had sent – one professing his love, the other proposing marriage – were no substitute for the heartfelt conversations about any manner of things that go on between young people who care for one another.

Now, after the hosts and neighbours had left and Yelizaveta Vasilyevna, tired from the journey, had laid down to rest in the next room, they talked for the first time and, as Krupskaya writes, "we talked long through the night".[534] One can detect echoes of that night-time conversation in her memoirs.

Later Krupskaya would say that from the moment "they began to live together, they had an agreement: never to question the other on anything – without the greatest trust they could not conceive of a life together. They also agreed on one other thing – never to hide any change in their feelings towards one another."[535]

Ulyanov only got round to writing to his mother three days later: "The guests have finally arrived, dearest Mother. They turned up on the evening of 7th May, just when I had contrived to spend the day hunting, so they did not find me at home. I found Nadezhda Konstantinovna looking poorly – she will need to look after her health better here. About me Yelizaveta Vasilyevna had this to say: 'My, you've filled out!' - an assessment of the kind, you will agree, it would have been preferable not to receive!"[536]

Krupskaya's letters to Maria Alexandrovna in those first weeks were even more cheerful and assuasive. On 14th June, she wrote, "I already feel like I've spent a lifetime in Shusha, I am so well acclimatised. Summer in Susha is actually very fine. We go for walks in the evening every day; Mother won't venture too far, but we sometimes go a little further afield. In the evening, there is no dampness in the air and the walking is splendid. There are a lot of mosquitoes, and we have sewn nets, but the mosquitoes seem to go for Volodya especially, though on the whole they let us live... Vladimir is not hunting at the moment (he's not an especially passionate hunter) ... even his hunting boots have been cast down to the basement... And what a marvel it was on the other side of the Yenisei! We went over there once and had all manner of adventures, it was splendid."[537]

---

534   Ibid. p. 224.
535   *V. Dridzo*. Nadezhda Konstantinovna. p. 62.
536   *V. I. Lenin*. Polnoye sobraniye sochineny. Vol. 55. p. 88.
537   Ibid. p. 391.

Relatives and friends were beginning to ask about the wedding, but there had been something of a hitch. To register the marriage, they needed documents, but Ulyanov, like all exiles, had no passport, this having been replaced with a particulars card [*stateiny spisok*]. The card had, as it turned out, been lost by someone in the Krasnoyarsk prison board.

The back and forth and red tape over the issue rumbled on for almost two months. In a June 30th petition to the head of Yenisei Province, Ulyanov wrote: "A very strange contradiction has arisen: on the one hand, the senior administration permits my request for my bride to be transferred to the village of Shushenskoye, stipulating that a condition of this permission is our *immediate* marriage; on the other hand I am wholly unable to obtain from the local authorities the document necessary for the marriage to take place; meanwhile, the responsibility is being shifted to my bride..."[538]

Finally, at the end of July, the documents were received. To their great pleasure, the clerk Stepan Zhuravlev and shopkeeper Ioanniky Zavertkin, Shushenskoye peasants whose acquaintance Ulyanov had made, were invited to act as witnesses and groomsmen. Oskar Engberg, who had once been apprenticed to a goldsmith, fashioned the wedding rings from a copper coin which he polished to a golden shine. On 10th July 1898, the priest Ioann Orestov carried out the sacrament of marriage in the local church. The ceremony was conducted in the proper fashion, with the priest placing the ring on the couple's fingers and leading them round the altar, after which they took communion and bowed to the icons of the Saviour and Mother of God at the holy doors to the iconostasis.[539]

538　Ibid. Vol. 46. p. 454.

539　Russian State Archive of Socio-Political History. Corpus 1. Inventory 1. Item. 46.

FAMILY

On the same day they held a house-warming party. They had spent their first two months living with the Zyryanovs, but the noisy drinking that the Zyryanov men indulged in forced them to look for alternative accommodation. On 10th July, the Ulyanovs took up residence with the peasant P. A. Petrova, who for four roubles rented them half the house and a vegetable plot.

Krupskaya recalled, "We began to live as a family. In the summer there was no-one to be found to help us around the house. My mother and I did battle with the Russian stove together. Initially, I would overturn the dumpling soup with the tongs, the dumplings scattering all over the bottom. I eventually got used to it. We had a proper variety of things growing in the vegetable plot – cucumbers, carrots, beetroot, pumpkins... We turned the yard into a garden – Ilyich and I headed into the forest, brought back some hops, and planted a garden together. In October a helper arrived, 13-year-old Pasha, a skinny girl with sharp elbows, who briskly took on all the domestic tasks. I taught her to read and write, and she decorated the walls under my mother's instruction: 'Ne'er, ne'er pour away the tea'..."540

It should be noted that the Ulyanovs were comfortable with local ways and customs and never overt in displaying urban practices such as their atheism. "'Although Vladimir is protesting,' Krupskaya wrote on the eve of Easter, 'I'm going to paint the eggs and make an Easter cake anyway. You know, there's a custom here – sweeping the room with a fir branch for Easter. It is a lovely one, so we are going to 'adhere to it.'"541

When they organised 'urban' curiosities such as a skating rink, these quickly became entertainments for the whole of Shushenskoye. "At Volodya and Oskar's initiative, and with assistance from the teacher and a few of the local inhabitants, a rink was laid out on the little river beside our house.

---

540   Vospominaniya o Vladimire Ilyiche Lenine. Vol. 1. p. 226.
541   V. I. Lenin. Polnoye sobraniye sochineny. Vol. 55. p. 410.

Vladimir is a wonderful skater... Oskar is a poor one, and rash to boot, so is continually falling, and I cannot skate at all... The teacher is still waiting for skates. For the locals, we are something of a free show: they marvel at Volodya, make fun of me and Oskar, and crack nuts unrelentingly, scattering the shells on our illustrious rink."[542]

But Siberia is an untamed land. Grandmother Zyryanova, seeing her tenant sitting in the evenings with his books at the open window, would fret, "God forbid someone takes a potshot..." Vladimir Ilyich laughed, but got a revolver to go along with his hunting rifle just in case.

The Siberian taiga could throw up surprises at any moment. On one occasion, Ulyanov found himself caught in a storm while in the forest. He wrote, "There has recently been very strong 'weather' [*pogoda*] – the cold, strong *wind* like a whirlwind coming from the west, which the Siberians refer to as 'weather' – blowing in from the Yenisei. In spring there are always twisters, which break fences, roofs and so on. I have been hunting in the forest lately – once when I was there, a twister tore up enormous birches and pine trees around me."[543] How he felt at that moment, Ulyanov does not say.

Initially it was assumed that the Ulyanovs would seek a transfer from Shusha to a more civilised place, at least to Minusinsk, which was at any rate a town. But the more time passed, the more resolutely Vladimir Ilyich began to resist the idea: an old and simple truth was revealing itself – that the intelligentsia, with its idle complacency, navel-gazing, endless talking and squabbling, was not the most ideal company in the extreme circumstances of exile.

Often, in-fighting literally tore exile colonies apart. This was tinged with a further unsavoury element: the way in which penal colonies and exile communities maintained their own hierarchy of authority. The old *Narodnaya Volya* members occupied a special place within it, as a kind of exile 'aristocracy'. The onrush to Siberia of these unknowns calling themselves social democrats, whose ranks included many semi-literate or poorly educated workers, created a common stigmatisation. "The old *Narodnaya Volya* exile community," recalled the worker A. Shapovalov, "believed that only they ... had breathed the gunpowder of revolution and viewed the Marxists rather contemptuously as people among whom there

---

542 Ibid. p. 404.
543 Ibid. p. 162.

was not a single individual willing to go to the gallows for the cause of revolution..."⁵⁴⁴

Ulyanov himself said to Krupskaya at the time, "'There is nothing worse than these exile intrigues, they hold everything up, and the old men have bad enough nerves, what with everything they've endured and the penal camps they've survived. Don't let yourself be sucked into these kinds of affairs – all our work is ahead of us, you cannot expend yourself on such episodes.' Vladimir Ilyich was pushing to break with these old men. I remember the meeting where that split took place. The decision to split had already been made, and now it was a matter of making it as painless as possible. We were breaking from them because we needed to, but we made the break without bad feeling, and with regret. Afterwards, we kept apart."⁵⁴⁵

In other exile colonies, similar splits had become far messier affairs. The tragic death of Nikolai Fedoseyev was one such scandal that greatly affected Ulyanov. In January 1898, Ulyanov learned of a quarrel which had erupted in Verkholensk, where Fedoseyev had been exiled. A certain Yukhotsky had virtually accused Fedoseyev of embezzling public money. Ulyanov wrote to his sister, "Some detestable troublemaker has appeared attacking N. Y."⁵⁴⁶ A 'hearing' took place in Verkholensk, at which the colony emphatically rejected Yukhotsky's false accusations, but he continued to spread them in other colonies.

"N. Y. was dreadfully shocked and distressed by all this," Ulyanov told Anna. "The slanderer has been strongly and publicly condemned by all comrades, and I never could have thought that N. Y. (who witnessed his share of exile scandals) would have taken everything so terribly to heart."⁵⁴⁷

Eventually, having received yet another odious missive from Yukhotsky, Fedoseyev broke down. He informed his comrade in exile Yakov Lyakhovsky that he was unable to work, and "having been certain he could no longer work, decided he could no longer live either". He then went into the forest and shot himself with a revolver. When the news of his death reached Arkhangelsk, his fiancée Maria Hopfenhaus committed suicide.⁵⁴⁸

---

544   O Lenine. Book 3. Moscow, 1925. p. 72.
545   Vospominaniya o Vladimire Ilyiche Lenine. Vol. 1. p. 231.
546   *V. I. Lenin.* Polnoye sobraniye sochineny. Vol. 55. p. 71.
547   Ibid. p. 98.
548   Ibid. pp. 97, 98.

"On 23. VI he was buried," Ulyanov wrote to his sister. "He left a letter to Gleb, as well as some manuscripts, and apparently he wanted me to know that he was dying 'with a wholehearted faith in life, and not from despair.'"[549]

After Fedoseyev's death, Ulyanov would hear no more talk of moving to a more 'civilised' place. Calling on friends, having them over, going for walks, talking, debating, playing a game or two of chess – by all means! But rubbing up against each other every day, and above all having constantly to repair relationships and resolve quarrels – no, thank you! "No, best not to hope for intellectuals as friends in Shushu!" he wrote to his sister angrily.[550]

As for the workers Promiński and Engberg, exiled in Shushenskoye, they remained close friends of Ulyanov until the end of his sentence, and for the household, the most welcome of guests. Krupskaya noted, "Over that time, we grew so thoroughly accustomed to our Shushenskoye comrades that if on any given day neither Oskar nor Promiński came to visit, it truly felt as if something was missing…"[551]

The people of Shushenskoye admired Ulyanov's sensitivity and his respectful manner. Stepanida Pleshkina, whose husband made pots for all of Shushenskoye, spoke often with Ulyanov and noted: "Our poverty did not make him uncomfortable. He was very courteous with us and all the other peasants."

After he began offering 'legal consultations' on Sundays, his circle of acquaintances only expanded. Rich and poor came to him for advice. "He was much sought after as a lawyer," writes Krupskaya, "after he helped a worker dismissed from the gold mine win a case against the mine owner. News of the victory spread quickly among the peasants. The men and womenfolk came and laid their troubles before him. Vladimir Ilyich listened attentively and considered everything carefully before offering his advice… Often, the mere threat of going to Ulyanov was enough to make an offender back down."

Naturally, such work did not pass without amusing incident: Krupskaya recalls an occasion when "a peasant travelled 20 *versts* for advice on taking action against an in-law who did not invite him to a

---

549   Ibid. p. 93.
550   Ibid. p. 71.
551   Ibid. p. 413.

particularly raucous wedding. 'And would your in-law offer you a glass if you were to visit him now?' 'I dare say he would now.' Ulyanov spent almost an hour persuading the man to make peace with his in-law."[552]

In August, Gleb Krzhizhanovsky and Zinaida Nevzorova were married. Towards the end of the year, the exiled social democrats dotted around the district made plans to gather in Minusinsk, where the Krzhizhanovskys and the Starkovs had moved, to celebrate Christmas together. The district police captain granted permission, and by 24th December they had all come together.

On 10th January, Krupskaya wrote to Maria Alexandrovna: "The festive period in Minus was wonderful, and really reinvigorated us. Almost the entire district came to town for Christmas, so we saw in New Year as a large group, and in fine fashion…The holidays were spent in a suitably festive way, Vladimir in battle on the chessboard from morning till evening… defeating all-comers, of course; we went skating (Volodya was sent Mercury skates from Krasnoyarsk as a present, on which one can perform figures and do all sorts of fancy things. I also have new skates, but I skate, or more accurately, strut like a chicken, as badly with the new ones as I did with the old – I'm finding it something of a tricky science!), sang together, and even rode on a *troika*!"[553]

Krupskaya's letters give an insight into all aspects of their life – she talks about collecting mushrooms and berries, infusing brandy with cherries and pickling the cucumbers which grew in the garden and vegetable plot, about the kitten and Dzhenka the dog – but most of all, particularly in her letters to Yelizarova, Kalmykova and Nina Struve, she writes about the work they are doing: about Ulyanov's monograph on markets, and their translation of Sidney and Beatrice Webb's *Industrial Democracy*, [translated as *The Theory & Practice of British Trade Unionism – trans.*], about the latest articles they were sending and proofs they were editing. It was the contents of these letters that made their acquaintances wonder about the nature of the newly-weds' relationship.

On 10th August 1898, Alexandra Mikhailovna Kalmykova wrote to Potresov: "The wedding of V. I. and N. K. has taken place. I saw his sister recently. I cannot decide whether this is a *mariage d'estime*

---

552   Vospominaniya o Vladimire Ilyiche Lenine. Vol. 1. p. 225.

553   V. I. Lenin. Polnoye sobraniye sochineny. Vol. 55. pp. 405, 406.

[a marriage of mutual respect], a *mariage de raison* [a marriage of reason], or a genuine *mariage* [a marriage for love]."[554]

In later times, as 'Leniniana' became the property of professional prudes, the restrained understatement of the letters was elevated to a distinct virtue. This is something Krupskaya mentions briefly, but earnestly: "We were a young couple, after all... The fact that I do not write about it in my memoirs does not by any means indicate that our life was without poetry or youthful passion."[555]

There was one other issue that was becoming an increasing cause for concern for the Ulyanov family, but about which Krupskaya wrote not a word.

Ariadna Tyrkova, an individual both observant and extremely precise and severe in her assessments of others, noted that Krupskaya did not possess a grain of vanity in her character. She was kind, sincere, and straightforward. She exhibited the kind of asceticism that defined many Russian revolutionaries. "But she had a unique femininity. She most fully expressed it in the integrity with which she devoted herself to her husband and leader. And in *love for children*."[556]

Their friends and colleagues – Peter Struve, Stepan Radchenko and the Krzhizhanovskys – were having their first children, but there were no new additions to the Ulyanov family.

Eventually, Maria Alexandrovna, who yearned for grandchildren, could no longer contain herself. After the New Year holidays, she wrote to Nadezhda and asked her directly whether she was well and if she had long to wait for "a little bird to fly in". Krupskaya replied, "As for my health, I am perfectly well, but the outlook is poor as regards the arrival of any little birds, alas: no little bird is on its way."[557]

There was no immediate panic over the issue, but a year later, when Krupskaya went to Ufa to complete her period of exile, she visited a doctor. Ulyanov wrote, "Nadya should be resting: the doctor discovered (as she wrote last week) that her condition (a female issue) requires continuous

---

554   Amsterdam. International Institute of Social History. Archive. Potresov papers collection. C2/II/20. 1898.

555   *V. Dridzo*. Nadezhda Krupskaya. p. 56; Istorichesky arkhiv. 1957. No. 2. p. 38.

556   *A. Tyrkova-Williams*. To, chego bol'she ne budet. pp. 194, 195.

557   *V. I. Lenin*. Polnoye sobraniye sochineny. Vol. 55. p. 409.

treatment and she should rest for two to *six weeks*."⁵⁵⁸ Lenin scholar Grigory Khant discovered a record of the final diagnosis made by a Doctor Fedotov in Ufa: "genital infantilism", for which there was no treatment at the time.

For Ulyanov and Krupskaya, this was a calamity. They both loved children. He had grown up surrounded by dozens of siblings and cousins of varying ages, while she had been preparing herself to go into teaching and had a propensity to fall in love with every bright, wide-eyed little girl she came across.⁵⁵⁹ Now it had become clear they would be unable to have their *own*.

---

558   Ibid. Vol. 55. p. 183; Vol. 46, p. 456.
559   Ibid. Vol. 55. p. 423.

WORK

The cheerful, matter-of-fact style of Ulyanov's letters to family, in particular his mother, has given birth to an entire branch of literature on the carefree life of 'politicals' in tsarist exile. Everything from Zyryanov's mutton to the black grouse he shot on his hunts have become part of it, as if mutton cutlets could make up for the loss of freedom and expulsion to the ends of the Earth. It renders incoherent the tragic martyrology for which the entire history of exile is noted. Looking only at those who were caught up in the League of Struggle case, the list of victims is extremely substantial.

Exile is exile: if rather than slip into despondency Ulyanov had managed to maintain his well-being and a certain cheerfulness of spirit, then it was not any inherent quality of his own character, or of human nature more generally, that had kept him from despair. It was to a large degree because in exile, as in prison, he kept himself busy on a daily basis with demanding work – or as he put it, an 'endeavour' [*delo*]. As he wrote to his sister, "It is better to apply oneself to the endeavour at hand: one would be lost in exile without it."[560]

He became a man of action in a more general sense. When the temperatures dropped and the wind began blowing in through all the cracks, "I even fetched a saw from the landlord and began sawing the door so it closed better".[561] Rather than howling with anguish at the greyness and squalidness of life in Shushenskoye, he got a shovel and went to clear the ice rink, a place that had become a source of amusement second only to festival days in the village. Instead of complaining about the lack of chess pieces in the local shops, he took a knife and whittled the intricate figures from bark himself. Rather than suffer the monotony of village food, he grabbed a gun and went hunting. Similarly, he learned to ride a horse rather than hire a cart for every journey.

---

560   Ibid. p. 94.
561   Ibid. p. 396.

In his three years in Shushenskoye, he wrote his landmark study *The Development of Capitalism in Russia*, a 500-page volume; he published a 290-page collection titled *Economic Studies & Essays*; he translated and edited the two-volume work by Sidney and Beatrice Webb *The Theory and Practice of British Trade Unionism* [English title: *Industrial Democracy*], which came in at 770 pages. He wrote around two dozen articles and reviews on the works of Kautsky, Hobson, Parvus, Bogdanov, Gvozdev, Struve and Tugan-Baranovsky, Bulgakov and others. These were all published in the St Petersburg journals *Novoye Slovo*, *Mir Bozhy*, *Nachalo*, *Zhizn'*, and *Nauchnoye Obozreniye* – in all, more than 100 pages of work. Finally, two pamphlets, "The New Factory Law", and "The Tasks of the Russian Social Democrats", were published in Geneva. This is not to mention the dozens of articles that were not published.

His was a full-time job – it was daily, laborious, and at times exhausting. The walks, skating and chess matches which he so loved to tell his relations about in letters would as a rule only happen when work was not going well, or, as Krupskaya put it, he was "all written out".[562]

On 22nd November 1898, Krupskaya wrote, "Vladimir has vanished quite fully and resolutely into his 'markets' and covets his time terribly, and we've not called on the Promińskis in several months. In the mornings, Ulyanov asks to be woken at 8, even 7:30, but my attempts to do so are usually unsuccessful: he will mumble a little, bury his head and go back to sleep. Last night he was saying something about ... subsistence farming in his sleep..."[563]

This kind of work offered a decent supplement to the measly eight-rouble entitlement that Ulyanov received as an exile. It is clear from his correspondence with relatives that he asked his mother at least three times for 'home loans' to help with his resettlement and the arrival of Krupskaya. However, the correspondence also makes clear that he repaid his debts. All royalties for his literary output – he received around 1,500 roubles for *The Development of Capitalism...* alone, and another 1,000 for his translation of the Webbs – were handled by his sister Anna, who used the money to settle his debts to his mother and to pay for the books that were sent to Shushenskoye. However, it should be stressed that Ulyanov was not writing for the sake of the royalties. A thousand *versts*

---

562   Ibid. p. 405.
563   Ibid. p. 404.

away, the Russian revolutionary movement was gathering steam. This was throwing up a multitude of problems and questions and here, in the Siberian wilds, he was attempting to offer responses to these – that was his central occupation.

The book was published in March 1899 in what was for the time a large print run – 2,400 copies. It appeared in spring, and "despite the coming summer and the tide of young people leaving the capital for Easter, the book sold out with remarkable rapidity... One cannot help but be gripped by the book."[564] Reviewers in both the capital and the provinces agreed unanimously that despite its polemical anti-*narodnik* tendency, "V. l. Ilyin's book merits attention for its rigorously scientific and objective research".[565]

There were many signs to suggest that the battle with the *narodnik* movement was entering its final phase. On 15th November 1897 Nikolai Mikhailovsky turned 55. Usually, however, he did not celebrate his birthday, instead marking his name day on 6th December. In earlier years this had been a day of celebration for radical intellectuals. A literal queue of people, from newspaper and magazine editorial staff, universities and institutes, and so on, would form at his door wishing to congratulate him.

This time, there was no queue. Editors from the liberal press were there, but of the academic institutions, only students of the Railway Institute made the effort. It was clear that the youth had gone over to the social democrats. This gave the *narodniki* cause to fall into despair and indulge in 'historical pessimism', as they perceived their defeat as nothing less than the end of the entire preceding era of liberation and the complete destruction of the great legacy of the democrats of the 1840s-1870s. "The further things progress like this, the worse it will be", they imagined. As such, "better stagnation than capitalist progress."[566]

That year, Ulyanov wrote a long article from exile titled "The Heritage We Renounce" by way of a response. In it, he singled out three defining characteristics in the legacy of those democratic torch bearers. The first was a complete rejection of and hostility towards serfdom "and everything it has engendered in the economic, social and legal spheres". The second: "a passionate defence of education, self-government, freedom, European

---

564   Vladimir Ilyich Lenin. Biograficheskaya khronika. Vol. 1. pp. 224-225.

565   Istoriya KPSS. Vol. 1. p. 320.

566   See: *V. I. Lenin*. Polnoye sobraniye sochineny. Vol. 2. pp. 534, 541; *B. I. Gorev*. Iz partiinogo proshlogo, p. 42.

modes of living and the wholesale Europeanisation of Russia". The third: "asserting the interests of the masses ... a sincere belief that the abolition of serfdom and its remnants will bring with it general prosperity and the genuine desire to facilitate this end." In this regard, concluded Ulyanov, it was not the liberal *narodniki*, but the social democrats who were the true custodians of that great legacy.[567]

Naturally, there was no uniformity of opinion among representatives of the liberal *narodnik* movement, but Ulyanov did identify certain common traits – those which touched on the most fundamental questions that united them.

Instead of recognising the inevitability of the 'Europeanisation' of Russia characteristic of the enlighteners of the 1860s-1870s, liberal *narodniki* of the 1880s-1890s believed firmly in the possibility of a kind of 'indigenous development'. They were convinced that capitalism represented "regression, error, deviation from a path supposedly prescribed by the entire historical existence of the nation, from a path consecrated on apparently age-old foundations, and so on". They believed that these unique traits, inherent to Russia, would allow her to take a different path to Europe, and in this sense, "backwardness [was] Russia's blessing".[568]

To deny the uniqueness of the rural Russian experience, Ulyanov believed, would be wrong. However, the trouble with talking about 'uniqueness' and 'age-old foundations' lay in the fact that the *narodniki* were closing their eyes to the new realities of rural life. The *narodnik* Alexander Engelhardt, while denying neither 'guild culture' [*artel'nost'*] nor communalism [*obshchinnost'*], wrote, "I have frequently pointed to the peasants' highly developed individualism, egoism, and tendency to exploit... Every one is proud to be a pike seeking a carp to devour." In other words, Ulyanov concludes, the peasantry's tendency is not towards 'communal' structures, but to "the most ordinary petty bourgeois arrangements common to all capitalist societies, as Engelhardt superbly demonstrates".[569]

The distinctive traits of the rural Russian experience far from negated the general laws of development, since much, if not all, of such 'distinctiveness' was merely a relic from earlier feudal relationships. Ulyanov identified with Vera Zasulich, who wrote that in attempting to fence off the community and

---

567   See: *V. I. Lenin*. Polnoye sobraniye sochineny. Vol. 2. pp. 519, 542.
568   Ibid. p. 532.
569   Ibid. p. 523.

preserve those patriarchal forms of economy that supposedly harmonised with the 'Russian soul', the *narodniki* were supporting the now indefensible 'regimentation' that had been generated by serfdom.[570]

Ulyanov writes that 'intellectual egotism' was one characteristic trait of the *narodnik* movement: "The *narodnik* always talks of which path 'we' should choose for the nation, which calamities might occur, were 'we' to steer the nation along one or another path, which outcomes 'we' could expect were 'we' to avoid the perils of the path old Europe has taken, if we were to 'take the good' from both Europe and from our ancient communal mode of living, and so on and so on. Hence the staggering levity with which the *narodnik* (ignoring the circumstances which surround him) embarks on all manner of social schemes..."[571]

Putting faith in "the reason and conscience, knowledge and patriotism of the governing classes," the *narodniki* exhorted the provincial administration and *zemstvos* to intervene more vigorously in the rural economy.

In contrast to the expectation of beneficial change 'from above' and faith in the conscience and patriotism of the 'governing classes', Ulyanov cites one of the most fundamental, or as he writes, "most profound and important provisions," of Marxist theory: that the more complex and radical the problems facing Russia are, the broader the mass of people – with all their attendant ideals and prejudices – will inevitably be drawn into this all-encompassing 'historic undertaking'.[572]

Would the social democrats be able to influence this path of development? Of course: Ulyanov was convinced that creating an organisation able to unite Russia's major proletarian centres, an organisation that wielded the kind of authority among workers that the St Petersburg-based League of Struggle enjoyed, "would be the most significant political factor in modern Russia – one which the government would be unable to ignore in its external and domestic policy..."[573]

The first thing required in the creation of such an organisation was a programme. While in prison, Ulyanov had written *Draft and Explanation of a Programme for the Social-Democratic Party*. In exile, as a continuation of this work, he would write *The Tasks of the Russian Social-Democrats* (1897).

---

570   Ibid. p. 538.
571   Ibid. p. 539.
572   Ibid. p. 539.
573   Ibid. p. 461.

A SPLIT IN THE SOCIAL DEMOCRATS

Working on material for the Russian social democrat programme, Ulyanov was confident that unification of their groups and organisations as a party was a matter of time. Krupskaya, having been in attendance, had told him about the meeting that had taken place between St Petersburg and Kiev-based social democrats in Poltava in summer 1896. He was also aware of attempts made by the Moscow-based Workers' Union to call an all-Russian congress in the same year, and of similar attempts made by the Kiev-based Workers' Cause the following year. He knew of the foundation of the *Rabochaya Gazeta* [Workers' Gazette] in Kiev, while Krupskaya also gave him an account of the First Congress of the RSDLP [Russian Social-Democratic Labour Party], which took place in Minsk in March 1898.

In the run-up to the congress, the organisers had decided they needed to issue a manifesto on the foundation of the party, providing a summary of its guiding principles. Initially, it seems Stepan Radchenko intended on using Ulyanov's *Draft and Explanation of a Programme for the Social-Democratic Party*. However, this pamphlet was apparently too broad to be distilled into a few lines of a short manifesto: the Kiev social democrats put forward their own alternative, and when Radchenko rejected that, they suggested asking Plekhanov. However, since communication with Plekhanov, and even more so Ulyanov, was rather difficult and would require a substantial amount of time, Stepan Radchenko was authorised to make arrangements with Struve for its composition.[574]

This manifesto marked the high point of Struve's "lapse into Marxism". Much later, he wrote by way of an exoneration of himself that he had sought not to express his personal beliefs, but merely the commonly-held "traditions of the social-democratic church": "I did everything in my power not to include in the manifesto any of those beliefs of my own

---

574   See: Istoriya KPSS. Vol. 1. pp. 261, 262, 265; *R. Pipes*. Struve: Liberal on the Left. p. 275 (Russian edition).

that could have been perceived as heresies, or were simply beyond the comprehension of the average social democrat."[575]

Plekhanov, Ulyanov, Martov and other prominent social democrats were nonetheless satisfied with the manifesto. Lepeshinsky recalled that Ulyanov "was as happy as a child. It was with great pride that he told us, his closest comrades in exile and those who shared his beliefs, that from that point onwards he was a member of the Russian Social-Democratic Labour Party. We also seized eagerly on this new cause, as if we had instantly grown in our own estimations."[576]

But as is often the case, bad news followed good: Krupskaya informed Ulyanov that immediately upon returning from the congress, Stepan Radchenko "prised the familiar manifesto, the one which Struve had drafted and the congress approved, from the spine of a book and broke down in tears: almost all participants in the congress – a good number of individuals – had been arrested".[577] It had all come full circle and now they were faced with the prospect of having to start all over again.

One major defect of an organisation such as the League of Struggle lay in the fact that everyone was party to *everything* that went on within it, while simultaneously being involved in *all* its activities. The same people gathered material for the factory leaflets, wrote the proclamations, printed them as hectographs, and then distributed them to the workers. Within such a system, each person was racking up enough charges to earn themselves a prison sentence and exile.

However, what if the entire process of illegal revolutionary activity was divided into separate parts? For example, one person to gather material, another to compose the leaflet, a third to organise their printing, and a fourth to distribute them. The person collecting the data would not know who was composing the flyers and who was printing them, while the one printing would be unaware of their distributor. Given such 'specialisation', each would become one part of a common revolutionary endeavour.[578]

The rationale for the kind of system set out by Ulyanov in his article "A Pressing Question", which appeared in the official party organ *Rabochaya Gazeta*, publication of which having been resumed after the arrests, lay not

---

575   R. *Pipes.* Struve: Liberal on the Left. p. 277-278 (Russian edition).
576   P. N. *Lepeshinsky.* Pervy s"ezd partii. Moscow, 1928. p. 26.
577   Vospominaniya o Vladimire Ilyiche Lenine. Vol. 1. p. 223.
578   V. I. *Lenin.* Polnoye sobraniye sochineny. Vol. 4. p. 196.

in a lack of trust in one another, but in the fact that such a system saved on effort. Moreover, breaking up tasks also reduced 'culpability', in that in the event of arrest each person involved in direct agitation and leafleting would be better off "insomuch as they *could not* be prosecuted for it". This applied to other forms of illegal work. Even if the chain was infiltrated by an agent, he would only be able to 'shine light' on a very limited area of the organisation's activities.[579]

With such clever use of 'specialisation', it was assumed the work of their organisations could be ramped up, communication between them re-established, and agreement reached on organising a second congress in the same manner as the first. Such attempts were repeatedly made in 1898, 1899 and 1900. However, these were unsuccessful: it was gradually becoming apparent that the method itself was the issue, the entire framework of the social-democratic movement having altered fundamentally.

The spread of Marxism had not only given organisations an enormous reserve of 'revolutionary recruits'; it had also diminished the theoretical, political and even practical activities of many social-democratic groups. One manifestation of this crisis within the movement was so-called 'economism'.

The first signs of the emergence of economism were noticed by Plekhanov and Ulyanov after the publication in Vilnius of a pamphlet titled "On Agitation", as well as in the activities of St Petersburg youth organisations. The resonance among even the most unsophisticated workers of earlier 'factory denunciations', which had sought to address the daily hardships faced by workers and had, more importantly, succeeded in earning a number of genuine concessions, certainly explains the fascination amongst some social democrats for supporting purely economic narratives. This narrowing of the field of agitation initially had a detrimental effect on their continuing efforts, but the 'old men' had been able to minimise its negative influence through their activities.

Later, in a letter to Plekhanov, Ulyanov wrote, "This economic *trend* ... was a legitimate and unavoidable companion of the *step forward* given the circumstances within our movement *present in Russia* at the end of the 1880s and early 1890s. The situation was more terrible than perhaps you could imagine and one cannot judge those who faltered in their attempt

---

579   Ibid. Vol. 2. pp. 468, 469.

to extricate themselves from it. A certain narrowing of the objectives while such attempts were being made was legitimate and necessary..."[580]

However, by 1897, 'economism' was beginning to emerge as a defined tendency in itself. The first editions of the illegal newspaper *Rabochaya Mysl* [Workers' Thought], which appeared in St Petersburg in October and December, brought the issue to the fore.

The youth's familiar motifs about the intelligentsia's stranglehold on the movement resounded from the very first edition of the newspaper. Political agitation was treated in the same vein as the rest of the intelligentsia's hobby horses, while economism was elevated to a virtue as the "true politics of the workers".

This was neither overzealousness nor mere error, but a conscious departure from the principles of the political struggle as professed by social democrats.

Meanwhile, despite dissatisfaction at the direction of the newspaper expressed by a host of influential workers' circles, the unification of the *Rabochaya Mysl* group with those members of the League of Struggle still at large took place in St Petersburg in December 1898, and the newspaper was designated the official organ of the St Petersburg committee of the RSDLP. However, disagreements immediately materialised.

Fierce disputes also emerged among émigré social democrats. Attacks by youth elements on Emancipation of Labour had begun as early as 1894, while the Union of Russian Social Democrats Abroad was being formed. However, at that stage the authority of Plekhanov and his colleagues had been too pronounced, and the campaign against them was largely nullified. Only in 1897, when the émigré community grew markedly, due largely to an influx of younger reinforcements, and, more significantly, when it became apparent that the economists were garnering support in Russia itself, did opposition to them begin to take on more robust forms.[581]

"This struggle against Emancipation of Labour," wrote Ulyanov later, "this sidelining of it, was carried out in hushed tones, furtively, and in private, through 'private' letters and conversations and, to put it bluntly, through scheming..."[582] As is often the case, intrigues proved more effective

---

580   Ibid. Vol. 46. pp. 67-68.

581   See: *G. S. Zhuikov, L. I. Komissarova, Y. R. Olkhovsky*. Bor'ba V. I. Lenina protiv "ekonomizma". Moscow, 1980. p. 55.

582   *V. I. Lenin*. Polnoye sobraniye sochineny. Vol. 46. p. 35.

than principles. At the first congress of the Union of Russian Social Democrats Abroad, which took place in Zürich in 1898, Emancipation of Labour suffered a crushing defeat and the leadership of the Union passed to the economists, who took the decision to replace *Rabotnik*, published by Emancipation of Labour, with *Rabocheye Delo*, edited by B. N. Krichevsky, P. F. Teplov (Sibiryak) and V. P. Ivanshin.[583]

---

583   G. S. Zhuikov, L. I. Komissarova, Y. R. Olkhovsky. Bor'ba V. I. Lenina protiv "ekonomizma". p. 103.

A NEW ERA

Later, as the significance of what had occurred finally became clear, it was apparent that 1897 marked the end of one stage in the history of social democracy.

One characteristic of this period had been the absence of any serious and irreconcilable differences among social democrats themselves. "Social democracy was at that point united ideologically and efforts had been made to achieve practical organisational unity as well (the foundation of the Russian Social Democratic Labour Party)." Moreover, victory over the *narodnik* movement had also been achieved.

However, Ulyanov noted the increasing manifestation from 1897-1898 of the "primacy (or at least significant expansion) of the 'economic' tendency", and as a consequence, "identifying and solving internal party issues" had now become a pressing issue.[584]

In opening a new chapter in the struggle, it was important to resist any clamour over showdowns between the 'youth' and the 'old men', and instead understand what was happening in the workers' movement itself: why the success of strikes that pushed minor, piecemeal demands, ones which were often supported by the state factory inspectorate itself, had led to the rejection of political slogans and the laying of fertile ground for the schismatic activities of the 'economists'.

By way of an analysis, Ulyanov penned a lengthy article titled "A Retrograde Trend in Russian Social Democracy".

To talk of the working class 'as a whole', he reflects, is to obscure the meaning of the processes taking place in the proletarian sphere. The sphere itself was clearly divided into three distinct strata of workers, exhibiting varying degrees of familiarity with the principles of social democracy.

The severity of the situation was down not only to the fact that as the movement broadened, the least politically conscious stratum of workers

---

584   *V. I. Lenin*. Polnoye sobraniye sochineny. Vol. 2. p. 438.

were becoming more involved – deep ideological differences were also emerging even among those who identified as social democrats. This ideological and organisational confusion had spread to almost every region of the country.[585]

As Ulyanov noted, a process of natural 'erosion' had begun within the social-democratic milieu. This had not come as a surprise. As he had written to Potresov, "'Erosion' is occurring, and I have no doubt that it will continue."[586] According to Axelrod, a number of "liberals in disguise" had gathered under the banner of Marxism by this stage. Now they were beginning to steer themselves away from social democracy.

There were of course a range of motivations for such splits away from the social democrats. Some, hungry for 'bold struggle', were simply turned off by the drab and wretched nature of economism. At this time the Socialist Revolutionary Party, which sought to combine political struggle with terrorism, was in the initial stages of its formation, and figures such as Boris Savinkov, Yegor Sazonov and Ivan Kalyaev decided to make the switch from the social democrats to the *Esery* [from the initials S.R., Socialist Revolutionary – *trans.*].

'Legal Marxists' such as Struve, Prokopovich, Bulgakov, Berdyaev and others also began to distance themselves more and more from the social democrats. The central figure within that contingent was, of course, Peter Struve.

It should be said that the relationship between Ulyanov and Struve was a somewhat curious one. Their working relationship during Ulyanov's years of exile had brought them closer together, with Struve taking it upon himself to send newly published literature to Shushenskoye. He had also procured the money for and negotiated the publication of a collection of articles, as well as Ulyanov's *The Development of Capitalism in Russia*. He published Ulyanov's pieces in the journals he edited, and his wife Nina had even proofread some of Ulyanov's articles for him. Vladimir Ilyich was grateful to them for undertaking such onerous tasks.

However, he was becoming increasingly irritated by articles written by Struve and, in particular, Tugan-Baranovsky: "God knows what this absurd, pretentious nonsense is! Devoid of any historical examination of

---

585   See: G. S. Zhuikov, L. I. Komissarova, Y. R. Olkhovsky. Bor'ba V. I. Lenina protiv "ekonomizma". pp. 81-101.

586   *V. I. Lenin*. Polnoye sobraniye sochineny. Vol. 46. p. 22.

Marxist doctrine, devoid of any original research ... making pronouncements about a 'new theory', Marx's errors, and restructuring..."

Ulyanov was in no doubt that "a proper conflict" with Struve was essential. In a letter to Potresov on 27th June 1899, he wrote, "It will, of course, be an enormous loss for all *Genossen* [comrades], as he is an extremely talented and knowledgeable person, but of course, 'friendship is friendship and service is service', and this does not negate the need for conflict."[587]

In response to Struve, Tugan-Baranovsky and Bulgakov's statements on political economy, Ulyanov wrote the articles "A Note on the Question of the Market Theory", "Once More on the Theory of Realisation", "Capitalism in Agriculture (on Kautsky's Book and Bulgakov's Article)" and others. As for questions of a more philosophical nature, Ulyanov left it to Plekhanov to offer a response, since, as he wrote to Potresov, "I am very well aware of my philosophical ignorance and do not intend to write on such subjects until I have learned more..."[588]

Krupskaya recalled, "In the evenings, Vladimir Ilyich usually read books on philosophy – Hegel, Kant, the French materialists..."[589] The more Ulyanov delved into philosophical problems, the clearer it became to him that, as he wrote to Potresov, "neo-Kantianism really needs to be reckoned with. I was no longer able to hold my tongue and attached comments and attacks on it in my response to Struve as well..."[590]

While studying neo-Kantian literature was something of a necessary undertaking, life continued to offer its own stimulating diversions. In February 1899, winter in Shushenskoye came to a sudden end. On 7th March, Krupskaya wrote, "Spring is in the air. The river ice continues to break up and the sparrows in the willows are twittering furiously, bulls are bellowing along the street, while the chicken under the landlady's stove clucks so loudly in the mornings that it wakes us up." Friends arrived from Minusinsk for the Shrove-tide festival and for five days they made merry, celebrating the holiday "in fine fashion", as Krupskaya put it.[591]

---

587   Ibid. p. 32.
588   Ibid. pp. 15, 31.
589   Vospominaniya o Vladimire Ilyiche Lenine. Vol. 1. p. 229.
590   *V. I. Lenin*. Polnoye sobraniye sochineny. Vol. 46. p. 30.
591   Ibid. Vol. 55. p. 147.

April marked the return of the dry weather, and on 1st May guests arrived to celebrate May Day.[592] After their departure, Ulyanov, who had continued to work on his article on Struve, wrote to his sister in St Petersburg: "Of course, disputes among our own are unsavoury, and I have tried to soften my tone, but glossing over disagreements is not only unpleasant, it is also *explicitly harmful...*"[593]

In fact, these disagreements had already travelled beyond Russia. In the years 1896-1898, while Ulyanov was in Siberia, Eduard Bernstein had written an article for *Die Neue Zeit*, a German social democrat journal, under the title "The Problems of Socialism". Many sensed that the world was entering a new era, one that would later be known as the age of imperialism. New vistas were opening up for capitalism – by means of capital export, the establishment of colonies and other factors.

Observing the emerging tendency among the liberal bourgeoisie to seek social compromise in their own countries, Bernstein posited the possibility of 'crude' capitalism's replacement with more orderly relationships, without the need for revolutionary upheaval. Therefore, he concluded, it was possible to discount a bloody socialist revolution and instead fight for reform: "progress is everything – the final goal is nothing."

The German left immediately evaluated "The Problems of Socialism" as a general revision of Marxist theory. However, the party central committee refrained from a public debate over the issue for some time. This was only begun in 1898, in Georgi Plekhanov's article titled "Bernstein and Materialism", which appeared in *Novoye Vremya*.

It was not by chance that Plekhanov was spearheading the debate. The disparateness of the Russian experience, where the newest elements of capitalism intermingled with remnants of the hoary Middle Ages; the intensity of the political and socio-economic conflicts that were raging; the elevated intellects of the leading figures in the revolutionary movement, plus a whole host of other factors – it all meant that many of the most significant issues in international social democracy at the turn of the 20th century first found expression in the theoretical discussions taking place in Russia, only later extending into Europe.

Given this, Ulyanov was fully prepared for all of Bernstein's vagaries. Back in 1894, Ulyanov had singled out a passage in Struve's *Critical Notes*

---

592 Vospominaniya o Vladimire Ilyiche Lenine. Vol. 1. pp. 226-227.

593 *V. I. Lenin*. Polnoye sobraniye sochineny. Vol. 55. pp. 160-161.

(Struve was by then already flirting with the 'unorthodox') in which he suggested that the idea of transition from capitalism to socialism via revolution (the "sharp decline") was already dated and that now "an important correction had been made" to the Marxist position: acknowledging the possibility of transition to a new order through reform.

Ulyanov had responded to Struve at the time: "The struggle for reform in no way indicates a 'correction', nor does it revise the doctrine of decline and fall, since this struggle is conducted with a clear and defined goal in mind: to reach this very 'fall'; that this would necessitate 'a whole series of transitions' – from one phase of the struggle to another, from one step to the next – Marx recognised back in the 1840s, noting in the Manifesto that progress towards a new order cannot be *isolated* from the labour movement (and consequently from the struggle for reform)..."[594]

It is worth noting that despite the testimony of his later memoirs, Struve not only greatly appreciated Ulyanov's intellectual capabilities, but also held out certain hopes for him, writing to Potresov in early 1899: "Ilyin [Ulyanov], after his criticism of my book, more departed from orthodoxy than drew nearer to it... However, I think that in terms of *Zusammenbruchstheorie* [the theory of the collapse and failure of capitalism] Ilyin is yet to renounce orthodoxy, though I hope that this will occur sooner or later... Ilyin has a lively and progressive mind and possesses true integrity of thought."[595]

At the same time Bernstein was brooding over "The Problems of Socialism" for *Die Neue Zeit*, Pope Leo XIII was appealing to his congregation with the encyclical *Rerum novarum* [The New Times]. Analysing the same processes as Bernstein, his conclusions offered little in the way of comfort and joy: "As a consequence of transformation and revolution, society has been split into two castes, and the gulf between them is growing ever wider. On the one hand a class has arisen which owns the wealth and therefore wields the power... On the other, the needy and dispossessed masses, embittered by suffering and ever ready for revolt."[596]

That a papal encyclical and the *Communist Manifesto* were finding common ground served as an indication that it was not a matter of adhering to one doctrine or another. Clearly, of significant importance

---

594   Ibid. Vol. 1. pp. 460-461.

595   A. N. Potresov. Posmertny sbornik proizvedeny. Paris, 1937. p. 33.

596   See: Svobodnaya mysl'. 1994. No. 7-8. p. 97.

was the moral aspect: through whose eyes did one view the world – the well-fed burgher's, or those of the 'dispossessed masses' that Leo XIII pointed to?

Adherents to 'economism' in Russia avoided expressing their views openly. However, in such cases, there are always those prone not only to give away the true nature of any opaque position, but also to take it – if not to the absurd – then at least to its logical limits. In this instance, that role was performed by Y. D. Kuskova.

THE ANTI-CREDO

Yekaterina Dmitriyevna Kuskova and her husband Sergey Nikolayevich Prokopovich, a recent graduate of Brussels University, returned to Russia after the victory of the economists at the first congress of the Union of Russian Social Democrats. In St Petersburg, they immediately found themselves at the centre of debates between 'youth' and 'orthodox' factions, Kuskova later recording that "quite a number were still ongoing at the time".

On one occasion, after a rather stormy debate, she was asked to "briefly formulate her views on issues of contention, so that there may be something comprehensive and concise to refer to during disputes". Kuskova threw together "a hasty and informal summary of her views". The document, titled "The Credo of the Young", found its way to Shushenskoye.[597] By 1st August, Ulyanov was requesting further details of the document, his intrigue matched only by his indignation at its content.[598]

There were reasonable grounds for his annoyance. For example, Kuskova had written that the proletariat of Western Europe had made progress in organising its forces and improving its material conditions only because the bourgeoisie had granted it political freedoms and access to parliament without the need for struggle. All of the Marxists' political pronouncements on 'seizures of power' and the 'fall of capitalism' had been mere sloganeering. She also claimed that it was vital to listen to Bernstein when he proposed augmenting the position of the party in society and striving for universal acceptance and support. To achieve this, the "desire to seize power" should once and for all make way for efforts to "reform society along democratic lines".[599]

Consequently, ineffectual attempts at creating an illegal political party should be abandoned in Russia too, and a reassessment undertaken of attitudes towards the bourgeoisie. This "demands from us a different

---

597 N. Lenin (V. Ulyanov). Sobraniye sochineny. Vol. 1. p. 665.
598 See: V. I. Lenin. Polnoye sobraniye sochineny. Vol. 55. pp. 168, 175.
599 Ibid. Vol. 4. p. 167.

Marxism, one that is appropriate and necessary for conditions in Russia". The final conclusion: "There is only one outlet for the Russian Marxist: engagement, i.e. supporting the economic struggle of the proletariat and participating in liberal-oppositional activity."[600]

Of course, Kuskova had compromised the economists: even in *Rabochaya Mysl* they had been more careful when formulating their views. But the deed was done. Ulyanov immediately sat down to compose "A Protest by Russian Social Democrats".

Firstly, he noted that it was incorrect to claim that workers in Europe had gained their freedom without struggle. They had been active participants in every revolution of the 19th century, and it had been this that had gained them political rights. It was also untrue to claim that the social democrats had forced political slogans onto strikers. These were advanced by the labour movement itself. The tsarist government offered economic concessions at exactly the point when the strikes took on a political significance. However, the main falsehood was the idea that the economists were claiming allegiance to social democracy while in fact contradicting the basic principles laid out in the manifesto adopted at the first congress of the RSDLP.[601]

The 'professorial socialism' preached by the authors of the Credo, in calling for support from "liberal opposition elements ... advocating legal reform", merely signified "the urge to conceal the class character of the proletarian struggle, weakening that struggle by a meaningless 'recognition of society', and the reduction of revolutionary Marxism to an unremarkable reform movement... The implementation of such a programme would be tantamount to political suicide for Russian social democracy..."[602]

At Ulyanov's request, those social democrats in exile in the Minusinsk district gathered in the village of Yermakovskoye on 20th August. In addition to Ulyanov and Krupskaya, the Vaneyevs, the Krzhizhanovskys, the Starkovs, the Lepeshinskys, Silvin, and three St Petersburg workers, Oskar Engberg, A. Shapovalov, and N. Panin, were all present. Ulyanov read out his "Protest", which was approved in principle, before a rather heated series of debates lasting almost three days commenced.

600	Ibid. p. 168.
601	Ibid. pp. 175-176.
602	Ibid. pp. 172, 173.

Initially, there were some among those present who believed that there was "no reason to turn an isolated personal opinion into a major event…" There were also those who had "no desire to quarrel with good people, dear comrades, even if they had deviated somewhat to the right".[603] In the end, all 17 ratified the "Protest". A copy was sent to Martov, and it was also approved by social democrats in the small colony at Turukhansk. A second copy, sent to the town of Orlov in Vyatka Province, was supported by Potresov, F. I. Gurvich (Dan), V. V. Vorovsky, N. E. Bauman, K. Y. Zakharova, V. G. and Y. P. Groman and others – 23 individuals in all.[604]

All three documents were sent abroad to Plekhanov. It was at this time that the new leadership of the Union of Russian Social Democrats Abroad were making a concerted effort to squeeze him and the other members of the Emancipation of Labour out of the active movement. It is easy to understand the genuine gratitude felt by Georgi Valentinovich and his colleagues, receiving such unexpected and vociferous support from Russia itself.

Meanwhile, exile was nearing its end for Ulyanov, Martov, Potresov, and the majority of those involved in the League of Struggle case. With events progressing as they were, it seemed a judicious time to rally their forces with a view to calling a new congress. But how, and on what basis?

Over the last few months of his exile, Ulyanov laboured over the issue of a programme, producing "Our Immediate Task", "Our Programme", and "A Draft Programme for Our Party". From the outset, he laid out the social democrats' attitude to theory: "A socialist party cannot be strong without the revolutionary theory which unites all socialists."

And if "one is sure in one's mind that [Marxist theory] holds true", then one is obliged to defend it "from unfounded attacks and attempts to degrade it". Of course, there will be those who seek to make accusations of "want[ing] to turn the socialist party into an order of 'true believers' who hunt down 'heretics' for deviating from the 'dogma', for every independent belief they hold, and so on. We know all those fashionable put-downs. But there is neither a grain of truth nor an iota of sense in them."[605]

Ulyanov warns that one cannot claim fidelity to a theory when it is the very essence of that theory that one attacks. This was precisely what the

---

603   M. A. Silvin. Lenin v period zarozhdeniya partii. p. 189.
604   See: V. I. Lenin. Polnoye sobraniye sochineny. Vol. 46. p. 479.
605   Ibid. Vol. 4. pp. 183, 184.

economists' rejection of the political nature of the proletariat's class struggle amounted to. It is in this regard that Ulyanov posits another fundamental Marxist position, one forgotten by his successors for many decades.

Ulyanov writes that the struggle against and overthrow of autocracy, and the backing of every revolutionary movement against absolutism, are "not only in the interests of the working class, but in the interests of societal development as a whole. Such a precept is vital ... since, from a fundamental Marxist standpoint, the interests of societal development are greater than those of the proletariat – the interests of the entire labour movement as a whole outweigh the interests of individual strata of workers, and are of more importance than individual phases of the movement..."[606]

The social democrat cannot be "hostile to *every* criticism. We do not regard Marxist theory as something complete and inviolable... We believe that *independent* development of Marx's theory is of particular importance to Russian socialists, since this theory only provides general *guiding* principles which will ... apply differently to England than to France, to France differently than to Germany, and to Germany differently than to Russia."[607]

For Ulyanov, the starting point for developing a programme was the draft programme published by Emancipation of Labour in 1895.[608]

The ultimate objectives – the transfer of political power to the proletariat, and the reversion of all means of production to public ownership, with a subsequent socialist reorganisation of all productive and social relations; the articulation of the specific circumstances of Russia, where the working masses experienced a two-fold burden; and the immediate overthrow of absolutism – these all needed to be preserved in the new programme.

Nonetheless, new additions to the programme were also very apparent. First, it was necessary to clarify that the expression 'seizure of power' in no way meant plotting coups. As Ulyanov writes, the social democrats believed that the battle against absolutism "should be led not by conspirators, but by a revolutionary party driven by the labour movement. They believe that the struggle against absolutism should not consist of plots, but be grounded in the education, discipline and organisation of the proletariat, and in political

---

606   Ibid. p. 220.
607   Ibid. p. 184.
608   Ibid. p. 216.

agitation among the workers, which stigmatises every manifestation of absolutism, pillories every knight of the police government, and forces that government into making concessions."[609]

Secondly, there was no need to set down in advance which means of struggle the workers' party and the labour movement might resort to, since that would depend on a multitude of disparate factors. "To argue in advance the means to which this organisation may resort in order to deliver the final blow to absolutism, whether it favours, for example, an uprising, or a large-scale political strike, or other means of attack – speculating on this in advance and resolving the question at the current time would be empty doctrinarianism."[610]

It was thus necessary to remove mention of "means of political struggle" and references to terror. "So as to leave no space for insinuation," Ulyanov clarifies, "let us now record that our personal view is that terror is *currently* an *in*expedient means of struggle, that the party must (*as a party*) reject it ... and concentrate *all its efforts* on strengthening the organisation..."[611]

Ulyanov returns to the question of methods and means of struggle in each article of the programme. "The editors of *Rabochaya Mysl*," he writes, "attribute to workers' socialism only what can be achieved by peaceful means, discounting the revolutionary path... The working class would of course prefer to take power peacefully... But to renounce the revolutionary seizure of power would from the standpoint of the proletariat, as well as from a theoretical and practical political point of view, be reckless... It is very probable, even likely, that the bourgeoisie will not offer concessions to the proletariat peacefully, but will resort at the decisive moment to violence to protect its privileges. In that case, the working class will be left with no other way of achieving its aims other than revolution."[612]

It was also necessary to remove from the Emancipation of Labour programme the thesis which associated "the victory of socialism with the *replacement* of parliamentarism by direct popular legislation..." As Ulyanov emphasises, given the conditions of Russian absolutism and the political immaturity of the bulk of the population, the danger of various forms of 'popular endorsement' degenerating into a demagogic 'imperial plebiscite'

---

609   Ibid. Vol. 2. p. 460; Vol. 4. p. 216.
610   Ibid. Vol. 2. p. 461.
611   Ibid. Vol. 4. p. 223.
612   Ibid. Vol. 4. p. 264.

was too great. It was therefore sufficient to restrict themselves to demanding a "democratic constitution".[613]

Ulyanov fully preserves and *supplements* the general democratic provisions of the programme with demands for: "full parity of men's and women's rights," "progressive income tax," "direct popular election of officials," and the right for any citizen to seek "prosecution of any official before the law". However, the main item was an undertaking to "support *all* those fighting absolutism". Russian social democracy, he writes, must raise "the banner of democracy as a rallying point for all elements and groups able to fight for political freedom, or at the very least support that struggle in some way".[614]

The peasant question was a particularly significant part of the draft programme he composed in exile. Contrary to false accusations that the Marxists welcomed the capitalist 'proletarianisation' of the countryside, Ulyanov writes that capitalist development would bring about the elimination of the remnants of feudalism "naturally, of its own accord". However, this would occur extremely slowly, and "crucially – this 'natural course' means nothing other than the extinction of the peasantry..." The social democrats would not tolerate this: "The workers' party has put *support* for the peasantry on its banner ... *since the peasantry is capable of revolutionary struggle against the remnants of serfdom as a whole and absolutism in particular.*"[615]

Fear of the terrible 'Russian rebellion', so fashionable in the modern era, was no less popular over 100 years ago. In Emancipation of Labour's programme, it was rightly stated that "the most important buttress of absolutism is precisely the political indifference and intellectual backwardness of the peasantry".[616]

However, Ulyanov continues, the presence of revolutionary elements within the peasantry is beyond doubt. "We are not overestimating the strength of these elements in any way, we do not forget the political underdevelopment and benightedness of the peasantry, and neither are we in any way whitewashing the difference between the 'Russian rebellion,

---

613	Ibid. Vol. 4. pp. 223, 224.
614	Ibid. Vol. 4. pp. 222, 224, 225.
615	Ibid. Vol. 4. pp. 227, 234.
616	Ibid. Vol. 4. p. 231.

pointless and pitiless,'[617] and revolutionary struggle… But all that may be taken from all this is that … the workers' party cannot, without violating the fundamental principles of Marxism and without committing a colossal error, *overlook* those revolutionary elements that exist within the peasantry, without offering them support… The question of how forcefully these elements within the peasantry manifest themselves will be resolved by history."[618]

As such, in contrast to previous works, which talked of the nationalisation and transfer of all landed estates to the peasantry, Ulyanov proposed removing concrete "precepts on the form peasant ownership should take" from the programme, instead leaving such questions for the peasantry itself to answer. Perhaps this was the "radical revision of agrarian relations" Emancipation of Labour's programme had referred to.[619]

Overall, the RSDLP's programme took on a more concise and defined structure. Now, it would be put forward for discussion, and then… Here, clarity was lacking on the terms of this discussion and, crucially, how to proceed from there.

Before, when no fundamental disagreements had existed among social democrats, unity had been achieved by establishing arrangements and agreements between all organisations and groups without any squabbling (what would be described in modern terms as a consensus model). But when infighting broke out, and disparate elements began to operate under the flag of social democracy, comprehending the fundamentals of party alignment became vital.

In his 1894 dispute with Struve, Ulyanov had written, "Upon which criteria can we judge the *real* 'thoughts and feelings' of *real* individuals? It is clear that there is only one such criterion: the *actions* of these individuals – and since we are only speaking of those social 'thoughts and feelings', we must also add: the *social actions* of these individuals…"[620] But in order to judge individuals on actions, that is, on their activities, it was clear that a common endeavour had to be proposed.

---

617 A quote from Alexander Sergeyevich Pushkin's *The Captain's Daughter*. (trans.)

618 V. I. Lenin. Polnoye sobraniye sochineny. Vol. 4. pp. 228-229, 231, 233.

619 Ibid. Vol. 1. p. 299; Vol. 4. pp. 222, 235.

620 Ibid. Vol. 1. pp. 423-424.

Ulyanov believed that publishing a Russia-wide illegal newspaper could be just the common endeavour to pull the party out of the swamp of economism, both ideologically and organisationally.

The idea seemingly arose in 1899 in the course of correspondence between Vladimir Ilyich and Potresov. Potresov's friendship with Struve had come to an end, specifically after the latter's split from Alexandra Kalmykova. The stinging attacks on Plekhanov in Struve's articles had on occasion infuriated Potresov, and he demanded a categorical split with the "critics" as a whole and Struve first and foremost.

In a reply dated 27th June 1899, Ulyanov stated, "Should the 'critics' cause an irrevocable split ... this cannot and will not come out" in legal publications such as *Nachalo* or *Zhizn'*. This would require a regularly published illegal newspaper – a party organ.

By the end of the year, Ulyanov had fully fleshed out the idea. He had discussed it in letters to Potresov and Martov, and in conversations with Krupskaya, Krzhizhanovsky and other exiled comrades. Finally, he outlined the idea in his articles "Our Immediate Task" and "An Urgent Question".

It would be on the pages of a "*regularly published party organ closely affiliated with all local groups*" that views on the party programme could be exchanged. Such a debate would help to illuminate "where the differences of opinion are and *how deep they lie*, whether these are of an essential nature, or related to specific issues, and whether they hinder cooperation within the ranks of a single party, or otherwise".[621]

Moreover, a collective publication would provide a rallying point for disparate organisations across Russia's expanses, from Petersburg to Vladivostok, and from Poland to Krasnoyarsk. These groups not only merely existed – they were active: they carried out propaganda work, distributed flyers, and directed strikes to the best of their abilities. But with such localised work, alliances between groups were either unnecessary, or of a purely ideological nature. "Consequently, the question is whether it is worth continuing work in this 'artisanal' way, or whether it should be coordinated by a single party", Ulyanov wrote.[622]

Regular correspondence, facilitating discussion of common concerns, setting up an illegal 'red post', as the Germans called it, to ensure passage

---

621   Ibid. Vol. 4. pp. 191, 215.

622   Ibid. Vol. 4. p. 193.

of material across the border, and organising distribution of the newspaper throughout the country – this would all go towards creating a system of interaction to carry the work of the groups beyond the local level, and coordinate activities as a whole, elevating their work to a Russia-wide significance.

It also opened up ample scope for the kind of 'specialisation' that would help the party avoid unnecessary casualties. Some party members would be involved in distributing the newspaper across Russia, others in distribution within the cities, even more in arranging safe houses, a fourth group in conveying correspondence, a fifth in collecting funds, and so on. Ulyanov wrote, "This kind of specialisation demands, as we know, a great deal more tenacity and the ability to concentrate on modest, unseen spade work, as well as far more genuine heroism, than the usual work that goes on in the circles."[623]

European workers, concluded Ulyanov, have, "a multitude of other means, aside from newspapers, of manifesting their activities, other ways of organising the movement: parliamentary activities, electoral agitation, popular assemblies, and participation in local institutions… *In place of all of this*, quite literally *all* of it until we achieve political freedom, we rely on our revolutionary newspaper, without which any large-scale organisation of the labour movement will be impossible."[624]

Nadezhda Krupskaya recalled, "Lev Tolstoy once wrote that the man travelling the first half of the journey thinks about what he has left behind, the second half about what lies ahead. Such is it in exile. In the beginning one reckons with the past. In the second half more thought goes into what lies ahead. Vladimir Ilyich was thinking ever more intently about what needed to be done to lead the party out of the state it found itself in… He had stopped sleeping and lost a terrible amount of weight. On sleepless nights he mulled over every detail of his plan… The longer it went on, the more impatient Vladimir Ilyich became, and the more devoted he became to his work."[625]

That summer, he began counting the days to the end of his exile. In June Ulyanov wrote to Potresov: "My sentence ends on 29.1.1900. As long as they don't extend my sentence – that is the greatest calamity that befalls those

---

623   Ibid. Vol. 4. p. 195.

624   Ibid. Vol. 4. p. 192.

625   Vospominaniya o Vladimire Ilyiche Lenine. Vol. 1. p. 232.

exiled in Eastern Siberia, and one that does frequently occur. I long for Pskov. Where for you?"[626]

Fears about such an extension were not unfounded. Ulyanov knew that the matter depended on a police report to the governor concerning an unauthorised visit to Minusinsk in autumn 1897. He also cast his mind back to an unscheduled search conducted in May 1899. Krupskaya's pre-emptive request to spend the rest of her exile in Pskov remained unanswered. There was much to be concerned about.

On 30th December, Viktor Kurnatovsky came to visit, and together they saw in the New Year, arranging a festive tree, a marvel in those parts, for the children. On 3rd January Vasily Starkov appeared, and relayed that according to his sources there was no indication that there would be any extension of Ulyanov's sentence. On 12th January, Ulyanov wrote to him in Minusinsk: "I hear reports from the district (in an off-the-record and oblique way) that papers have arrived for my release and Nadya's transfer to 'the Ufa area.'"[627]

"Finally, the issue has been cleared up: we can travel to Russia," Krupskaya wrote to Maria Alexandrovna on 19th January 1900. "There will be no extension of the sentence. We are sending our things on 28th, and travelling ourselves on 29th. Now all that is left to do is have a conversation about the journey. We packed the books into a crate and weighed it – it comes in at around 15 *poods* [approximately 240kg – *trans*.]. We are sending the books and a portion of our things by transport, so by the looks of things we won't have much with us... Our departure is now so close that Mother was about to cook *pelmeni* for the road today. We have been advised that we really should take *pelmeni* with us for the journey, as anything else will freeze."[628]

On 29th January they set off for Minusinsk as scheduled. Krupskaya recalls, "There our brothers-in-exile had already assembled and one sensed that mood that arises when an exile departs for Russia... Thoughts turned to Russia, though the talk was of more trivial matters. ... Finally, done up in our fur boots, coats and so on, we set out off."[629]

They travelled by horse in two covered sleighs. "300 *versts* with the horses following the course of the Yenisei, day and night, the moonlight a blessing," wrote Krupskaya. "We raced on at great speed, and Vladimir

---

626	*V. I. Lenin*. Polnoye sobraniye sochineny. Vol. 46. p. 32.
627	Vladimir Ilyich Lenin. Biograficheskaya khronika. Vol. 1. p. 240.
628	*V. I. Lenin*. Polnoye sobraniye sochineny. Vol. 55. pp. 180, 181.
629	Vospominaniya o Vladimire Ilyiche Lenine. Vol. 1. p. 233.

Ilyich, he travelled without his fur coat, convinced he would be too hot in it; stuffing his hands into the muff he had borrowed from my mother, he spurred himself on with thoughts of reaching Russia..."[630]

They made Achinsk station just in time. At seven in the morning on 2nd February 1900, the Irkutsk – Moscow passenger and mail service set off. They travelled in third class, a taciturn Ulyanov in the upper bunk reading the whole way.

---

[630]   Ibid; *M. A. Silvin*. Lenin v period zarozhdeniya partii. pp. 202, 203.

PART FIVE – THE TURN OF THE 20ᵀᴴ CENTURY

THE TRIPLE ALLIANCE

On 6th February, the train pulled into Ufa.

There, they found a hotel and Krupskaya and Ulyanov went to meet *Narodnaya Volya* affiliate Maria Chetvergova, whose circle he had been part of back in Kazan. Now, in Ufa, she was running a bookshop and serving out her permanent exile. They had not seen each other for 12 years, but memories of their long conversations on Chernyshevsky and about life persisted. Now, on meeting again, "there was a certain peculiar softness in his voice and expression when he spoke with her," Krupskaya recalled.

But there was none of the previous intimacy and understanding. Recalling their meeting, Krupskaya was reminded of a passage from Lenin's *What Is To Be Done?*, in which he acknowledged that many social democrat leaders "had begun their revolutionary thinking as followers of *Narodnaya Volya*... The abandonment of this fascination with that heroic tradition ... was accompanied by the breaking off of relations with those people who would not yield in their loyalty to *Narodnaya Volya*, people whom young social democrats had deeply admired." This passage, concludes Krupskaya, "is a piece of Vladimir Ilyich's own biography".[631]

Ulyanov was not permitted to remain in Ufa, so leaving his wife and mother-in-law behind, he left for Moscow after a few days.

"At that time, we were living on the outskirts of Moscow, on Bakhmetyevskaya Street in the Kamer-Kollezhsky Val," wrote Anna Ulyanova-Yelizarova. "Seeing the driver pull up, we all ran to the stairs to greet Vladimir Ilyich. My mother's anguished voice was the first to cry out:

'How could you write that you are well again! Look how thin you are!'

---

631   Vospominaniya o Vladimire Ilyiche Lenine. Vol. 1. p. 234.

'I did get well. Only in the lead-up to my departure did I succumb once more.'"[632]

The preceding few months had utterly drained Maria Alexandrovna. Her youngest son Dmitry – a fifth-year university student – had been sent to Tula after nine months of solitary confinement, and she had only just managed to secure him a transfer to Podolsk. Meanwhile, her youngest daughter Maria was arrested and her passport seized upon returning from Brussels for the holidays – she had been sent to Nizhny Novgorod. As a consequence, their mother was regularly having to travel between Nizhny Novgorod, Tula, and Podolsk.

Everyone had gathered in Moscow for Vladimir's return and, as Anna Ulyanova-Yelizarova observed, Maria Alexandrovna wanted a little time "to have Vladimir Ilyich all to herself". But after the initial embraces and the usual enquiries after health and family business, Vladimir began rattling off a series of completely different questions: "Has Yuliy [Martov] come? Have there been any letters? Telegrams?" Learning there had been no word from Martov, he grew agitated: "What could that mean?" He immediately sat down to compose a telegram, and sent his brother to the post office with it.

Only after this had been done did they take a seat at the table for the questions and stories about exile to begin again. He then began to hum the new tunes that he had brought from Siberia. Anna Ulyanova-Yelizarova relates how he "sang us a song that Tsederbaum [Martov] had come up with in exile:

Far away in Russia, some folk may cut a dash,
Heroically splendid, with uniforms to match,
But carted off to distant lands for many a long year,
Such gilding quickly rubs away and counts for nothing here,
And any gallant flourishes are cleanly cancelled out
By alcohol, so rich infused with rough makhorka snout.

With my sister following his lead on the piano, Ilyich also sang some Polish revolutionary songs he had learned from exiled Polish workers, partly in Polish, partly in Russian translations done for him by Krzhizhanovsky...

---

632   Ibid. p. 59.

I vividly recall Ilyich pacing from one corner of our small dining room to the other, singing with gusto..."[633]

Meanwhile, Moscow was in a festive mood. "The height of Shrove-tide," wrote *Novosti Dnya* [News of the Day] - "At last, the buoyant, carefree, boundless Moscow Shrove-tide is upon us! It is a blessing. No, no German could conceive such a holiday. Compare our Shrove-tide with its western European equivalent. There Shrove-tide is a mere allegory. They hold processions, with crowds of satyrs and Pierrots scurrying around. Here, there is no mocking, no denouncing of anyone. Here it is only doctors' advice that is scorned..."[634]

On 17th February Ulyanov went to see Herman Krasin, who had introduced him to the Moscow Marxist circle more than six years before. However, as during his meeting with Chetvergova, conversation did not come easily. Krasin had moved away from the movement, and his interests had shifted onto a different plane, becoming more renowned as an up-and-coming engineer than for his illegal activities.[635]

The following day, Isaak Lalayants, his old friend from his days in Samara, arrived from Yekaterinoslav. It was a Friday, and as the *Russky Listok* wrote:

What goes on on Friday -
The pen cannot expound:
When theatre seats are gold dust,
And drunkenness abounds...

But tickets were nonetheless acquired, and on the evening of 18th they set off to the Hermitage Garden on Karetny Ryad for a performance of Gerhart Hauptmann's *Drayman Henschel* by the Moscow Art Theatre. A year later, Ulyanov was still writing to his mother: "What fine performers they are at the Art Theatre – I have fine memories of my visit there last year..."[636]

---

633   Ibid. pp. 59, 60.
634   *S. Dreiden.* V zritel'nom zale – Vladimir Ilyich. Moscow, 1986. Book 1. p. 31.
635   See: *M. A. Silvin.* Lenin v period zarozhdeniya partii. p. 130.
636   *V. I. Lenin.* Polnoye sobraniye sochineny. Vol. 55. p. 204; *S. Dreiden.* V zritel'nom zale – Vladimir Ilyich. Moscow, 1986. Book 1. p. 31.

However, Ulyanov's family were plainly aware that he was more preoccupied with affairs of a very different kind, and that Lalayants was there not simply as an old friend, but also as a member of the Yekaterinoslav Committee and editor of a popular underground newspaper, the *Yuzhny Rabochy* [Southern Worker]. He left two days later, and Ulyanov departed for Nizhny Novgorod, and from there to St Petersburg. There, in Alexandra Kalmykova's apartment, he met with Vera Ivanovna Zasulich.

Ulyanov also spoke with Struve. Only afterwards, on 26th February, did Ulyanov arrive in Pskov, where he should have gone to be monitored by police immediately upon returning from exile.[637]

At that time Pskov was perhaps one of the smallest and most unsophisticated of Russia's provincial cities, but its proximity to St Petersburg made it an attractive destination for those under surveillance, so Ulyanov immediately came across acquaintances there.

Most importantly, it was Potresov's destination after his return from exile, and now the two finally had the opportunity to discuss everything they had been unable to in their correspondence.

Initially, Lenin stayed with Obolensky – a childhood friend of Potresov. Many years later, Obolensky wrote that Ulyanov "had a very unprepossessing appearance. He was short, as bald as a kneecap, despite his young age, with a grey face, rather prominent cheekbones, a yellowish beard and cunning little eyes, and in appearance reminded me more of a grain store clerk than an intellectual."

An alternative portrait from the time was also provided: on 2nd April, Ulyanov travelled in secret from Izborsk to Riga to meet Silvin and some Latvian social democrats. Silvin writes, "It was around midday when Ulyanov appeared in the doorway to our room, wearing a soft felt hat and gloves and carrying a cane, every bit the gentleman... We then set off to see the Latvians... There I was once again struck by his ability to captivate and make an impression on others..." This is followed by an entire page describing his "immense charisma," and so forth.[638]

In addition to Obolensky, the Pskov circle of social democrats included A. M. Stopani, N. M. Kislyakov, P. A. Blinov, N. F. Lopatin, V. V. Bartenev, and the student N. N. Lokhov, a vehement 'economist' sent back from

---

637   See: Byloye. 1926. No. 1. p. 67; Perepiska G. V. Plekhanova i P. B. Axelroda. Vol. 2. pp. 102-105.

638   See: *M. A. Silvin*. Lenin v period zarozhdeniya partii. p. 130.

St Petersburg to his parents. The moment Ulyanov joined the group, continues Obolensky, "he immediately became the central figure, thanks to his erudition in economic matters and, in particular, their Marxist interpretation".

Obolensky goes on, "These closed meetings, open to only around ten trusted individuals, took place in my apartment. Usually we were silent as [Ulyanov] argued with Lokhov. Both were brilliant polemicists and extremely well versed in Marxist literature. However, there was no doubt [Ulyanov] had the upper hand over his young opponent. Lokhov's position was especially difficult, since he was having to defend a point of view held by no-one else at the meeting. I, too, was entirely on the side of Ulyanov..."[639]

However Ulyanov himself had little interest in such gatherings. The time for making presentations and holding discussions within the circles had long past, and now there were more important things to focus on. He moved from Obolensky's apartment to that of a local pharmacist, K. V. Luryi, from whom he rented a 15m^2 room, and preferred visiting the library and taking walks to evenings at the Obolenskys or the Bartenevs. As he wrote to his mother, there were "no shortage of beautiful spots" in Pskov and its surrounds.[640] By way of confirmation, he sent her a postcard with a view of the city's famous Trinity Cathedral. When at the suggestion of local statisticians Ulyanov began assisting in the development of a survey on peasant farming, he began regular visits to Izborsk.

There, much was a novelty: the ancient churches in the Novgorod style, with their green, helm-shaped domes, and bell gables instead of towers, the menfolk with their shaved napes and trimmed whiskers, the women in old-fashioned dress, and the Pskov dialect, which, especially in western regions, swapped "ch" sounds for "ts", and as in days of yore, called local landowners "boyars" rather than lords [*barin*].[641]

However, time was of the essence. Ulyanov visited St Petersburg with Potresov in secret. A number of urgent issued needed to be addressed, but with only Ulyanov and Potresov, there was still not enough to make up a 'quorum'. Finally, after having been in Omsk and Samara, Martov arrived in Pskov from St Petersburg at the end of March.

---

639 *V. A. Obolensky*. Moya zhizn'. Moi sovremenniki. pp. 177, 178, 179.

640 *V. I. Lenin*. Polnoye sobraniye sochineny. Vol. 55. pp. 182, 183.

641 See: *V. A. Obolensky*. Moya zhizn'. Moi sovremenniki. p. 171.

If meetings can truly be *long-awaited*, then this was precisely what the encounter between Ulyanov, Potresov and Martov was. Telling his mother about Martov's arrival in Pskov, Ulyanov wrote, "...I was spurred into action at the long-awaited traveller's arrival."[642]

Life in Shushenskoye had been insulated from the intellectual squabbling among exiles, but also limited completely his sphere of communication. Ulyanov had tried to compensate for that by corresponding by letter with dozens of others, but he had only grown close to two of them – in spirit, in their common understanding of the tasks they faced, and in their perception of life in general. These were Alexander Potresov and Yuliy Martov.

Prior to their arrest, none of them had felt any particularly close affinity to each other. It is possible that something of the sort developed between Ulyanov and Martov after their release from prison and their long night-time conversation. In exile, their correspondence grew more intensive, and their voluminous letters read more like an extensive, unhurried conversation in which even the slightest interruption seems like a break in continuity.

"A mass of questions worth discussing have piled up," wrote Ulyanov to Potresov on 27th April 1899, "and one cannot talk about subjects of a chiefly literary character here. One feels too detached from the writing when one cannot converse with colleagues. Here, only Yuliy alone feels so passionately about it all, but with him the damnable 'great distances' prevent us from talking in any depth."[643]

Naturally, all three were very different characters, but in some ways they complemented each other. Certainly, Ulyanov was impressed by Potresov's intellectualism and vast knowledge, and by Martov's journalistic talent and vitality. Meanwhile, both were attracted to Ulyanov's scrupulousness and his understanding of real life, a trait perhaps nowadays described as earthiness. Their shared efforts on Ulyanov's Anti-Credo was what finally brought them together. This commonality of attitude was on the whole what made it possible for them to come to an agreement, while in exile, on the foundation of a 'literary group'.

As Martov recalled, "At the end of the final year of exile, I received a letter from V. I. Ulyanov in which he quietly suggested 'forming a triple alliance', which would also include A. N. Potresov, to battle revisionism and 'economism'. This union was to join forces with Emancipation of Labour

---

642   V. I. Lenin. Polnoye sobraniye sochineny. Vol. 55. p. 182.
643   Ibid. Vol. 46. p. 22.

in the first instance. Between the lines of the letter, I discerned allusions to a journalistic undertaking. I naturally responded with my full agreement and put my energies at my comrades' disposal, promising not to delay a single day in going to where I would be needed upon completion of my period of exile."[644]

And now, finally, they were meeting in person.

Reactions to initial meetings and encounters could prove rather unexpected: Boris Nikolaevsky wrote, "Alexander Potresov and Ulyanov were in fact a little stunned by the reception they received in the most varied of circles. They had returned from exile with the expectation that they would be met, if not with hostility, then at least with a great deal of wariness. It had seemed to them from a distance that the young activists had been behind the 'critics' they viewed as direct opponents, and had been prepared to fight against this new scourge as a minority. But it suddenly became apparent that not only the young activists, but also the theoretically-minded 'critics' themselves, treated them as the recognised leaders of the movement..."[645]

No less unexpected was the conduct of Struve and Tugan-Baranovsky, the main 'assumed opponents'. "It was not without surprise that I learned from my comrades," Martov wrote, "that much like the *Rabocheye Delo* set, our 'legal Marxists' had greeted them very cordially, clearly demonstrating that they are prepared to view our group as the natural leaders of social-democratic party and are inclined to support our initiatives..."[646]

Ulyanov relayed to Potresov and Martov the details of his meeting with Lalayants in Moscow. The Yekaterinoslav Committee, having begun issuing the *Yuzhny Rabochy* in January, had made contact with the Jewish social-democratic party Bund and took the initiative in calling for a second congress of the RSDLP to be held in Smolensk in late April. Ulyanov was officially invited to the congress and offered the editorship of the newspaper – the party's central organ.

Ulyanov replied that he was "not alone, but part of a small group of three ... with Martov and Potresov" – they would take part in the congress only as a "special, independent group that would not commit itself in advance to the congress's resolutions". As regards the newspaper, "they

---

644   Y. *Martov*. Zapiski sotsial-demokrata. p. 411.
645   A. N. *Potresov*. Posmertny sbornik proizvedeny. p. 36.
646   Leninsky sbornik, IV. Moscow, Leningrad. p. 55.

were more than willing to take the task on, but again only on the condition that they would lead it in the spirit and direction they believed it should be taken, making their views clear on the matter in advance of the congress."

Eventually, Ulyanov opened up about the reasons for his doubts and reservations, telling Lalayants that in his opinion "proper restoration of the party had to be preceded by lengthy preparatory work to establish and develop the basic principles of organisation, programme and tactics upon which the party should be built, and only then, after such work was complete, should a congress be called".[647]

There was no cause to doubt the sincerity of Lalayants' offer. However, another meeting – with Pyotr Maslov, a representative of the émigré *Rabocheye Delo* who had arrived in Pskov in March and someone with whom Ulyanov had shared correspondence since the 1880s – raised a significant number of questions.

It emerged that the editorial group of *Rabocheye Delo* had split into two factions. One, led by Teplov, regarded cooperation with Plekhanov feasible, but knowing his temperament, objected to "his exclusive direction of the [central] organ". The other group – Kuskova, Prokopovich and Ivanshin – considered it impossible to work with Plekhanov, as he was "inclined to be unyielding to all the young people".

In politics there is no position more wrong-headed and degrading than acting as a plaything or bargaining chip in another's game, and Martov immediately suspected something Machiavellian and underhand in the behaviour of the *Rabocheye Delo* set and the 'Struvists' – an attempt to isolate and oust Plekhanov. However, Ulyanov and Potresov reassured him, claiming that the behaviour of the "friendly enemies" was not so much indicative of a desire to set them at odds with Emancipation of Labour, as it was a wish to "build bridges towards reconciliation with it".[648]

Any plots to drive a wedge between the 'literary group' and Plekhanov would have been senseless, since agreement with Zasulich over the substantive issues had already been reached. Ulyanov described his February conversation with her in St Petersburg: she had made it clear that having lost the strong ties with Russian organisations, Emancipation of Labour found itself in a difficult situation. However, they did not lose heart. In

---

647   Proletarskaya revolyutsiya. 1929. No. 1. p. 69; *V. I. Lenin*. Polnoye sobraniye sochineny. Vol. 6. p. 159.
648   Ibid. p. 53.

February Plekhanov published a pamphlet titled "*Vademecum* [Guide] for the Editors of *Rabocheye Delo*", which featured Ulyanov's Anti-Credo, while Axelrod released "An Open Letter to the Editors of *Rabocheye Delo*"; both proved very popular in Russia.

Ulyanov in turn told her about the attempts by those in Yekaterinoslav and Bund to organise a congress, about the plans of his 'literary group', and of the fact that with the situation as it was, they would be maintaining their independence and not merging with Emancipation of Labour. He concluded not only by strongly affirming their support for Plekhanov, but stating that as a matter of principle they considered it impossible "to conduct business without such forces as Plekhanov and Emancipation of Labour...", and with that laid out their position.[649]

But all this manoeuvring in the upper echelons of the party would have been less significant had Ulyanov, Potresov and Martov not been of one mind when it came to the main issue – in assessing what was going on in the lower rungs of the social-democratic sphere.

The meetings in St Petersburg, Moscow, Ufa, Samara and Omsk had demonstrated that the apparent dominance of the 'economists' was not so much a consequence of their strength as it was a direct result of the weakness of the organisations. In other words, self-restraint over issues surrounding the ongoing economic struggle was perceived by many social democrats not as an 'ideological position', but as a statement of their inability to focus in a practical sense on the issues that needed to be addressed in the struggle against autocracy. Therefore, it was necessary not to shy from such weaknesses, but to provide assistance and win support.[650]

"Having discussed the matter comprehensively," said Martov, "we decided to accept the invitation to the congress ... and immediately begin correspondence with the Emancipation of Labour group. At the congress we had to make a thorough 'confession of faith' which clearly expressed the revolutionary tasks of the party as we understand them to be, and accept our collective candidacy for the editorship of the party organ only on the basis of the congress's approval of this programme."[651]

A dispute arose over the issue of cooperating with Struve and his friends. Martov, who had a general dislike for Struve, believed that the

---

649   V. I. Lenin. Polnoye sobraniye sochineny. Vol. 46. pp. 42, 43.
650   See: Leninsky sbornik, IV. pp. 50-53, 55, 57.
651   Ibid. p. 53.

legal Marxists' conversion to liberalism was a certainty and working with them would be worthless and damaging, since even in collaboration with the social democrats they would attempt to further their own ends first and foremost.

However, Alexander Potresov believed that under certain circumstances an alliance with Struve was vital and that it was necessary to remain flexible and tolerant towards him.[652]

Ulyanov maintained a different position. He did not regard it necessary to remain diplomatic, demonstrate any loyalty, or enter into an alliance. In January 1899 he had written to Potresov: "It is my belief that 'utilising' is a far more accurate and appropriate word…",[653] that is confining the relationship to a purely practical one which benefited both sides.

In the end, all three agreed that "conversations with Struve and his colleagues, who were soon to arrive in Pskov, should be conducted on the basis of our clearly articulated Credo, in which our position must be unequivocally emphasised… I predicted that in this instance the agreement would be broken at the very outset. 'Let's see,' my comrades told me."[654]

---

652 See: Leninsky sbornik, IV. pp. 56-58; R. Pipes. Struve: liberal on the left, 1870-1905.

653 V. I. Lenin. Polnoye sobraniye sochineny. Vol. 46. p. 20.

654 Leninsky sbornik, IV. p. 57.

TWO PASSPORTS

Ulyanov immediately set to work penning a statement of the principles of the 'literary group', and with everything already having been agreed, the document was quickly ready. Nowadays the piece is normally titled "Draft statement of the editorial board of *Iskra* and *Zarya*". However, perhaps more accurate is the title given in Vol. IV of Lenin's Collected Works: "Draft statement 'From the Editors'", since in 1900 *Iskra* and *Zarya* were not openly discussed. Here it was a reference to the editorial board of *Rabochaya Gazeta* – the party's central organ – membership of which was to be ratified at the Smolensk congress, as well as to the journal published abroad.

The "From the Editors" draft statement was an attempt at formulating the position of both publications. "Our movement," wrote Ulyanov, was at a "critical stage". On the one hand, despite the widespread arrests, it was rapidly "penetrating ever more deeply into the working class" and "sprouting vigorously all around Russia". On the other, the movement was fragmented, crude in nature, and local groups were isolated from one another; in the interests of the movement, it required a transition to a higher form of organisation – the foundation of a party.[655]

While not denying the significance of the first congress of the RSDLP, and remaining supportive the ideas of its Manifesto, Ulyanov wrote that they nonetheless believed that restoring the former central leadership was not the issue, and that "unity cannot simply be decreed ... it must be developed." For this to happen, it was important to grapple with the various divergent intellectual currents. It was with this in mind that a Russia-wide newspaper and journal were proposed.[656]

In his memoirs, published many years later, Obolensky writes that Ulyanov was deeply intolerant of those who did not agree with the 'orthodox' position: "He was utterly unpleasant in arguments – haughty

---

655   V. I. Lenin. Polnoye sobraniye sochineny. Vol. 4. pp. 322, 323.
656   Ibid. pp. 325, 327, 329, 330.

and contemptuous, peppering his flowing speech with caustic and often vulgar flourishes..."[657]

However, in "From the Editors," there is no trace of this intolerance. Quite the contrary: alongside an explicit demonstration of his 'orthodox' position, the statement also reflected the impressions Ulyanov had garnered from the meetings in St Petersburg, Moscow, Ufa and Nizhny Novgorod, as well as from speaking to Potresov, Martov, Obolensky and his colleagues in Pskov. This is manifested most of all in Ulyanov's resolute refusal to break with the wavering and genuinely misguided social democrats, leaving open for them "the possibility of working together".

With the draft approved, Ulyanov, Potresov and Martov waited for their 'guests' to arrive. The next day, Stepan Radchenko arrived from St Petersburg and announced that Struve and Tugan-Baranovsky were coming on the next train. Yuliy Martov offers a vivid account of the meeting:

Ulyanov read out the draft. Martov writes, "As he read it, I observed the faces of our guests... There was something between dismay and bewilderment etched on the face of Mikhail Tugan-Baranovsky, and at times it was clear he was holding himself back so as not to interrupt the reading. On the other hand, Struve maintained an Olympian calm, through which one was at times able to discern a slightly scornful flash in his eyes...

'What are your thoughts on all this, gentlemen?' Ulyanov asked.

Struve said something vague and general. He spoke somewhat reluctantly, dragging the words out... For the unsophisticated Mikhail Tugan-Baranovsky, diplomacy clearly did not come naturally. He launched into an impassioned speech to the effect that he could see that the entire section of the declaration dedicated to the state of social democracy and Marxism was directed against him and Struve personally, and that this was extremely unfair... Even their characterisation as critics of Marxism was made in such a way that Tugan was forced to ask himself: could he and Struve support our endeavour if this passage remained in the declaration? Struve, still silent, allowed the expression on his face to endorse Tugan as he sallied forth."

However, no major row erupted. Ulyanov and Potresov, citing the facts, replied that it was the legal Marxists, in being "ideologically supportive of the rebellion against 'orthodoxy' and thereby seducing the youngsters of the social-democratic youth", that were undoubtedly contributing to the

---

657   V. A. Obolensky. Moya zhizn'. Moi sovremenniki. p. 179.

disarray and the intensification of the intra-party struggle. They spoke firmly, but tactfully. "Generally, the conversation was conducted in a very mild tone and when Ulyanov indicated his willingness to slightly soften the passage which dealt with the roles played by the 'critics of Marxism', to my surprise they came to a clear agreement...

And when we asked: what is your ultimate attitude towards our endeavour, I was surprised to hear Struve's firm statement: we consider it vital and we will offer reasonable support, after which I asked him for a monthly contribution of five roubles, as I recall. Tugan-Baranovsky, who was evidently not averse to an argument or the odd haggle, said with a rather sulking expression that he would also contribute ten roubles monthly."[658]

After their guests departed, agreement was reached on immediate practical steps. Potresov was to go to Switzerland as soon as he received a foreign passport, meet there with Plekhanov and Axelrod, and "attend to the publication of a theoretical journal which was certainly for issue abroad. As far as the political newspaper was concerned," Martov writes, "we for the time being had to be responsive to the wishes of the activists and attempt publication in Russia... Ulyanov was to stay in Pskov until the congress, and then represent our group there, either by himself or with me..."[659]

However, other events soon put paid to these plans. As they had feared, nothing came from the convocation of the Smolensk congress: in the middle of April, police carried out arrests in St Petersburg, Moscow, Kiev, Kharkov, and other cities, while on the night of 17th April the main organisers – members of the Yekaterinoslav Committee headed by Lalayants – were also rounded up. As a result, none of the major local RSDLP committee membership were in attendance at the congress. "Having waited in vain for several days, we decided to disperse, considering any further work on organising the congress hopeless."[660]

Shortly before, on 10th April, Ulyanov had turned 30. It was not the first birthday he had spent apart from his relatives, in a strange city, surrounded by many acquaintances but few friends. Martov had left at the very start of April. His friendship with Potresov was still at an early stage. None of the multitude of memoirs left by those in Pskov make any mention of a celebration to mark the occasion.

---

658   Leninsky sbornik, IV. pp. 58-60.
659   Ibid. p. 60.
660   O Lenine. Book 3. p. 26.

30 years old is no age at all, yet among his achievements he could already list university, a legal career, solitary confinement and Siberian exile, the first revolutionary circles, and the creation of a major – for the time – social democrat organisation, as well as authorship of pamphlets, a respectable collection of articles, and a major scientific monograph published in the capital: no small feat for a man of 30.

He gave little thought to this himself. As he said to Plekhanov: "It is better to pay more attention to what is to come, than what has been."[661]

When Krupskaya came to him a year later, they developed a custom of spending his birthday in the forest, going to nature. Krupskaya recalled, "We formed a regular routine that on his birthdays he and I would go on long walks somewhere deep into the forest, and he would tell me about what he was busy with at the time. The spring air, the blossoming forest, the swollen buds – it all created a special air, moving thoughts forward to the future."[662]

The beginnings of this 'tradition' can perhaps be traced to his time in Pskov. On 18th May, Ulyanov wrote to his mother: "I walk a lot, given the magnificent weather; after two-three days of rain, everything has turned green, the dust has not yet lifted, and the air is wonderful – and this draws us *ins Grüne* [into the bosom of nature]."[663]

With the failure of the Smolensk congress, it had finally become clear how next to proceed. This could only mean fulfilling their original plan – the publication abroad of a Russia-wide newspaper. It would seem that this was when they settled on a name: *Iskra* [Spark]. Their "Statement from the editors of *Iskra*" included the line: "uniting under its banner all democratic elements in the country" for victory "over the hated regime".[664]

Potresov left for Switzerland at the end of April as agreed. On 5th May, Ulyanov finally received a foreign passport. On 19th May Martov arrived from Poltava, and that evening they set off for St Petersburg.

Ulyanov only had permission to visit his mother in Podolsk, so the trip to St Petersburg was clearly an illegal one. If he had been aware that the police were close on his heels, it is unlikely he would have risked

---

661   *V. I. Lenin*. Polnoye sobraniye sochineny. Vol. 4. p. 350.
662   *N. K. Krupskaya*. O Lenine. pp. 66-67.
663   *V. I. Lenin*. Polnoye sobraniye sochineny. Vol. 55. p. 188.
664   Ibid. Vol. 4. p. 359.

such a journey, though it seems neither Martov nor Ulyanov noticed the surveillance.

Meanwhile, those tailing them were reporting: "Ulyanov and Martov set off in great secrecy for St Petersburg on train No.18 at 7.26 in the morning of 20th May, exiting at Alexandrovskaya station and then weaving about the parkways of Tsarskoye Selo, trying to avoid detection, until 9.00am; having arrived in St Petersburg by the Tsarskoye Selo road, here they left a small hand basket they had in their possession in a building where the statistical committee of the national census is located (Kozachy Lane) and departed separately..."[665]

On the morning of 21st, Ulyanov was arrested leaving Alexander Malchenko's apartment, where he had spent the night. As he recounted later, he was immediately seized "by the arms, one taking the left and another taking the right, grabbed so you are unable to move... (H)ad I needed to swallow anything, I would have been unable to. I was taken to the municipality buildings, searched and questioned: 'What is the purpose of your coming here? Aren't you aware that you are not permitted to enter the capital?' Colonel Piramidov, head of the St Petersburg secret police, sneered: 'You chose your route, there's nothing left for you to say! Through Tsarskoye Selo! Didn't you know that we were tracking you there behind every bush?'"[666]

So it goes: plans years in the making, every detail finely honed, and then some minor incident occurs to ruin everything. Anna Ulyanova-Yelizarova recalled, "It meant he would not be able to go abroad! But naturally Vladimir Ilyich was more worried about the chemical letter to Plekhanov, written on a sheet of notepaper with some kind of bill on it... This could have given him away... He was most worried by the fact that the chemical ink can sometimes appear by itself over time."[667]

Ulyanov was placed in a miserable solitary confinement cell. He wrote: "Night or day there is no peace from the insects, and the filth is insufferable, while the nights are noisy and filled with angry shouting; every night the policemen, snoops and the rest sit round and play cards just outside the cell."[668]

---

665   Krasnaya letopis'. 1924. No. 1. pp. 21, 22-23.
666   Vospominaniya o Vladimire Ilyiche Lenine. Vol. 1. p. 121.
667   Ibid. pp. 62, 63.
668   Ibid. p. 121.

In the end, the situation was resolved without much trouble. No attention was paid to the 'chemical' letter, though gendarmes were suspicious of the 1,300 roubles they discovered in the lining of his waistcoat. During interrogation on 23rd May, Ulyanov explained: "I always carry large sums in this way [sewn up], something that can be verified easily by examining my other waistcoats." The money itself was a fee received for a translation done for the publisher Popova, and "savings leftovers". The gendarmes checked and a fee of 963 roubles 75 kopecks was confirmed.[669]

Of course this was not the fee that Anna Ulyanova-Yelizarova had collected back in October 1899. It appears that the money sewn up in his waistcoat was the 1,000 roubles Ulyanov had been given by Nikolai Lopatin for publishing the newspaper on the day he left Pskov.[670] But such 'small details' were unknown to the gendarmes.

In his situation, it would seem prudent to keep quiet and not make a fuss, but this was not in his nature. He proceeded to protest the "conditions of detention" in prison, after which his cell was treated with insecticide, an experience that stuck in his memory for some time…

20 years later, as delegates at the III International were complaining of the fact that they were being eaten by bedbugs in the 4th House of Soviets, he dictated to the secretary of the Council of People's Commissars: "Vladimir Ilyich points out that even under tsarism, it was possible to extirpate bedbugs using a device which resembled a samovar, and this in an institution not designed to host guests, but a prison, something he could testify to himself. And if we in Soviet Russia are unable to extirpate bedbugs, this should elicit neither a grin nor a wry lampoon, but a sense of embarrassment."[671]

On 31st May, Ulyanov was released for "lack of evidence" and, accompanied by an "escorting warden", taken to Podolsk, where he had been ordered in accordance with Department of Police directives. On 1st June, the warden delivered him directly to the police captain of Podolsk district as instructed.

Dmitry Ulyanov writes, "The police chief, a certain Perfiliev, an old bureaucrat who enjoyed throwing thunder and lightning around

---

669   See: Krasnaya letopis'. 1924. No. 1. pp. 22-23.
670   See: Vladimir Ilyich Lenin. Biograficheskaya khronika. Vol. 1. p. 253.
671   Russian State Archive of Socio-Political History. Col. 1. Inventory 1. Dep. Item. 511. P. 1.

on occasion, but was by nature a coward, demanded Vladimir Ilyich's documents. He presented his foreign passport. Having leafed through it, he placed it on his desk and said: 'Now you can go, the passport will stay with me.' This was the worst possible thing that could happen to Ulyanov: his foreign passport had been taken from him, and who had taken it? Some district police chief! 'I need that document,' Ulyanov said, 'return it to me.' The captain responded imperiously: 'You heard me: the document stays with me, and you may go.'"[672]

He had good reason to be furious, but Ulyanov maintained his composure and stated firmly: "According to the articles of the law (followed by numerous citations of these) you have no right to confiscate my passport! If you do not return it to me immediately, I will make a complaint, I will not leave it like this!" This said, he turned abruptly and exited. However, he had not gone ten steps before the policeman caught up with him and handed him the priceless passport.[673] His legal training and self-restraint had helped him on this occasion.

Anna Ulyanova-Yelizarova recalled: "He stayed with us for a week, joining us on our walks and on a boat in Podolsk's picturesque surrounds, and enjoying croquet in the yard." His comrades arrived: "Vladimir Ilyich agreed a cypher with everyone and urged the need for the right material for the planned Russia-wide newspaper..."[674]

On 7th June, accompanied by his mother and eldest sister, Ulyanov travelled to Ufa to see his wife. They went by train to Nizhny Novgorod, where they boarded the steamer *Ost*. Anna writes, "It was June, and the river was in spate, and travelling by steamer along the Volga, then the Kama, and finally the Belaya River, was a singular delight. We spent all those days on deck. Vladimir was in the most positive spirits, taking deep, joyous breaths of the wonderful air of the river and surrounding forests. I remember our long night-time conversations on the deserted upper deck of the small steamer as it moved along the Kama and Belaya. My mother would go down to her cabin when she was tired. The few passengers would vanish even earlier. The deck was left for the two of us..."[675]

672	Vospominaniya o Vladimire Ilyiche Lenine. Vol. 1. p. 122.
673	See: Ob Ilyiche. Book 3. Moscow; Leningrad, 1924. p. 46.
674	Vospominaniya o Vladimire Ilyiche Lenine. Vol. 1. p. 63.
675	Ibid. p. 64.

As if making up for the bug-ridden police cells and constant nervous tension of the preceding months, fate was, as it were, now smiling on them. He knew that he would be abroad for a while, and they did not know when they would see each other again. But the even hum from the engine room and gentle splashing of the paddles on the water brought him peace and quiet, and memories of the journey stayed with him for many years.

"How fine a summer on the Volga would be! How splendid was that spring of 1900 with you and Anna!" he wrote to his mother in Samara from London in 1902. Or this to his mother in Mikhnevo, near Moscow, in 1910: "I send my warmest wishes from Naples. I arrived by ferry from Marseilles: pleasant and inexpensive it was. Like travelling along the Volga."

Those intimate conversations between him and his sister on the upper deck also included talk of a purely practical nature. "I pointed out to him," writes Anna Ulyanova-Yelizarova, "as Shesternin and other activist workers had, that we couldn't break ties with *Rabocheye Delo*, since only it was providing us with popular literature, printing our correspondence, and carrying out orders... We got neither hide nor hair from Emancipation of Labour, not even so much as a letter of reply. Vladimir said that, of course, these were people too old and infirm to carry out any practical work and that the young people should provide assistance to them in this regard, but without isolating themselves in a separate group, and recognising in full their rightful, time-served theoretical authority."[676]

In Ufa, they were immediately dragged into an unending torrent of meetings and gatherings, with people coming and going continuously. Alexander Tsyurupa writes, "There were arguments and even heated fights" at the meetings. But Ulyanov turned virtually every conversation towards the same thing – the need to assist the future newspaper: by collecting money, producing material, and dealing with logistics.

Ulyanov left Ufa in early July. He stopped over for a short period in Samara, before going to Syzran, where he met with Alexei Yeramasov, who had promised to provide money for the newspaper. By 10th July, Ulyanov was in Podolsk bidding farewell to his family, before arriving in Smolensk on 13th. There he held a series of meetings (with Vladimir Rozanov and Ivan Babushkin) and possibly with Peter Struve.

Ulyanov's time in Smolensk is known to us from reports in the local newspaper *Smolensky Vestnik*, which was published by an acquaintance of

---

676   Ibid. p. 64.

Nadezhda Krupskaya, Y. P. Azanchevskaya. In the paper's daily summary, it reported that a "Mr Ulyanov" arrived on 14th, stayed at the European Hotel, and departed on 15th. A "Mr Struve" also arrived and departed on these dates, staying at the more expensive Grand Hotel. It seems he was bringing the 2,000 roubles that Ulyanov was unable to obtain from Kalmykova due to his arrest. It is unlikely that having been in such close proximity to each other for two days that Ulyanov and Struve did not discuss further plans.

Now he could depart: the money was collected, everything had been arranged with friends and colleagues, and his passport was safe in his pocket. In fact, it is likely he was carrying not one passport, but two.

For decades, the question of how Ulyanov came to use the pseudonym Nikolai Lenin in spring 1901 remained unanswered, with a multitude of differing explanations put forth. Some are toponymic: after the river Lena (see also Plekhanov as 'Volgin'), or the village of Lehnin, near Berlin. Lepeshinsky hinted that the pseudonym was derived from the name of his daughter, Lenochka. With the emergence of professional 'Lenin-bashing', 'amorous' sources were sought, with one claim being that it stemmed from the Kazan beauty Yelena Lenina – in another version, it was the Mariinsky Theatre chorus girl Yelena Zaretskaya who was the inspiration, and so on. However, none of these claims stand up to the slightest serious scrutiny.

Mikhail Shtein has discussed all of these theories in his book *Ulyanovy i Leniny. Tainy rodoslovnoi i psevdonima* [The Ulyanovs and the Lenins. Secrets of the Family Tree and Pseudonym]. He was the first to solve definitively the puzzle of the origins of Ulyanov's pseudonym.[677]

The Lenin line begins with the Cossack Posnik, who was awarded noble status, the surname Lenin, and an estate in Vologda Province for his services in the conquest of Siberia and the development of winter quarters on the banks of the river Lena. His numerous descendants frequently distinguished themselves in military and civilian service. One of them – Nikolai Yegorovich Lenin – who attained the rank of State Councillor, fell ill and retired to Yaroslavl Province in the 1880s.

His daughter – Olga Nikolayevna – graduated from the History and Philology Faculty of the Bestuzhev Courses in 1883 and went to work in the Smolenskaya evening school for workers in St Petersburg, where she met Krupskaya. When it became a possibility that the authorities would refuse Ulyanov a foreign passport, and Kalmykova began exploring illicit

---

677   See: *M. G. Shtein*. Ulyanovy i Leniny, pp. 176-230.

means of crossing the border, Nadezhda turned to Lenina for help. Olga Nikolayevna passed on the request to her brother, the agronomist Sergey Nikolayevich Lenin, a prominent official in the Ministry of Agriculture. It seems his friend, the statistician Alexander Dmitriyevich Tsyurupa, who had made Ulyanov's acquaintance in Ufa, also approached him with a similar request.

Sergey Nikolayevich knew Ulyanov personally from meetings of the Free Economic Society in 1895, and was also aware of his work. In his turn, Ulyanov was aware of Lenin and had referenced his articles three times in *The Development of Capitalism in Russia*. After discussing the matter, the Lenin siblings decided to offer Ulyanov the passport of their father, Nikolai Yegorovich, who was by this stage in seriously ill health (he died on 6th April 1902).

According to family legend, Sergey Nikolayevich was in Pskov on official business. "There, on behalf of the Ministry of Agriculture, he was to accept delivery from Germany of Sack ploughs and other agricultural machinery. In one of Pskov's hotels, S. N. Lenin also passed on the passport of his father, with the date of birth altered, to Vladimir Ilyich, who was living in Pskov at the time."[678]

Given the timing of events, this version is quite conceivable and this would appear to be the precise origin of Ulyanov's main pseudonym – N. Lenin. On 16th July 1900, Ulyanov left the country.

---

678   Ibid. p. 207.

A MORAL DOUSING

Ulyanov provides a detailed account of his first few weeks abroad: "I arrived initially in Zürich... In Zürich P. B. [Axelrod] greeted me with open arms, and we spent two days in intimate conversation. The conversation was one of two friends long parted: it covered everything and more besides, with no structure, and wholly unrelated to serious business.

...P. B. 'fawned' awfully (excuse the expression) and said that for them, everything connected to our enterprise was a revival for them and that 'we' would now have an opportunity to argue against the 'extremes' of G. B. [Plekhanov] – this last point particularly stood out for me, and the whole 'story' that followed demonstrated how remarkable those words were."[679]

From Zürich Ulyanov made his way to Geneva, where he met with Potresov – he had also been to see Axelrod, and then later on Plekhanov, laying out for him the agenda and plans of the 'literary group'. He had also given Plekhanov the draft statement of "From the Editors". Georgi Valentinovich had read it through and "did not object to anything in principle. He merely expressed a desire to correct the style, to give it a lift, while maintaining the sense as a whole." However, Potresov was left with a sense that Plekhanov was deeply dissatisfied, extremely suspicious, and that they "need(ed) to be very careful" with him.[680]

This conversation with Potresov aside, there were plenty of other reasons for Plekhanov's dark mood. At the second congress of the Union of Russian Social Democrats Abroad in Geneva in April 1900, a decisive split had occurred between Emancipation of Labour and the economist leadership, along with the majority of the Union's 'young' members. With a few supporters, Plekhanov formed the independent Russian Social-Democratic Union, later renamed to Revolutionary Organisation "Social Democrat".

---

679   *V. I. Lenin*. Polnoye sobraniye sochineny. Vol. 4. p. 334.
680   Ibid. pp. 334, 338.

Any split is inevitably accompanied by a round of squabbling, and Ulyanov found himself immediately caught up, against his wishes, in the émigré scene's tumultuous atmosphere, with its endless rounds of discussions and infighting. "I am living in quite a significant, even undue level of turmoil," he wrote to Krupskaya in Ufa, "and this (NB) despite the enormous and extraordinary lengths I have gone to in order to protect myself from turmoil! One could say I am living in virtual solitude, but a tumultuous one all the same!"[681]

Acquaintances, and friends of acquaintances, from among the 'youth' tried to tell him that the reason for all the discord in the émigré ranks was Plekhanov's malign character, and that his conduct amounted to "a continuous personal attack, and in the same vein, an utterly domineering attitude, inflating minor issues due to [his] vilification of individuals..."[682]

It was common knowledge that Plekhanov was not always the easiest to deal with. He had a remarkable knack of setting others against him. Ulyanov wrote, "Vera Ivanovna [Zasulich] very subtly remarked that G. V. always argues in such a way that the reader sympathises with his opponent."[683]

The venerable anarchist Prince Peter Kropotkin, who had observed Plekhanov for many years in emigration, once rather darkly joked: "Had Kropotkin returned to Russia under Nicholas II, he would have sent him to Sakhalin to conduct geological surveys; had Plekhanov been in charge of Russia, he would simply have hanged him."[684]

Deciding it was best to 'marshal their forces', Ulyanov, Martov and Potresov had agreed back in Russia to keep their distance and maintain their independence. "We want to remain independent. We do not consider it possible to conduct business without forces such as Plekhanov and Emancipation of Labour, but *no-one has the right to conclude* from that *that we are giving up the slightest part of our independence.*"[685]

In Pskov they had firmly resolved: "We shall be the editors, and they – our closest contributors," Ulyanov wrote. "We should be the editors, given the intolerance of the 'old men' and their inability to accurately conduct

---

681   Ibid. Vol. 46. p. 34.
682   Ibid.
683   Ibid. Vol. 4. p. 339.
684   R. *Pipes*. Struve: liberal on the left.
685   V. I. *Lenin*. Polnoye sobraniye sochineny. Vol. 46. p. 42.

the heavy spade work of editing: these were the only considerations that mattered to us, as we were quite ready to recognise their ideological leadership."[686]

Having arrived into such a highly charged atmosphere abroad, one which had led to literal hysterics and fist-fights, Potresov for one found himself becoming jaded. Ulyanov's reaction was different. "I could rail at the heavens," he wrote to Krupskaya, "but it is a blessing I am not as neurotic as our dear bookseller [Potresov], who sinks into a black melancholy and is instantly laid low by all this mayhem."[687]

Eventually, Ulyanov met with Plekhanov. Initially, it was all perfectly amiable: they spent a lot of time on walks; Georgi Valentinovich, as always, gently teased his conversation partners, albeit not always successfully. Yuri Steklov tells of how, on one of these walks, Plekhanov began to mock Ulyanov, quoting Gleb Uspensky, whose work he knew inside out, on the reasons for men going bald. But having begun the quote, he suddenly halted, realising that it would not end well for him...

Ulyanov instantly noticed this, and "rolling with laughter on the grass" continued: "What is it, Georgi Valentinovich, aren't you going to finish? Allow me to continue the quote. Uspensky has it: 'The man whose baldness begins on the brow is one of great intellect (he pointed to his pate, which was itself balding from the front). But the man who balds from the nape (and here he made a cruel jab at Plekhanov, whose baldness spreads from both his forehead and the nape of his neck) betrays a life ill-led."[688]

However, when conversation turned to matters concerning the publication of *Iskra* and *Zarya*, the jocularity ended.

Over the course of almost three weeks, they had at least *seven* meetings. A few days after the conclusion of negotiations, on 20th August, Ulyanov, genuinely dazed by what had taken place, wrote out on station café stationery a detailed summary of these meetings for Krupskaya. He called the piece, quoted in the following passages, "How the 'Spark' [*Iskra*] Was Nearly Extinguished".

First, though, a preliminary remark:

In previous chapters, effort has been made to avoid making forays into other people's souls or attempts at mind-reading. What Ulyanov was

---

686   Ibid. Vol. 4. p. 342.
687   Ibid. Vol. 46. p. 34.
688   Proletarskaya revolyutsiya. 1923. No. 5. p. 222.

feeling or experiencing is referenced strictly when reliable data is available to support it. There is very little of this, as he was as little inclined to 'self-searching' as he was to bickering. On this basis, some authors have concluded that he was a 'soulless' individual, completely devoid of the most subtle emotional impulses and feelings.

The document in question is something of an exception. It was not intended for publication, nor for anyone else's eyes. Ulyanov needed to 'pour out his soul' immediately, and he wrote it in one sitting, in defiance of his usual practice, almost without correction or deletion. It only saw the light of day after Ulyanov had died.

From the outset of his conversations with Plekhanov, Ulyanov writes, "it was immediately apparent that he really was suspicious, mistrustful, and [always considers himself completely in the right]. I tried to maintain a degree of caution, avoiding 'sore' points, but this constant guardedness could of course not fail to have a severe effect on his mood. From time to time there were small 'tensions' in the form of G. V.'s sharp retorts to every remark... G. V. demonstrated complete intolerance, and an inability and unwillingness to try and understand the arguments of others..."[689]

"Towards his 'allies' [the Union of Russian Social Democrats Abroad] he exhibited a hatred that verged on the obscene (suspecting them of espionage, calling them swindlers and scoundrels, stating that he would not hesitate in 'shooting' such 'traitors', and so on)..."

As regards his attitude towards the Bund, Plekhanov "demonstrated a phenomenal intolerance, declaring explicitly that it was not a social-democratic organisation, merely a group looking to exploit Russians, saying our aim should be to kick them out of the party and that Jews were complete chauvinists and nationalists, that a Russian party should be Russian and not let itself be 'taken captive' by a 'clutch of snakes' and so on. None of our objections to such unpleasant talk had any effect, and G. V. stuck steadfastly to his position, saying that we simply lacked knowledge of Jewry and life experience in dealing with Jews."[690]

By this stage, it was utterly impossible to enter into a conversation on his relations with Struve and Tugan-Baranovsky. Firstly, "G. V. tried to make out that we wanted to avoid savage conflict with Struve, that we wanted to 'come to an accommodation with everyone' and so on."

---

689   *V. I. Lenin*. Polnoye sobraniye sochineny. Vol. 4. pp. 334, 337.
690   Ibid. pp. 337, 338-339.

When he was presented with the fact that in 1895 and 1897 it had been he who had ducked out of the dispute, and not Ulyanov, "G. V., after a heated discussion, laid his hand on my shoulder and said, 'Gentlemen, I am not setting conditions, we will discuss everything there ... and come to a decision together.' This touched me at the time."[691]

It was becoming clear that the Pskov formula - "we are the editors, they – our closest contributors" - could not be the basis for consensus. Both Ulyanov and Potresov suggested working as 'co-editors', though Plekhanov's attitude indicated that he was unlikely to accept that either.

After Plekhanov's remark that the issue of Struve and Tugan-Baranovsky would be solved collectively, Ulyanov and Potresov offered their "conditional invitation", to which "G. V. very coldly and dryly declared his complete opposition and made a point of sitting in silence as we conducted rather prolonged discussions with P. B. [Axelrod] and V. I. [Zasulich], who had no objections. The whole morning passed in this strained atmosphere: it began to become apparent that G. V. was presenting us with an ultimatum – it was either him, or we invited the 'scoundrels.'"[692]

Ulyanov and Potresov found themselves becoming more obstinate the more Plekhanov toughened his stance: "G. V.'s incredible brusqueness somehow instinctively pushes one towards objecting, and defending his opponents." But this was already becoming immaterial, as the atmosphere was now threatening to obscure the matter. "Becoming aware of that, Arsenyev [Potresov] and I decided to concede and at the outset of the evening session stated that 'at the insistence of G. V.' we were withdrawing [the invitation to Struve]. This announcement was met with silence (as if our giving way was the natural outcome!). We were thoroughly irritated by this 'atmosphere of ultimatums' (as Arsenyev called it later) – G. V.'s desire to rule unchecked was quite apparent."[693]

The following day, on the Sunday, "our meeting was scheduled to take place not at our cottage, but at Plekhanov's. We arrived there... Plekhanov entered and called us into his room. There he stated that it was better he be a contributor, merely a contributor, as there would only be tensions otherwise, that it was clear he saw the matter differently from us, that he

---

691	Ibid. pp. 337, 340.
692	Ibid. pp. 339-340.
693	Ibid. pp. 339, 340.

understood and respected our viewpoint as a party, but could not endorse it. Let us be the editors, and he a contributor.

We were utterly taken aback by this, immediately so, and began to protest. Then G. V. said: 'Well, if we are to vote together, how shall we vote? How many votes do we have?' 'Six.' 'Six is no good.' 'Well, let G. V. have two votes,' V. I. [Zasulich] interceded, 'otherwise he will always be on his own – two votes on matters of tactics.' We agreed.

At that point G. V. takes the reins and then in the tone of an editor begins issuing departments and articles for the journal, assigning these departments to those present – this tone is not one that permits objections.

We sat there dejected, impassively agreeing to everything, unable to digest what had happened. We felt taken for fools, that our comments were becoming increasingly timid and that G. V. was 'side-lining' them (not rejecting them, but putting them to the side) ever more casually; that this 'new system' was in effect G. V. taking total control, and G. V., fully aware of this, would not hesitate to dominate and not stand on ceremony about it. We realised that we had been completely deceived and outflanked..."[694]

"As soon as we were alone, as soon as we disembarked from the steamer and went to our cottage, we both immediately snapped... The heavy atmosphere broke out into a thunderstorm. We walked till late from one end of our little village to the other, the night was rather dark, and all around the thunder and lightning crashed and flickered. We walked and fumed. As I recall, Arsenyev began by stating he considered personal relations with Plekhanov ruptured once and for all, and could never be resumed... His behaviour is an insult... He is treating us with contempt, and so on. I fully agreed with these charges.

We realised now that it was perfectly clear that Plekhanov's statement that morning on refusing co-editorship was a simple trap, calculated like a chess move, a snare for naïve 'buffoons': there is no question of this, since if Plekhanov was genuinely worried about being co-editor, and feared slowing up the endeavour and creating unnecessary tension between us, then he would not have been able, a minute later, to display (and so rudely) the fact that his *co*-editorship was wholly tantamount to his *sole* editorship.

Well, if the man with whom we want to work together in a common endeavour ... employs a chess move against his comrades, then there is no

---

694   Ibid. pp. 341-342.

doubt that this is a person of bad character, bad is the word, powerfully motivated by his personal, petty vanities and conceit – an insincere person."[695]

In that case, was it best to seize on Plekhanov's morning 'resignation' and return to the Pskov model, whereby Ulyanov take over the editorship himself? No! As he wrote, "taking on the editorial role myself would be unspeakable, it would seem that we were merely grasping for editorial spots as if we really were *Streber*, careerists, as if the same vanity was driving us, only to a smaller scale..."[696]

Those that claim that Ulyanov, with his 'ironclad single-mindedness', was incapable of any kind of intellectual introspection have never read this document. Just as Vladimir Obolensky was wrong when he enviously and maliciously observed, having heard it said while in Pskov that Ulyanov and Potresov lived "soul to soul", that: "they do not live soul to soul, but mind to mind, as [Ulyanov] has no soul."[697] From this evidence he did possess a soul, and rather a sensitive one to boot.

"It is difficult to describe with sufficient accuracy," Ulyanov wrote, "our state that evening: such a confused, heavy, troubled state of mind! It was a genuine drama, a complete break with that which we had treated as a beloved child for so many years...

Never, never in my life have I felt such respect, reverence and *vénération* for a person, never have I carried myself more 'humbly' in anyone's presence, and never have I felt such a vicious 'kick'.

And this was all because we had loved Plekhanov: had this love not been there, had we been more dispassionate and level-headed in our dealings with him, we would have seen him more objectively, and this ruin, in the literal sense of the word, this 'moral dousing', as Arsenyev rightly called it, would not have befallen us. It was the harshest of life lessons – painfully harsh, and painfully savage."[698]

Having realised this, they came to a resolution: "This is impossible! We do not want to, we will not, we cannot work together in such circumstances... We will give it all up and return to Russia, and there we

---

695   Ibid. pp. 343-344.
696   Ibid. p. 344.
697   *V. A. Obolensky*. Moya zhizn'. Moi sovremenniki. p. 178.
698   *V. I. Lenin*. Polnoye sobraniye sochineny. Vol. 46. pp. 343, 344-345.

will start again afresh and restrict ourselves to the newspaper. We will not be pawns in this man's hands..."[699]

The following morning Axelrod arrived. Ulyanov writes, "I heard Arsenyev [Potresov] answer the door – hearing this I think to myself: will Arsenyev have the heart to come out with everything straight away? It's better to come out with it, vital to come out with it, not drag it out. After washing and dressing, I went to Arsenyev's room… Axelrod is sitting in an armchair with a rather strained expression. Arsenyev says to me, 'Now, N. N., I have told P. B. about our decision to return to Russia and our belief that we cannot work in this way.' Of course, I fully subscribed to this and supported Arsenyev… Axelrod shook his head sadly, demonstrating a certain degree of general empathy for our position, and seemed thoroughly dejected, bewildered, and disconcerted… poor P. B. looked thoroughly miserable when he recognised that we were resolved in our decision."[700]

They went to Vera Zasulich. Ulyanov writes, "I will never forget the mood in which we three set off: 'It is as if we are going to a funeral,' I said to myself. And indeed, we walked as if we were following a coffin, in silence, eyes lowered, laid to the very lowest degree by the absurdity, savagery and senselessness of our loss… It was at times so hard that it seemed I might weep… One is brought to tears most easily at funerals when words of condolence and despair are uttered…"

They arrived at Zasulich's and told her of their decision. Zasulich "was terribly dejected, and pleaded, almost begged, for us to go back on our decision… It was excruciatingly hard to hear such earnest exhortations from someone who, though weak before Plekhanov, was so genuinely sincere and passionately dedicated to the cause, an individual with the 'heroism of a slave' (Arsenyev's words) who bore the yoke of Plekhanovism."[701]

After lunch, they met Plekhanov at the appointed hour. "Arsenyev began talking – he was composed, dry and succinct, saying we were so dismayed at the possibility that affairs would be conducted in the way they had been the previous day that we had decided to return to Russia to consult with comrades there, as decisions could no longer be made by us alone…

Plekhanov was clearly somewhat annoyed. He had not expected such a tone, such dryness, and such direct accusations: 'Well, you have made

---

699 Ibid. p. 344.
700 Ibid. pp. 345, 346.
701 Ibid. pp. 346, 347.

your decision to leave, what more is there to discuss? I have nothing to say, I am left in a strange position: you have your impressions, and impressions are what they are, nothing more: you have gotten the idea that I am a bad man. What am I supposed to do now?.. *Do not count on me.* If you leave, then I will not sit idly by and shall move on to a different enterprise until your return.'

Nothing lowered Plekhanov as much in my eyes as this statement. It was such a blunt threat, such a poorly calculated intimidation, that it merely delivered the 'kiss of death' for Plekhanov and made clear his 'policy' towards us: giving them a good fright will do the trick...

But we did not pay the *slightest bit of attention* to this threat. I merely pursed my lips in silence... Seeing that the threat had had no effect, Plekhanov tried a different gambit. How could one not call it a gambit, when in a matter of minutes he began saying that our breaking with him was for him tantamount to his complete withdrawal from political activity, that he would renounce it and move into scientific, purely scientific literature, since if he could not work with us, then he could not work with anyone... If intimidation didn't work, why not try flattery!.. But after trying to threaten us, this could only leave us repelled... The conversation was short and did nothing for the situation... What was left of the evening passed emptily and gloomily."[702]

The story could have ended like this. At precisely the moment when it seemed everything was falling into place, Ulyanov began to realise that something incredible and bizarre had occurred: "It is as if we are cursed! Everything seemed to be progressing, working out after so many years of adversity and failure, and suddenly a whirlwind descends and it's the end, everything is ruined again. I simply could not bring myself to believe it (just as one cannot bring oneself to comprehend the death of a close one) – could I, an ardent admirer of Plekhanov, really be speaking about him with such venom, going to him with clenched mouth and cold heart and saying such cold, cutting things to him, practically announcing the 'end of our relationship'? Was this really happening, and not merely a nightmare?"[703]

At some ungodly hour of the morning, Potresov came. He was also in complete mental disarray. They recalled Axelrod's words: "Plekhanov is also finished and now it is on our conscience if we leave like this, and so on."

---

702   Ibid. pp. 347-349.
703   Ibid. pp. 346-347.

They remembered Zasulich begging them: "Couldn't we try? Perhaps in practice things will not be so bad, and getting on with the work will improve relations and the unpleasant aspects of [Plekhanov's] character will not be so apparent..." Potresov said that during the night he had "come up with the last possible scenario for somehow rectifying the matter and saving a party endeavour from falling to pieces due to the deterioration of a *personal* relationship... If Plekhanov digs his heels in, then hell mend him – we will know that we did everything we could... This was agreed on."[704]

They left the small village of Vésenaz, along with Axelrod and Zasulich, to return to Geneva once more. Plekhanov immediately "assumed the kind of tone that suggested it had all been a sad misunderstanding born of nerves. He asked sympathetically after Arsenyev's health and almost embraced him – he in turn almost recoiled... We said that there were three possible alternatives for dealing with the question of editorship: (1. We be the editors, he a contributor; 2. We are all co-editors; 3. He be the editor and we the contributors), and that we would discuss all three possibilities in Russia, work out a plan, and bring it back here.

Plekhanov stated that he categorically rejected the third option, strongly insisted that it be completely excluded, and agreed to the first two. A decision was made: for now, until the submission of a draft editorial arrangement, we would keep the old system (all six of us as co-editors, with two votes for Plekhanov)."[705]

It seemed as if everything had come full circle. "Plekhanov exhibited all his cunning, all the brilliance of his examples, similes, jokes and quotations, making us laugh despite ourselves... We decided not to speak of what had taken place with anyone beyond those closest to us, - ... so as not to give our opponents cause for celebration. From the outside, it is as if nothing has happened, and the whole machinery must continue running as before – only a wire has snapped inside..." And while Plekhanov span his yarns, Ulyanov thought: "You are a fool, if you cannot see that we are no longer the same people we were before, that we have been completely reborn overnight."[706]

Note how this part of the letter resonates: "An enamoured youth receives from the object of his affection a bitter lesson: one must treat everyone 'without sentimentality', and be ready to strike back. An endless

---

704   Ibid. pp. 347, 349, 350.
705   Ibid. p. 350.
706   Ibid. pp. 349, 351.

stream of bitter words were spoken that night. The suddenness of the breakdown naturally led to a great deal of hyperbole, but the basis for these bitter words held true."[707]

These "*bitter words*" were just that, nothing more. But the 'life lesson' that Ulyanov spoke of lay elsewhere: "We had both loved Plekhanov up to that point, and like a loved one, forgave him everything, closed our eyes to every shortcoming, doing all we could to convince ourselves that these shortcomings were not there, that they were minor, and that only those who placed no value in principles would focus on them. And now, we had been forced to see for ourselves how such 'minor' shortcomings could repel his most loyal friends, how no acknowledgement of his theoretical correctness was capable of making us forget his repellent traits... The ideal was shattered, and we zealously trampled it underfoot like a toppled idol..."

His conclusion: "Blinded by our love, we in essence let ourselves become *slaves*, and it is contemptible to be a slave..."[708]

---

707   Ibid. p. 345.

708   Ibid. pp. 344, 345.

PERSONAL RELATIONS

On 15th August, Ulyanov left Geneva for Munich, but stopped off in Nuremberg to make arrangements with German social democrats on the technical assistance they were providing in the publication of *Iskra* and *Zarya*.

The shock from the conflict with Plekhanov lingered for the first few days, but ongoing concerns gradually pushed that experience into the background.

"Today is 2nd September [20th August]," he wrote to Krupskaya from Nuremberg, "so it has *only* been a week since it all happened!!! It feels like a year has passed. It already seems so far away." He continues: "As we began to move on from what had taken place, we started to view it in a more measured fashion and came to the conclusion that this was no grounds to abandon the endeavour and that there was nothing to fear from taking on the editorship… [and thus] prevent the enterprise from dying a death as a result of Plekhanov's disorganising 'qualities'."[709]

While on the road to Nuremberg, he began penning a draft agreement between Emancipation of Labour, now renamed Social Democrat, and a Russian group which he referred to for the first time as Iskra. "In view of the solidarity in our fundamental views and the commonality of our practical objectives," the document stated, both "organisations are forming an alliance." Plekhanov's group would "participate very closely in editorial work" for *Iskra* and *Zarya*, as well as assist in their circulation, in broadening their network of connections, and in "the sourcing of material resources".[710]

The editorial group's voting procedure was outlined by Ulyanov later, on 6th October. It stipulated parity in the voting rights of both groups, and in cases of disagreement, provided recourse to publish dissenting opinions, either as a group or as individual members. There was no more reference

---

709   V. I. Lenin. Polnoye sobraniye sochineny. Vol. 4. pp. 341, 352.
710   Ibid. p. 353.

to Plekhanov's two votes.[711] There was one additional item: it was finally agreed that the editing of *Iskra* would be done not in Switzerland, near Plekhanov, but in Munich, where Vera Zasulich was to move.

Ulyanov also set about reworking the original draft of "From the Editors", written back in Pskov. He not only halved the length of the text, but made it more uncompromising. Plekhanov had knocked out of him any weakness in phrasing and anything that, in his view, might give off the impression of "opportunism".

"Before uniting, and in order to unite," wrote Ulyanov, "we must definitively and distinctly define our position. Otherwise, our association would merely be a fiction cloaking the current confusion… We do not intend to make our organ a mere repository for differing viewpoints. On the contrary, we will run it with a strictly defined direction in mind. This direction can be expressed in one word: Marxism…"[712]

The key point remained: "The unification of all Russian social democrats … cannot be by decree, it cannot be brought into being by a single decision taken by a gathering of some or other representatives, it must be developed. Firm ideological unification must be developed first of all… Secondly, we must develop an organisation…" Only then will "the party be on a solid footing and become a proper entity, and consequently, a powerful force."[713]

There was another difference apparent in this redraft. While the previous Pskov draft was known simply as "From the Editors", this was given a more fleshed-out title: "Declaration of the Editorial Board of *Iskra*".

It is hard to say whether or not rumours of the conflict with Plekhanov were known in émigré circles. However, it was clear to anyone who met Ulyanov at that time: Potresov writes, "He stopped eating and sleeping, and became drawn and sallow, even sombre."[714] Equally noticeable was the fact that Potresov himself was beginning to slip back into a "black melancholy" on occasion.

Immediately after his arrival in Nuremberg, Ulyanov was attacked by representatives of the Union of Russian Social Democrats, who wanted a 'merger', or at the very least, a 'federation' with his entire 'literary group'.

---

711   Ibid. p. 484.
712   Ibid. p. 358.
713   Ibid. p. 357.
714   N. Valentinov. Nedorisovanny portret… p. 520.

Their missive ended with a melodramatic appeal: "The eyes of the Union are on you."

However, their calculation that insults and assertions were reasonable grounds to bring about rapprochement was not vindicated. On 23rd August [5th September], Ulyanov replied: "Our decision remains *unchanged* – to remain an independent group and enjoy a very close working relationship with Emancipation of Labour... At the present time, when all our lifeblood must be expended on nurturing our new-born [*Iskra*], we cannot take on the nursing of the offspring of others."

Ulyanov confirmed the same to Takhtarev, representative of the Union of Russian Social Democrats Abroad. Between 23rd - 27th September, the International Socialist Congress took place in Paris. Takhtarev invited Plekhanov to run *Rabochaya Mysl*. He wrote, "Georgi Valentinovich, as it became clear to me from several conversations with him, was prepared to accept my offer and become editor of *Rabochaya Mysl* on the condition, of course, that it change direction."[715] The entire plan for the publication of *Iskra* was once again left hanging in the air.

Ulyanov "was at that time living in Munich," recalls Takhtarev, "and I went there for talks on *Rabochaya Mysl* without knowing how he would receive me, a person ... he naturally considered one of his opponents. However, he greeted me in a comradely fashion."[716]

For Ulyanov, this was another lesson in 'big politics', but he had made a firm decision not to let himself be drawn into any intrigues, instead adopting an outspoken and transparent position.

The plan proposed by Takhtarev, as he himself writes, "had the potential to spoil Ulyanov's hand, and complicate and hinder the struggle he was waging at the time... It could even have changed its final outcome." As a result, Ulyanov "opposed in the most vigorous manner Plekhanov's taking charge of *Rabochaya Mysl*... Vladimir Ilyich expressed quite frankly the reasons why my plan was unacceptable to him. I understood that this plan was unfeasible while he dissented. I also recognised that the main leader of the Russian social-democratic movement was no longer Plekhanov, but Ulyanov."[717]

---

715   *K. M. Takhtarev*. Rabocheye dvizheniye v Peterburge. pp. 172-173.

716   Ibid.

717   Ibid. p. 173.

Many years later, Nadezhda Krupskaya would write that "personal attachment to people made the schisms very difficult for Vladimir Ilyich," but breaking with a person politically, "he broke with them on a personal level – it could not be any other way when his entire life had been tied to the political struggle..."[718] But this observation is more true of the culmination of his years of struggle. At that point – at the turn of the century – he still felt that ideological struggle did not necessarily need to affect personal relationships.

It was necessary to persevere, and correspondence between Munich and Geneva became regular, composed, and constructive, although, in contrast to his letters to Axelrod, he eschewed any expression of emotion in correspondence with Plekhanov.

Martov only managed to leave Russia later, in March 1901, so Ulyanov was the only one of the 'holy trinity', as Axelrod called them, in Munich at that time.

---

718   *N. K. Krupskaya*. O Lenine. pp. 22, 23.

THE WIND OF CHANGE

On 11th [24th] December, the first issue of *Iskra* was published.[719] The month and a half leading up to publication had been a major source of difficulty for Ulyanov. The German social democrats had held up proceedings by dragging their feet on guaranteeing use of their printing press. Ulyanov wrote to Axelrod: "My nerves are really rather shot. The main issue is this tedious uncertainty, these damned Germans are fobbing me off – oh, what I'd like to do to them!..."[720] It took until November to come to an agreement on the printing of *Iskra* in the Leipzig printworks of H. W. Dietz, and typesetting only began on 27th November.

The process of editing the paper, and the back-and-forth correspondence this necessitated, took up a great deal of time. Every one of its venerable contributors – those 'founding fathers' – was desperate to offer journal-length articles to the newspaper, and they were extremely sensitive to any abridgements and corrections. There was a plethora of responses for every editorial remark, and that is not to mention their approach to deadlines: Axelrod sent an extensive article for the first issue of *Iskra* at quite literally the last possible moment.

It is necessary to note that harshness during ideological disputes was a general characteristic of Russian democrat-leaning journalism. Justifying this harshness, Belinsky had written: "Ugly and vulgar these personal disputes may be, but the battle for ideas is a sacred undertaking, and woe to those who did not fight."

No less a scholar of Struve's work as Richard Pipes noted at the time that Struve "adopted [a] manner of debating, and frequently used a tone of biting sarcasm which suggested that anyone who did not agree with him was a fool or a hypocrite or both."[721]

---

719   See: V. I. Lenin. Polnoye sobraniye sochineny. Vol. 46. p. 75.
720   Ibid. p. 51.
721   R. Pipes. Struve: Liberal on the Left, 1870-1905. Harvard, 1970. p. 180.

By contrast, Ulyanov's articles were becoming more restrained. While in exile, he had come to the realisation that the time for the kind of essays and provocative pieces he had written in Samara had passed. In a letter to Anna Ulyanova-Yelizarova he wrote, "As for harsh language, I am now broadly in favour of toning it down and reducing its use. I am convinced that sharp words in print are immeasurably more powerful than when spoken or in letters, so one must be more measured in this regard." Even in disputes with noted opponents, he "as much as possible tried to soften his tone…"[722]

Ulyanov stated his position thus: "…we now need to be more careful: not in the sense that we compromise so much as a scintilla of our principles, but in the sense that we do not needlessly embitter those people working, as they see it, for social democracy."[723]

While in Pskov, as they exchanged impressions from their journeys around Russia, all three – Ulyanov, Potresov and Martov – could sense the 'wind of change' in the air.

The industrial upsurge of the 1890s, which was bound up in the success of the economic strikes, was grinding to a halt. In the boom years, the inevitable disruption of deliveries to customers wrought by the strikes caused far more damage than small handouts to workers. Now, with the worsening economic conditions, manufacturers were no longer making concessions, instead utilising strikes as grounds for mass lay-offs. In 1900, as the number of strikes decreased, instances of clashes between workers and the police and authorities increased. The process of 'politicising' the movement gathered pace, signalling a clear portent of the bankruptcy of 'economism'.

"One does not need to be a prophet," Ulyanov had written back in 1897, "to predict the inevitability of the (rather sharp) collapse that should follow this 'prospering' of industry. Such a collapse … thus presents before the working masses in acute form those questions of socialism and democracy that have long faced every class-conscious, thinking worker."[724]

For the first issue of *Iskra*, Ulyanov wrote an editorial titled "The Urgent Tasks of Our Movement." In it he noted, "Russian social democracy is going through a period of hesitation, a period of doubt verging on abnegation."

---

722   V. I. Lenin. Polnoye sobraniye sochineny. Vol. 55. pp. 139, 158.
723   Ibid. Vol. 46. p. 38.
724   Ibid. Vol. 2. p. 466.

These hesitations were being caused by problems in the relationship between the socialist intelligentsia and the labour movement. This disconnect existed in many countries, and in each it had been resolved "in its own way, dependent on the conditions extant in that place and time". One thing was beyond doubt: "In all countries, such detachment has led to the weakness of socialism and of the labour movement..."[725]

In this vein, Ulyanov came to a conclusion that would later form the basis for his work *What Is To Be Done?* (1902): "Cut off from social democracy, the labour movement is diminished and must slide into bourgeoisness: conducting merely an economic struggle, the working class loses its political independence and becomes a tail of other parties, betraying the great maxim: 'the emancipation of the workers must be an undertaking of the workers themselves.'"[726]

"No class in history," he writes in the *Iskra* editorial, "achieved supremacy without advancing its own political leaders, its own key figures, capable of organising the movement and leading it. And the Russian working class has already shown that is capable of producing such people..."[727]

The dearth of guile demonstrated by his opponents suggests that social-democratic organisations of the time were made up exclusively of intellectuals far removed from the working masses. Yet it is enough to glance at a list of those activists from Emancipation of Labour who had suffered repression to see what proportion of the organisation were workers: of its 74 convictions, 34 had been members of the intelligentsia and 46 were workers – 63%.[728]

In addition, we have the representative Russia-wide estimates of Mark Volin, which indicate that at the turn of the century workers made up 61% of the total membership of social-democrat groups. This was the cream of the Russian proletariat: 48% were metalworkers, 18% worked in the textile industry, 10% worked in printing trades, and so on. Members of the intelligentsia accounted for 36% of party members. Of these, 40% were students and school pupils, 21% were teachers, 20% were doctors, and so on. Social democrats were young – a quarter were under the age

---

[725] Ibid. p. 372, 373.
[726] Ibid. p. 373.
[727] Ibid. Vol. 4. p. 375.
[728] See: *N. Lenin (V. Ulyanov). Sobraniye sochineny*. Vol. 1. pp. 603-617.

of 20, 40% were between the ages of 21 and 25, and over 21% were 26 to 30 years old.[729]

Ulyanov wrote in *Iskra* that "the struggle of the Russian workers over the past five to six years has demonstrated how much revolutionary force there is in the working class, how the most desperate government harassment has not reduced but increased the number of workers stirring for socialism, striving for political consciousness and spoiling for political struggle."[730]

Ulyanov cited an episode from that year's May Day, when in response to a factory inspector's inquiry as to what it was the workers were demanding, a solitary cry broke forth from the crowd: "A constitution!" The correspondent himself had described the reply as "semi-comical". To that, Ulyanov noted, "In fact, there was nothing amusing in this response: the only thing that could be construed as amusing is the incongruity between this solitary call to overhaul an entire state system and demands for a shortening of the working day by half an hour and to be paid for hours worked. But the connection between these last demands and the call for a constitution is beyond doubt, and if we succeed (and we will certainly succeed) in making the masses aware of this connection, then that cry of 'A constitution!' will no longer be a solitary one, but will be heard on the lips of thousands, hundreds of thousands, and then that cry will no longer be amusing, but formidable."[731]

In his *Iskra* editorial, Ulyanov wrote, "Social democracy does not bind its own hands, nor does it narrow its own activity to some preconceived plan or method of political struggle – it recognises all means of struggle provided they accord with the available forces of the party and present an opportunity to achieve the best results possible in the given conditions."[732]

Did this imply that in order to succeed in a great and noble cause, any means, including those that may be considered 'ignoble', were valid? Did, as the Jesuits might say, "the end justify the means"? This accusation is as popular among Marxism's opponents as it is – in theory at

---

[729] See: Revolyutsiya 1905-1907 godov v Rossii i yeyo vsemirnoye-istoricheskoye znacheniye. Moscow, 1976. pp. 176-181.

[730] V. I. Lenin. Polnoye sobraniye sochineny. Vol. 4. p. 375.

[731] Ibid. p. 369.

[732] Ibid. p. 376.

least – groundless. As Marx himself wrote, "Truth resides not only in the result, but also in the path to it."

The paper's publication on 11th (24th) December was a cause for celebration for everyone involved in *Iskra*. Three articles by Ulyanov, two from Martov, articles by Axelrod and Christian Rakovsky, an extensive chronicle of working life and the liberation movement... After a year spent mustering forces and resources, months of exhaustive work, dangerous journeys across Russia, and the arrest of many associates and colleagues, they had achieved what they had set out to do. However, in a letter to Axelrod, Ulyanov wrote, "If this undertaking [*Iskra*] is destined to be a success ... then my earlier 'optimism' ... has been considerably knocked by the 'prose of life'."[733] And this "prose of life" somewhat dampened the festivities.

On 16th (29th) December, Struve arrived in Munich.

---

733   Ibid. Vol. 46. p. 63.

LENIN

After the release of the first issue of *Iskra*, it became clear that there was neither the money nor the 'political' content for continued publication. During the meetings held in November between Potresov and Struve in St Petersburg, Struve had hinted that he had a solution to this problem and could source the money and content to guarantee publication, having contacts in the highest institutions able to provide sensational material. Buoyed by these promises, Potresov returned to Munich.

Ulyanov wrote, "It turned out completely the other way round. This strange error probably stemmed from the fact that Arsenyev [Potresov] was desperate for what the twin [Struve] was waving before him – political material, reports, etcetera, and 'one believes in what one desires' – Arsenyev believed in the potential of what the twin was presenting, wanted to believe in the twin's sincerity, in the potential for a decent *modus vivendi* with him."[734]

At the very outset of their meeting, which took place on 16th (29th) December, Ulyanov began by asking Struve for his thoughts on their continuing relationship, and whether he was willing to work together on *Iskra* and *Zarya*. Struve replied firmly "that it was psychologically impossible for him to work at a journal where he would be 'dressed down' (this was the expression he used), that we shouldn't think that we can berate him, that he would be writing 'political articles' (literally) for us, that cooperation could only be discussed on condition of full parity..., that before he had wanted to confine himself to a role of 'benevolent assistance', but no longer intended to limit himself to this..."[735]

What had happened? Why was what had been acceptable in March intolerable come December? After all, there had been attacks directed at Struve and the other 'critics' in the past.

---

734   Ibid. p. 386.
735   Ibid. p. 387.

From 1899, the relatively turbulent student movement had resurfaced. At St Petersburg University, this had reached such a degree that clashes with police had occurred. *Zemstvo* student fraternities were beginning to agitate. In the same year, they had formed the organisation Beseda [Conversation], which began forging links across Russia. However, authorities were far more concerned about another issue altogether. In surveys conducted by government officials, landowners unanimously repeated: "It is not the unrest in the cities, the factories, or even the capital that are a threat to the state – the danger is emerging *from the countryside.*"[736] A little more than a year later, in spring 1902, peasant unrest erupted in Poltava and Kharkov Provinces. The unrest spread to the Central Black Earth [*Chernozem*] Region, the Volga Region, and Georgia, as landlords' estates went up in flames...

Meanwhile, Struve had become convinced that the time for revolution had passed, that "from a theoretical standpoint socialist revolution is not only wrong – it is diversionary". The only route that offered promise was reform. This "in no way represents a 'feeble stop gap' – it is conversely merely a link in an organic chain leading from one socio-economic formation to another".[737]

No-one was arguing that reform was not necessary and worthwhile, or that a 'peaceful way' was not preferable – Ulyanov himself acknowledged this. But were there any real grounds to expect reform from above? And given that this had not occurred in Germany or France, why would it in Russia, of all places?

In response to the student riots of 1899, the government had introduced 'temporary provisions' that authorised expulsion from educational institutions and military conscription for 'riotous crowd disorder'. As a retaliation to the relatively timid protests of the *zemstvos* and their attempts at forging an alliance, the government dismissed a number of prominent *zemstvo* members and scaled back the financial rights of the *zemstvos* themselves. In a memorandum to the tsar, Sergey Witte proposed shutting down the *zemstvos* outright as threats to the very idea of autocracy. And when unrest flared in Kharkov and Poltava Provinces, around 10,000 soldiers were despatched and more than 1,000 peasants put on trial.

---

736   Istoriya VKP(b). Vol. 1. Issue 2. Moscow; Leningrad, 1926. pp. 230, 231, 232.
737   *P. Struve*, Na raznyye temy. St Petersburg, 1902.

Later, concessions were offered – promises were made to simplify the process for peasants to leave their village community and joint taxation liability. But all this once again reinforced the fact that reform could not come about through the good will of a monarch, but only as a consequence of revolutionary struggle, and that the government would yield only to force. Looking further ahead, one can add that basic political freedom and the State Duma would only emerge in Russia *after* the working class took up arms and the flames from peasant uprisings took hold throughout virtually the entire country.

For Struve, the path of revolutionary struggle was one he found impossible to endorse. He therefore sought contacts with liberal *zemstvo* members, meeting with Shakhovsky and Rodichev. At the end of 1899 he had begun working with the newspaper *Severny Kurier* [Northern Courier], founded by Prince V. V. Baryatinsky. His articles received a warm response in liberal circles, and *zemstvo* members began developing plans for a printed organ abroad, with two candidates nominated for post of editor-in-chief: [the future liberal leader] Pavel Milyukov and Struve.[738]

Those involved in Beseda were household names throughout Russia: Pyotr and Pavel Dolgorukov, Y. N. and C. N. Trubetskoy, P. S. Sheremetyev, D. I. Shakhovskoy, and Y. A. Novosiltsev – all were renowned not only for their aristocratic backgrounds, but for their wealth.

It is hard to say whether Struve himself was aware of the potential opportunities opening up before him (given how informed he was, and the connections he boasted, it is likely he had an inkling), but now a role playing 'second fiddle' to a social-democrat orchestra was no longer any kind of enticement.

Moreover, involvement with social democrats was beginning to become a hindrance. He wrote later: "I was fully aware that my influence among both liberals and democrats would lessen, even disappear, or alternatively become an altogether negative one, if I became one of the 'orthodoxalists'. This is why I remained so firm and resolute."[739]

Thanks to Richard Pipes' major study, we can now trace virtually every step of Struve's evolution. Yet one question remains open: his motivations. Pipes makes repeated reference to the memoirs of Prince Vladimir Obolensky, who had been friends with Struve for over 40 years. However,

---

738 R. Pipes. Struve, Liberal on the Left.
739 Ibid.

Pipes left untouched one fragment of these recollections which offered an answer to precisely this question.

"It was not so much a search for truth and justice," writes Obolensky, "that led [Struve] to Marxism, as it was the theoretical harmony and schematic logic of his teaching that drew him in... The admiration of the masses never appealed to Struve, a factor that did not hinder him from being a somewhat ambitious person. But his ambition was of a peculiar kind. It made him inclined to reject the hackneyed modes of thinking of the multitude, and drew him to originality and paradox... Such an individual is by nature alien to genuine democracy, and if Struve had once been a democrat and a socialist, then it was merely as an accident of coming across these doctrines on the journey his thinking was on."[740]

Struve understood from his St Petersburg meetings with Potresov that *Iskra* and *Zarya* were in a tricky position, and decided not to stand on ceremony. As Potresov garnered from their negotiations, "he had appeared with full confidence in our powerlessness. The twin had come sure of our impotence and was there to offer us terms of surrender..."[741] He stated that he was no longer satisfied with being a mere contributor, and wished to be made editor, though neither of *Iskra* nor *Zarya*, but of a third new journal, *Sovremennoye Obozreniye* [Modern View].

As he saw it, *Zarya*, where Plekhanov would be in charge, should be a purely theoretical journal. *Iskra*, run by Ulyanov, was to be more 'popular' in form and more 'worker-oriented' in content. *Sovremennoye Obozreniye* was to focus on socio-political topics, while *Zarya* and *Iskra* were to "give over to this organ all of their general political material". A special condition was also stipulated: "There must be nothing social-democratic, nothing indicating our enterprise, on the cover [of *Sovremennoye Obozreniye*]."[742]

Even after five years of a rather fraught working and personal relationship, this about turn came out of the blue for Ulyanov. He wrote, "When the matter was first relayed by Arsenyev, I was of the understanding that the twin was coming over to us... It was this meeting that finally and irrevocably disproved that belief. The twin showed himself in a completely different light, showed himself to be a consummate 'politician',

---

740   V. A. Obolensky. Moya zhin'. Moi sovremenniki. p. 135.
741   V. I. Lenin. Polnoye sobraniye sochineny. Vol. 4. pp. 386-387.
742   Ibid. p. 387.

a 'politician' in the worst sense of the word, a political opportunist, a scoundrel, a wheeler-dealer, and a cocksure fellow."[743]

Struve spoke like the master of the house, with enough strength and resources to demand his own way. He had made his about turn in an exquisitely elegant and graceful fashion: as Ulyanov wrote, "he carried it out in the most perfectly proficient manner, without a single harsh word, but revealing nevertheless what a crass, mercenary nature this most ordinary of liberals kept hidden underneath the refined, civilised exterior of a sophisticated 'critic'."[744]

The implementation of Struve's plan meant only one thing: the migration of all political issues relating to other classes and likely to affect 'public opinion' in the country from *Iskra* and *Zarya* to a *non*-social democratic, liberal bourgeois organ. Therein lay the crux of the matter.

Ulyanov knew nothing of the behind-the-scenes vicissitudes going on in the liberal camp, but seized on the essence of the problem immediately: He wrote, "I said straight out that there can be no question of the foundation of a third organ, that the situation boils down to whether social democracy should lead the political struggle, or the liberals independently and self-sufficiently (I expressed myself more clearly, more exactly and in more detail). The twin understood, grew angry and stated that since I had expressed myself with *anerkennenswerte Klarheit* [a commendable clarity] (his exact words!) there was nothing else to say on the matter... Arsenyev and Velika [V. I. Zasulich] pressed him and demanded explanations; they argued, I was more quiet, and chuckled (so that the twin clearly saw it)..."[745]

In the ensuing negotiations, the pressure from Potresov and Zasulich garnered some results – Struve yielded and agreed to print on the cover of *Sovremennoye Obozreniye*: "An appendix to the social-democratic journal *Zarya*". Zasulich, Potresov, and then Axelrod celebrated this as a victory - "We've taken what's ours."

Ulyanov turned to Plekhanov for support. In one letter to him, he stopped referring to Struve as 'the twin', and now called him what Plekhanov himself would refer to him as in correspondence - "Judas". For them, he was no longer a comrade who had lost his way, but a traitor.[746]

743	Ibid. p. 386.
744	Ibid. p. 387.
745	Ibid. p. 388.
746	See: Leninsky sbornik, III. p. 126.

"The situation is clear," Ulyanov wrote, "competition is directed not so much against *Zarya* as it is against *Iskra*: the same prevalence of political material, the same style of newspaper – a review of current events... We will be dancing to the tune of Judas, who in his dominion over *Sovremennoye Obozreniye*... will forge a magnificent liberal career and make an attempt to wipe out not only the heavyweight *Zarya*, but *Iskra* as well. We will be the ones scurrying around, putting the effort in, making the corrections, and shifting it, while his Excellency Mr Judas will be *rédacteur en chef* of the most influential journal (in wider *so genannten* [so-called] 'public' opinion). ... With this in mind, one asks – could the fabled 'hegemony' of social democracy prove to be mere cant?...

If we are destined to have the chance at real hegemony, then it will exclusively be with the assistance of a political newspaper (backed by a theoretical organ), and when we are told, with breathtaking arrogance, that the political department of our organ must not present competition to the political venture of the gentlemen liberals, then the wretchedness of our role is as clear as day." In other words, "We are selling our primacy for lentil soup and finding ourselves *genasführt* [led by the nose] by Judas..."[747]

Plekhanov had his reasons for referring to Stuve as Judas. After all, in this instance, this was not simply a matter of tolerating the views of others, but of Peter Struve's switch to another camp entirely. Given that Struve had so recently pledged his allegiance to the RSDLP, without having been dragged kicking and screaming to do so, in this instance treachery *was* a reasonable charge. A split with Struve had therefore become necessary.

Struve himself was in fact well aware of this. When later on he returned to Munich and only Krupskaya came to meet him, "he spoke of the fact that he was considered a traitor, something else of that ilk, and mocked himself". Krupskaya writes that there was "something very Dostoevskian" about the meeting.[748]

Ulyanov suggested to Plekhanov that he "raise the standard of revolt" against Struve. However, Plekhanov, who feared a break with Struve might cut off sources of financial support, replied: "The circumstances *now* are such that a split will destroy us; we will make an assessment *later*."[749] Ulyanov submitted to the majority. However, as events transpired, Struve

---

747   V. I. Lenin. Polnoye sobraniye sochineny. Vol. 46. pp. 80, 81.

748   Vospominaniya o Vladimire Ilyiche Lenine. Vol. 1. p. 244.

749   Leninsky sbornik, III. p. 133.

was arrested shortly after his return to Russia and exiled to Tver, and *Sovremennoye Obozreniye* collapsed. *Iskra* gained a firm footing without Struve's assistance.

From the outset, the approaching 20th century promised great upheaval in Russia. As one participant of the 1900 Kharkov May Day demonstration remarked: "Every worker to a man talks ceaselessly of this only being the beginning, that a storm is coming..." Five years later, the first Russian revolution began, its echoes heard around the world from Mexico to China. But at the turn of the century, the smell of smoke was already hanging over Russia.

"There is something ominous in the air around us: each day there is the glow of fires on the horizon, a bloody haze is spreading across the earth, making it hard to live and breathe, as before a thunderstorm. The peasant is dismally silent, and if he utters the odd word from time to time, it is only to clear the frost from his flesh," ran a letter from Voronezh Province. This letter comes from Tambov: "We need to leave, before they begin hanging us from the gates... Some kind of Pugachev rebellion is happening..."[750] The 'Red Wheel' of peasant uprisings, sometimes quickening pace, sometimes slowing, would roll its way across Russia for almost two decades.

The question was no longer whether reform from above or revolutionary struggle was preferable, or whether or not to employ violent means. With its policy of repression, the government had made violence a part of the paradigm.

The struggle had begun, and now it was time to choose sides. It would be harsh to blame the theoreticians of the 19th century workers' movement for the 20th century's brusque abandoning of many of their noble ideas, just as Christ cannot be held responsible for the bloody Crusades or the brutality of the Inquisition. It seems the key to such a metamorphosis lies in the historical conditions which distort and prevent the realisation of such worthy teachings. In this sense, Dostoevsky was correct to have one of the Karamazov brothers joke bitterly that if Christ was to return to Earth with his sermons, he would be crucified again – and this time by the Christians.

Ulyanov had chosen his objective in the coming struggle. Recognising the growing hatred "among the masses of common people" for the existing regime, he wrote – yet again – that the task of revolutionaries was first and foremost to educate these masses, bring to them "a ray of awareness of their

---

750 Istoriya VKP(b). Vol. 1. Issue. 1. pp. 230, 231, 232.

rights and faith in their own strength". Only then, he stressed, "with this awareness and belief in their own strength embedded, can the hatred of the people find an outlet not in bestial vengeance, but in the struggle for freedom."[751]

All that had been argued in the circles, every dispute that had driven a wedge between, in particular, Struve and Ulyanov – who would lead the people, or rather, who would the people follow – would no longer be mere theory, but put to the test in real political struggle. The overarching task facing Russia's working class was channelling its peasant 'Pugachev rebellion' into a wider national liberation movement, conscious of its political objectives.

Just a few days before Struve's arrival, the Christmas holidays had begun. Ulyanov wrote to his mother on 26th December, "Here it is already *Weihnachten* [Christmas], there are *Christbäume* [Christmas trees] everywhere, and there is an unusual vivacity in the streets at the moment… However, it is an unpleasant winter, devoid of snow. In fact, it's no winter at all, more of a poor imitation of autumn, a hanging dampness… I am growing tired of the slush and think back to proper Russian winter with fondness – sleigh rides and the crisp frost in the clean air. This is my first winter abroad, my first un-wintery winter, and I cannot say that I am especially pleased with it, although there are sometimes splendid days that remind me of a fine Russian autumn.

I am living as I did before, in a rather lonely fashion … and in an alas rather slapdash one. I hope to organise everything more systematically, but for some reason I have been unable to… Having hurtled around Russia and Europe after my Shushenskoye repose, I now long once more for the peaceful toil of a book, and only the unfamiliarity of my foreign predicament prevents me from making a proper start."[752]

This was written on 26th December. After his split with Struve a few days later, it became necessary to make some adjustments to these plans…

Over the previous five years, despite prison and exile, he had managed to emerge from the confines of the underground and publish a slew of academic works, making his name and his ideas familiar to what was then a vast reading public.

The break with Struve also snapped many of the threads that connected Ulyanov to the legal, academic sphere and that particular part of Russian

---

751 V. I. Lenin. Polnoye sobraniye sochineny. Vol. 4. p. 416.
752 Ibid. Vol. 55. pp. 197-198.

society. So was this voluntary 'self-isolation', an 'estrangement' from society? He had addressed this point while in exile: "To me it seems," he had written to Potresov, "that 'estrangement from society' certainly does not mean 'isolation', for there is society and there is society..."[753]

A short time passed, and in February 1903 Ulyanov delivered four lectures on the agrarian question in Russia and Europe at the Russian Higher School of Social Sciences in Paris. In fact, the school's sponsors, the renowned Russian scientists Maxim Kovalevsky and Yuri Gambarov, who were both hostile to Marxists and generally inclined to shy away from 'politics', had invited one V. Ilyin, author of *The Development of Capitalism in Russia* and other respected economic works. The lectures were a success.

One attendee recalled: "Vladimir Ilyich concluded his first lecture to thunderous applause, which transformed into a roaring extended ovation, the likes of which had never been heard within the school's walls." Learning that the lecturer V. Ilyin was in fact V. Ulyanov, almost the very embodiment of the underground, Maxim Kovalevsky became very aggrieved: "What a fine professor he would have made," he remarked. "This coming from Professor Kovalevsky," wrote Grigory Zinoviev, a student of the school, "was the highest possible praise."[754]

But Ulyanov had made his choice.

On the night of 29th to 30th December, as he recorded his impressions of those discussions with Struve, he noted: "This was a significant and in its own way 'historic' meeting ... at least historic in my lifetime, bringing to a close an entire – if not epoch, then chapter of my life, determining my future actions and the path my life would take for a long time to come."[755]

In spring 1901, as the 20th century dawned, he began signing his works with a new pseudonym – LENIN.

---

753   Ibid. Vol. 46. p. 16.

754   Proletarskaya revolyutsiya. 1924. No. 3. p. 146; *G. Zinoviev.* Lenin. 2nd edition. Leningrad, 1925. p. 14.

755   *V. I. Lenin.* Polnoye sobraniye sochineny. Vol. 4. p. 386.

INDEX OF NAMES

Abramova, A. – 87
Afanasyev, Fyodor – 130
Alexander II (Romanov, A. N.) – 8, 10, 35, 37, 39, 40, 65, 66, 216
Alexander III (Romanov, A. A.) – 8, 9, 10, 66, 67, 77, 78, 80, 81, 112, 114, 163
Alexander the Great – 94
Alexandrov, Pyotr A. – 52
Ammosov, Konstantin M. – 67
Andreyushkin, Pakhomy I. – 75, 78, 81, 88
Apraksin, Alexander – 30, 37
Ardasheva-Ponomareva, Lyubov A. – 31
Aristov, A. P. – 34
Armand, Inessa – 102, 221, 223, 224
Aronson, Naum D. – 21, 22
Arsenyev *see* Potresov, Alexander N.
Arzt (Krutovsky, V. M.) – 209
Axelrod, Pavel B. – 154, 174, 178, 180, 182, 199, 249, 268, 273, 277, 285, 289, 292, 293, 294, 299-300, 304, 309
Azanchevskaya, Y. P. – 283

Babushkin, Ivan V. – 161, 163, 182, 193, 282
Bakunin, Mikhail A. – 38, 91
Baranov, Dmitry Osipovich – 29, 30
Barsov, Fyodor – 30
Bartenev, V. V. – 268
Bauman, N. E. – 256
Bebel, August – 140
Beethoven, Ludwig van – 31
Beketov, Nikolai Nikolayevich – 58
Belinsky, V. G. – 300
Belova, Y. – 87
Beltov *see* Plekhanov, Georgi Valentinovich

Belyakov, Alexei A. – 117
Bernstein, Eduard – 16, 153, 251, 252, 254
Beshkin, G. L. – 102
Billroth, Teodor – 215
Blagoev, Dmitry – 159, 160, 182
Blank, Alexander (Israel) Dmitriyevich – 25, 28, 29, 30-33, 36, 43, 44
Blank, Dmitry (Abel) Dmitriyevich – 28, 29, 30, 31
Blank, Dmitry Alexandrovich – 31
Blank, Maria Alexandrovna *see* Ulyanova, Maria Alexandrovna
Blank, Moshe (Dmitry) Itskovich – 28-29, 36, 44
Blank, Sofia Alexandrovna (married name Lavrova) – 31
Blinov, P. A. – 268
Bogatyrev, Yevgeny G. – 159
Bogdanov, Nikolai Dementyevich – 130, 159, 239
Bogolyubov, Alexei – 52
Bogoraz, L. – 87, 88
Bonch-Bruevich, Vladimir D. – 176
Bragin, Yefim – 215, 216
Braginsky, M. – 76
Brusnev, M. I. – 129
Bulgakov, S. N. – 239, 249, 250
Bunakov, Nikolai F. – 68
Bunge, Nikolai K. – 58

Chebotarev, Ivan N. – 74, 136
Chebotareva, Alexandra K. – 136, 187
Chekhov, Anton Pavlovich – 54, 128, 132, 133
Chernov, Viktor M. – 144
Chernyshevsky, Nikolai Gavrilovich – 9-10, 11, 12, 13, 35, 84, 85, 93-94, 95, 99, 122, 129, 140, 265
Chertkov, Ivan Dmitriyevich – 32
Chetvergova, Maria Pavlovna (née Orlova) – 99, 101, 104, 265, 267
Chinov, P. G. – 127
Chirikov, Yevgeny N. – 89
Clémence, Adolphe – 176
Conring, Hermann – 110
Cui, César Antonovich – 58
Curtius, Ernst – 31

Danielson, Nikolai F. (also Nikolai-on) – 119, 131, 140-141
Davydova, Lidiya Karlovna (married name Tugan-Baranovskaya) – 151, 221
Delyanov, Ivan Davydovich – 54, 70, 88, 90, 95, 109
Dietz, H. W. – 300
Dobrolyubov, N. A. – 35, 75-76
Dolgorukov, Pavel D. – 114, 307
Dolgorukov, Pyotr D. – 114, 307
Dostoevsky, F. M. – 311
Dreiden, S. – 267
Dridzo, Vera S. – 226, 227, 229, 236
Dubasov, F. V. – 47
Dunin, I. N. – 67
Durnovo, I. N. – 95
Durnovo, Pyotr N. – 79, 109, 112

Engberg, Oskar A. – 219, 228, 230, 231, 232, 234, 255
Engelhardt, Alexander N. – 241
Engels, Friedrich – 69, 93, 101, 102, 125, 140, 173, 176, 178
Essen, Maria – 84

Fedoseyev, Nikolai Yevgrafovich – 99, 101, 102, 104, 131, 133, 134, 213, 214, 233, 234
Fedotov, N. K. – 237
Fet, Afanasy Afanasyevich (Shenshin) – 114
Feuerbach, Ludwig Andreas von – 121
Fisher, Matvei – 169
Foerster, Otfrid – 22
Foss, Y. N. – 90
Friedrich Wilhelm III – 31
Froimovich, Mariam (Marem) (married name Blank) – 28, 29

Gambarov, Yuri – 313
Geiden, Pyotr A. – 114
Generalov, Vasily D. – 75, 78, 81
Genghis Khan – 95
George V – 167
Gerd, Nina A. *see* Struve, Nina A.
Godunov, Boris F. – 81

Gofman, S. A. – 181, 193
Goldman-Gorev, Boris I. *see* Gorev, Boris I.
Golitsyn, Prince A. N. – 30
Golubev, M. P. – 144
Golubeva-(Yasneva), Maria P. – 143, 145
Goncharov, Dmitry A. – 105
Goncharov, Ivan A. – 52
Goremykin, Alexander D. – 209, 211
Gorev, Boris I. – 181, 203, 205, 206, 240
Gorky, Maxim (Peshkov, Alexei Maximovich) – 19, 88, 89, 173, 187, 196
Govorukhin, Orest M. – 75, 77, 78
Granovsky, T. N. – 35
Gresser, Y. V. – 76, 77
Gringmut, Vladimir A. – 29
Groman, V. G. – 256
Groman, Y. P. – 256
Großschopf, Alexandra I. – 31
Großschopf, Amalia I. – 31
Großschopf, Anna I. (married name Blank) – 31, 32
Großschopf, Gustav I. – 31
Großschopf, Ivan Fyodorovich (Johann Gottlieb) – 30, 31
Großschopf, Johann I. – 31
Großschopf, Karl I. – 31
Großschopf, Karolina I. (married name Biuberg) – 31
Großschopf, Yekaterina I. *see* von Essen, Yekaterina I.
Guesde, Jules – 176
Gurevich-Dan, Fyodor I. – 181, 193, 256
Gurko, I. V. – 47
Gusev – 127
Gvozdev, R. – 239

Hauptmann, Gerhart – 267
Hayek, Friedrich August von – 122
Hegel, Georg Wilhelm Friedrich – 76, 93, 147, 250
Heine, Christian Johann Heinrich – 80
Herzen, Alexander Ivanovich – 35, 38, 121, 140
Hopfenhaus, Maria G. – 233

Ilyin, V. *see* Lenin, Vladimir Ilyich
Ionov, V. A. – 153
Ishersky, Ivan Vladimirovich – 82, 83
Ishutin, Nikolai A. – 41, 42
Ivanshin, V. P. – 247, 272

Kalashnikov, Vasily Andreyevich – 49
Kalmykov, D. A. – 150
Kalmykova, Alexandra Mikhailovna – 150, 151, 152, 204, 207, 221, 235, 261, 268, 283
Kalyaev, Ivan P. – 249
Kant, Immanuel – 250
Karakozov, Dmitry Vladimirovich – 40, 41, 42
Karamyshev, Pyotr I. – 184
Kareyev, N. I. – 119
Kashkadamova, Vera V. – 74, 79, 80, 82
Kasvinov, M. K. – 166, 167, 196, 202
Kautsky, Karl – 140, 146, 161, 239, 250
Kerensky, Alexander Fyodorovich – 55
Kerensky, Fyodor Mikhailovich – 55, 59, 64, 69, 82, 86
Khalturin, Stepan N. – 65
Khardin, Andrei Nikolayevich – 126, 128, 131, 136
Kichin, A. Y. – 186, 187, 190
Kislyakov, N. M. – 268
Klasson, Robert – 151, 153, 172, 221, 224
Klements, Grigory A. – 21
Klimanov, Yegor A. – 130
Klobukov – 151
Klykov – 186
Knyazev – 80
Knyazev, Vladimir A. – 160, 161
Komissarov, Osip – 40, 41, 42, 51
Komissarova, L. I. – 246, 247, 249
Kon, Feliks Yakovlevich – 216
Kondratyev, I. – 90, 91
Kopyakov – 127
Korinfsky, Apollon A. – 59, 61, 69
Korobko, Y. P. – 151

Korsak – 151
Kotovshchikov, Nikolai I. – 103
Kovalevsky, Maxim M. – 313
Krasikov, Fyodor – 127
Krasikov, Pyotr A. – 211
Krasilnikov, Ignat – 127
Krasin, Herman B. – 137, 138, 140-142, 159, 170, 267
Krasin, Leonid B. – 137, 139, 140
Krasnoperov, I. M. – 120
Kremlev, N. A. – 89
Krichevsky, B. N. – 247
Krivenko, Sergey N. – 115, 146
Kropotkin, Peter A. – 36, 41, 286
Krupskaya, Nadezhda K. – 18, 46, 60, 61, 72, 84, 93, 99, 151, 161, 181, 190, 193, 218, 219, 221-229, 231, 233-237, 239, 243, 244, 250, 255, 261, 262, 263-264, 265, 278, 283, 286, 287, 296, 299, 310
Krupskaya, Yelizaveta Vasilyevna – 221, 222, 225, 228, 229
Krupsky, Alexander I. – 222
Krupsky, Konstantin I. – 221
Krzhizhanovskaya, Zinaida P. *see* Nevzorova-Krzhizhanovskaya, Zinaida P.
Krzhizhanovsky, Gleb M. – 19, 20, 21, 135, 137-138, 142, 163, 170, 181, 184, 191, 192, 203, 207, 212, 213, 214, 215, 217, 220, 221, 226, 227, 235, 236, 255, 261, 266
Kukleyev, F. I. – 127
Kuprin, Alexander Ivanovich – 20
Kurnatovsky, Viktor K. – 263
Kuskova, Yekaterina Dmitriyevna – 16, 253, 254, 255, 272
Kuzyutkin, Kuzma – 160

Lafargue, Paul – 175, 176
Lalayants, Isaak Khristoforovich (Columbus) – 118, 119, 131, 132, 138, 267, 268, 271, 272, 277
Laptev, Filipp Y. – 128
Lassalle, Ferdinand – 69, 172
Lavrov, Pyotr L. – 91, 140
Lavrov, S. Y. – 127
Lavrov, V. M. – 132
Lefrançais, Gustave Adolphe – 176
Lengnik, Friedrich – 159

Lenin, N. *see* Lenin, Vladimir Ilyich
Lenin, S. N. – 284
Lenin, Vladimir Ilyich (Ilyin; "baldy"; Lenin, N.; Nikolai Petrovich; Tulin, K.; "the old man" [starik]) – 7-313
Lenina, Olga Nikolayevna – 283, 284
Lenina, Yelena – 283
Leo XIII, Pope – 252, 253
Léo, André – 176
Leonidov, O. L. – 20
Lepeshinsky, P. N. – 213, 244, 255, 283
Leskov, Nikolai S. – 132
Levitsky, V. (Tsederbaum, V. O.) – 206
Liebknecht, Wilhelm – 179
Lissagaray, Prosper Olivier – 176
Livanov, Nikolai – 34
Lobachevsky, N. I. – 27
Lokhov, N. N. – 268, 269
Lopatin, N. F. – 268, 280
Lukashevich, Iosif D. – 75, 77, 81
Lunacharsky, A. V. – 21, 22
Luria, M. A. – 181
Lvov, I. A. – 193
Lyakhovsky, Yakov M. – 181, 192, 193, 203, 207, 212, 233
Lyustikh, V. O. – 187

Malchenko, Alexander L. – 137, 181, 184, 279
Malon, Benoît – 176
Mandelshtam, M. L. – 100, 101
Maria Feodorovna, Dowager Empress – 166
Martov, L. (Tsederbaum, Yuliy O.) – 13, 17, 130, 145, 149, 162, 163, 168, 169, 175, 176, 181, 182, 184, 186, 190, 191, 192, 193, 199, 203, 204, 205, 206, 213, 214, 244, 256, 261, 266, 269, 270-271, 272, 273, 276, 277, 278, 279, 286, 299, 301, 304
Martyanov, Nikolai M. – 216
Marx, Karl Heinrich – 11, 69, 76, 81, 93, 100-102, 121, 122, 124, 131, 139, 140, 141, 147, 148, 151, 153, 155, 161, 173, 175, 176, 250, 252, 257, 304
Maslov, Pyotr P. – 131, 272
Matov – 218

Mendelssohn, Moses – 99
Merkulov, Nikita Y. – 161, 184
Meshchersky, Prince V. P. – 67, 68
Mikhailov, Nikolai N. – 159, 190
Mikhailovsky, Nikolai K. – 93, 115, 117, 119, 129, 145, 146, 147, 199, 200, 203, 221, 240
Mill, John Stuart – 93
Milyukov, Pavel N. – 307
Milyutin, Dmitry A. – 53
Model, Otto Moritz Walter – 31
Mukhin – 215
Mulenkov, Vasily F. – 126
Muratov, V. I. – 69
Muravyov, N. V. – 204
Muromov, Sergey – 159
Murzin – 127

N. Y. *see* Fedoseyev, Nikolai Yevgrafovich
Nafigov, R. I. – 83, 87, 89, 91, 95, 98, 99, 101, 103, 104
Napoleon I – 94, 95
Naumov, Alexander N. – 47, 61, 62, 63, 82
Nazaryev, Valerian Nikanorovich – 44, 45
Nazvanov, Mikhail K. – 137
Nechayev, P. – 124
Nechayev, S. G. – 122
Nefedyev, N. G. – 51
Nekrasov, N. A. – 50, 66, 93
Nevzorova, Sofia P. – 141
Nevzorova-Krzhizhanovskaya, Zinaida P. – 111, 141, 181, 221, 225, 226, 235, 236, 255
Nicholas I, Emperor (Romanov, N. P.) – 29, 34, 35, 37, 66
Nicholas II, Emperor (Romanov, N. A.) – 61, 114, 163, 166, 167, 195, 202, 286
Nikolaevsky, Boris – 271
Nikolai Nikolayevich, Grand Prince (the elder) – 47
Nikolai Petrovich *see* Lenin, Vladimir I.
Nikolai-on *see* Danielson, Nikolai F.
Nikonov, Sergey – 77
Nordau, Max (Südfeld, Simon Maximilian) – 151

Novorussky, M. V. – 81
Novosiltsev, Y. A. – 307

Obolensky, Prince Vladimir A. – 47, 112, 114, 166, 167, 204, 268-269, 275, 276, 291, 307, 308
Okhotnikov, Nikofor Mikhailovich – 57
Olkhovsky, Y. R. – 246, 247, 249
Oparin, Mikhail V. – 127
Orestov, Ioann – 230
Orlov-Sokolovsky, Alexander A. – 98
Osipanov, Vasily S. – 78, 81
Oskar *see* Engberg, Oskar A.

Panin, N. N. – 255
Parvus, A. L. (Gelfand, Israel Lazarevich) – 239
Pasha (Mezina, P. A.) – 231
Pasternak, Boris Leonidovich – 19
Perfliev – 280
Perovskaya, Sofia L. – 91
Peskovsky, Matvei Leontyevich – 79, 80
Petrov, Alexander G. – 27
Petrova, P. A. – 231
Philip II of Spain – 224
Pipes, Richard Edgar – 221, 243, 244, 274, 286, 300, 307, 308
Piramidov, V. M. – 279
Pisarev, Alexander – 82
Plato – 110
Plekhanov, Georgi Valentinovich (Beltov; Volgin; Kuznetsov, D.; Utis) – 18, 22, 76, 93, 102, 111, 113, 114, 115-116, 121, 122, 125, 137, 138, 140, 150, 152, 153, 154, 156, 157, 172, 173-174, 175, 176, 177, 178, 179, 182, 198, 199, 204, 211, 243, 244, 245, 246, 250, 251, 256, 261, 268, 272-273, 277, 278, 279, 283, 285-289, 290, 291, 292-298, 299, 308-310
Pleshkina, Stepanida – 234
Pobedonostsev, Konstantin P. – 58, 166
Polyansky, S. – 87, 90
Ponomarev, Yakov P. – 137, 181, 193
Ponomareva, L. A. *see* Ardasheva-Ponomareva, L. A.
Popov, Ivan F. – 22, 50

Popova, Klavdiya G. – 211
Popova, O. N. – 280
Posnik – 283
Postnikov, V. Y. – 120-121, 123, 132
Potresov, Alexander N. (Arsenyev) – 17, 151, 153, 167, 168, 170, 176, 177, 188, 198, 199, 235, 236, 249, 250, 252, 256, 261, 262, 268, 269, 270-271, 272, 273, 274, 276, 277, 278, 285, 286, 287, 289, 291, 292, 293, 294, 297, 301, 305, 308, 309, 313
Preobrazhensky, Alexei A. – 105, 106, 131
Pribylovskaya, A. I. – 43
Prokopovich, Sergey Nikolayevich – 249, 254, 272
Promiński, Jan (I. L.) – 217, 219, 234
Pushkin, Alexander Sergeyevich – 30, 81, 260

Rachinsky, Sergey A. – 66
Radchenko, Lyubov N. – 181
Radchenko, Stepan I. – 137, 181, 183, 192, 193, 205, 236, 243, 244, 276
Radek, Karl B. – 100, 108
Radetsky, Fyodor Fyodorovich – 47
Rakovsky, Christian G. – 304
Repin, Ilya Y. – 132
Repin, Stepan – 127
Rodichev – 307
Rosenberg, Elvira E. – 214
Roßmäßler, E. A. – 224
Rozanov, Vladimir N. – 282
Rozental', I. S. – 159
Rudakov, M. I. – 225
Rusanov, Nikolai S. – 52

Sakharov, Timofei I. – 127
Saltykov-Shchedrin, Mikhail Y. – 57, 75
Samoilov, A. I. – 106
Sarbatova, Varvara Grigoryevna – 44, 46, 47, 49
Savelyev, A. A. – 166
Savinkov, Boris V. – 249
Sazonov, Yegor – 249
Semenov, Matvei I. – 106, 107, 108, 118
Semevsky, Vasily I. – 75

Serebrovsky, S. M. – 151
Sergiyevsky, Nikolai L. – 133
Seryozhnikov, V. K. – 181
Shaginyan, Marietta S. – 26, 27
Shakhovskoy, D. I. – 307
Shalaginov, V. K. – 127
Shalyapin, Fyodor I. – 204
Shapovalov, A. I. – 232, 255
Shchapov, Afanasy P. – 38
Shcherbo, Alexandra – 60
Shelgunov, Nikolai Vasilyevich – 38, 129, 130
Shelgunov, Vasily Andreyevich – 159, 160, 161, 162, 169, 181, 182, 184
Shepelev, S. P. – 129
Sheremetyev, P. S. – 307
Shesternin, S. P. – 282
Shestopalov, A. I. – 181
Shevyrev, Pyotr Y. – 77, 78, 81
Shtein, Mikhail G. – 27, 29, 30, 31, 81, 283
Shteingauer, Yakob Mikhailovich – 172
Shukht, Apollon A. – 107, 136
Silvin, M. A. – 136, 137, 139, 140, 141, 145, 168, 181, 183, 184, 186, 189, 191, 192, 193, 197, 205, 255, 256, 264, 267, 268
Sklyarenko, Alexei Pavlovich (Popov, A. V.) – 106, 107, 108, 118, 119, 120, 131, 132
Skobelev, M. D. – 47
Skvortsov, A. I. – 87, 88
Skvortsov, Pavel N. – 102, 132, 136, 138, 153
Smidovich, I. – 181
Smidovich, Inna G. – 181
Smirnov, Alexei Lukyanovich – 26
Smirnova, Anna Alexeyevna *see* Ulyanova, Anna Alexeyevna
Smirnova, Tatyana Alexeyevna – 26
Socrates – 22
Sokolov, B. – 222, 223, 224
Sokolov, N. P. – 112, 113, 114
Solovyov, Alexander K. – 65
Solovyov, S. M. – 34, 35
Sponti, Yevgeny I. – 173

Stalin, Joseph Vissarionovich (Dzhugashvili) – 28
Starkovs – 235, 255
Starkov, Vasily V. – 137, 139, 181, 184, 191, 203, 212, 213, 214, 221, 263
Starkov, Vladimir V. – 138
Steklov, Yuri M. – 287
Stepniak, Sergius (Stepnyak-Kravchinsky, Sergey Mikhaylovich) – 53
Sternik, I. B. – 127
Stopani, A. M. – 268
Stranden, N. P. – 41
Struve, Nina A. – 221-222, 235
Struve, Peter B. ("the twin") – 150-153, 154, 168, 169, 170, 199, 203, 204, 221, 236, 239, 243, 244, 249-250, 251-252, 260, 261, 268, 271, 273, 274, 276, 277, 282, 283, 286, 288, 289, 300, 304, 305-310, 311, 312, 313
Strzhalkovskaya, Nina – 83
Suvorov, A. V. – 94

Takhtarev, Konstantin M. – 14, 15, 16, 17, 161, 162, 165, 169, 183, 193, 194, 197, 198, 199, 201, 202, 205, 298
Teplov, P. F. (Sibiryak) – 247, 272
Thornton (factory) – 182, 193
Tikhomirov, Lev A. – 140
Timofeyev, Alexander Vasilyevich – 42
Tkachev, P. N. – 122
Tochissky, Pavel V. – 159
Tolstoy, Count Dmitry Andreyevich – 54, 57, 67
Tolstoy, Lev N. – 73, 114, 196, 262
Trenyukhin, V. M. – 181
Trepov, Fyodor F. – 52, 53
Trofimov, Zhores A. – 44, 45, 46, 55, 56, 64, 67, 68, 69, 70, 73, 75, 77, 78, 79, 82, 86
Trubetskoy, C. N. – 307
Trubetskoy, Y. N. – 307
Trukhovskaya, Dominika V. – 221
Tsaplin, V. V. – 28
Tsederbaum, Lidia O. – 203
Tsederbaum, V. O. *see* Levitsky
Tsederbaum, Yuliy O. *see* Martov, L.
Tsyurupa, Alexander Dmitriyevich – 282, 284

Tugan-Baranovskaya, Lidiya Karlovna – 151
Tugan-Baranovsky, Mikhail I. – 150, 151, 162, 203, 204, 221, 239, 249, 250, 271, 276, 277, 288, 289
Tulin, K. *see* Lenin, Vladimir I.
Turgenev, I. S. – 219
Tyrkov, Arkady V. – 216
Tyrkova, Ariadna V. (Tyrkova-Williams) – 151, 222, 223, 224, 236
Tyutchev, Fyodor I. – 36
Tyutyukin, S. V. – 177

Ulyanin, Nikita Grigoryevich – 25
Ulyanin, Nikolai Vasilyevich (Ulyaninov; Ulyanov) – 25, 26, 34
Ulyanin, Vasily Nikitich – 25
Ulyanov, Alexander Ilyich – 40, 42, 46, 48, 49, 50, 66, 68, 69, 74, 76, 77, 78, 79, 81, 83, 87, 88, 104, 106, 107, 137, 138
Ulyanov, Alexander Nikolayevich – 26
Ulyanov, Dmytry Ilyich – 44, 68, 145, 266
Ulyanov, Feodosiya Nikolayevna – 26
Ulyanov, Ilya Nikolayevich – 25, 26, 27, 33, 34, 37, 39-42, 43, 44-45, 46, 48, 51, 52, 54, 55, 56, 57, 61, 66, 67, 68, 69, 70, 71, 72, 73, 74, 82, 98, 105, 126, 145
Ulyanov, Vasily Nikolayevich – 26, 27, 34
Ulyanova-(Yelizarova), Anna Ilyinishna – 25, 27, 28, 36, 37, 39, 40, 42, 43, 46, 54, 55, 57, 66, 68, 70, 71, 72, 74, 79, 80, 92, 101, 102, 104, 117, 124-125, 130-133, 143-144, 185, 189, 191, 194, 201, 207, 208, 210, 226, 235, 265-226, 279, 280, 281, 282, 301
Ulyanova, Anna Alexeyevna (née Smirnova) – 26, 28, 34, 44
Ulyanova, Maria Alexandrovna (née Blank) – 25, 27, 28, 31, 33, 40, 41, 43, 44, 46, 48, 49, 50, 56, 69, 73, 79, 80, 82, 95, 98, 103, 105, 109, 145, 146, 161, 185, 188, 189, 206, 207, 208, 217, 223, 229, 235, 236, 263, 266
Ulyanova, Maria Ilyinishna – 25, 27, 28, 44, 45, 70, 81, 145, 188, 189, 208, 217
Ulyanova, Maria Nikolayevna – 26
Ulyanova, Olga Ilyinishna – 44, 49, 50, 83, 91, 110
Umov, Vasily – 43
Uspensky, Gleb I. – 287
Uzhdin, Ilya I. – 127

V. V. *see* Vorontsov, Vasily P.
Valentinov, Nikolai V. – 10, 11, 12, 47, 60, 81, 82, 84, 94, 99, 101, 102, 121, 129, 132, 297
Vaneyev, Anatoly A. – 137, 181, 184, 203, 213, 214, 221, 255
Veretennikov, Alexander I. – 59
Veretennikov, Ivan Dmitriyevich – 27
Veretennikov, Nikolai I. – 50, 51, 56, 57
Veretennikova, Anna Alexandrovna (née Blank) – 27
Veretennikova, Anna I. – 31, 96
Verkhovsky, V. P. – 164
Voden, Alexander M. – 177
Vodovozov, Vasily V. – 131
Volgin *see* Plekhanov, Georgi Valentinovich
Volin, Mark – 302
Volkenshtein, Mikhail Filippovich – 136
Volkogonov, D. A. – 20, 31
von Essen, Yekaterina I. (née Großschopf) – 31, 32, 33, 44, 57
Vorontsov, Vasily P. (V. V.) – 117, 119, 131, 144-145
Vorovsky, Vatslav V. – 92, 93, 256
Voskresensky, I. – 87, 88
Voyeikov, Dmitry – 67
Vygornitsky, K. – 87, 88

Webb, Beatrice – 16, 235, 239
Webb, Sidney – 16, 235, 239
Weber, Georg – 94, 95
Wetzel, Faina – 127
Witmer, Olga K. – 223
Witte, Sergey Y. – 202, 306
Wylie, Baronet Sir James – 32

Yakovlev, B. V. – 46, 60, 61, 176, 214, 216
Yakovlev, Ivan I. – 184
Yakovlev, Y. V. – 34, 36, 37, 39, 45, 48, 49, 51, 57, 60, 66, 67, 68, 70, 80, 83, 84, 97
Yakubova, Apollinariya Alexandrovna – 181, 226
Yashchenko – 127
Yelizarov, Mark Timofeyevich – 104, 124, 143, 145, 208

Yelizarov, Pavel T. – 124
Yelizarova, A. I. *see* Ulyanova-Yelizarova, A. I.
Yeramasov, Alexei I. – 282
Yudin, Gennady V. – 212
Yukhotskaya, V. – 213
Yukhotsky – 233
Yuzhakov, Sergei N. – 146, 203

Zaichnevsky, Pyotr G. – 38, 91
Zaitsev, Kuzma F. – 127
Zakharov, V. I. – 41
Zakharova, K. Y. – 256
Zakrzhevsky, Yulian – 98
Zalesskaya – 143
Zalezhskaya, Yekaterina – 31
Zaporozhets, Pyotr K. – 137, 181, 184
Zaretskaya, Yelena – 283
Zasulich, Vera Ivanovna – 52, 53, 129, 241, 268, 272, 286, 289, 290, 292, 294, 297, 309
Zavertkin, I. I. – 218, 230
Zhelyabov, Andrei I. – 65
Zhuikov, G. S. – 246, 247, 249
Zhukovsky, V. A. – 93
Zhuravlev, Stepan N. – 219, 230
Zilbershtein, I. S. – 33, 100, 103, 106, 107, 109, 126
Zinoviev, Boris I. – 182, 184, 190, 191, 206
Zinoviev, G. E. – 313
Znamensky, Vladimir – 43
Zyryanov, Apollon D. – 217, 218, 221, 227, 228, 231, 238

Leo Tolstoy – Flight from Paradise
by Pavel Basinsky

Over a hundred years ago, something truly outrageous occurred at Yasnaya Polyana. Count Leo Tolstoy, a famous author aged eighty-two at the time, took off, destination unknown. Since then, the circumstances surrounding the writer's whereabouts during his final days and his eventual death have given rise to many myths and legends. In this book, popular Russian writer and reporter Pavel Basinsky delves into the archives and presents his interpretation of the situation prior to Leo Tolstoy's mysterious disappearance. Basinsky follows Leo Tolstoy throughout his life, right up to his final moments. Reconstructing the story from historical documents, he creates a visionary account of the events that led to the Tolstoys' family drama.

Flight from Paradise will be of particular interest to international researchers studying Leo Tolstoy's life and works, and is highly recommended to a broader audience worldwide.

Buy it > www.glagoslav.com

A Brown Man in Russia
Lessons Learned on the Trans-Siberian
by Vijay Menon

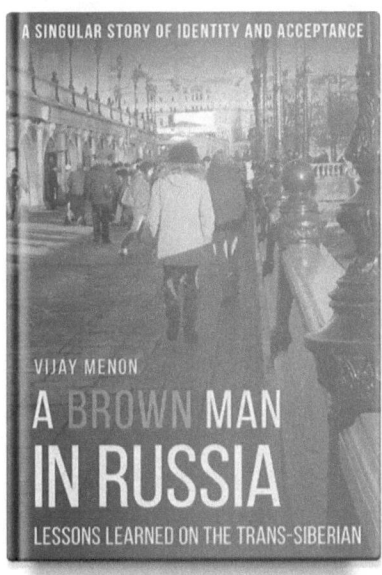

A Brown Man in Russia describes the fantastical travels of a young, colored American traveler as he backpacks across Russia in the middle of winter via the Trans-Siberian. The book is a hybrid between the curmudgeonly travelogues of Paul Theroux and the philosophical works of Robert Pirsig. Styled in the vein of Hofstadter, the author lays out a series of absurd, but true stories followed by a deeper rumination on what they mean and why they matter. Each chapter presents a vivid anecdote from the perspective of the fumbling traveler and concludes with a deeper lesson to be gleaned. For those who recognize the discordant nature of our world in a time ripe for demagoguery and for those who want to make it better, the book is an all too welcome antidote. It explores the current global climate of despair over differences and outputs a very different message – one of hope and shared understanding. At times surreal, at times inappropriate, at times hilarious, and at times deeply human, A Brown Man in Russia is a reminder to those who feel marginalized, hopeless, or endlessly divided that harmony is achievable even in the most unlikely of places.

Buy it > www.glagoslav.com

A Man of Change –
A study of the political life of Boris Yeltsin

A Man of Change is a gift from the Foundation of the First President of the Russian Federation B.N. Yeltsin otherwise known as The Yeltsin Fund, produced in cooperation with Glagoslav Publications and distributed with the aim to preserve the knowledge and memory of Russia's first President.

Boris Yeltsin will be remembered as the fierce, daring political leader who fought for democratic ideals of his nation during an unprecedented crisis when the Soviet empire had already fallen apart and new emerging nations had not yet firmly established themselves in the region. Russia took over from the previously mighty union of nations, but the country had to be rebuilt and its leadership needed to be reaffirmed.

During the years when others were abandoning the sinking ship, Boris Yeltsin showed a remarkable strength of character and took it upon himself to salvage the nation despite unfavorable odds. Yeltsin created a stronghold for the new Russian governance, and

Buy it > www.glagoslav.com

Dear Reader,

Thank you for purchasing this book.

We at Glagoslav Publications are glad to welcome you, and hope that you find our books to be a source of knowledge and inspiration.

We want to show the beauty and depth of the Slavic region to everyone looking to expand their horizon and learn something new about different cultures, different people, and we believe that with this book we have managed to do just that.

Now that you've got to know us, we want to get to know you. We value communication with our readers and want to hear from you! We offer several options:

– Join our Book Club on Goodreads, Library Thing and Shelfari, and receive special offers and information about our giveaways;

– Share your opinion about our books on Amazon, Barnes & Noble, Waterstones and other bookstores;

– Join us on Facebook and Twitter for updates on our publications and news about our authors;

– Visit our site www.glagoslav.com to check out our Catalogue and subscribe to our Newsletter.

Glagoslav Publications is getting ready to release a new collection and planning some interesting surprises — stay with us to find out!

Glagoslav Publications
Email: contact@glagoslav.com

Glagoslav Publications Catalogue

- *The Time of Women* by Elena Chizhova
- *Andrei Tarkovsky: The Collector of Dreams* by Layla Alexander-Garrett
- *Andrei Tarkovsky - A Life on the Cross* by Lyudmila Boyadzhieva
- *Sin* by Zakhar Prilepin
- *Hardly Ever Otherwise* by Maria Matios
- *Khatyn* by Ales Adamovich
- *The Lost Button* by Irene Rozdobudko
- *Christened with Crosses* by Eduard Kochergin
- *The Vital Needs of the Dead* by Igor Sakhnovsky
- *The Sarabande of Sara's Band* by Larysa Denysenko
- *A Poet and Bin Laden* by Hamid Ismailov
- *Watching The Russians (Dutch Edition)* by Maria Konyukova
- *Kobzar* by Taras Shevchenko
- *The Stone Bridge* by Alexander Terekhov
- *Moryak* by Lee Mandel
- *King Stakh's Wild Hunt* by Uladzimir Karatkevich
- *The Hawks of Peace* by Dmitry Rogozin
- *Harlequin's Costume* by Leonid Yuzefovich
- *Depeche Mode* by Serhii Zhadan
- *The Grand Slam and other stories (Dutch Edition)* by Leonid Andreev
- *METRO 2033 (Dutch Edition)* by Dmitry Glukhovsky
- *METRO 2034 (Dutch Edition)* by Dmitry Glukhovsky
- *A Russian Story* by Eugenia Kononenko
- *Herstories, An Anthology of New Ukrainian Women Prose Writers*
- *The Battle of the Sexes Russian Style* by Nadezhda Ptushkina
- *A Book Without Photographs* by Sergey Shargunov
- *Down Among The Fishes* by Natalka Babina
- *disUNITY* by Anatoly Kudryavitsky
- *Sankya* by Zakhar Prilepin
- *Wolf Messing* by Tatiana Lungin
- *Good Stalin* by Victor Erofeyev

- *Solar Plexus* by Rustam Ibragimbekov
- *Don't Call me a Victim!* by Dina Yafasova
- *Poetin (Dutch Edition)* by Chris Hutchins and Alexander Korobko
- *A History of Belarus* by Lubov Bazan
- *Children's Fashion of the Russian Empire* by Alexander Vasiliev
- *Empire of Corruption - The Russian National Pastime* by Vladimir Soloviev
- *Heroes of the 90s - People and Money. The Modern History of Russian Capitalism*
- *Fifty Highlights from the Russian Literature (Dutch Edition)* by Maarten Tengbergen
- *Bajesvolk (Dutch Edition)* by Mikhail Khodorkovsky
- *Tsarina Alexandra's Diary (Dutch Edition)*
- *Myths about Russia* by Vladimir Medinskiy
- *Boris Yeltsin - The Decade that Shook the World* by Boris Minaev
- *A Man Of Change - A study of the political life of Boris Yeltsin*
- *Sberbank - The Rebirth of Russia's Financial Giant* by Evgeny Karasyuk
- *To Get Ukraine* by Oleksandr Shyshko
- *Asystole* by Oleg Pavlov
- *Gnedich* by Maria Rybakova
- *Marina Tsvetaeva - The Essential Poetry*
- *Multiple Personalities* by Tatyana Shcherbina
- *The Investigator* by Margarita Khemlin
- *The Exile* by Zinaida Tulub
- *Leo Tolstoy – Flight from paradise* by Pavel Basinsky
- *Moscow in the 1930* by Natalia Gromova
- *Laurus (Dutch edition)* by Evgenij Vodolazkin
- *Prisoner* by Anna Nemzer
- *The Crime of Chernobyl - The Nuclear Goulag* by Wladimir Tchertkoff
- *Alpine Ballad* by Vasil Bykau
- *The Complete Correspondence of Hryhory Skovoroda*

- *The Tale of Aypi* by Ak Welsapar
- *Selected Poems* by Lydia Grigorieva
- *The Fantastic Worlds of Yuri Vynnychuk*
- *The Garden of Divine Songs and Collected Poetry of Hryhory Skovoroda*
- *Adventures in the Slavic Kitchen: A Book of Essays with Recipes*
- *Seven Signs of the Lion* by Michael M. Naydan
- *Forefathers' Eve* by Adam Mickiewicz
- *One-Two* by Igor Eliseev
- *Girls, be Good* by Bojan Babić
- *Time of the Octopus* by Anatoly Kucherena
- *The Grand Harmony* by Bohdan Ihor Antonych
- *The Selected Lyric Poetry Of Maksym Rylsky*
- *The Shining Light* by Galymkair Mutanov
- *The Frontier: 28 Contemporary Ukrainian Poets - An Anthology*
- *Acropolis - The Wawel Plays* by Stanisław Wyspiański
- *Contours of the City* by Attyla Mohylny
- *Conversations Before Silence: The Selected Poetry of Oles Ilchenko*
- *The Secret History of my Sojourn in Russia* by Jaroslav HašekCharles S. Kraszewski
- *Mirror Sand - An Anthology of Russian Short Poems in English Translation* (A Bilingual Edition)
- *Maybe We're Leaving* by Jan Balaban
- *A Brown Man in Russia - Perambulations Through A Siberian Winter* by Vijay Menon
- *Hard Times* by Ostap Vyshnia
- *The Flying Dutchman* by Anatoly Kudryavitsky
- *Nikolai Gumilev's Africa* by Nikolai Gumilev
- *Zinnober's Poppets* by Elena Chizhova
- *Soghomon Tehlirian Memories - The Assassination of Talaat*
- *The Hemingway Game* by Evgeni Grishkovets

More coming soon...

www.ingramcontent.com/pod-product-compliance
Lightning Source LLC
Chambersburg PA
CBHW020901080526
44589CB00011B/385